THE ETHICAL CASE AGAINST ANIMAL EXPERIMENTS

WITHDRAWN FROM
THE LIBRARY

UNIVERSITY OF
WINCHESTER

UNIVERSITY OF WINCHESTER
LIBRARY

KA 0437375 8

UNIVERSITY OF ILLINOIS
PRESS

THE **ETHICAL CASE**

AGAINST ANIMAL EXPERIMENTS

Edited by

ANDREW LINZEY and **CLAIR LINZEY**

UNIVERSITY OF ILLINOIS PRESS
Urbana, Chicago, and Springfield

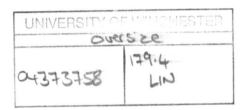

UNIVERSITY OF WINCHESTER

oversize

04373758

179.4
LIN

© 2018 by the Board of Trustees
of the University of Illinois
All rights reserved
1 2 3 4 5 C P 5 4 3 2 1

Printed and bound in Great Britain by
Marston Book Services Ltd, Oxfordshire

♾ This book is printed on acid-free paper.

Library of Congress Control Number: 2017955135
ISBN 978-0-252-04132-7 (hardcover)
ISBN 978-0-252-08285-6 (paperback)
ISBN 978-0-252-09992-2 (e-book)

For Michelle Thew
for her vision and courage

Contents

PART 2 THE SUPPORTING ESSAYS

THE ETHICAL CASE AGAINST ANIMAL EXPERIMENTS

INTRODUCTION

Oxford: The Home of Controversy about Animals

Andrew Linzey and Clair Linzey

I

"IT IS THE RAREST THING in the world to hear a rational discussion of vivisection." So began the famous antivivisectionist tract Oxford don C. S. Lewis penned in 1947. Lewis did not mince his words: "The victory of vivisection marks a great advance in the triumph of ruthless, non-moral utilitarianism over the old world of ethical law; a triumph in which we, as well as animals, are already the victims, and of which Dachau and Hiroshima mark the more recent achievements."[1]

People are sometimes surprised to learn that such a noted Christian apologist was an ardent opponent of vivisection (or, as we say today, animal experimentation), but they shouldn't be. The initial nudge came from no less a person than Sir Richard W. Livingstone, then the vice chancellor of Oxford University. Livingstone drew the attention of his friend George R. Farnum, then president of the New England Anti-Vivisection Society, to Lewis's book *The Problem of Pain*.[2] Farnum subsequently wrote to Lewis and invited him to write for the cause.[3]

The Problem of Pain was one of Lewis's most successful books and dealt at length with how the existence of suffering could be reconciled with belief in God. Lewis devoted a long chapter specifically to the problem of animal suffering and recognized that the suffering of innocent, uncomprehending, and vulnerable nonhuman creatures constituted a serious obstacle to Christian theism. That humans should *add* to the existing suffering in the animal world by deliberately inflicting pain was abhorrent to Lewis.

Lewis's interest in animals was not limited just to the theological problem; indeed, the issue of animals, their moral status, and their eternal destiny informed his personal life, his fiction, and his books for children. For example, in *Perelandra*, the villain is a scientist, Dr. Weston, who seeks to colonize other planets for the service of humankind and effectively deifies himself: "I, Weston, am your God and your Devil."[4] It was a view of the scientific enterprise that hardly endeared Lewis to his scientific colleagues at Magdalen College, Oxford. Indeed, he ends his tract on vivisection with these provocative words: "We must first decide what should be allowed: after that it is for the police to discover what is already being done."[5]

II

Lewis did not write in a vacuum, of course. As recently as 2006, there were stormy protests about the establishment of the new "animal lab" in Oxford, leading to the establishment of Voice for Ethical Research at Oxford (VERO), with distinguished patrons such as the Nobel laureate John Coetzee.[6] There were frequent, even daily, protests against the building of the new Biomedical Sciences Building, as the university described it. The protesters alleged the university intimidated and abused them, and the High Court even granted an injunction against the protesters them-

UNIVERSITY OF WINCHESTER
LIBRARY

selves. The vice chancellor wrote to all academics, asking them to support the lab, and university policy was formulated to specifically support animal experiments.[7] The campaign in opposition failed. The new Oxford lab was built.

To those who lived through those days, at least those with a sense of history, it all seemed eerily familiar. The establishment of the very first Oxford animal laboratory in 1885 also occasioned stormy protests both within and without the university. After Convocation (the university's governing body) hastily passed a motion establishing a vivisection laboratory by only three votes, a circular was issued by the opposition ahead of the following Convocation on March 10, 1885. The new motion was to secure further funds for the physiological laboratory. The aim of the circular was to rally Convocation members to vote "*non placet*." The circular's appeal was plainly a moral one and affected Oxford's standing:

> It is hard to over-estimate the influence on popular opinion which is exerted by the attitude of a University such as ours. Will you then allow it to go forth to the world that Oxford sanctions the doctrine of the Physiologists that knowledge may justly be acquired at the cost of torturing God's creatures?[8]

The signatures on the circular (known as a "fly-post" in British university speak) represented a roll call of some of Oxford's most distinguished names: John Ruskin, Slade Professor of Fine Art; Charles L. Dodgson (Lewis Carroll), student (meaning "fellow") of Christ Church; S. R. Driver, Regius Professor of Hebrew; Edward King, Regius Professor of Pastoral Theology and also founder of St. Stephen's House, Oxford, and subsequently bishop of Lincoln; E. A. Freeman, Regius Professor of Modern History; H. W. Chandler, Waynflete Professor of Moral and Metaphysical Philosophy; and E. B. Nicholson, Bodley's Librarian (librarian of the Bodleian library). To these were added four heads of colleges and many college fellows and tutors.[9]

This sensitivity to animals had many antecedents. The renowned Oxford scientist Robert Boyle, despite his later experimental work on animals, ascribed reason to animals, holding that they "partake of that Beame of Divinity as well as we" and maintaining, "I have ever esteem'd Mercy to Beasts to be one of the Purest acts of Charity."[10] As far back as 1772, James Granger, a vicar of Shiplake, Oxfordshire, preached the first recorded sermon against cruelty to animals.[11] John Wesley, founder of Methodism and a fellow of Lincoln College, Oxford, made known his detestation of animal cruelty, especially blood sports. In 1781 he also preached in favor of animal immortality.[12] The vicar of the University Church, John Henry Newman (later Cardinal Newman), preached a sermon in 1842 comparing the innocent suffering of Christ on the cross to that of a vivisected animal. "Think then, my brethren," Newman declared, "of your feelings at cruelty practised on brute animals, and you will gain one sort of feeling which the history of Christ's Cross and Passion ought to excite within you."[13] Dodgson penned his own satirical tract *Some Popular Fallacies about Vivisection* in 1875. His last and thirteenth fallacy—"that the practice of vivisection will never be extended so as to include human subjects"—was met with this mocking reply:

> In other words that while science arrogates to herself the right of torturing at her pleasure the whole sentient creation[,] to man himself some inscrutable line is there drawn over which she will never venture to pass. . . .
>
> And when that day shall come, O my brother-man, you who claim for yourself and for me so proud an ancestry—tracing our pedigree through the anthropomorphoid ape up to the primeval zoophyte—what potent spell have you in store to win exemption from the common doom? Will you represent to that grim spectre, as he gloats over you, scalpel in hand, the inalienable rights of man? He will tell you that this is merely a question of relative expediency,—that, with so feeble a physique as yours, you have only to be thankful that natural selection has spared you so long. Will you reproach him with the needless torture he proposes to inflict upon you? He will smilingly assure you that the hyperæsthesia, which he hopes to induce, is in itself a most interesting phenomenon, deserving much patient study. Will you then, gathering up all your strength for one last desperate appeal, plead with him as with a fellow-man, and with an agonized cry for "Mercy!" seek to rouse some dormant spark of pity in that icy breast? Ask it rather of the nether mill-stone.[14]

Not to be overlooked is Nicholson's *The Rights of an Animal: A New Essay in Ethics*, published in 1879, six years before the Convocation debate at Oxford. His book, radical for its time, anticipated philosophical discussion at Oxford in the 1970s.[15]

In the end, H. P. Liddon, the well-respected Dean Ireland Professor of the Exegesis of Holy Scripture (and a personal friend of Dodgson), was prevailed upon to lead the opposition,[16] cheered on by the then bishop of Oxford John Mackarness and Freeman,[17] in particular, but it was all to no avail. A counterpetition had also been launched, not with such distinguished names, perhaps, but with more muscle and official university support.[18]

The fallout was bitter and long-lasting. Ruskin resigned his Slade Chair, in his own words, "following the vote endowing vivisection in the University."[19] Although some have doubted that this was his real reason,[20] he had a year earlier made clear his detestation of the practice of experiments on animals: "These scientific pursuits are now defiantly, insultingly separated from the science of religion; they are all carried on in defiance of what has been hitherto held to be compassion and pity, and of the great link which binds together the creation from its Maker to the lowest creature."[21]

On the national stage, the debate had already been lost. The 1876 Cruelty to Animals Act had legalized animal experiments in the United Kingdom, also despite fierce debate. This was the first legislation in the world explicitly legalizing animal testing. The leading person in the opposition was Frances Power Cobbe, who founded the Victoria Street Society for the Protection of Animals from Vivisection, later the National Anti-Vivisection Society, in 1875 and the British Union for the Abolition of Vivisection in 1898. She was closely associated with Manchester (now Harris Manchester) College, Oxford, and her spiritual mentor was principal James Martineau. But it was Christ Church graduate Lord Shaftesbury, the famous alumnus of humanitarian causes, who led the parliamentary battle. As Cobbe said after Lord Shaftesbury's death, he "never joined the Victory Street Society; it was the society which joined Lord Shaftesbury."[22] A marble memorial to Cobbe herself can be found on the wall of the ground-floor corridor at Harris Manchester College. The inscription reads,

"Writer on philosophy and religion and a pioneer in social reform." The memorial was presented to the college by Mrs. S. Woolcott Browne in 1908, four years after Cobbe's death.[23]

After 1876 a wide range of antivivisection societies emerged worldwide, also in response to legislation enabling animal research, notably the American Anti-Vivisection Society in 1883, the New England Anti-Vivisection Society in 1895, and the National Anti-Vivisection Society in 1929. In Europe other societies mushroomed, including the Swiss League against Vivisection in 1883, the Société Française Contre la Vivisection in 1883, the Scandinavian League against the Scientific Torture of Animals in 1883, and the Unione Antivivisezionista Italiana in Italy in 1929. By the end of the nineteenth century, the antivivisection movement had virtually become a worldwide phenomenon.

III

The historical narrative would not be complete, however, without some mention of the so-called Oxford Group that emerged in the late 1960s and early 1970s. Although it would be a mistake to think that there was no progress between the 1870s and the 1970s, since the cause was able to pressure for two Royal Commissions on the subject in 1875 and 1906,[24] it was only with the reemergence of intellectual interest in the 1970s that the issue became a topic of ethical interest.

As we have written elsewhere,

> it was the 1971 book *Animals, Men and Morals: An Enquiry into the Maltreatment of Non-Humans*, edited by three Oxford graduate students [Ros Godlovitch, Stanley Godlovitch, and John Harris] . . . that really put animals on the intellectual agenda. It was later dubbed by Peter Singer as "a manifesto for an Animal Liberation movement." The book was one result of the so-called Oxford Group, composed largely of students and academics. The term "Oxford Group," coined by Richard D. Ryder, is something of a misnomer since the various individuals never met all together and had no plan, strategy, or program as such. But it was a time of intellectual ferment, and from that rather unlikely collection of people (philosophers, a sociologist, a psychologist, and a theologian) emerged a cluster of pioneering books, including

Peter Singer's *Animal Liberation*, Richard D. Ryder's *Victims of Science*, Andrew Linzey's *Animal Rights: A Christian Assessment*, and Stephen R. L. Clark's *The Moral Status of Animals*.[25]

A symposium, The Rights of Animals, held under the auspices of the Royal Society for the Prevention of Cruelty to Animals (RSPCA) at Trinity College in Cambridge in 1977 and organized by Andrew Linzey (then, with Ryder, a council member of the RSPCA), concluded with a "Declaration against Speciesism":

> Inasmuch as we believe that there is ample evidence that many other species are capable of feeling, we condemn totally the infliction of suffering upon our brother animals, and the curtailment of their enjoyment, unless it be necessary for their own individual benefit.
>
> We do not accept that a difference of species alone (any more than a difference in race) can justify wanton exploitation or oppression in the name of science or sport, or for food, commercial profit or other human gain.
>
> We believe in the evolutionary and moral kinship of all animals and we declare our belief that all sentient creatures have rights to life, liberty and the quest for happiness.
>
> We call for the protection of these rights.[26]

IV

The purpose of this book is to rearticulate the ethical case pioneered by our Oxford forebears against animal experiments. In our view, the historic debate is unfinished, and the case against experiments far too frequently dismissed. And one of the reasons the case is so frequently dismissed was identified by C. S. Lewis when he stressed that "the alarming thing is that the vivisectors have won the first round," and hence we hardly dare to use the "calmly stern language" of Dodgson or Dr. Johnson (Samuel Johnson, a famous London diarist referred to simply as Dr. Johnson).[27] Another reason, also identified by Lewis, is simply the lack of rational debate.

Although it is true that Oxford was the first university to host a fierce controversy about experiments, it was certainly not the last, as accounts of controversies elsewhere have shown.[28] Universities have traditionally been places of open inquiry and critical thought—powerhouses for generating new ideas and their dissemination in wider society. And yet, most universities in the United States and Europe (and the rest of the world) are not characterized by free and open debate about the ethics of using animals in research. Of course, there are honorable exceptions, especially where academic posts have been created in animal ethics, animal studies, or animals in philosophy. But in most universities where scientific work is increasingly funded by pharmaceutical companies and research councils that support animal experimentation, there is little interest in, let alone support for, opening up the issue for rational debate. A regrettable moral lacuna has opened up. Universities need some critical self-reflection in this regard.

A myriad of ethical arguments appear in the following pages, but one at least is worth emphasizing. At the heart of the historic opposition to animal experiments was the sense that a line was being crossed to the detriment of animals—but not only animals. It is impossible to read the work of opponents without being struck by their concern that experimentation would not stop at animals. Lewis himself echoes this concern:

> No argument for experiments on animals can be found which is not also an argument for experimentation on inferior men. If we cut up beasts simply because they cannot prevent us and because we are backing up our own side in the struggle for existence, it is only logical to cut up imbeciles, criminals, or capitalists for the same reason. Indeed experiments on men have already begun. We all hear that Nazi scientists have done them. We all suspect that our own scientists may begin to do so, in secret, at any moment.[29]

These words may sound stern, even alarmist. But consider this: on October 4, 1995, President Bill Clinton publicly apologized to the survivors and families of those who unknowingly were subjects of US government–sponsored radiation experiments that began in 1944 and continued for three decades. According to a *Los Angeles Times* article published at the time,

> Clinton made the remarks as he accepted the recommendations of an advisory committee he ap-

pointed to study the secret experiments. Although the panel studied about 4,000 radiation experiments that took place during that period, it recommended that only a handful of victims receive compensation. Panel members specifically cited three experiments, including one project where 18 hospital patients, most of them terminally ill, were unknowingly injected with plutonium to determine how long the substance would remain in their body. . . .

Nevertheless, Administration officials appeared to leave the door open for additional restitution. Energy Secretary Hazel O'Leary said in an interview that there could be "thousands, many thousands" of individuals who deserve payment but stressed that both the government and the panel have been hampered by poor or nonexistent record-keeping during that time. . . .

Clinton also ordered a review of the procedures for government-sponsored research on humans and said he will create a bioethics advisory panel to police the research process to "see to it that never again do we stray from the basic values of protecting our people and being straight with them."

He acknowledged that medical and scientific progress "depends upon learning about people's responses to new medicines, to new cutting-edge treatments . . . but there is a right way and a wrong way to do it."[30]

This report raised many questions, but there was one question that no journalist ever asked: if researchers could use human subjects in such a way that was plainly cruel and illegal, what hope can we have that animals in legal experiments are protected from cruelty? The twentieth century that saw an explosion of experiments on animals also saw experiments on human subjects, including prisoners of war, soldiers, gay people, Jewish people, children, the mentally challenged, and people of color.[31] If there are, in Clinton's words, "a right way and a wrong way" to perform experiments and if regulations and safeguards have not been enforced even in regard to thousands of human subjects, why should we believe claims about regulation and enforcement in relation to animals? In arguing that the logic of experimentation, if morally valid, would lead to experimentation on humans, opponents have been more than vindicated.

V

This book falls into two parts.

The first is a report, "Normalizing the Unthinkable: The Ethics of Using Animals in Research: A Report of the Working Group of the Oxford Centre for Animal Ethics," produced by the Oxford Centre for Animal Ethics in 2015. Founded in 2006 to pioneer ethical perspectives on animals through academic teaching, research, and publication, the center is independent and is not under the aegis, control, or sanction of the University of Oxford. The center comprises an international fellowship of more than ninety academics drawn from the sciences and the humanities and more than one hundred academic advisers. A working group of twenty academics from six countries, all but one of whom are fellows of the center, wrote the report, and all members volunteered their services.

The report is the most comprehensive ethical critique of the practice of animal experiments. The full report is included in this book,[32] and the major conclusions are worth emphasizing.

The report's basic contention is that the deliberate and routine abuse of innocent, sentient animals involving harm, pain, suffering, stressful confinement, manipulation, trade, and death should be unthinkable. Yet, animal experiments are just that: the normalization of the unthinkable.[33]

- This normalization is reinforced by the institutionalization of animal experiments through legislation, institutional and establishment thinking, public and private funding, the partiality of the media, and the language of animal research, which obscures, justifies, exonerates, and minimizes what actually takes place in laboratories. The result of these factors is moral stagnation and resistance to change. We cannot avoid the conclusion that animal experiments represent the institutionalization of a preethical view of animals.
- This normalization flies in the face of what is now known about the extent and range of how animals can be harmed. The issue of the complexity of animal awareness, especially of animal sentience (defined as the capacity to experience pain and pleasure), cannot be ignored. Unlike our forebears, we now know,

as reasonably as we can know of humans, that animals (mammals and birds especially) experience not only pain but also shock, fear, foreboding, trauma, anxiety, stress, distress, anticipation, and terror to a greater or lesser extent than humans do. This is the conclusion of many scientific books and articles in peer-reviewed scientific journals.

- This normalization is protected by a range of regulations and controls that in reality do very little to protect animals and indeed often do the reverse. Inspection of animal experiments is flawed, licensing creates a false sense of legitimacy, supervised self-regulation in the European Union (EU) is inadequate, the Three Rs principles (refinement, reduction, and replacement) are not enforced, and care and ethics committees do not provide rigorous evaluation of proposals from an ethical perspective and are fundamentally flawed in not addressing the basic ethical issue. The Three Rs, which are endorsed by the EU and to which lip service is paid by governments (and which might have provided some impetus to change), are in practice massively underfunded, so that alternatives are the Cinderella of scientific research. Even where controls exist, we find them wanting.

- This normalization is justified by the oft-repeated assertion that human interest requires such experiments, but it has to be questioned whether humans are ever benefited by the abuse of animals. The new scientific evidence must make us challenge the claim of utility, since we now know that many experiments have provided misleading or erroneous results.

In terms of harm, pain, suffering, and death, animal experiments constitute one of the major moral issues of our time. It is estimated that 115.3 million animals are used yearly in experiments worldwide.[34] The use of animals in invasive, regulated research represents the institutionalization of a preethical view of animals. The normalization of animal experiments over the last 150 years has been based on flawed moral arguments that can no longer be justified given deeper contemporary understanding of animal sentience. The only logical conclusion is that animals must be afforded special moral consideration that precludes them from use in experiments.

VI

The second part of this book consists of eleven original essays that engage with or elaborate on aspects of the Oxford Centre's report.

The first two, by Simon Pulleyn and Robyn Hederman, address historical aspects that are not covered by the report. Pulleyn, in "Animal Experimentation in Classical Antiquity," illustrates the emotional and psychological distance displayed by some of the first experimenters—notably Galen, who advises anatomists against pity in these rather chilling words: "Every cut that you impose should travel in a straight line . . . and the cut should *without pity or compassion* penetrate into the deep tissues in order that within a single stroke you may lay free and uncovered the skull of the animal."[35] Thus began to emerge a practice devoid of moral or emotional constraints. Hederman illustrates this point further in "Gender and the Animal Experiments Controversy in Nineteenth-Century America" and shows how opponents were classed as suffering from a mental disease called "zoophil-psychosis."[36] Although this condition apparently applied to both sexes, American neurologist Charles Loomis Dana maintained that women were particularly susceptible to the "disease." Opponents were thus characterized as emotionally and mentally unstable. Compassion for animal suffering was pathologized.

But are there not such things as "necessary cruelties"? This issue is discussed in the report, and bioethicists John Rossi and Samual A. Garner, in "Is 'Necessity' a Useful Concept in Animal Research Ethics?" further analyze this question. Despite its common currency in debates about animal research, the notion of necessity is much more philosophically tendentious than its proponents suppose. Rossi and Garner argue that the concept of necessity is vague and requires considerable discussion simply to make intelligible, rendering it unhelpful as a rhetorical counterpoint to ethical criticism of animal research. As well, appeals to the putative necessity of animal research in securing medical benefits merely sidestep relevant ethical issues instead of engaging them directly. Finally, Rossi and Garner consider whether the pursuit of medical progress might be an unconditional moral imperative—making animal research "necessary" in the process—and conclude in the negative.[37] In other words, even if some morally worthy goal can be achieved through animal testing, the issue of its ethical permissibility still remains. As Clinton pointed out, there are right and wrong ways to achieve even laudable goals.

The issue of necessity justifying harms is also explored by Kay Peggs in "Science Fiction and Science Fact: Ethics and Nonhuman Animal Experiments." By focusing on science fiction, notably an episode of *Star Trek: The Next Generation*, Peggs shows how this genre helps us confront the sheer arbitrariness of anthropocentric moral assumptions whereby one species is cherished and another mutilated. The point is reinforced by Katy D. Taylor, "Harms versus Benefits: A Practical Critique of Utilitarian Calculations," who addresses the practical difficulty in formulating, let alone enforcing, some harm-benefit analysis. Even if the system can be improved by greater transparency, clearer criteria, and wider evaluation involving wider society, the crux issue remains that "this process is dominated by the opinions of those set to benefit and not by the perspective of those set to be harmed."[38]

Putative "utilitarian benefit" also receives a lengthy analysis from Robert Patrick Stone Lazo in "Utilitarian Benefit and Uncertainty under Emergent Systems." Unpredictability, Lazo reminds us, is at the very heart of animal testing:

> The behavior of an emergent system can be predicted only by simulation. There is no algorithm, no magic percentage of shared genetic material that can be relied upon as predictive. Even if the translation statistics were better than they are, there would still be no way to know, except by actually running the experiment, . . . whether or not some treatment would be effective for nonhuman animals and for humans. At the very best, a high probability could be offered, but even then, the potential benefit would still be theoretical, whereas the suffering caused by the experiment would be all too real.[39]

In other words, the very unpredictability of an experiment should tell against it morally, since hypothetical benefits cannot outweigh actual harms.

As a former animal experimenter, Nedim C. Buyukmihci, in "Do Moral Principles Permit Experimenting on Nonconsenting Beings?" recounts his painful journey from researcher to opponent, highlighting the institutional resistance to change. At the heart of his conversion was the realization that "human beings do not have a moral right to use other animals if human beings are unwilling to apply the same treatment to fellow human beings."[40] Jarrod Bailey, in "Can Animal Experiments Be Ethically Acceptable When They Are Not Scientifically Defensible?" on the other hand, argues that the lack of human benefit constitutes one of the major objections to animal testing. In his view, the scientific evidence when critically and comparatively analyzed is simply wanting, due to the key differences in all aspects of gene expression and function, affecting many biological systems—in particular, the immune system—so that even monkeys cannot serve as predictive "models" for humans.

In "A Rawlsian Case against Animal Experimentation," Carlos Frederico Ramos de Jesus addresses John Rawls's well-known theory of justice, which has influenced many philosophers and ethicists and which notably excludes animals from the direct sphere of moral obligation. Morality conceived as a form of contract between equals obviously excludes animals because they cannot have a sense of justice or agree to human contracts. But Ramos de Jesus shows that a Rawlsian concept of justice can and should encompass interspecies justice, by reference to Rawls's notions of "parties," not persons, and his emphasis on moral lotteries. Experimentation on animals therefore becomes as "unthinkable" as experiments on children.

One of the issues highlighted by the report is discussed by Elizabeth Tyson in "The Harms of Captivity within Laboratories and Afterward." The question of animal suffering in laboratories is usually centered on the actual experiments that animals have to undergo, but as the report explains, animals suffer not just through invasive experiments but also through the conditions in which they are kept, including captivity, close confinement, handling, and transport. Tyson concentrates on the situations of nonhuman primates and selects four case studies of confinement within the laboratory and afterward. The essay demonstrates how the "physiological and behavioral needs" of nonhuman primates—including but not limited to "the need to live in specific (and often very large and complex) social groups, the need to develop interpersonal relationships, the need to travel over a home range freely (sometimes covering long distances), the need to eat a certain diet, the need to live in a particular climate or habitat, and the need to procreate and raise offspring"—are all necessarily frustrated both by confinement within the laboratory and outside it.[41] The result is harm that is seldom taken into account even by cost-benefit analyses.

The issue of moral distance, raised by Pulleyn in the book's first essay, is illustrated further by Kurt Remele in "When Harry Meets Harry: An Ethical Assessment of Harry Harlow's Maternal Deprivation Experiments." In a notorious series of experiments, Harlow subjected rhesus monkeys to extreme forms of deprivation, including isolation and separation, and yet was wholly unmoved by the suffering he helped to create. Remele compares Harry Harlow with Harry Lime, the latter being the racketeer and diluter of penicillin from the 1949 movie *The Third Man*. In the fictional case, Harry Lime is regarded with opprobrium and finally prosecuted, whereas Harry Harlow is acclaimed as a great scientist and awarded various prizes, including the National Medal of Science in 1967. Yet, both display—in Remele's words—"an alarming, possibly pathological detachment from the suffering and deaths of their victims."[42] Because of this, we believe that it is the right chapter to conclude the second section. Moral distance facilitates moral dissociation.

VII

Given our concern about language, articulated in the report,[43] and because most of our historic language denigrates animals—for example, as "brutes," "beasts," "beastly," "dumb animals," and "subhumans"—we have strived to use ethically sensitive language. The term "companion animals" is used rather than "pets," "free-living" or "free-ranging" rather than "wild" (or "wild" in quotation marks rather than "wild" alone), and "caregiver" rather than "owners." "He" or "she" is utilized in relation to individual animals rather than "it." Also, we have placed the words "model" and "models" as applied to animals, as well as "animal model" and "animals models," in quotation marks because these terms suggest the commodification or objectification of animals (in addition to assuming what needs to be demonstrated).

Our work would have been impossible without the support of Cruelty Free International and especially its chief executive, Michelle Thew, and her colleague Carla Owen. Cruelty Free International acknowledges the generous support of Jane Livesey, who helped to make this project happen. Cruelty Free International both commissioned the original report by the Oxford Centre and also partnered with the center in organizing the 2015 Oxford Summer School from which the essays in this volume are drawn. Cruelty Free International is not a neutral bystander in the debate about animal testing, of course, but it is all to its credit that it was prepared to commission independent academic research on this topic. We have requested and received research information from Cruelty Free International, and it has at no point sought to place restrictions on the nature and type of our deliberations, the selection of essays, or the nature of our conclusions.

Our special thanks go to fellows of the Oxford Centre for their time and expertise in the writing of the report (and its many drafts), as well as to the individual essayists. Details regarding the membership of the working group, the editors, and the essayists are listed at the end of the book. Producing the report was a lengthy process, and since the working group was self-selected (and included experts from many disciplines), we could not at any point be sure of what our collective judgment would be—or indeed whether we would be able to agree on a final text. That we all reached agreement and all signed the report is a result of an impressive convergence that emerged after many months of ethical deliberation.

The report also attracted public endorsement from more than 150 academics and intellectuals worldwide. Although there are too many to list here, at least some should be mentioned: Keith Ward, emeritus professor of divinity, University of Oxford; Nobel laureate John Coetzee; Winchester University vice chancellor Joy Carter; Daniel A. Dombrowski, professor of philosophy, Seattle University; University of South California Upstate associate vice chancellor Clifton N. Flynn; Conor Gearty, professor of human rights, London School of Economics; Stanley Hauerwas, emeritus professor of divinity and law, Duke Divinity School; Richard Llewellin, former bishop at Lambeth, London; David Madden, former British ambassador to

Greece and senior member, St. Antony's College, Oxford; International University of the Caribbean vice president Adrian McFarlane; John Pritchard, former bishop of Oxford; John P. Gluck, emeritus professor of psychology, University of New Mexico; Éric Baratay, professor of contemporary history, Jean Moulin Lyon III University, France; and Jan Wetlesen, emeritus professor of philosophy, University of Oslo.

Finally, our grateful thanks also go to Stephanie A. Ernst for her expert copyediting and advice on the text. Thanks also to the expert team at the University of Illinois Press, including James Engelhardt, Jennifer Comeau, and Dustin Hubbart, and freelance copy editor Mary Lou Kowaleski for their painstaking and thorough work.

Andrew Linzey and Clair Linzey
Oxford Centre for Animal Ethics

Notes

1. C. S. Lewis, *Vivisection*, foreword by George R. Farnum (Boston: New England Anti-Vivisection Society, 1947), 11. Farnum's foreword explains the history of the booklet. Reproduced in Andrew Linzey and Tom Regan, eds., *Animals and Christianity: A Book of Readings* (New York: Crossroads, 1990), 160–64.

2. C. S. Lewis, *The Problem of Pain* (London: Collins, 1940).

3. See discussion in Andrew Linzey, "C. S. Lewis's Theology of Animals," *Anglican Theological Review* 80, no. 1 (1998): 62–63, note 5.

4. C. S. Lewis, *Out of the Silent Planet* (London: Pan Books, 1960), 109, first published by Bodley Head, 1938. Cited and discussed in Linzey, "C. S. Lewis's Theology," 80.

5. Lewis, *Vivisection*, 164.

6. See Voice for Ethical Research at Oxford, "VERO's Patrons," accessed January 11, 2016, http://www.vero.org.uk/who.asp.

7. University of Oxford, "University Policy on the Use of Animals in Scientific Research," accessed January 11, 2016, http://www.ox.ac.uk/news-and-events/animal-research/university-policy-on-the-use-of-animals-in-scientific-research.

8. "Vivisection in Oxford," a flypost distributed ahead of the Convocation of the university on Tuesday, March 10, 1885, box 2/5/3, Pusey House, Oxford. We are grateful to Father Barry Orford for his assistance.

9. Ibid., 3.

10. Robert Boyle, *The Boyle Papers*, Royal Society Library, London, vol. 37, fol. 186r–86v. See also Malcolm Oster, "The 'Beame of Divinity': Animal Suffering in the Early Thought of Robert Boyle," *British Journal for the History of Science* 22 (1989): 151–80. We are grateful to Oster for this reference.

Also cited and discussed in Andrew Linzey, "Ethical Concern for Animals," brochure, Mansfield College, Oxford, 1994, 5.

11. James Granger, "An Apology for the Brute Creation or Abuse of Animals Censured; in a Sermon on Proverbs xii.10," preached in the Parish Church of Shiplake, Oxfordshire, October 18, 1772. Second ed. printed by T. Davies (1773). In a postscript, Granger writes, "The foregoing discourse gave almost universal disgust to two considerable congregations. The mention of dogs and horses was censured as a prostitution of the dignity of the pulpit, and considered as proof of the author's growing insanity" (26).

12. John Wesley, "The General Deliverance," *Sermons on Several Occasions*, with biographical note by John Beecham (London: Wesleyan Conference Office, 1874), 2:60.

13. John Henry Newman, "The Crucifixion," *Parochial and Plain Sermons* (London: Rivingtons, 1868), 2:138. Also cited and discussed in Andrew Linzey, *Why Animal Suffering Matters* (Oxford: Oxford University Press, 2009), 37–40.

14. Lewis Carroll (Charles L. Dodgson), *Some Popular Fallacies about Vivisection*, printed for private circulation (Oxford, June 1875), 14–16.

15. E. B. Nicholson, *The Rights of an Animal: A New Essay in Ethics* (London: C. Kegan Paul, 1879).

16. Liddon noted in his diary, "Bright [regius professor of ecclesiastical history], Freeman, and Moore [principal of St. Edmund Hall] called on me to beg me to lead the opposition to the front for vivisection. Consented with some understandable reluctance." H. P. Liddon, diaries, Sunday, March 8, 1885, Pusey House, Oxford.

17. From Liddon's diary: "Spoke in Convocation against the Decree for Endowing Professor B. Sanderson with an additional £500 without exacting safeguards against cruelties in vivisection. The Dean [of Christ Church, H. G. Liddell], Acland [H. W. Acland, regius professor of medicine], Dicey [academic unknown], [and] W. Anson [W. R. Anson, Warden of All Souls] on the other side. The Bishop of Oxford spoke for us and Freeman. Only we three. The whole Keble vote (alas!) for the decree." Liddon diaries, Tuesday, March 10, 1885, Pusey House, Oxford.

18. "The Physiological Laboratory and Oxford Medical Teaching," flypost, n.d., Liddon papers, box 2/5/1A, Pusey House, Oxford.

19. John Ruskin, letter in *Pall Mall Gazette*, April 21, 1885, reproduced and discussed in *Library Edition of the Works of John Ruskin*, 33:1vi.

20. John Bowker suggests that Ruskin's resignation was not as simple as he himself suggested. See Bowker, "Religions and the Rights of Animals," introduction to *Animal Sacrifices: Religious Perspectives on the Use of Animals in Science*, ed. Tom Regan (Philadelphia: Temple University Press, 1986), 3.

21. John Ruskin, speech, December 1884, cited in M. M. Johnson, ed., *These Also: An Anthology* (Cambridge: Cambridge University Press, 1949), 21; also cited and discussed in Bowker, "Religions," 3.

22. Frances Power Cobbe, *In Memoriam: The Late Earl of Shaftesbury, K. G. First President of the Victoria Street Society* (London: 1885), 3.

23. See Andrew Linzey, "Making Peace with Creation: A Sermon at Harris Manchester College," *The Expository Times* 110, no. 9 (1999): 283.

24. See E. Westacott, *A Century of Vivisection and Anti-Vivisection* (Ashingdon, UK: C. W. Daniel, 1949).

25. Andrew Linzey and Clair Linzey, "The Challenge of Animal Ethics," introduction to *The Handbook of Practical Animal Ethics*, ed. Linzey and Linzey (Basingstoke, UK: Palgrave Macmillan, forthcoming).

26. David Paterson and Richard D. Ryder, eds., *Animals' Rights—A Symposium* (London: Centaur, 1979), viii.

27. Lewis, "Vivisection," in A. Linzey and Regan, *Animals and Christianity*, 163–64. The reference to Dr. Johnson is his note on *Cymbeline*, act 1, scene 5, where the queen says that she would like experiments on "such creatures as We count not worth the hanging,—but none human" (Shakespeare, *Cymbeline*, act 1, sc. 5, lines 19–20). Dr. Johnson comments, "The thought would probably have been more amplified, had our author lived to be shocked with such experiments as have been published in later times, by a race of men that have practised tortures without pity, and related them without shame, and are yet suffered to erect their heads among human beings." Walter Raleigh, ed., *Johnson on Shakespeare: Essays and Notes Selected and Set Forth with an Introduction by Sir Walter Raleigh* (London: Oxford University Press, 1908), 181.

28. See, for example, Deborah Blum, *The Monkey Wars* (Oxford: Oxford University Press, 1995), and Deborah Rudacille, *The Scalpel and the Butterfly: The War between Animal Research and Animal Protection* (New York: Farrar, Straus, and Giroux, 2000).

29. Lewis, "Vivisection," in A. Linzey and Regan, *Animals and Christianity*, 163.

30. Marlene Cimons, "Clinton Apologizes for Radiation Tests, Experiments: Cabinet Will Study Compensation for Some Victims and Their Families: About 4,000 Secret Studies through 1974 Were Disclosed," *Los Angeles Times*, October 4, 1995, accessed January 12, 2016, http://articles.latimes.com/1995–10–04/news/mn-53213_1_radiation-experiments. Clinton's public statement can be viewed on YouTube, https://www.youtube.com/watch?v=KRTOB8JPwa8, accessed January 12, 2016.

31. See p. 49.

32. See Part 1, pp. 11–100.

33. Lisa Peattie, "Normalizing the Unthinkable," *Bulletin of Atomic Scientists* (1984): 32–36.

34. Katy Taylor, Nicky Gordon, Gill Langley, and Wendy Higgins, "Estimates for Worldwide Laboratory Animal Use in 2005," *Alternative to Laboratory Animals* 36 (2008): 327–42.

35. See p. 112 (editors' emphasis).

36. See p. 112.

37. See p. 131.

38. See p. 156.

39. See p. 165.

40. See p. 168.

41. See p. 192.

42. See p. 204.

43. See pp. 58–61.

PART 1

NORMALIZING THE UNTHINKABLE

THE ETHICS OF USING ANIMALS IN RESEARCH

A Report of the Working Group
of the Oxford Centre for Animal Ethics

Introduction to the Report

EACH YEAR MILLIONS of nonhuman animals (hereafter "animals") are used in research. Animal experimentation generates public and political concern worldwide. In this report, we offer a new assessment of the central ethical issue, namely, whether such experiments can be justified morally. There have been some recent reports in the United Kingdom that address the ethics of our use of animals in research, notably the *Review of Cost-Benefit Assessment* by the Animal Procedures Committee in 2003, the Select Committee of the House of Lords report in 2002, and the report of the Weatherall Committee in 2006,[1] all of which we address in detail, as well as reports by the Nuffield Council and the Boyd group.[2] But we find that these reports insufficiently address the deeper ethical issues raised by animal experimentation. Our report is also one of the very few to focus on the ethical dimension and to do so from a variety of disciplines, including philosophy, science, history, theology, law, critical animal studies, and sociology. We especially consider arguments that arise from changing ethical views based on recent discussions of the status of animals, the moral relevance of animal sentience, and the limits that morality imposes on the treatment of sentient creatures.

With the insights of various disciplines, we have endeavored to raise the fundamental ethical question in relation to almost all aspects of animal experimentation, not only examining the procedures themselves but also addressing such questions as animal experimentation's history, scientific validity, philosophy, institutionalization, and purported controls, including legislation, regulation, inspection, licensing, and regulation. In doing so, we have had to challenge much conventional wisdom and many standard justifications. Examining the evidence and thinking outside the box has not been an easy experience, and we deeply wish we could have published a more emollient and less controversial report. But we have felt constrained to follow the evidence as it has led us and, most of all, to be faithful to where we believe the weight of moral argument resides.

We commend our report to fellow academics, governments, and the media in the hope that it will engender a more progressive discussion of the morality of animal testing.

Notes

1. Animal Procedures Committee (APC), *Review of Cost-Benefit Assessment in the Use of Animals in Research* (2003), accessed September 29, 2014, https://www.gov.uk/government/uploads/system/uploads/attachment_data/file/119027/cost-benefit-assessment.pdf; House of Lords, *Select Committee on Animals in Scientific Procedures, Volume 1—Report* (London, 2002), accessed September 29, 2014, http://www.publications.parliament.uk/pa/ld200102/ldselect/ldanimal/150/150.pdf; D. Weatherall et al., *The Use of Non-Human Primates in Research*, accessed September 29, 2014, https://royalsociety.org/~/media/Royal_Society_Content/policy/publications/2006/Weatherall-Report.pdf.

2. Nuffield Council on Bioethics, *The Ethics of Research involving Animals* (2005), accessed May 13, 2014, http://nuffieldbioethics.org/wp-content/uploads/The-ethics-of-research-involving-animals-full-report.pdf; J. A. Smith and K. M. Boyd, *Lives in the Balance: The Ethics of Using Animals in Biomedical Research* (Oxford: Oxford University Press, 1991).

1.1

The Scale of the Problem

THE ANIMAL RESEARCH we consider should be distinguished from purely observational studies in which the animals are not harmed. In this report, we use the terms "animal experimentation," "animal tests," and "animal research" interchangeably to denote procedures that entail, inter alia, the capture, handling, transport, confinement, and manipulation of living sentient beings and the subjection of these beings to procedures against their own individual interests, including those that involve the deliberate infliction of suffering, harm, and/or death.

We intend our report to be relevant to experimentation worldwide, and although we make references to research in various countries, we principally focus on animal experimentation in the United Kingdom. We have done this for two reasons. In the first place, the United Kingdom (rightly or wrongly) is often held up as a model for how animal experimentation should be regulated. For example, Lord Winston, speaking in the House of Lords, claimed that "the overall standard of inspection, control and regulation conditions for laboratory animals are remarkably high" in Britain compared with six other countries in which he has worked.[1] In order to avoid any accusation of bias, we have therefore tried to focus on the country that many scientists themselves apparently believe to exhibit "best practice."

Second, if animal experiments can be effectively regulated, then the United Kingdom—with its detailed laws, licensing procedures, inspectorate, and

ethical review committees—ought to achieve this. Hence, we analyze the ethical rationale provided by UK advisory bodies and provide examples of various experiments in the United Kingdom, as well as focusing on the methods of regulation and control.

We begin by outlining the scale and diversity of the usage of animals in research.

Numbers and Uses Worldwide

It is important to grasp the scale of animal usage in research, including the numbers of animals used worldwide, the range of animals used, and the variety of uses to which animals are subjected. Relatively few countries collate and publish statistics on the number of animal subjects used in research laboratories. Estimates are often based on little more than guesswork. Using a range of statistical techniques, some authors estimate that 115.3 million animals are used every year worldwide. However, they also caution that this is likely to be an underestimate.[2]

It is hard to accurately estimate the number of animals used in research worldwide for two main reasons. First, relatively few countries produce statistics on the numbers of animals used or the purposes for which they are used. Second, among those countries that do keep statistics on animal research, the definitions of the terms "animal" and "use" vary widely. For example, the United States publishes statistics on animals used in research, but those statistics do not include mice, rats, birds, fish, reptiles, and amphibians (i.e., the vast majority of animals used).

To date, only one journal article has attempted to calculate the scale of worldwide animal use.[3] The study calculated the estimates for animal use in research using the definitions of "animals," "purposes," and "an experiment" given in the *Glossary of Terms and Guidelines for Statistical Tables* for European Union (EU) statistical reports.[4] The definition of "animal" includes mammals, birds, reptiles, amphibians, and fish but excludes their respective fetal or embryonic forms. Purposes include biological studies, research and development of products for human medicine, dentistry, veterinary medicine, military uses, toxicology, disease diagnosis, education, and training. The EU definitions exclude animals killed solely to provide tissue; "surplus" conventional animals bred but then killed; animals exploited in behavioral research, including in the marking of "wild" fish; and genetically modified (GM) animals bred to maintain GM strains. The definitions exclude, as well, most invertebrates (cyclostomes and cephalopods are included in the definitions).

The study estimates that under the aforementioned EU definitions, there are conservatively 58.3 million animals being used in research in 179 countries worldwide. However, if animals being killed for the provision of tissue, animals used to maintain GM strains, and animals considered "surplus" who are bred for laboratory use are included, that figure rises to a more comprehensive estimate of 115.3 million animals.

A wide variety of animals are used in research globally, varying by country. In the EU, categories of animals include all kinds of mammals—including nonhuman primates, mice, rats, guinea pigs, hamsters, other rodents, rabbits, cats, dogs, ferrets, other carnivores, equids, pigs, goats, sheep, and cattle—as well as birds, reptiles, amphibians, fish,[5] and more recently, cyclostomes and cephalopods.[6] Because many countries in which animal experiments occur do not publish statistics on animal use—for example, the People's Republic of China, Egypt, Iran, India, and Thailand—it is hard to give an accurate account of all the animals used. However, it seems reasonable on the basis of the EU list to conclude that animals from all biological categories are used.

Although many countries do not publish statistics on animal use in experiments, Taylor et al. provide informed estimates of the numbers of animals in laboratories who were used per country in 2005.[7] The top ten users (ranked in order of standardized, estimated number of animals used per year) are as follows: United States, 17,317,147; Japan, 11,154,961; People's Republic of China, 2,975,122; Australia, 2,389,813; France, 2,325,398; Canada, 2,316,281; United Kingdom, 1,874,207; Germany, 1,822,424; Taiwan, 1,237,337; and Brazil, 1,169,517.

Two general conclusions may be gleaned from the foregoing. In the first place, the use of animals in research is a worldwide phenomenon. Almost every country allows the practice. Second, in many countries no information or actual figures are provided regarding the number of animals or number of experiments.

Examples of Experiments

We detail here experiments drawn from twelve selected categories of use during 2010–15. The examples are taken from six countries but principally focus on the United Kingdom, and they have been drawn from published scientific reports. These experiments range from the standard to the nonstandard and were chosen to illustrate the breadth of the use of animals. The examples by no means illustrate the most (or least) severe types of experiments.

a. Military

In order to simulate the effects of explosions on soldiers and civilians in terrorist attacks, researchers subjected large white pigs to bomb blasts to induce severe blast injuries. Pigs were anesthetized and then wrapped in protective blankets before they were left on trolleys [buses] two and a half meters [about eight feet] away from explosives that were then detonated remotely. Immediately after the blast, 30 percent of the pigs' total blood content was pumped out through an artery in their legs. The researchers then tried to resuscitate the pigs using two different techniques. However, eleven pigs (out of twenty-eight) died despite the resuscitation. All of the animals were killed and dissected at the end of the experiment (*Porton Down, England, United Kingdom*).[8]

Guinea pigs were poisoned with an extremely toxic nerve agent (VX) so that researchers could test the efficacy of a combination of drugs and human enzyme as a treatment after exposure. VX is a lethal substance that can be used as a chemical weapon and enters the body through the skin or the lungs, where it causes severe systemic damage leading to seizures, breathing difficulties, coma, and eventually death. VX was applied to the shaved backs of conscious guinea pigs before drugs were injected into their muscles. The animals received treatment only when they displayed observational signs of poisoning, which included severe tremors, tearing, salivation, and seizures followed by rapid physical and/or mental impairment. No mention of pain relief was given. Some of the guinea pigs died because of the nerve agent, and the ones who survived were killed at the end of the study. All of the animals were dissected, and most (even those who survived) showed signs of internal damage to the lungs such as bleeding, swelling, and excess fluid buildup (*Porton Down, England, United Kingdom*).[9]

b. Food/drink

To investigate whether Lipton black tea could reduce diarrhea caused by the bacteria *E. coli*, researchers housed ninety-six one-month-old piglets in isolation and fed them a diet containing the tea for six days before force-feeding them the bacteria in order to induce diarrhea. The daily prevalence of diarrhea and the piglets' weight and behavior were measured while they were kept on the diet for a further twenty-one days. During the experiment, eight piglets died from severe diarrhea, and some of the surviving animals developed skin abnormalities and behavioral problems (*Unilever, the Netherlands*).[10]

To investigate whether black cumin seed extract could alleviate the symptoms of food allergies in humans, researchers force-fed the extract to mice daily through a tube down their throats, for forty-three days. During this period the mice were forced to become allergic to a protein found in chicken eggs after it was injected into their abdomens twice and force-fed to them six times. The animals were examined throughout the experiment and given scores based on the severity of their diarrhea. They were then killed

so that their intestines could be dissected for further analysis (*Nestlé, Switzerland*).[11]

c. Recreational drugs

So that researchers could investigate the effects of age and nicotine on the brain, both young and old rats had pumps surgically implanted under their skin for the administration of nicotine. The rats were separated into two groups; animals in the high-dose group were infused with enough nicotine to mimic "heavy smokers," which according to data from a different study would be the equivalent of 266 cigarettes per day (*University of Dundee, Scotland, United Kingdom*).[12]

In an attempt to discover a treatment for alcohol abuse, researchers used a strain of male mice who "like" alcohol as well as standard male rats in a series of experiments. Substances thought to encourage an aversion to alcohol were injected into the rats' abdomens. One hour later, the rats were injected with a large dose of alcohol equivalent to seventeen and a half units of alcohol in a seventy-kilogram [154-pound] human (the recommended daily allowance in the United Kingdom is three to four units). Blood samples were then taken from the rats' tails every hour for three hours. In another experiment, one of the alcohol-aversion drugs was injected into the rats' abdomens every day for four days. On the third day, the rats were deprived of water for eighteen hours before being tested to see how much alcohol-laced water they would drink two hours after the final injection (*University of Cardiff, Wales, United Kingdom*).[13]

d. Stem cells

So that researchers could discover whether stem cells could be found in the spaces between the joints after a knee injury, mice were subjected to surgery to purposefully damage their knees. Under anesthesia their knee joint was dislocated, and a deep wound was carved into their kneecap before the knee was relocated and the joint capsule and skin were sewn back up. The mice were injected with stem cell–detecting chemicals after surgery to help the researchers detect the presence of stem cells after the mice had been killed and dissected (*University of Aberdeen, Scotland, UK*).[14]

e. Genetics

Some Asian people carry a mutated version of a gene that is known to play a key role in the development of hair, sweat glands, and other skin features. The mutation is common in people from East Asia and is thought to have arisen thirty thousand years ago as an adaptation to the humid environment. To demonstrate the effects of the mutation, a group of international researchers from the United States, China, and the United Kingdom genetically modified mice to possess the mutated gene. As anticipated, the mice developed thicker hair, more sweat glands, and denser mammary glands. The six-week-old animals were then killed, and their eyelids, mammary glands, and skin were dissected for examination (*Harvard Medical School, United States*).[15]

Researchers in China have used a new technology to create GM monkeys, which they have claimed will help produce better models to mimic human diseases. The GM work was carried out using a genetic engineering system called CRISPR/Cas9, which allows researchers to cut and paste DNA to create specific mutations. To produce just two GM monkeys, researchers collected 198 eggs from an unknown number of donor females and then modified them to possess three mutations using the CRISPR system. Eighty-three embryos were found to have developed the desired mutations and were subsequently surgically implanted into twenty-nine surrogate mothers. Only ten monkeys became pregnant, with a total of nineteen fetuses, and as of this writing, five of the mothers have already miscarried while four are still "waiting" to give birth. Only one female, who gave birth to twins, carried two of the three mutations that the researchers had originally expected (*Nanjing Medical University, China*).[16]

f. Chemical testing

Bisphenol A (BPA) is a chemical that has been used for over sixty years to produce polycarbonate plastics and epoxy resins that are found in many consumer products. Scientists have become increasingly concerned about its widespread use because BPA is thought to be an endocrine disruptor that can lead to fertility and developmental problems. In order to examine the effect of prenatal BPA exposure on egg formation, scientists from Washington State University forced pregnant rhesus macaques to ingest pieces of fruit containing the chemical every day throughout their pregnancy. Another group of pregnant monkeys received continuous BPA exposure through tubes implanted into their bloodstream. At the end of the study, the fetuses were removed by caesarean section and dissected and examined (*Washington State University, United States*).[17]

Triclosan is an antibacterial chemical commonly used in lipsticks, soaps, deodorants, toothpastes, mouthwashes, detergents, and thousands of other cosmetic and household products. Although it has been widely used for over forty years, scientists have recently begun to question its safety. Researchers from the University of California found that in mice, triclosan hinders the process by which muscles, including the heart, receive signals from the brain. In their experiment, eight ten-week-old male mice were anesthetized before undergoing surgery in which the carotid artery in their neck was exposed. A pump was inserted into the artery to measure the volume and pressure of blood that passed through. With the mice under anesthesia, various doses of the chemical were then injected into their abdomens. During the surgery their hearts were punctured to collect blood for analysis, and they were then killed. In another procedure, conscious three-month-old male mice were injected with triclosan in their abdomens before being subjected to a grip-strength test in which they were made to grab onto a wire mesh with all four paws before being pulled away by their tails (*University of California, United States*).[18]

g. Product testing

Researchers forced two different types of mouthwash into the mouths of rats via syringe twice a day for fourteen days to see whether either mouthwash had an effect on healing after tooth extraction. One contained chlorhexidine, which is an active ingredient found in most commercially available mouthwashes, and the other was an herbal mouthwash containing persica plant extract. On the eighth day of the study, the rats were placed in closed chambers, where they were anesthetized with a gas before their molars were pulled out using forceps. The animals were then killed, and their tooth sockets were dissected. During the study, one of the rats choked on the mouthwash and died (*University of Dundee, Scotland, United Kingdom*).[19]

h. Food toxicology

In an attempt to test the safety of aloe vera juice (produced by a US company called Herbalife), researchers forced ninety-six rats to drink various concentrations of the juice in their drinking water for three months. They were observed to see whether they would die over this period and at the end were anesthetized and bled out through a puncture in their hearts so that their tissues could be removed and examined (*Huntingdon Life Sciences, England, United Kingdom*).[20]

Researchers carried out a carcinogenicity test on GM maize using rats. They fed two hundred rats for their entire lifetime (two years) a diet of one of the best-selling strains of GM maize produced by agricultural biotechnology giant Monsanto, along with the company's popular weed killer Roundup, in order to induce cancer in the animals. The rats developed large, cancerous tumors that led to multiple organ damage and premature death in 50 percent of males and 70 percent of females. No mention of pain relief was given (*Caen University, France*).[21]

i. Brain research

To investigate how the cells in the brain process information, researchers surgically implanted electrodes into the brains of two macaque monkeys. Researchers required the monkeys to sit still for hours in restraint chairs where their heads were fixed into place. Their brain activity and eye movements were monitored as they were made to stare at color pictures of animals, nature scenes, patterns, and everyday objects presented on a computer screen. They were given juice-drop rewards throughout the procedure in order to keep them working. They had been deliberately deprived of water to make them thirsty prior to each experimental session (*University of St. Andrews, Scotland, United Kingdom*).[22]

To find out whether childhood stress leads to an increased risk of developing psychiatric disorders in adulthood, researchers subjected baby rats to a sequence of stressful tests. On the first day (when the rats were twenty-five days old), the rats were forced to swim in a water-filled tank from which they could not escape for ten minutes. The next day, they were pushed into narrow plastic tubes to restrain them for three periods of thirty minutes each. On the final day, they were placed in chambers where they were given electric foot shocks every thirty seconds for three minutes. When the rats became adults, they were subjected to various behavioral tests and assessed for signs of anxiety (*University of Edinburgh, Scotland, United Kingdom*).[23]

j. Medical research

So that researchers could investigate changes in heart wall stress and stretching associated with heart disease, mixed-breed dogs were anesthetized before undergoing open-chest surgery where part of their heart was stretched by 22 percent for six hours by a stretching device that was sewed directly onto their heart muscle. The dogs in one group were injected with a blood pressure–lowering drug before the stretch and again three hours after the stretch. The dogs were then killed by electrical stimulation of the heart before their hearts were dissected. The experiment was funded by the British Heart Foundation and the [National Institute for Health Research] NIHR Biomedical Research Centre in the United Kingdom but was probably conducted in the United States.[24]

In a study supported by Breast Cancer Research Scotland, breast tissue excised from twenty human patients with breast cancer was surgically implanted under the skin of mice (six to twelve mice per patient). Four days after surgery, the mice were placed in chambers where they were subjected to four hours of radiation, so that researchers could study the radiation's effect on cancerous breast tissue. The mice were then killed four hours after radiation exposure so that the xenografted breast tissue could be harvested (*University of Dundee, Scotland, United Kingdom*).[25]

k. Drug testing

To test a potential drug treatment for lazy eye in humans, researchers anesthetized fourteen kittens (twenty to twenty-six days old) in order to sew one of each kitten's eyes shut. The kittens were left in that state for two months before they were subjected to brain surgery at the age of three months. The kittens were anesthetized, and each kitten's eye was reopened. Both eyes of each kitten were covered with a contact lens to help the eyes focus on a computer screen placed fifty centimeters [about twenty inches] away from the kittens' faces. The kittens were injected with a neuromuscular blocking agent (NBA) so that their eyes would not move. NBAs pose additional risks to animals because they cause paralysis and prevent animals from indicating to researchers by movement or vocalization that they are actually coming around from the anesthetic. The kittens' scalps were cut to expose their skulls so that a piece of skull could be removed to expose their brains. The researchers then cemented a metal recording device into their skulls and covered it with a glass "window" so that they could see the kittens' brains. A head-restraining device was also glued onto their skulls to keep their heads still during recording. Images were then presented on the screens to stimulate the eyes while recordings were made for two hours. The test substance was also injected into the kittens' brains throughout the recording session. The kittens were woken up and then subjected to further recording sessions one and two weeks later. At the end of the final session, all of the kittens were killed, and their brains were dissected (*University of Cardiff, Wales, United Kingdom*).[26]

Eleven sheep had tubes surgically implanted into their spines for the administration of a new drug that was thought to reduce pain sensitivity. Fourteen days after surgery, their legs were injected with formalin, which slowly damaged the tissues, causing serious pain to the animals. Researchers recorded how often the sheep flinched in pain or how long they held their legs up because they were unable to put any weight on them. Blunt pins were also pushed into their skin with increasing force until the sheep lifted up their legs in pain. Because the point of the experiment was to assess pain reactions, there was no mention of pain relief during the tests, but there was no mention of pain relief afterward either (*University of Glasgow, Scotland, United Kingdom*).[27]

I. Eating disorders

Researchers have used sheep as a model of human obesity. In one experiment they kept eighteen young (ten-month-old) female sheep on their own in individual pens. Tubes were surgically implanted into their heads so that drugs could be delivered directly into their brains. Over the next forty weeks, some of the sheep were then allowed to consume a high-calorie diet consisting of three times the normal amount of food required, whereas the others were fed a restricted diet for forty weeks. Members of the "obese group" were then "put on a diet" and had their food restricted for sixteen weeks, and the others were given high-calorie food to fatten them up for the remaining weeks. The sheep were subjected to regular anesthesia so that their bodies could be scanned by a machine. They also had to undergo repeated blood-sample draws via cannulas in their jugulars as well as insulin injections directly into their brains. At the end of this experiment, all of the sheep were killed, and their fat was taken off their bodies and weighed (*University of Aberdeen, Scotland, United Kingdom*).[28]

In an attempt to mimic anorexia, researchers fed mice severely restricted diets and encouraged them to exercise, leading to severe weight loss. Mice were kept on an increasingly restricted feeding schedule for three months, until they were being given access to food for only two hours per day. Mice whose body weight dropped below 70 percent of the normal body weight were killed. In one experiment, mice were kept in cages with running wheels, where they were encouraged to exercise excessively. In another experiment, a chemical derived from cannabis was injected into the animals daily to see whether it would increase their appetite. Some of the mice had to be killed due to the severe weight loss (*University of Strathclyde, Scotland, United Kingdom*).[29]

Two conclusions can be drawn from these examples and from the numbers and uses worldwide. First, the range of uses to which animals are subjected is very wide, and second, all biological categories of animals are utilized. Almost all of these animals are sentient. Indeed, sentiency is a precondition of the need for a license to experiment under UK law and the current EU directive. These sentient beings experience suffering, distress, harm, and death, as illustrated by the preceding examples.

Since these experiments cause not only physical and/or psychological harm but also death, it follows that they require strong moral justification. We shall explore whether such justification is available to researchers, but first we shall look briefly at the history of the debate.

Notes

1. R. Winston, *Hansard*, House of Lords, October 24, 2011, col, 623, accessed January 2, 2015, http://www.publications.parliament.uk/pa/ld201011/ldhansrd/text/111024-0002.htm#11102443000399. Cited and discussed in A. Linzey and P. N. Cohn, "Wanted: Full Disclosure," *Journal of Animal Ethics* 2, no. 2 (2012): v.

2. K. Taylor, N. Gordon, G. Langley, and W. Higgins, "Estimates for Worldwide Laboratory Animal Use in 2005," *Alternatives to Laboratory Animals* 36 (2008): 327–42.

3. Ibid.

4. European Commission, *Glossary of Terms and Guidelines for Statistical Tables by Member States*, XI/411/97 (1997).

5. Ibid.

6. European Commission, *Eurobarometer Science and Technology Report* (2010), accessed May 9, 2014, http://ec.europa.eu/public_opinion/archives/ebs/ebs_340_en.pdf; European Parliament, *Directive 2010/63/EU of the European Parliament and of the Council of 22 September 2010 on the Protection of Animals Used for Scientific Purposes* (2010), accessed January 3, 2015, http://eur-lex.europa.eu/legal-content/EN/TXT/PDF/?uri=CELEX:32010L0063&from=EN. For discussion, see K. Peggs, *Experiments, Animal Bodies, and Human Values* (London: Routledge, 2017).

7. Taylor, Gordon, et al., "Estimates."

8. J. Garner, S. Watts, C. Parry, J. Bird, G. Cooper, and E. Kirkman, "Prolonged Permissive Hypotensive Resuscitation Is Associated with Poor Outcome in Primary Blast Injury with Controlled Haemorrhage," *Annals of Surgery* 251, no. 6 (2010): 1131–39.

9. H. Mumford, C. J. Docx, M. E. Price, A. C. Green, J. E. H. Tattersall, and S. J. Armstrong, "Human Plasma-Derived BuChE as a Stoichiometric Bioscavenger for Treatment of Nerve Agent Poisoning," *Chemico-Biological Interactions* 203, no. 1 (2013): 160–66.

10. M. J. Bruins, M. A. M. Vente-Spreeuwenberg, C. H. Smits, and L. G. J. Frenken, "Black Tea Reduces Diarrhoea Prevalence but Decreases Growth Performance in Enterotoxigenic Escherichia Coli–Infected Post-Weaning Piglets," *Journal of Animal Physiology and Animal Nutrition* 95, no. 3 (2011): 388–98.

11. S. C. Duncker, D. Philippe, C. Martin-Paschoud, M. Moser, A. Mercenier, and S. Nutten, "*Nigella sativa* (Black Cumin) Seed Extract Alleviates Symptoms of Allergic Diarrhoea in Mice, Involving Opioid Receptors," *PLoS One* 7, no. 6 (2012): e39841.

12. C. Scerri, C. A. Stewart, D. J. K. Balfour, and K. C. Breen, "Nicotine Modifies In Vivo and In Vitro Rat Hippocampal Amyloid Precursor Protein Processing in Young but Not Old Rats," *Neuroscience Letters* 514, no. 1 (2012): 22–26.

13. A. B. A. Badawy, S. Bano, and A. Steptoe, "Tryptophan in Alcoholism Treatment I: Kynurenine Metabolites Inhibit the Rat Liver Mitochondrial Low Km Aldehyde Dehydrogenase Activity, Elevate Blood Acetaldehyde Concentration and Induce Aversion to Alcohol," *Alcohol and Alcoholism* 46, no. 6 (2011): 651–60.

14. T. B. Kurth, F. Dell'Accio, V. Crouch, A. Augello, P. T. Sharpe, and C. De Bari, "Functional Mesenchymal Stem Cell Niches in Adult Mouse Knee Joint Synovium In Vivo," *Arthritis and Rheumatology* 63, no. 5 (2011): 1289–1300.

15. Y. G. Kamberov, S. Wang, J. Tan, P. Gerbault, A. Wark, L. Tan, Y. Yang, et al., "Modelling Recent Human Evolution in Mice by Expression of a Selected EDAR Variant," *Cell* 152 (2013): 691–702.

16. Y. Niu, B. Shen, Y. Cui, Y. Chen, J. Wang, L. Wang, Y. Kang, et al., "Generation of Gene-Modified Cynomolgus Monkey via Cas9/RNA-Mediated Gene Targeting in One-Cell Embryos," *Cell* 156, no. 4 (2014): 836–43.

17. P. A. Hunt, C. Lawson, M. Gieske, B. Murdoch, H. Smith, A. Marre, T. Hassold, and C. A. VandeVoort, "Bisphenol A Alters Early Oogenesis and Follicle Formation in the Fetal Ovary of the Rhesus Monkey," *Proceedings of the National Academy of Sciences* 109, no. 43 (2012): 17525–30.

18. G. Cherednichenko, R. Zhang, R. A. Bannister, V. Timofeyev, N. Li, E. B. Fritsch, W. Feng, et al., "Triclosan Impairs Excitation-Contraction Coupling and Ca^{2+} Dynamics in Striated Muscle," *Proceedings of the National Academy of Sciences* 109, no. 35 (2012): 14158–63.

19. M. Dorri, S. Shahrabi, and A. Navabazam, "Comparing the Effects of Chlorhexidine and Persica on Alveolar Bone Healing following Tooth Extraction in Rats: A Randomised Controlled Trial," *Clinical Oral Investigation* 16, no. 1 (2010): 25–31.

20. A. Shao, A. Broadmeadow, G. Goddard, E. Bejar, and V. Frankos, "Safety of Purified Decolorized (Low Anthraquinone) Whole Leaf Aloe Vera (L) Burm. F. Juice in a 3-Month Drinking Water Toxicity Study in F344 Rats," *Food and Chemical Toxicology* 57 (2013): 21–31.

21. G. E. Séralini, E. Clair, R. Mesnage, S. Gress, N. Defarge, M. Malatesta, D. Hennequin, and J. Spiroux de Vendômois, "Long-Term Toxicity of a Roundup Herbicide and a Roundup-Tolerant Genetically Modified Maize," *Food and Chemical Toxicology* 50, no. 11 (2012): 4221–31.

22. M. W. Oram, "Visual Stimulation Decorrelates Neuronal Activity," *Journal of Neurophysiology* 105 (2011): 942–57.

23. N. M. Brydges, L. Hall, R. Nicolson, M. C. Holmes, and J. Hall, "The Effects of Juvenile Stress on Anxiety, Cognitive Bias, and Decision Making in Adulthood: A Rat Model," *PLoS One* 7, no. 10 (2012): e48143.

24. W. Hussain, P. M. Patel, R. Chowdury, C. Cabo, E. J. Ciaccio, M. J. Lab, H. S. Duffy, A. L. Wit, and N. S. Peters, "The Renin-Angiotensin System Mediates the Effects of Stretch on Conduction Velocity, Connexin43 Expression, and Redistribution in Intact Ventricle," *Journal of Cardiovascular Electrophysiology* 21, no. 11 (2010): 1276–83; British Heart Foundation, *Animals and Heart Research*, leaflet, (2010).

25. P. J. Coates, M. V. Appleyard, K. Murray, C. Ackland, J. Gardner, D. C. Brown, D. J. Adamson, et al., "Differential Contextual Responses of Normal Human Breast Epithelium to Ionizing Radiation in a Mouse Xenograft Model," *Cancer Research* 70, no. 23 (2010): 9808–15.

26. V. Vorobyov, J. C. F. Kwok, J. W. Fawcett, and F. Sengpiel, "Effects of Digesting Chondroitin Sulphate Proteoglycans on Plasticity in Cat Primary Visual Cortex," *Journal of Neuroscience* 33, no. 1 (2013): 234–43.

27. S. Dolan, M. D. Gunn, C. Crossan, and A. M. Nolan, "Activation of Metabotropic Glutamate Receptor 7 in Spinal Cord Inhibits Pain and Hyperalgesia in a Novel Formalin Model in Sheep," *Behavioural Pharmacology* 22 (2011): 582–88.

28. C. L. Adam, P. Findlay, R. Aitken, J. Milne, and J. Wallace, "In Vivo Changes in Central and Peripheral Insulin Sensitivity in a Large Animal Model of Obesity," *Journal of Endocrinology* 153, no. 7 (2012): 3147–57.

29. D. Y. Lewis and R. R. Brett, "Activity-Based Anorexia in C57/BL6 Mice: Effects of the Phytocannaboid, Delta-9-Tetrahydrocannabinol (THC) and the Anandamide Analogue, OMDM-2," *European Neuropsychopharmacology* 20 (2010): 622–31.

The Old Debate

ANIMAL EXPERIMENTATION has been practiced since the time of the Greeks and possibly even before.[1] But it was only in the nineteenth century that experimentation began to be officially regulated through legislation. Since passage of the Cruelty to Animals Act 1876 in the United Kingdom, there has been a long, and frequently acrimonious, debate between supporters and opponents of the practice. This old debate provides lessons for us and provides impetus for a new assessment. Numerous aspects of the old debate have effectively blocked progress in the discussion. Here we center on four major aspects.

Four Blocks to Ethical Discussion

The first block is nomenclature. The words "vivisection" (meaning the practice of cutting a live animal) and "antivivisection" (opposition to such a practice) became the standard terms of the pre- and post-1876 debate. In context, when the first uses of animals were preponderantly of this kind, the terms had some relevance. But the use of animals now, as already shown, widely exceeds such strictly invasive techniques. As such, sole concentration on these outdated terms now obscures the nature of the debate, which encompasses myriad factors, including the antecedent conditions of actual use (capture, rearing, transport, handling, and conditions of captivity) as well as the uses themselves, including any reuse and the killing of the animals who can no longer be used. Clarity of terms helps to ensure clarity of ethical analysis.

The second aspect blocking discussion is the limited ethical framework within which many of the previous debates were (and continue to be) conducted. Many opponents of animal experiments focused on such considerations as the need to promote kindness and prevent cruelty. Although, of course, promotion of kindness and prevention of cruelty both are admirable goals, this approach did not challenge many of the underlying assumptions about the moral priority of human interests or indeed about the nature and status of animals. It is worth noting that the Society for the Prevention of Cruelty to Animals (SPCA, founded in 1824) sought the extension of charity to what they termed the "inferior classes of animated beings," namely animals.[2] We shall return to this issue in a subsequent part of our report (see section 1.5).

The third issue concerns the fascination with the newly emerging sciences—for example, pathology and immunization—and the promise they held for human betterment. It is impossible to read the history of the debates pre- and post-1876 without being struck by the optimism of scientists that human ills could be prevented and disease could be vanquished with the use of animal research.[3] Such claims were not entirely unfounded, of course. In the nineteenth and twentieth centuries, there were great strides in the development of treatments and drugs that have undoubtedly benefited humankind. But it is also true that some of the earlier claims were exaggerated. We are only now, with hindsight, beginning to assess more critically the role of animal research and its practical benefits. We have to confront the fact that animal research may have hindered progress, at least in some respects. Indeed, it is inevitable, given that over 90 percent of drugs passed for safety and efficacy in animal tests do not pass clinical trials, that some, probably many, treatments wrongly have been rejected after animal tests. Therefore, the earlier claims regarding the indispensability of animal research must be addressed critically. We address this further in section 1.4.

The fourth issue that has tended to stymie ethical discussion relates to the complexity of animal awareness, especially animal sentience (defined as the capacity to experience pain and pleasure). Unlike our forebears, we now know, as reasonably as we can know of humans, that animals (notably, mammals, birds, and reptiles) experience not only pain but also shock, fear, foreboding, trauma, anxiety, stress, distress, anticipation, and terror to a greater or lesser extent than humans do. This is the conclusion of many scientific books and scientific articles in peer-reviewed scientific journals. In a comprehensive study, David DeGrazia concludes,

> The available evidence, taken together, suggests that many species of animal—indeed, there is some reason to think, most or all vertebrates—can experience anxious states of mind. . . . Additionally, given the close—probably overlapping—relationship between fear and anxiety, it is reasonable to conclude that these animals can also experience fear. Supporting this proposition is the fact that all vertebrates have automatic-nervous systems and limbic systems, which contain the basic substrates of anxiety and fear. In conclusion, the available evidence suggests that most or all vertebrates, and perhaps some invertebrates, can suffer.[4]

Ironically, animal experiments have themselves helped reveal the extent of animal sentience and also animal sapience (the capacity for intelligence). There is scientific evidence to support not only animal awareness but also the kinds of cognitive capacities required for the ascription of mental states such as self-awareness and rationality. Along with this body of scientific research, there is the argument from evolutionary continuity to support these claims. There is no distinct difference in kind between humans and other animals: we are all on the same biological continuum. It is rather a matter of degree. The old debate's characterization of animals in such terms as "beasts," "brutes," and "subhumans" relies on prescientific depictions that no longer do justice to our understanding of animals.

Allied to this is the greater appreciation of the ways in which animals can be harmed. In the nineteenth century, a rather limited notion of "cruelty" was employed that focused on the adverse physical harm inflicted on animals in research experiments. "Cruelty" was defined, wholly or largely, in terms of stabbing, kicking, or hitting another creature, for example. That it was possible to harm animals by emotional or psychological means was almost entirely absent from the notion of cruelty as previously defined. Thus, the literature in relation to animal research, both for and against, was for many years almost entirely focused on the nature of the physical cruelties inflicted by experiments, rather than, for example, the psychological harms that animals had to endure or the conditions under which they were kept. The narrow view of cruelty is now outdated: when assessing the harms done by experiments, we must take into account a range of factors, such as trade, capture, control, conditions, and killing as well as psychological and emotional pain. Without taking these myriad factors into account, we cannot conduct a proper moral assessment of the ethics of animal research.

This view is buttressed by the increasingly acknowledged link between animal abuse and human violence.[5] There has also been growing awareness of the connection between the treatment of animals and public health at large.[6] It is only right to take account of the empirical evidence that animal abuse has socially unwelcome effects. Exploration of the link was pioneered by the FBI among others in the 1970s, when the agency began to systematically interview serious offenders as to their past history of animal cruelty, if any.[7] The results showed that high proportions of serious criminals had histories of animal abuse, and in the light of that information, the FBI now includes animal cruelty as one of its diagnostic criteria for assessing dangerousness. Of course, this does not mean that researchers who experiment on animals will experiment on humans nonconsensually (though some have) or will develop antisocial traits, but it does mean that we must question the old assumption that there is an absolute dividing line between what is done to "them" (animals) and how it might affect "us" (humans). We can no longer assume that abuse of animals in any context is socially cost-free.

In support of this, it is worth recalling the long history of anticruelty law since the nineteenth century, which has been predicated on, inter alia, the basis that humans have an interest in the creation of a cruelty-free society. Even philosophers and theologians not known as supporters of animal protection (e.g., Aquinas) still saw the possibility of adverse social consequences from allowing animal cruelty to flourish. Now this previously largely un-evidenced assumption has received empirical confirmation.[8]

All in all, these features of the old debate have contributed to an intellectual impasse and have helped obscure the underlying moral issue.

Early Controversy

It is also interesting to note the relative unimportance accorded by the scientific community to Charles Darwin's *The Expression of the Emotions in Man and Animals* (1872),[9] which cannot be explained merely by reference to the rejection of Lamarckism. Evolution more generally is probably the single most influential underpinning of modern scientific thought in zoology, biology, botany, and physiology, yet this work, which Darwin thought just as important as *The Origin of Species*, was afforded little notice until the recent growth in the discipline of evolutionary psychology. It is tempting to conclude that this is because ignoring Darwin's subsequent book enables an emotion-free zone when it comes to "animal modeling" and a more comforting outcome for experimenters. Daniel M. Gross has pointed out,

> Though initially a bestseller, the *Expression* lapsed into relative obscurity during the next century as Darwin's evolutionary theory established itself primarily on other terms, including, most im-

portantly, the fossil record, homologies across related life-forms, geographic distribution of related species, and artificial selection like dog breeding. Meanwhile the ambiguities of studying emotion rendered it a difficult and even suspect science for the next century.[10]

Animal testing has long been a subject of public revulsion. Even some physiologists found the work of vivisection distasteful. Robert Hooke (who performed many animal experiments in the pursuit of his understanding of the circulation of blood) was unhappy about the cruelty involved in an experiment he regularly conducted with Richard Lower, which involved the opening of a dog's thorax. In the 1660s Robert Boyle conducted many experiments involving an air pump, and these all led to the deaths of animals. One such experiment was depicted much later in Joseph Wright's painting *An Experiment with a Bird in the Air Pump* (1768). Here a wild-haired natural philosopher (sometimes said to be a portrait of Joseph Priestley) suffocates a bird while a bourgeois family looks on. Two young girls are tearful, and another gentleman sits pensively with his eyes fixed on the table and not on the dying bird, while a servant operates the bellows, looking fearfully over his shoulder. The audience for the experiment is clearly not uniformly happy with what is happening to the bird, and of course, the experiment is needless because the effects of depriving an animal of oxygen had been demonstrated many times over the previous century.[11]

Dr. George Hoggan, one of the earliest proponents within the medical camp of a humanitarian approach to research, was moved to remark after his visits to Claude Bernard's laboratory that he was "prepared to see not only science, but even mankind, perish rather than have recourse to such means of saving it." In a letter to the newspaper *Morning Post* in 1875, Hoggan added,

> We [i.e., the scientists in Bernard's laboratory] sacrificed daily from one to three dogs, besides rabbits and other animals, and after four years' experience I am of the opinion that not one of these experiments on animals was justified or necessary. The idea of the good of humanity was simply out of the question, and would be laughed at, the great aim being to keep up with, or get ahead of, one's

contemporaries in science, even at the price of an incalculable amount of torture needlessly and iniquitously inflicted on the poor animals.[12]

Bernard himself claimed,

> The physiologist is no ordinary man. He is a learned man, a man possessed and absorbed by a scientific idea. He does not hear the animals' cries of pain. He is blind to the blood that flows. He sees nothing but his idea, and organisms, which conceal from him the secrets he is resolved to discover.[13]

By the late nineteenth century, a complex number of humanitarian causes (animal welfare, vegetarianism, feminism, and early manifestations of the gay rights and green movements) had come together to create a climate in which a more active response to experimentation might be enacted. In fact, it was the interventions of the feminist Frances Power Cobbe that led to the foundation of the National Anti-Vivisection Society in 1875 and the British Union for the Abolition of Vivisection in 1898. In 1895 and 1896, the *Animals' Friend Magazine* published a series of articles, each titled "Why I Oppose Vivisection." These included three by physicians (Dr. Arthur Beale, Dr. Lawson Tait, and Dr. John Makinson), all of whom argued that not only was experimentation cruel, but that also it was medically valueless and led to no discoveries that could not have been made by diligent clinical observation. In the United States, Dr. Albert Leffingwell was publishing material along the same lines at much the same time. Middle-class women had shown in their letter-writing campaigns to other women wearing hats with feathers—what the humanitarian Henry Salt called "murderous millinery"— that campaigning could be effective on animal issues. This campaign also led to the formation of the Society for the Protection of Birds in 1889.[14]

But the most spectacular eruption of public feeling about experiments came in the form of the "Brown Dog affair."[15] In 1903, the physiologist William Bayliss successfully defended himself against the charge of unnecessary cruelty and won damages for libel. But the controversy rumbled on in the press, and public protest resulted, so much so that in 1907 full-scale rioting between medical students and radicals (especially feminists) broke out around a London monu-

ment to a specific dog who had been the subject of the case. The monument had the following inscription:

> In Memory of the Brown Terrier
> Dog Done to Death in the Laboratories
> of University College in February
> 1903 after having endured Vivisection
> extending over more than Two Months
> and having been handed over from
> one Vivisector to Another
> Till Death came to his Release.
>
> Also in Memory of the 232 dogs Vivisected
> at the same place during the year 1902.
> Men and Women of England
> how long shall these Things be?[16]

The monument was removed in 1910, but a new one was erected in 1985 with the original inscription restored and the following addition:

> This monument replaces the original memorial of the brown dog erected by public subscription in Latchmere Recreation Ground, Battersea in 1906. The sufferings of the brown dog at the hands of the vivisectors generated much protest and mass demonstrations. It represented the revulsion of the people of London to vivisection and animal experimentation. This new monument is dedicated to the continuing struggle to end these practices. After much controversy the former monument was removed in the early hours of 10 March 1910. This was the result of a decision taken by the then Battersea Metropolitan Borough Council, the previous council having supported the erection of the memorial.
>
> Animal experimentation is one of the greatest moral issues of our time and should have no place in a civilized society. In 1903, 19,084 animals suffered and died in British laboratories. During 1984, 3,497,355 animals were burned, blinded, irradiated, poisoned and subjected to countless other horrifyingly cruel experiments in Great Britain.[17]

Historically, then, we can readily trace a pattern in which the public expresses distaste for live animal experiments, scientists who doubt the value of such experiments register objections, and other scientists defend the experiments on the grounds of the greater good for humankind. This offers some background for understanding the contemporary debate.

Notes

1. E. Westacott, *A Century of Vivisection and Anti-Vivisection: A Study of Their Effect upon Science, Medicine, and Human Life during the Past Hundred Years* (Ashingdon, UK: C. W. Daniel, 1949); B. J. Cohen and F. M. Loew, "Laboratory Animal Medicine: Historical Perspectives," in *Laboratory Animal Medicine*, ed. J. G. Fox, B. J. Cohen, and F. M. Loew (New York: Academic Press, 1984), 1–18.

2. H. Kean, *Animal Rights: Political and Social Change in Britain since 1800* (London: Reaktion Books, 1998), 36.

3. Westacott, *Century*.

4. D. DeGrazia, *Taking Animals Seriously: Mental Life and Moral Status* (Cambridge: Cambridge University Press, 1996), 123. See chapters 4–7 of DeGrazia's book for a survey and analysis of the empirical evidence about animal consciousness and sentiency.

5. See, for example, C. P. Flynn, "Examining the Links between Animal Abuse and Human Violence," *Crime, Law, and Social Change* (Special issue: Animal Abuse and Criminology) 55 (2011): 453–68.

6. A. Akhtar, "The Need to Include Animal Protection in Public Health Policies," *Journal of Public Health Policy* 34, no. 4 (2013): 549–59.

7. R. Lockwood and A. W. Church, "An FBI Perspective on Animal Cruelty: Alan C. Brantley Interviewed by Randall Lockwood and Ann W. Church," in *The Link between Animal Abuse and Human Violence*, ed. A Linzey (Brighton, UK: Sussex Academic Press, 2009), 223–27.

8. F. R. Ascione and P. Arkow, eds., *Child Abuse, Domestic Violence, and Animal Abuse* (West Lafayette, IN: Purdue University Press, 1999); P. Beirne, "For a Nonspeciesist Criminology: Animal Abuse as an Object of Study," *Criminology* 37, no. 1 (1999): 117–47; A. Linzey, ed., *The Link between Animal Abuse and Human Violence* (Brighton, UK: Sussex Academic Press, 2009); S. L. Nelson, "The Connection between Animal Abuse and Family Violence: A Selected Annotated Bibliography," *Animal Law Review* 17, no. 2 (2011): 369–414; E. Gullone, *Animal Cruelty, Antisocial Behaviour, and Aggression: More Than a Link* (Basingstoke, UK: Palgrave Macmillan, 2012).

9. C. Darwin, *The Expression of the Emotions in Man and Animals* (London: John Murray, 1872), accessed August 11, 2014, http://darwin-online.org.uk/content/frameset?itemID=F1142&viewtype=side&pageseq=1.

10. D. M. Gross, "Defending the Humanities with Charles Darwin's *The Expression of the Emotions in Man and Animals* (1872)," *Critical Inquiry* 37 (2010): 36, accessed August 11, 2014, http://iicas.ucsd.edu/_files/conferences/science-emotions/abstracts/Gross_abstract.pdf.

11. A. Guerrini, "Natural History, Natural Philosophy, and Animals, 1600–1800," in *A Cultural History of Animals in the Age of Enlightenment*, ed. M. Senior (Oxford: Berg, 2007), 121–44.

12. G. Hoggan, letter, *Morning Post*, February 2, 1875.

13. Quoted in R. Preece, *Awe for the Tiger, Love for the Lamb: A Chronicle of Sensibility to Animals* (Vancouver: University of British Columbia Press, 2002), 309.

14. S. Moss, *Birds Britannia: Why the British Fell in Love with Birds* (London: Collins, 2011).

15. C. Lansbury, *The Old Brown Dog: Women, Workers, and Vivisection in Edwardian England* (Madison: University of Wisconsin Press, 1985); Kean, *Animal Rights*.

16. Lansbury, *Old Brown Dog*, 14.

17. Lansbury, *Old Brown Dog*; P. Mason, *The Brown Dog Affair: The Story of a Monument That Divided the Nation* (London: Two Sevens, 1997).

The New Scientific Critiques

THE TERMS OF THE old debate have been challenged in recent years by the emergence of scientific critiques of the validity of animal experimentation. We need to attend to these critiques if we are to understand why a reassessment of the morality of animal research is so important.

The Unreliability of Animal Experiments

The first factor in the scientific critiques of animal experimentation is the scientific debate on the utility of animal tests.[1] At the outset of legalized animal testing, the issue of utilitarian justification was in its infancy. It was impossible at that time to know with certainty whether animal tests would yield the results that many claimed and would unambiguously lead to scientific progress. In the intervening years, many assumed that such utilitarian justifications contributed so decisively to new discoveries that the issue hardly bore further scrutiny. But this assumption has now been radically questioned from two angles: (1) the growing evidence regarding animal tests that have not proved beneficial and that may indeed have hindered scientific progress and (2) the issue of whether "animal models," as they are sometimes termed, are themselves satisfactory models for human disease.[2]

In recent decades, "evidence-based medicine" has become the mantra of sound, scientifically based medical research and practice. Evidence-based medicine is implemented in virtually every facet of health research, ethics, and practice save one—the use of animal experimentation to inform human health. Animal experimentation is most often viewed as the default or "gold standard" method of testing. Yet despite this or perhaps because of it, animal testing does not receive the critical examination needed to determine its relevance to human health. As a result, there is a dearth of published, peer-reviewed evidence that supports the usefulness and validity of animal experimentation. The Nuffield Council on Bioethics has noted this lack of critical studies examining the relevance of animal experiments.[3] Nevertheless, the work that has been done tends to demonstrate the unreliability of animal experiments, and we shall now review some of those studies.

In 2006, the *Journal of the American Medical Association* reported, "While investment in basic research in the United States doubled from 1993 to 2003, the number of therapeutics entering the clinic has actually declined."[4] New compounds entering phase 1 trials (almost exclusively in vivo animal assays) have about an 8 percent chance of reaching the market. Many drug candidates that enter later phases of the drug development process are also falling by the wayside. Overall, in the United States, 92 percent of drugs that pass preclinical tests, mostly animal tests, fail to make it to the market because they are proven to be ineffective and/or unsafe in people.[5] This information is supplied by the 2004 US Food and Drug Administration (FDA) "Critical Path" report.[6] This report also

UNIVERSITY OF WINCHESTER
LIBRARY

notes that if topical medicines are excluded, the failure rate is around 97 percent. In response to the standard reply in support of animal research—namely, "That's just the way it is with research"—it is worth noting that this was emphatically not the FDA's conclusion.

Leaders in the biotechnology and pharmaceutical industries published a paper outlining the major problems underlying the drug development process in 2002.[7] They concluded that the poor predictability of animal experiments is one of the major challenges facing the drug discovery community. One of the more notable studies highlighting the lack of relevancy of animal experiments to the human condition is a *British Medical Journal* (BMJ) systematic review that examined the clinical (human) data of six different interventions to treat head injury, respiratory distress syndrome, osteoporosis, stroke, and hemorrhage.[8] The investigators compared the human results with the published animal experimental results and found that the human and animal results were in concordance only half of the time. In other words, the animal experiments were no more likely to predict whether those interventions would benefit humans than a flip of the coin. The study authors suggested, among other things, that the discordance between human and animal results might reflect biases in reporting and publication. As LaFollette and Shanks comment, "many researchers do not interpret the failure to correlate findings in nonhuman animals as humans as suggesting *disanalogies* between model and subject modeled."[9]

Notably, a 2014 review published in the BMJ found that over the preceding decade, despite rigorous discussion of the foregoing problems in animal experimentation, these problems had remained ubiquitous throughout the field, and systematic studies examining the validity of animal experiments remain few. As a result, it is "nearly impossible to rely on most animal data to predict whether or not an intervention will have a favourable clinical benefit-risk ratio in human subjects."[10] An accompanying editorial in the BMJ by editor in chief Fiona Godlee reports,

> Better conduct and reporting of animal research will help, say [review authors] Pound and Bracken. This could come from better training and education of basic researchers and from a cultural change fuelled by greater scrutiny and public accountability. But how much would this really improve the rate of successful translation from animals to humans? Not much, it seems. Even if the research were conducted faultlessly, argue the authors, our ability to predict human responses from animal models will be limited by interspecies differences in molecular and metabolic pathways.

Funds might be better directed towards clinical rather than basic research, where there is a clearer return on investment in terms of effects on patient care. The authors conclude: "If research conducted on animals continues to be unable to reasonably predict what can be expected in humans, the public's continuing endorsement and funding of preclinical animal research seems misplaced."[11]

As highlighted in the BMJ editorial, although biases and poor quality of animal research certainly may play a role, there are immutable factors inherent in the use of animals in experimentation that are more likely to account for the unreliable nature of the testing results. These factors include (*a*) unpredictable influences of laboratory environments and procedures on experimental results, (*b*) discordance between human diseases and "animal models" of disease, and (*c*) interspecies differences in physiology and genetic function. We shall now explore these in turn.

a. Unpredictable influences of laboratory environments and procedures on experimental results

Elements of the laboratory environments and procedures may cause unpredictable influences on animal experimental results.[12] Arguably, every procedure conducted on animals in laboratories causes them substantial distress.[13] Mice in laboratories commonly show clear signs of distress, and at the New England Regional Primate Research Center, almost 90 percent of monkeys showed behavioral abnormalities.[14]

Routine laboratory procedures, such as catching an animal and removing him or her from the cage, in addition to the experiments themselves, cause significant and prolonged elevations in animals' stress markers.[15] These stress-related changes in physiological parameters as a result of the laboratory procedures and environment can have a significant effect on test results.[16] An article in *New Scientist* argues that stressed rats develop lasting inflammatory conditions, which cause their intestines to leak: "This inflammation adds uncontrollable variables to experiments . . . confounding the data."[17]

Conditions in the laboratory are shown to cause unpredictable changes in neurochemistry, genetic expression, and nerve regeneration.[18] In one study, mice were genetically altered to develop defects in their hearts.[19] But when the mice were put in larger cages, those defects almost completely disappeared. It has also been shown that the noise levels in laboratories damage blood vessels in animals.[20] Even the type of flooring on which animals are tested in spinal-cord injury experiments can affect whether a drug shows a benefit or not. The cumulative effect is that these stressors cause animals to be less reliable and less representative of human biology.

b. Discordance between human diseases and "animal models" of disease

Additionally, the lack of sufficient congruency between "animal models" and human disease is another frequent and significant obstacle. In the laboratory, diseases that occur naturally in humans are artificially induced as substitute diseases in animals. The inability to reproduce the complexity of human diseases in animals is a crucial hindrance to the use of animals.[21] Even if design and conduct of an animal experiment are sound and standardized, the translation of its results to the clinic may fail because of disparities between the "animal model" and the clinical trials.[22]

In stroke research, for example, frequent disparities include preexisting diseases in humans that lead to stroke, such as diabetes and atherosclerosis, use of additional medications to treat these risk factors in humans, and nuances in the pathology of the disease that are absent in animals. As a result of the recognition of these discrepancies, several publications argue for the need to use animals who also have the co-diseases (co-morbidities) that occur naturally in humans and who are given medications that are part of standard clinical care for human patients.[23] Reproducing the co-diseases, however, leads to roadblocks as well because of the inability to replicate the complexity of these co-diseases. For example, most animals do not naturally develop significant atherosclerosis, which is characterized by a narrowing of blood vessels. In order to reproduce the effects of atherosclerosis in animals, researchers ubiquitously clamp their blood vessels or artificially insert clots. These mechanisms to induce disease, however, do not replicate the elaborate pathology of atherosclerosis and the causes behind it.

In attempts to reproduce the complexity of human diseases in animals, the complexity of the predisposing diseases and physiology must be reproduced, which also proves difficult to accomplish. Every time an "animal model" is found to be lacking, no shortage of reasons is proffered to explain what went wrong—poor methodology, publication bias, lack of co-disease and medications, wrong gender or age, and so on. Recognition of each potential difference between the "animal model" and the human disease creates a renewed effort to eliminate these differences. What is too often ignored is that these "models" are intrinsically lacking relevancy to human diseases.[24]

c. Interspecies differences in physiology and genetic function

Ultimately, interspecies differences in physiology, metabolism, pharmacokinetics, and genetic function cause insurmountable obstacles in translation to human physiology. In spinal cord injury, for example, drug testing results vary according to which species, and even which strain within a species, is used because of numerous interspecies and interstrain differences in neurophysiology, anatomy, and behavior.[25] Again, the micropathology of the spinal cord injury, injury repair mechanisms, and recovery from injury vary greatly between different strains of rats and mice. Surprisingly, even rats from the same strain, but purchased from different suppliers, produce different test results.[26] In one study, responses to twelve different behavioral measures on pain sensitivity varied among eleven strains of mice, with no clear-cut patterns that would allow prediction of how each strain would respond.[27] Each of these and numerous other differences influenced not only how the animals responded to the injury but also how they responded to any potential therapy being tested. A drug might be shown to help one strain of mice recover but not another.

Although we share most of our genes with other mammals, there are critical differences in how our genes actually function. The best analogy is perhaps a piano: just as pianos have the same keys, humans and animals share the same genes. Where we mostly differ is in the way the genes or keys are expressed. Play the keys in a certain order, and you hear Chopin; play them in a different order, and you hear Ray Charles; choose yet a different order, and it is Jerry Lee Lewis. In other words, the same keys or genes are "played," but their different order results in very different outcomes.

To circumvent these differences, experimenters alter animals' genes in attempts to make them more "humanlike." Mice are used extensively because of their ostensible genetic similarity with humans and because their entire genome has been mapped. Their genes are modified to make them more "human." However, if a human gene is inserted into the mouse genome, that gene is likely going to function quite differently from how it functions in humans. A study published in *Science* found that a crucial protein that controls blood sugar in humans is missing in mice.[28] When the human gene that produces this protein was expressed in genetically altered mice, it behaved differently. In fact, the effect in mice was opposite: the gene caused *loss* of blood sugar control in mice. To continue the piano analogy, the key that had been playing Chopin (in humans) was now playing Ray Charles (in mice).

Even among mice, corresponding genes can behave very differently. The disruption of a gene in one strain of mice is lethal, whereas disruption of that gene in another strain has no deleterious effect.[29] Six strains of mice who share the same genetic mutation that causes Fragile X syndrome (a genetic condition that causes intellectual disability and behavioral problems) show radically different behaviors.[30] In other words, one strain of mice is not predictive of another strain of mice. Such findings question the wisdom of extrapolating data that is obtained in mice to other species, most notably humans. "If one mouse gene is so difficult to understand in a mouse context," asks Dr. David Horrobin, "and if the genome of a different inbred strain of mouse has so much impact on the consequences of that single gene's expression, how unlikely is it that genetically modified mice are going

to provide insights into complex gene interactions in the . . . human species?"[31]

Genetically engineered "animal models" are not living up to their promise. Perhaps the major reason GM animals will not solve the problems of animal experimentation translation to humans is the fact that the "humanized" genes are still in nonhuman animals. When a "humanized" gene is introduced into a mouse, that gene may be expressed quite differently from how it is expressed in humans, and the gene will be affected by all of the physiological mechanisms that are unique to the mouse.

Instead of mice, many experimenters use nonhuman primates (NHPs), hoping they will better mimic human results. Chimpanzees share at least 98 percent of our genes, yet there are many differences between chimpanzees and humans in DNA sequence and how our genes function.[32] These genetic differences ultimately cause differences in physiology. HIV/AIDS vaccine research using NHPs is one of the most notable failures in animal experimentation. Immense resources have been devoted to studying HIV in chimpanzees and other NHPs. Yet all of about ninety HIV vaccines tested so far that worked in animals have failed in human trials.[33]

Hormone replacement therapy (HRT) was originally hailed for preventing heart disease and strokes. The campaign to prescribe HRT to millions of women was based in large part on experiments on NHPs. HRT is now known to *increase* the risk of these diseases in women.[34] In March 2006, six human volunteers were injected with TGN 1412, an experimental therapy created by TeGenero. The results were described by *Slate*:

> Within minutes, the human test subjects were writhing on the floor in agony. The compound was designed to dampen the immune response, but it had supercharged theirs, unleashing a cascade of chemicals that sent all six to the hospital. Several of the men suffered permanent organ damage, and one man's head swelled up so horribly that British tabloids refer to the case as the "elephant man trial."[35]

TGN 1412 had been tested in mice, rabbits, rats, and NHPs with no ill effects. Cynomolgus monkeys had been used because they best replicated the human mechanisms specifically targeted by TGN 1412.[36]

Thus, not only had several different species been used; those deemed most relevant to humans had been used. NHPs also had undergone repeat-dose toxicity studies and in fact had been given five hundred times the dose given to the human volunteers for not less than four consecutive weeks. Still, none of the NHPs manifested the ill effects that humans showed within minutes of receiving a miniscule amount of the test drug. Experiments using NHPs have proved to be no more predictive of human responses than those using other animals.

In summary, in addition to extrinsic factors, such as publication biases and the poor quality of animal experiments, such tests fail for three primary and inherent reasons:

1. Stressed animals yield poor data. The unnatural laboratory environments and procedures cause animals substantial stress. Their distress causes changes in their physiology that affect research data in very unpredictable ways.[37]
2. Animals do not naturally develop most human diseases. The inability to re-create human diseases accurately in other animals is a fundamental flaw in the use of animal experiments.
3. Animals are not miniature humans. Despite attempts to genetically alter animals to mimic human physiology or use closer genetic species, such as NHPs, physiological and genetic differences that are unalterable and inherent to species diversity remain an insurmountable obstacle to using animals to predict human outcomes.

The Development of More Predictive Human-Based Testing

The second factor in the scientific critiques of the validity of animal experimentation is the development of alternatives to animal testing. In the nineteenth century, the scientific community did little to seek alternatives to the then-emerging (and largely unproven) scientific techniques involving animals. Indeed, the whole idea of developing alternatives had to wait until the 1960s and 1970s. But such alternative techniques and methodologies have now emerged, largely through the efforts of animal protection organizations. It is these bodies that have principally funded (indeed were the only initial funders of) the main alternative research bodies in the United Kingdom, such as the Fund for the Replacement of Animals in Medical Experiments (FRAME), the Lord Dowding Fund, the Dr. Hadwen Trust, and the Humane Research Trust. It is often unacknowledged that animal protectionists have pioneered new fields of scientific research and have contributed many millions of pounds in the process. The range of alternatives to animal research offers new possibilities. Examples include adult stem cell research, human organs-on-a-chip, lab-grown human organs, and systems biology.

Currently, many of these testing methods are being used in conjunction with animal experiments prior to clinical trials. The problem with using both human-based research and animal experiments, however, is that the animal experiments may contradict findings from the human-based tests. When this occurs, as is often the case, the animal experimental results may be incorrectly favored (leading researchers down the wrong path of investigation) because they represent "whole animal system" results. However, the animal tests provide the wrong whole systems. For genetic and physiological reasons that are immutable, animal experiments are less trustworthy than even incomplete systems of the human body.

Some have argued that in vitro or other similar testing methods are simplistic and cannot accurately mimic the complexities of the human body—hence the need for animal experiments. In vitro tests certainly are prone to some of the same problems as animal experiments in that they can be relatively simplistic models of disease or physiological mechanisms and are not always very accurate. But are the animal experiments necessarily *more* accurate or predictive?

A multicenter team of researchers evaluated sixty-eight different methods to predict the toxicity of fifty different chemicals.[38] The animal tests were only 59 percent accurate, whereas a combined human cell in vitro test was 83 percent accurate in predicting actual human toxicity. Again, cultured human skin cells outperformed live rabbit tests in detecting chemical skin irritants. Tests in rabbits misclassified ten of twenty-five chemical irritants, whereas the cultured cells classified all irritants correctly.[39] Other researchers compared in vitro human tumor cell lines with mouse cancer "models" for their reliability in predicting clinical phase 2 trial results of thirty-one potential cancer drugs. The study found that the in vitro tests were reliable in predicting the clinical utility of these drugs for all four cancer types tested, whereas the mouse allograft cancer "model" (in which cancerous tissue from one mouse is transplanted into another) was not predictive.[40]

The human xenograft mouse "model" (in which cancerous tissue from a human is transplanted into a mouse) was predictive for only two of the four cancer types studied. The study authors concluded that cancer drug–development emphasis should be placed on in vitro cell lines. An in vitro test developed by UK researchers could have predicted TGN 1412's serious adverse effects before it was ever tested in humans.[41] In all of these examples, in vitro tests were far more accurate than whole "animal model" systems. This is because of the simple fact that nonhuman animal "models" are not the correct systems. At a fundamental level, nonhuman "models" *cannot* be accurate—and cannot be made to be accurate—because of distinctions in genetic makeup and expression and evolutionary issues, such as causal disanalogy between species, which makes "animal models" insufficient for making reliable predictions in humans.[42] An understanding of *human* physiology is critical.

Although there is no perfect predictive approach to human medicine, a combination of human-based testing methods, including in vitro tests, will bring us closer to the true answers than animal experiments, which are inherently flawed. Human-based in vitro tests may not always be accurate predictors of human responses, but they have great potential to become more accurate, particularly as new methods are developed that are closer to depicting whole human systems. Perhaps the most exciting new development is human organs-on-a-chip, microchips lined by human cells connected by microfluidic channels that could revolutionize medical testing and drug development. In addition, there is an array of emerging methods that can replace animals, including, for example, microdosing.

The upshot of these scientific developments in cutting-edge human-based testing methods is that it is no longer accurate or reasonable (if it ever was) to say that the only moral choice is between experimenting on animals and giving up on medical progress. This is a false dilemma. The choice instead is between experimenting on animals and using improved human-based methods of testing.

Notes

1. H. LaFollette and N. Shanks, *Brute Science: Dilemmas of Animal Experimentation* (London: Routledge, 1996).

2. The obvious example is thalidomide, which was first used in the late 1950s to alleviate nausea in pregnant women. It was developed by the German drug company Chemie Grünenthal. The first reports that thalidomide caused severe congenital anomalies in babies born to those women who took the drug were made independently by W. G. McBride and W. Lenz. W. G. McBride, "Thalidomide and Congenital Abnormalities," letter, *The Lancet* 278, no. 7216 (1961): 1358; W. Lenz, "Thalidomide and Congenital Anomalies," *The Lancet* 279, no. 7219 (1962): 45–46.

3. Nuffield Council on Bioethics, *Ethics of Research*.

4. T. Hampton, "Targeted Cancer Therapies Lagging: Better Trial Design Could Boost Success Rate," *Journal of the American Medical Association* 296, no. 16 (2006): 1951–52.

5. K. Archibald and R. Coleman, "How Human Biology Can Prevent Drug Deaths," *New Scientist* 2895 (2012), accessed November 27, 2014, http://www.newscientist.com/article/mg21628950.200-how-human-biology-can-prevent-drug-deaths.html#.

6. US Food and Drug Administration, *Innovation or Stagnation: Challenge and Opportunity on the Critical Path to New Medical Products* (2004), accessed January 2, 2015, http://www.fda.gov/ScienceResearch/SpecialTopics/CriticalPath Initiative/CriticalPathOpportunitiesReports/ucm077262.htm.

7. M. G. Palfreyman, V. Charles, and J. Blander, "The Importance of Using Human-Based Models in Gene and Drug Discovery," *Drug Discovery World* (2002), accessed May 13, 2014, http://www.ddw-online.com/fall-2002/p148472-the-importance-of-using-human-based-models-in-gene-and-drug-discovery.html.

8. P. Perel, I. Roberts, E. Sena, P. Wheble, C. Briscoe, P. Sandercock, M. Macleod, L. E. Mignini, P. Jayaram, and K. S. Khan, "Comparison of Treatment Effects between Animal Experiments and Clinical Trials: Systematic Review," *British Medical Journal* 334, no. 7586 (2007): 197.

9. LaFollette and Shanks, *Brute Science*, 25, emphasis in original.

10. P. Pound, M. B. Bracken, and S. D. Bliss, "Is Animal Research Sufficiently Evidence Based to Be a Cornerstone of Biomedical Research?" *British Medical Journal* 348, no. 3387 (2014).

11. F. Godlee, "How Predictive and Productive Is Animal Research?" *British Medical Journal* 348, no. 3719 (2014).

12. A. Akhtar, J. J. Pippin, and C. B. Sandusky, "Animal Models in Spinal Cord Injury: A Review," *Reviews in the Neurosciences* 19, no. 1 (2008): 47–60.

13. K. N. Morgan and C. T. Tromborg, "Sources of Stress in Captivity," *Applied Animal Behaviour Science* 102, no. 3–4 (2007): 262–302.

14. P. C. Hart, C. L. Bergner, B. D. Dufour, A. N. Smolinsky, R. J. Egan, J. L. LaPorte, and A. V. Kalueff, "Analysis of Abnormal Repetitive Behaviors in Experimental Animal Models," in *Translational Neuroscience in Animal Research: Advancement, Challenges, and Research Ethics*, ed. J. E. Warnik and A. V. Kalueff (New York: Nova Science, 2009), 71–82; C. Lutz, A. Well, and M. Novak, "Stereotypic and Self-Injurious Behavior in Rhesus Macaques: A Survey and Retrospective Analysis of Environment and Early Experience," *American Journal of Primatology* 60, no. 1 (2003): 1–15.

15. J. P. Balcombe, N. D. Barnard, and C. Sandusky, "Laboratory Routines Cause Animal Stress," *Contemporary Topics in Laboratory Animal Science* 43 (2004): 42–51.

16. A. Baldwin and M. Bekoff, "Too Stressed to Work," *New Scientist* 194 (2007): 24.

17. Ibid.

18. Akhtar, Pippin, and Sandusky, "Animal Models."

19. Baldwin and Bekoff, "Too Stressed."

20. Akhtar, Pippin, and Sandusky, "Animal Models."

21. S. H. Curry, "Why Have So Many Drugs with Stellar Results in Laboratory Stroke Models Failed in Clinical Trials? A Theory Based on Allometric Relationships," *Annals of the New York Academy of Sciences* 993 (2003): 69–74; U. Dirnagl, "Bench to Bedside: The Quest for Quality in Experimental Stroke Research," *Journal of Cerebral Blood Flow and Metabolism* 26 (2006): 1465–78.

22. H. B. van der Worp, D. W. Howells, E. S. Sena, M. J. Porritt, S. Rewell, V. O'Collins, and M. R. Macleod, "Can Animal Models of Disease Reliably Inform Human Studies?" *PLoS Medicine* 7, no. 3 (2010): e1000245.

23. Dirnagl, "Bench to Bedside"; E. S. Sena, B. van der Worp, D. Howells, and M. Macleod, "How Can We Improve the Pre-clinical Development of Drugs for Stroke?" *Trends in Neurosciences* 30 (2007): 433–39.

24. D. O. Wiebers, H. P. Adams, and J. P. Whisnant, "Animal Models of Stroke: Are They Relevant to Human Disease?" *Stroke* 21 (1990): 1–3.

25. Akhtar, Pippin, and Sandusky, "Animal Models."

26. Ibid.

27. J. S. Mogil, S. G. Wilson, K. Bon, S. E. Lee, K. Chung, P. Raber, J. O. Pieper, et al., "Heritability of Nociception I: Responses of 11 Inbred Mouse Strains on 12 Measures of Nociception," *Pain* 80, no. 1–2 (1999): 67–82.

28. H. Ledford, "Flaws Found in Mouse Model of Diabetes," *Nature*, May 28, 2009, accessed May 13, 2014, http://www.nature.com/news/2009/090528/full/news.2009.523.html.

29. D. F. Horrobin, "Modern Biomedical Research: An Internally Self-Consistent Universe with Little Contact with Medical Reality?" *Nature Reviews Drug Discovery* 2 (2003): 151–54.

30. C. M. Spencer, O. Alekseyenko, S. M. Hamilton, A. M. Thomas, E. Serysheva, L. A. Yuva-Paylor, and R. Paylor, "Modifying Behavioral Phenotypes in Fmr1KO Mice: Genetic Background Differences Reveal Autistic-Like Responses," *Autism Research* 4, no. 1 (2011): 40–56.

31. Horrobin, "Modern Biomedical Research."

32. A. Akhtar, *Animals and Public Health: Why Treating Animals Better Is Critical to Human Welfare* (Basingstoke, UK: Palgrave Macmillan, 2012), 148.

33. J. Bailey, "An Assessment of the Role of Chimpanzees in AIDS Vaccine Research," *Alternatives to Laboratory Animals* 36, no. 4 (2008): 381–428.

34. J. Pippin, "Animal Research in Medical Sciences: Seeking a Convergence of Science, Medicine, and Animal Law," *South Texas Law Review* 54 (2013): 469–511.

35. A. Allen, "Of Mice and Men: The Problems with Animal Testing," *Slate*, June 1, 2006, accessed May 13, 2014, http://www.slate.com/articles/health_and_science/medical_examiner/2006/06/of_mice_or_men.html.

36. H. Attarwala, "TGN1412: From Discovery to Disaster," *Journal of Young Pharmacists* 2, no. 3 (2010): 332–36; T. Hanke, "Lessons from TGN1412," *The Lancet* 368, no. 9547 (2006): 1569–70.

37. J. P. Garner, "Stereotypies and Other Abnormal Repetitive Behaviors: Potential Impact on Validity, Reliability, and Replicability of Scientific Outcomes," *Institute for Laboratory Animal Research Journal* 46, no. 2 (2005): 106–17.

38. C. Clemedson, E. McFarlane-Abdulla, M. Andersson, F. A. Barile, M. C. Calleja, C. Chesne, R. Clothier, et al., "MEIC Evaluation of Acute Systemic Toxicity; Part II: In Vitro Results from 68 Toxicity Assays Used to Test the First 30 Reference Chemicals and a Comparative Cytotoxicity Analysis," *Alternatives to Laboratory Animals* 24, Suppl. 1 (1996): 273–311; C. E. Clemedson, F. A. Barile, C. Chesne, M. Cottin, R. Curren, B. Eckwall, M. Ferro, et al., "MEIC Evaluation of Acute Systemic Toxicity; Part VII: Prediction of Human Toxicity by Results from Testing of the First 30 Reference Chemicals with 27 Further In Vitro Assay," *Alternatives to Laboratory Animals* 28 (2000): 161–200.

39. MatTek Corporation, reports presented at the annual Society of Toxicology meeting in Seattle, March 16–20, 2008, accessed July 20, 2008, http://www.mattek.com.

40. T. Voskoglou-Nomikos, J. L. Pater, and L. Seymour, "Clinical Predictive Value of the *In Vitro* Cell Line, Human Xenograft, and Mouse Allograft Preclinical Cancer Models," *Clinical Cancer Research* 9, no. 11 (2003): 4227–39.

41. S. Mayor, "Researchers Refine In Vitro Test That Will Reduce Risk of 'First in Humans' Drug Trial," *British Medical Journal* 337 (2008): 3016.

42. LaFollette and Shanks, *Brute Science.*

The Changing Ethical Paradigm

WE NOW TURN TO the most important change of all, namely the emergence of a new ethical paradigm.

During the last forty years, there has been considerable growth in intellectual work on the ethical status of animals. Philosophers have led the way, and there is now a multidisciplinary corpus of hundreds of academic books and articles that argue for changes in the ways in which we use animals. Of course, they are not all in agreement, but it is fair to say that there is a growing consensus among ethicists and philosophers about the need for fundamental change. The intellectual context in which we discuss the issue of animals today is considerably different from the one that operated a hundred or even fifty years ago.

In order to understand this change, it is important to engage with the intellectual legacy to which these philosophers and ethicists have responded and are still responding. We can delineate three dominant tendencies in their responses.

The Challenge to Moral Anthropocentrism

By "moral anthropocentrism," we mean the assumption that human needs, wants, or desires should have absolute or near-absolute priority in our moral calculations. Of course, there have been thinkers who have challenged moral anthropocentrism in almost every age, stretching right back to the pre-Socratics, but such ideas have often lacked any organizational or institutional backing and have therefore had limited social influence.

Perhaps the most obvious example of moral anthropocentrism stems from the perceived relation between justice and friendship. Aristotle was clear that there could be no friendship between the ruler and the ruled—"for where there is nothing in common to ruler and ruled," he continues, "there is not friendship either, since there is no justice."[1] Aristotle provides examples of how there is no justice between humans and inanimate ("lifeless") objects, since "each case is benefited by that which uses it." He further explains that "neither is there friendship towards a horse or an ox, nor to a slave *qua slave*."[2] Aristotle avers that perhaps owners and slaves can be friends insofar as they can "share a system of law or be a party to agreements" and insofar as they are humans, but animals are not obviously included within those stipulations.[3]

St. Thomas Aquinas develops this line of thought by proposing that charity (which is defined as a kind of friendship) extends only to God and fellow humans. We cannot have friendships with "irrational animals." But he does stipulate that "we can love irrational creatures out of charity" but only "if we regard them as good things *for others*"—namely, "as we wish for their preservation, to God's honour *and man's use*."[4] Put more simply, animals are considered "irrational," and because of their lack of reason, humans cannot be friends with them, and neither can animals *in themselves* deserve justice or charity.

This Aristotelian-Thomist core, despite various challenges, remains at the heart of much philosophical and theological thought about animals. Thomas Hobbes, for example, argues that because there can be no social contract with animals, so humans can have no duties toward them.[5] David Hume also argues that there is no society with animals and hence no possibility of an equal claim to justice. Our "intercourse with [animals] could not be called society, which supposes a degree of equality, but absolute command on one side, and servile obedience on the other."[6]

To bring the issue up to date, John Rawls argues that animals are outside the scope of a proper theory of justice. In only a mild departure from the Thomist-Aristotelian tradition, he argues that only human persons are entitled to equal justice. He writes that "it is wrong to be cruel to animals and [that] the destruction of a whole species can be a great evil," but "it does not seem possible to extend the contract doctrine so as to include them in a natural way."[7]

At root, then, contractualists conceive morality as a set of rules that are derived from the unanimous consent of rational, self-interested individuals who share the aim of living in a stable society that encourages human flourishing. In such a picture, animals—as creatures incapable of the rationality required for participation in such a conference—may be accorded indirect and derivative moral status, if any status at all. Of course, contractualism does not always entail such a low view of animals. Contractualism can include animals if it is allowed that rational agents can represent the interests of other nonrational or less-than-rational beings. For example, in the work of Mark Rowlands, animals have direct moral status that can be championed by others.[8] But in its classical form, contractualism, like most philosophy and theology, has been morally anthropocentric.

The obvious weakness of moral anthropocentrism is that it fails to take account of the interests of animals, or if it accepts that animals have interests, it denies that these interests have any moral weight. Unsurprisingly, Albert Schweitzer likened the history of Western philosophy to that of a person who cleans the kitchen floor, only to find that the dog comes in and muddies it with paw prints.[9] The problem of how to square obligations to humans with obligations to other sentient beings is resolved by not addressing them. Thus conceived, morality becomes a humans-only affair in which animals are locked out. The arbitrariness of moral anthropocentrism can be shown by selecting some other feature or characteristic of human beings, or of a particular race or nation, and then erecting a system of exclusion based on that feature or characteristic alone. There is an obvious self-serving aspect to all such exclusions that belies the supposed objectivity of the exercise. Most importantly, such exclusions most usually overlook the common ability of humans and animals to experience pain and suffering.

The Challenge to Instrumentalism

By "instrumentalism," we mean the assumption that animals exist for human beings, to serve their interests and wants. This idea also has a long intellectual history and has become one of the dominant lenses through which humans perceive other species. The notion that we "own" animals has been a direct result of this assumption and has been codified in almost all legislation worldwide.

Instrumentalism, like moral anthropocentrism, has both philosophical and religious roots. Some believe that the religious root can be found in the first creation saga in Genesis 1, where God gives humans "dominion" over animals. Although there is good reason to suppose that dominion in its original context did not mean despotism (see the related discussion in section 1.9, "Consideration of Counterarguments"), it cannot be doubted that historically this view has provided a kind of biblical proof-text to justify human exploitation of animals.

The philosophical root of instrumentalism reaches as far back as Aristotle (if not earlier), who famously wrote, "Since nature makes nothing without some end in view, nothing to no purpose, it must be that nature has made them [animals and plants] for the sake of man."[10] St. Thomas's use of Aristotle's view (by combining it with the earlier idea of dominion) baptized the notion within the Christian tradition. Compare the preceding quotation with St. Thomas's view in the *Summa contra Gentiles*: "By divine providence, they [animals] are intended for man's use according to the order of nature. Hence it is not wrong for man to make use of them, either by killing *or in any other way whatever*."[11] What was thought "natural" or "according to nature" in Aristotle becomes in Aquinas a matter of "divine providence" as well.

Aquinas also argues that "dumb animals and plants are devoid of the life of reason whereby to set themselves in motion." He continues, "They are moved, as it were by another, by a kind of natural impulse, a sign of which is that they are naturally enslaved and accommodated to the uses of others."[12] Notice the development of the argument: animals are on the same level as plants in being nonrational (or "irrational" as St. Thomas actually puts it). Rationality is a sphere entirely reserved for the human species; everything else within creation is "devoid of the life of reason." What directs or "moves" animated beings (animals and plants) is not rational direction or any self-chosen goal (because animals cannot rationally choose anything), but the movement of others or "a kind of natural impulse." Animals, in other words, act "naturally," or as occasioned by others, rather than through deliberate will. And the proof of this is that they are "naturally enslaved" and "accommodated to the uses of humans." The logic is plainly circular, of course: how do we know that animals, like plants, are slaves for human use? The answer is because we can enslave them.[13]

It would be a mistake to minimize the influence of this teaching of St. Thomas. In relation to animals, Thomistic formulations have held sway for subsequent centuries of Christian thought. His idea that animals have no mental life and act not by conscious will, but by "nature" or "instinct," has been persuasive right up to the present day.

St. Thomas's negative theology undoubtedly contributed to a dismissive Christian view of animal welfare. Historic Catholic moral textbooks deny that humans have any *direct* duties to animals. *Dictionary of Moral Theology*, written as recently as 1962, explains why: "Zoophilists [animal lovers] often lose sight of the end for which animals, irrational creatures, were created by God, viz., the service and use of man. In fact, Catholic moral doctrine teaches that animals have no rights on the part of man."[14] Notice how animals are deemed to have no independent worth other than their service to human beings. Their end (*telos*) is understood entirely in instrumentalist terms. It should not come as a surprise then to discover that Pope Pius IX, in the nineteenth century, reputedly forbade the opening of an animal protection office in Rome on the grounds that humans had duties to other humans but none to animals.[15]

Although the Christian tradition is very diverse and comprises many traditions that are favorable to animals, the dominant voices in Western Christianity have laid great emphasis on instrumentalism. But it is not only within the Christian tradition that instrumentalist attitudes have persisted. Immanuel Kant, for example, held that "inasmuch as crops (for example, potatoes) and domestic animals are products of human labour, at least as far as their quantity is concerned, we can say that they may be used, consumed, or destroyed [killed]."[16] Kant divides the moral universe into persons and things: Persons are rational beings, and things are nonrational beings. Morality is, in this view, a reciprocal relationship among persons; thus, we have no moral obligations to animals, understood as nonrational beings. Kant's fundamental moral principle—the categorical imperative—is that persons are to be treated as ends in themselves, not merely as means to an end. This principle does not apply to our interactions with animals because they are things, or mere means to human ends.

It does not follow, however, that we may not hold some *indirect* duties to animals insofar as some human interest is involved. Aquinas held that cruelty to animals may be wrong if it dehumanizes the perpetrator.[17] Kant judged likewise: "Our duties towards animals are merely indirect duties towards humanity." He provided an example of how it would not be wrong to kill a dog who could no longer provide service, but the owner must be careful not to stifle humane feelings since "he who is cruel to animals becomes hard also in his dealings with men."[18] Some contemporary Kantians, such as Christine Korsgaard, have attempted to include animals in the moral universe by considering what animals would consent to if they could consent.[19]

Again, the obvious weakness in instrumentalism is its circularity: we know that animals are slaves because they are enslavable. As such, the argument seems to be little more than the working out of the notion that might is right—that power is its own justification.

Both anthropocentrism and instrumentalism reject the idea that we have direct duties to animals and that we should consider their interests independently of human wants or needs. But it is not obvious (as it was for Aristotle and Aquinas) that there exists (or should exist) a rational hierarchy in the world such that the rationally "inferior" should exist for or serve the "superior." At the very least, the contrary implication should be enjoined—namely, that the species blessed with greater rationality should demonstrate that "superiority" (if such there be) by a particular regard for the weak of all species. As Alexander Pope argued, "I cannot think it is extravagant to imagine that mankind are no less, in proportion, accountable for the ill use of their dominion over creatures of the lower rank of beings, than for the exercise of tyranny over their own species."[20]

The Challenge to Dualism

By "dualism" in this context, we mean the tendency to distinguish and separate humans from other animals in terms of a binary "us" and "them." In dualistic perspectives, animals are invariably judged to be inferior to humans. Animals are judged to be devoid of immortal souls, minds, rational capacities, and language. There are, of course, differences (sometimes important ones) within and between species. Nevertheless, such distinctions have often been used to explain and bolster the presumed moral priority of the human species to the detriment of others.

The distinction between "rational" and "nonrational" has led to entrenched dualisms in Christian thought that separate humans from the rest of creation. The view emerged that animals are "just animals." For example, whereas humans have "spirit," animals have only "flesh"; humans have "minds," whereas animals are just "matter"; humans are "persons," and animals are mere "things"; humans have rational immortal souls, and animals have nonrational souls. These distinctions in favor of humans are reinforced by the historic language we use about animals: "brutes," "beasts," "irrational," and "dumb." Dualistic distinctions have always tended to disadvantage animals and elevate humans.

It is worth noting that the foregoing arguments do not of themselves necessarily lead to the justification of animal cruelty or abuse. Lack of rationality and absence of an immortal soul should logically lead to greater solicitude. If animals are not rational, then this may increase their suffering since they experience the raw terror of confinement or injury without knowing why they are suffering or for what purpose. If animals are really nonrational, it follows that their suffering cannot be softened by intellectual comprehension of the circumstances. Also, as C. S. Lewis observed, if animals are not to be recompensed with an eternal paradise for the sufferings that they have to undergo in the present world, then that surely makes their current suffering of greater, not lesser, significance.[21]

From the denial of mental life and rational soulfulness in animals, it was only a short step to the idea that animals had insufficient consciousness to feel pain. The suspicion that animals did not really feel "like us," if at all, was given impetus by René Descartes. According to Descartes, animals "act naturally and mechanically, like a clock which tells the time better than our own judgement does."[22] Animals, in short, are automatons, without consciousness, rationality, or feeling. It is sometimes claimed that Descartes was more well-intentioned toward animals than the plain reading of his work might suggest. But closer examination shows that he put his own idea into practice since he himself performed vivisections.[23] It is said of his followers, the Port Royalists, that "they kicked about their dogs and dissected their cats without mercy, laughing at any compassion for them, and calling their screams the noise of breaking machinery."[24]

Doubtless, this view represents the Christian tradition at its worst and would be held by few Christians today, but it is worth remembering that various forms of Cartesianism have been implicitly or explicitly accepted by many theologians. In the twentieth century, even the celebrated biologist, natural theologian, and Cambridge professor of divinity Charles Raven doubted whether animals could feel pain without a frontal cortex.[25] And Raven was not alone among theologians in the twentieth century.

It is important to stress that Cartesianism would not have been possible without the ground laid by Aquinas and subsequent Thomists. As we have seen, the strength of Thomism consists in its circularity:

God put animals here for our use; we know that they are meant to be slaves because they are enslavable; and because they are without reason and therefore only merely means to human ends, they cannot have individual worth or a rational soul. Thus, to posit that they also have insufficient consciousness to know pain, or anything like what humans experience when we experience pain, was a significant step, but not a surprising or illogical one.

Neither is Cartesianism wholly disavowed in contemporary philosophy. The contemporary philosopher Peter Carruthers shows the influence of Descartes when he suggests that animals can experience pain, but that because they lack "phenomenal consciousness," their pain has no "subjective feel" to them. They experience pain, but they are not aware that they experience pain.[26]

The common theme in the mainstream history of Western ethics is that humans, by virtue of their reason, are morally special and that animals, because they lack reason, are properly subordinated to and used by humans. Yet even among contemporary philosophers working in these traditions, there are attempts to extend the moral realm to include obligations to animals. Working in the Aristotelian virtue ethics tradition, Rosalind Hursthouse rejects the concept of moral status and argues that a well-developed account of the virtues would require compassion for animals.[27]

Grounds for Extending Moral Solicitude

In contrast to these dominant tendencies in Western thought, the consensus among ethicists has moved toward embracing three positions.

The first is that animals have worth in themselves, what may be termed "inherent" or "intrinsic" value. Sentient beings, or sentients, are not just things, objects, machines, or tools; they have their own interior life that deserves respect. This view extends worth to sentients as individuals, not just as collectivities or as part of a community.

The second position is that, given the conceding of sentience, there can be no rational grounds for not taking animals' sentience into account or for excluding individual animals from the same basic moral consideration that we extend to individual human beings.

The third position is that it follows that causing harm to individual sentients (except when it is for their own good—for example, in a veterinary operation) requires strong moral justification. Some would argue that such acts of harming innocent (i.e., morally blameless) sentients is wrong in itself, and such acts are usually termed "intrinsically wrong" or "intrinsically evil."

There are a number of considerations that provide grounds for granting animals moral solicitude.[28]

a. Animals cannot give or withhold their consent

It is commonly accepted that informed consent is required in advance from an individual when anyone wishes to override the legitimate interests of that individual. The absence of this factor requires, at the very least, that we exercise extraordinary care and thoughtfulness. The very (obvious) fact that animals cannot agree to the purposes to which they are put increases our responsibility.

It may be claimed that although animals cannot talk about consent, their actions may manifest consent and the lack thereof. So, for example, it may be presumed that an animal who fights (and howls perhaps) to stay out of a kennel is registering her will against being placed in a kennel. So maybe an animal can behaviorally, and even vocally, manifest his or her lack of consent.

Although we cannot deny the importance of these behavioral indications, they obviously fall short of what humans mean when they speak of voluntary, informed consent. Consent makes sense, logically, only if an individual is presented with alternative possibilities and has both the knowledge of what these possibilities represent and the freedom to choose one of them—and to do so without coercion. When an animal cries or howls or reels in pain, she registers displeasure at her predicament, but registering displeasure (or pleasure) is not voluntary consent or non-consent. In short, we can sometimes know how animals feel—largely negatively—about their state (and we do well to be sensitive to such indications). In that sense we do often (rightly or wrongly) presume consent, but *presumed* consent is still a long way from *voluntary*, verbal consent as we know it between human beings.

It is pertinent to look at how the issue of consent has evolved historically in relation to the ethics of research involving human subjects. The 1931 German Guidelines on Human Experimentation, which preceded the Nuremberg Code, were claimed to be the first of their kind in providing protection for human subjects of scientific research, even though the 1900 Berlin Code briefly preceded them.[29] Of note are the following paragraphs:

5. Innovative therapy may be carried out only after the subject or his legal representative has unambiguously consented to the procedure in the light of relevant information provided in advance. Where consent is refused, innovative therapy may be initiated only if it constitutes an urgent procedure to preserve life or prevent serious damage to health and prior consent could not be obtained under the circumstances.
6. The question of whether to use innovative therapy must be examined with particular care where the subject is a child or a person under eighteen years of age.[30]

The Nuremberg Code was drafted at the end of World War II. The code was a landmark document in the development of the ethics of research involving human subjects. Six out of the ten points of the Nuremberg Code were derived from the 1931 guidelines. Although the Nuremberg Code was not a legal document, it was the first international document to advocate voluntary participation and informed consent. The Nuremberg Code states that "the voluntary consent of the human participant is absolutely essential" and that the benefits of research must outweigh the risks.[31]

In 1964 the World Medical Association established recommendations guiding doctors in biomedical research involving human participants. These recommendations were set down in the Declaration of Helsinki,[32] which governs international research ethics and defines rules for research combined with clinical care and for nontherapeutic research. The declaration has been updated regularly, the last update being in 2013. One ethical stipulation is especially relevant: "Informed consent from research participants is necessary."[33]

In response to the prejudice (unjustifiable bias) that had been shown to occur during the Tuskegee Syphilis Study (1932–72), the National Research Act was passed in the United States in 1974. This act created the National Commission for the Protection of Human Subjects of Biomedical and Behavioural Research (National Commission). The National Commission was charged with identifying the basic ethical principles that should underlie the conduct of biomedical and behavioral research involving human subjects and with developing guidelines that should be followed to ensure such research is conducted in accordance with those principles. The National Commission drafted the *Belmont Report* in 1979, which was to become a foundational document for the ethics of research involving human participants in the United States. It is pertinent to note that the *Belmont Report* established three basic ethical principles, as follows: (1) respect for persons, (2) beneficence, and (3) justice.[34]

The report's first principle, "respect for persons," encapsulates the issue well: "Individuals should be treated as autonomous agents," and "persons with diminished autonomy are entitled to protection."[35] Of note is that an autonomous person is defined in the *Belmont Report* as an individual who is "capable of deliberation about personal goals and of acting under the direction of such deliberation."[36] The application of this particular ethical principle is in informed consent, as follows: (1) participants, "to the degree that they are capable," must be "given the opportunity to choose what shall or shall not happen to them"; and (2) the consent process must include the following three elements: information, comprehension, and voluntary participation.[37]

But the question must be asked: if these principles are sound, why should they not apply to nonhuman subjects as well? The irony is rendered acute when it is appreciated that the Declaration of Helsinki expressly endorses experiments on animals as a precursor to ethical experiments on humans.

The fact that it is impossible to obtain informed consent (with all that it should entail) highlights the moral difficulty of using animals. Constitutionally, animals are unable to give fully informed, voluntary consent for the following reasons:

1. It is not possible to communicate the relevant information to them.
2. It is reasonable to argue that they may not fully comprehend the information, even if it were possible to communicate the information to them.
3. Therefore, they are not in a position to make sound judgments between alternative (long-term) future optional courses of action.

In other words, the animals are being coerced, and coercion is an example of pathogenic (situational) vulnerability.[38]

b. Animals cannot represent or vocalize their own interests

Animals cannot vocalize their own interests except by behavioral indicators, as illustrated previously. Individuals who cannot adequately represent themselves have to depend on others to represent them. The plight of animals, like that of children or the elderly who suffer from dementia, should invoke a heightened sense of obligation—precisely because they cannot articulate their needs or represent their interests.

Again, it may be claimed that animals can and do represent their interests—for example, an animal found scouring rubbish bins may be said to "represent his interest" in getting food. In such ways, animals may be said to "speak to us" so that we have some sense of their interests. But one cannot logically insist on the "linguistic deficiency" of animals (as so many philosophers have done) and then refuse its conclusion that animals cannot properly represent themselves—at least in terms that humans can verbally understand. Of course, those who wish to exploit animals pretend to know only too well what "their" animals "want." But in fact, although we can and should take behavioral indications seriously, our general (and sometimes specific) unknowing should be counted in the animals' favor.

c. Animals cannot understand or rationalize their suffering

The underlying assumption (at least as it is utilized in contemporary debate) is that rational incomprehension makes suffering less morally considerable because the suffering of rational beings is incomparably greater. Rational comprehension might heighten suffering if, for example, it involves anticipation of harm or death, which animals cannot experience. It is sometimes claimed, for example, that animals have no anticipation of death and are therefore spared that ontological anxiety that besets human beings. If that is true, then it must be granted that humans may be liable to more suffering in those situations.

Another example is when a prisoner of war is told that his country has been destroyed or that his family has been killed or will be killed. Verbal threats or abusive comments may cause considerable suffering for a human, whereas such threats (as long as they remain purely verbal) would not increase the suffering of an animal. Again, in these cases, it should be accepted that humans suffer more, or rather that they suffer in ways in which animals cannot.

But is it true that rational comprehension always or generally heightens suffering? The general claim is less well founded. Consider the case of free-living animals—for example, nonhuman primates who are captured, taken from their natural state, and then subjected to captivity in zoos or laboratories. The animals concerned do not know why they have been captured, why they are being transported, or what will happen to them. They experience the raw terror of not knowing. And since the implication of the argument is that animals live closer to their bodily senses than we do, the frustration of their natural freedoms may well induce more suffering than we allow. Human suffering, on the other hand, can be softened by an intellectual comprehension of the circumstances. When, for example, a human visits the dentist, who then performs procedures ranging from the uncomfortable to the traumatic, the patient can at least console himself or herself that the procedures are for his or her own putative good. No such consolations are available to animals who are denied their liberty and who have procedures performed upon them that are equally, if not more, uncomfortable or traumatic.

It seems reasonable that the imposition of captivity upon free-ranging animals constitutes a considerable harm—what has been termed "harms as deprivation."[39] Captive animals are frequently denied the opportunity to express even elementary patterns of behavior. Is that harm lessened by intellectual incomprehension? Not obviously. If it is true that animals are nonrational, then it follows that they have no means of rationalizing their deprivation, boredom, and frustration. They have no intellectual means of escaping their circumstances—for example (as far as we can tell), by use of the imagination. They cannot, like Terry Waite in captivity, intellectually appreciate the forces that led to their capture and resign themselves, as he did, to a heroic policy of "no self-pity."[40] Waite at least had the benefit of communication, however limited, with his captors—an amelioration always unavailable to captive animals. Neither can they, like Waite, write novels in their heads.[41] Such considerations also extend to a range of situations in which we manage or use animals.

The claim, then, that rational incomprehension is a morally relevant difference stands only if it can be shown that comprehension increases liability to suffering or that its absence makes the experience of suffering less acute. In some instances, this surely is the case, but in others, there are equal grounds for supposing that the contrary is true. The bottom line is that animals and humans suffer in varying ways. Humans will suffer more in some situations, animals more in others. Rationality is only one of many factors (including, notably, bodily sensibility) that may intensify suffering. It cannot be singled out as the only, or even main, factor capable of justifying the privileged position that human suffering now occupies.

d. Animals are morally innocent

Some animals may possess moral sense,[42] but we can be confident that they are not moral agents. Because animals are not moral agents with free will, they cannot be regarded as morally responsible. That granted, it follows that they (unlike, arguably, adult humans) can never deserve suffering or be improved morally by it. Animals can never merit suffering; proper recognition of this consideration makes any infliction of suffering upon them problematic.

Inflicting pain on those who can never deserve or merit it increases our responsibility; it raises the bar of moral acceptability even higher, and that is true even if some decide that infliction of pain may still be justified by reference to the greater good. The point is that we have as much need to justify intentional infliction of suffering on animals as we do to justify infliction of suffering on humans.

e. Animals are vulnerable and (relatively) defenseless

Animals are wholly, or almost wholly, within our power and entirely subject to our will. Except in rare circumstances, animals pose us no threat, constitute no risk to our life, and possess no means of offense or defense. Moral solicitude should properly relate to, and be commensurate with, the relative vulnerability of the subjects concerned, or with what might be termed "ontologies of vulnerability."

The massive vulnerability of animals to humans is like and unlike other vulnerabilities. It is *like* the vulnerability of children (particularly infants), comatose patients, and the mentally unwell. These individuals are most readily subjected to us; in fact, almost everything we do to them is done without consent. Such actions incur heavy responsibilities when they involve calculations of the subjects' own interests, especially when the activity involves harm. Few would dissent from this line of reasoning in relation to these subjects.

But in relation to animals, the case is equally strong, if not stronger. Animal vulnerabilities are *unlike* others in that animals, especially managed animals, are almost completely vulnerable and subject to exploitation. We do not breed, choose to create, artificially inseminate, or genetically engineer infants or the mentally unwell. Our institutional control of animal lives is without parallel. In the case of many animals used on farms, as well as in laboratories, we not only determine that they should exist but also determine the pattern and shape of their lives. We change the "nature" or physical appearance of animals through, inter alia, genetic manipulation. Our almost total control over billions of animals, properly understood, involves us in a near-total moral responsibility to them.

Briefly summarized, then, the rational considerations for granting sentients moral solicitude are as follows:

a. Animals cannot give or withhold their consent.
b. They cannot represent or vocalize their own interests.
c. They cannot understand or rationalize their suffering.
d. They are morally innocent or blameless, and
e. They are vulnerable and relatively defenseless.

The presence of just one of the factors so far discussed forms the rational basis for a compelling case for further discussion about moral consideration for animals, and all these considerations make the infliction of suffering on animals not *easier* but *harder* to justify.[43]

As with children (especially infants), these considerations provide the rational basis for regarding animals as cases of special moral concern. Simply put, the factors that are usually employed to argue against consideration of animals (such as their inability to talk, to claim their interests, or to act as moral agents) mean that they should be granted not weaker but stronger moral solicitude. Rather than adopting a "might makes right" mentality, we need to recognize that our dominance over animals means that we have special responsibilities to take care of them.

It is the difficulty in justifying harm to animals that renders animals (like infants) a special moral case. Strictly speaking (because they are not moral agents), animals cannot merit or deserve suffering, and they cannot be morally improved by it. This means that all the usual justifications for inflicting suffering simply do not apply in the case of animals. Now, it is true that some utilitarians may justify inflicting such suffering by appeal to the alleged fact that greater positive good would result from such infliction—as in medical experiments—than would result without such infliction of suffering. But that is not the morally usual or accepted way we would act toward humans. The utilitarian response simply shows how such an ethical theory cannot reconcile well with our ordinary (non-utilitarian) notion of justice. In other words, it is inconsistent to suppose that species alone can justify the maltreatment of animals while opposing maltreatment of humans.

We shall see how this new thinking radically changes our moral assessment in our subsequent discussion.

Notes

1. Aristotle, "Nicomachean Ethics," in *The Works of Aristotle*, vol. 9, trans. W. D. Ross (London: Oxford University Press, 1915), 1161a–b.

2. Ibid., emphasis in the original.

3. Ibid.

4. T. Aquinas, *Summa Theologiae*, ed. the English Dominican Fathers (New York: Benzinger Brothers, 1918), part 1, question 65.3, emphasis added.

5. T. Hobbes, "De Cive [1642]," in *The English Works of Thomas Hobbes of Malmesbury*, vol. 2, ed. W. Molesworth (London: John Bohn, 1841), 63–75. Cited and discussed in A. Linzey and P. B. Clarke, *Animal Rights: A Historical Anthology* (New York: Columbia University Press, 2004), xix.

6. D. Hume, *Enquiry concerning the Principles of Morals*, ed. L. A. Selby-Brigge (Oxford: Clarendon Press, 1902), 189–92. Originally published in 1751. Cited and discussed in Linzey and Clarke, *Animal Rights*, xix.

7. J. Rawls, *A Theory of Justice* (Oxford: Oxford University Press, 1972), 504–12. Cited and discussed in Linzey and Clarke, *Animal Rights*, xix.

8. M. Rowlands, *Animal Rights: A Philosophical Defence*, 2nd rev. ed. (Basingstoke, UK: Palgrave Macmillan, 1998); M. Rowlands, *Animals like Us* (London: Verso, 2002); M. Rowlands, *Animal Rights: Moral Theory and Practice* (Basingstoke, UK: Palgrave Macmillan, 2009).

9. A. Schweitzer, *Civilisation and Ethics*, trans. C. T. Campion (London: Allen and Unwin, 1923), 119.

10. Aristotle, *The Politics*, trans. T. A. Sinclair (London: Penguin, 1985), 1.viii, 79.

11. T. Aquinas, *Summa contra Gentiles*, in *Basic Writings of Saint Thomas Aquinas*, vol. 2, trans. A. C. Pegis (New York: Random House, 1945), 221–22, emphasis added.

12. Aquinas, *Summa Theologiae*, part 1, question 64.1.

13. Some material in this section has been borrowed from C. Linzey, "Animals in Catholic Thought: A New Sensitivity?" in *The Animals in Us: We in Animals*, ed. S. Wróbel (Frankfurt, Germany: Peter Lang, 2014), 187–202.

14. P. Palazzini, ed., *Dictionary of Moral Theology* (London: Burns and Oates, 1962), 73.

15. J. Gaffney, "The Relevance of Animal Experimentation to Roman Catholic Methodology," in *Animal Sacrifices: Religious Perspectives on the Use of Animals in Science*, ed. T. Regan (Philadelphia: Temple University Press, 1986), 149, 159–60.

16. I. Kant, *Metaphysics of Morals*, trans. J. Ladd (New York: Bobbs-Merrill, 1965), 345–46.

17. Aquinas, *Summa contra Gentiles*, 220–24.

18. I. Kant, *Lectures on Ethics: Duties towards Animals and Other Spirits*, trans. L. Infield (New York: Harper and Row, 1963), 239–41.

19. C. Korsgaard, "Interacting with Animals: A Kantian Account," in *The Oxford Handbook of Animal Ethics*, ed. T. L. Beauchamp and R. G. Frey (Oxford: Oxford University Press, 2011), 91–118.

20. A. Pope, "Of Cruelty to Animals," in *A Hundred English Essays*, ed. R. Vallance (London: Thomas Nelson, 1950), 159–65.

21. C. S. Lewis, *Vivisection* (Boston: New England Anti-Vivisection Society, 1947).

22. E. S. Haldane and G. R. T. Ross, eds., *Discourse on Method in Philosophical Works of Descartes* (London: Cambridge University Press, 1950), 115ff.

23. A. Gombay, *Descartes* (Oxford: Blackwell, 2007), 43.

24. J. P. Mahaffy, *Descartes* (London: Blackwood, 1901), 118.

25. C. Raven, *The Creator Spirit* (London: Longmans, 1927), 120.

26. P. Carruthers, "Brute Experience," *Journal of Philosophy* 86, no. 5 (1989): 258–69; P. Carruthers, "Animal Mentality: Its Character, Extent, and Moral Significance," in *The Oxford Handbook of Animal Ethics*, ed. T. L. Beauchamp and R. G. Frey (Oxford: Oxford University Press, 2011), 373–406.

27. R. Hursthouse, "Virtue Ethics and the Treatment of Animals," in *The Oxford Handbook of Animal Ethics*, ed. T. L. Beauchamp and R. G. Frey (Oxford: Oxford University Press, 2011), 119–43.

28. The following rationale is adapted from A. Linzey, *Why Animal Suffering Matters: Philosophy, Theology, and Practical Ethics* (Oxford: Oxford University Press, 2009).

29. R. B. Ghooi, "The Nuremberg Code—A Critique," *Perspectives on Clinical Research* 2, no. 2 (2011): 72–76.

30. Ibid., 74.

31. "The Nuremberg Code," para. 1, accessed January 2, 2015, http://www.hhs.gov/ohrp/archive/nurcode.html. Originally published in *Trials of War Criminals before the Nuremberg Military Tribunals under Control Council Law No. 10*, vol. 2 (Washington, DC: US Government Printing Office), 181–82.

32. World Medical Association, "Declaration of Helsinki—Ethical Principles for Medical Research involving Human Subjects" (2013), accessed November 27, 2014, http://www.wma.net/en/30publications/10policies/b3/.

33. Ibid.

34. National Commission for the Protection of Human Subjects of Biomedical and Behavioural Research, *The Belmont Report: Ethical Principles and Guidelines for the Protection of Human Subjects of Research* (US Department of Health and Human Services, 1979), accessed November 27, 2014, http://www.hhs.gov/ohrp/humansubjects/guidance/belmont.html.

35. Ibid.

36. Ibid.

37. Ibid.

38. C. MacKenzie, "The Importance of Relational Autonomy and Capabilities for an Ethics of Vulnerability," in *Vulnerability: New Essays in Ethics and Feminist Philosophy*, ed. C. MacKenzie, W. Rogers, and S. Dodds (Oxford: Oxford University Press, 2014), 39.

39. T. Regan, *The Case for Animal Rights* (London: Routledge and Kegan Paul, 1983), 96.

40. T. Waite, *Taken on Trust* (London: Hodder and Stoughton, 1993).

41. Ibid.

42. M. Rowlands, *Can Animals Be Moral?* (Oxford: Oxford University Press, 2012).

43. The section on grounds for extending moral solicitude draws on and extends the argument in chapter 1 of A. Linzey, *Why Animal Suffering Matters*.

1.5

The Putative Justifications

WE NOW TURN TO consider arguments for the use of animals in research. In order to avoid the charge of bias, we have selected the most considered arguments in three authoritative reports, two of which are UK governmental reports. We believe that these arguments represent the pro-animal experimentation case in a more considered and cautious way than may be articulated by individual philosophers and scientists. We therefore judge that we have selected the best arguments for the pro-animal experimentation case. These reports are the *Review of Cost-Benefit Assessment in the Use of Animals in Research* of the Animal Procedures Committee (APC), published by the Home Office in the United Kingdom;[1] the 2001–2 report of the Select Committee on Animals in Scientific Procedures of the House of Lords (SCHOL);[2] and the working group report chaired by Sir David Weatherall, *The Use of Non-Human Primates in Research* in 2006 (hereafter "Weatherall report" or "Weatherall").[3]

We begin by turning to the lengthy assessment of the morality of animal testing in the APC review.

Cost-Benefit Assessment

The function of the APC was "to provide Ministers with independent advice about the workings of the [Animals (Scientific Procedures) Act 1986] . . . and their functions within the Act."[4] One of the roles of the APC was to consider the morality of using ani-

mal subjects in experiments. The committee included some animal welfare representatives, including ethicists (of various hues), but they were in the minority, and most committee members were pro-animal research scientists. In reply to the statement by the British Union for the Abolition of Vivisection that "it is indefensible to knowingly inflict suffering on innocent sentient animals other than in their own [individual] interests," the APC states,

> Even if this claim were accepted, it would not imply that animal experiments should never be carried out. As pointed out in the APC Biotechnology Report (Home Office 2001, para 44), actions that are inherently or intrinsically wrong are not therefore absolutely wrong, in the sense that there are no circumstances in which they could be justified. For example, an action that is judged to be wrong might nevertheless be justified if it could be shown to be the lesser of two wrongs that we have to choose between. Moreover, the claim does not seem to rule out experiments on animals provided that they are anaesthetised.[5]

The distinction between "intrinsic" and "absolute" may be problematic—at least to those who hold deontological theories of ethics. If something is wrong "intrinsically" or "inherently," this logically implies that the action or set of actions *in itself and of itself* is morally illicit. From a deontological perspective, there are some actions that should never be performed, whatever the consequences.

This deontological perspective finds its classic expression in the encyclical *Veritatis Splendor* of John Paul II, which opposes teleological ethical theories that "maintain that it is never possible to formulate an absolute prohibition of particular kinds of behaviour which would be in conflict, in every circumstance and in every culture, with those values."[6] The encyclical argues that "there exist acts which *per se* and in themselves, independently of circumstances, are always seriously wrong by reason of their object."[7] Again:

If acts are intrinsically evil, a good intention or particular circumstances can diminish their evil, but they cannot remove it. They remain "irremediably" evil acts *per se* and in themselves they are not capable of being ordered to God and to the good of the person.[8]

From such a deontological perspective, then, the distinction between "intrinsic" and "absolute" is not plain sailing. However, one of the tasks of deontological approaches to ethics is to develop a ranking system of rights or obligations—a system of principles that shows when one right can be overridden by another (Regan's miniride and worse-off principles are good examples[9]). In such versions of deontological theory, the distinction between intrinsic and absolute wrong is supported.

But not in all. For some, the deliberate infliction of suffering on innocent sentients (human or animal) can never be morally licit. This position deserves much more consideration than is usually given to it. The moral considerations previously outlined indicate that there are good rational grounds for supposing that certain kinds of activity, directed against vulnerable subjects, are so morally outrageous that they ought never to be countenanced, whatever the circumstances. The deliberate infliction of suffering on captive creatures is, from this perspective, intrinsically objectionable or intrinsically evil. Circumstances, benefits, or compensating factors may limit the offense, but they can never make the practice morally licit.[10]

The perspective of teleological ethics, however, is typically different. To say that an action is "intrinsically" wrong or "wrong in itself" means that the performance of such an action has a moral mark against it and so should not be performed unless there are overriding reasons. An action that is wrong in itself is usually classed as "defeasibly" wrong.

From this perspective, the APC is right in claiming that there are conceivable circumstances in which an act that is inherently (or intrinsically) wrong is justifiable. The APC argues that "an action that is judged to be [intrinsically] wrong might nevertheless be justified *if it could be shown to be the lesser of two wrongs that we have to choose between.*"[11] This qualifier again invites a number of questions. Let us consider the subordinate clause "that we have to choose between." This language suggests that we have to make a direct or immediate choice between two wrongs (bad options). But a moment's reflection will show us that there is no "direct" choice involved. A direct choice is precisely that—a choice that *has* to be made; there is no alternative to making it. To live one further minute or second is to make a choice. That is why (as the APC admits) the "your child or your dog" argument has no real relevance to judging the morality of animal experiments. As the APC states, "in animal research we are rarely, if ever, presented with the stark situation in which we can save the life of a child by taking the life of an animal."[12] In reality, what we are presented with is an actual harm and a hypothetical good. In fact, in the entire history of experimentation on both humans and animals, there is not one direct choice of the kind supposed. It is not a question of "if ever" but one simply of "never." As argued by early antivivisectionists, who were equally concerned about experimentation on human subjects, "It is NOT a question of Your Dog or Your Baby, but one of Your Dog AND Your Baby."[13]

This consideration is often overlooked in discussions in the media and even in scientific analyses of animal experiments. But it requires much more ethical probing. Let us try to focus the point by way of an example. Suppose an aged professor (who happens to teach ethics) hears a noise in his house one night and comes down to discover a person stealing his books. On closer encounter he discovers that the thief is actually a former ethics student.

"Now, Stephen, what are you doing?"
"Well, very good to see you, Professor Noggins, but I would like to defend what I am doing."
They both sit down and begin some philosophical discourse.

"As you may know," begins Stephen, "I have always been attracted by consequentialist ethical theory."

"I know that," says Professor Noggins.

"Well, I have decided to begin to act on this theory," the student says, "and implement some consequentialist thinking in my life."

"I see," says Professor Noggins, "but what has this to do with you rifling through my books?"

"Well, everything," says Stephen. "I'm not just rifling through them. I'm taking them, at least a thousand or so—hence all the noise and the boxes everywhere."

"And what exactly are you going to do with them?" asks Professor Noggins.

"Well, that's the point, or rather the consequentialist point. I intend to sell them and give all the money to Oxfam. Consider, whatever small harm stealing your books involves is outweighed by the benefit stealing them will bring to starving people in desperate need of water, food, and proper sanitation. I judge it to be a simple and readily understood moral assessment."

"But what about the injustice *to me*?" questions Noggins in a state of some alarm.

"Yes, I'm sorry about that," says Stephen reassuringly. "But there is a higher choice here. It is plainly wrong for you to enjoy something which, when properly stolen and utilized, can relieve the suffering of others."

Many of us (not only academics) would feel keenly the injustice done to Professor Noggins. But most glaringly, we would want to question the moral assessment that allows an actual harm in the hope (or even reasonable chance) of some hypothetical good. We would judge that the weakness of consequentialism as an ethical theory consists in just that: a failure to take *sufficient* account of actual harm. The student "takes account" of the harm but thinks that it is "overcome" by all the good that may, even probably will, be produced. So it is the case with animal experiments; by various mechanisms (some real, others partly so), the harms are minimized, but the hypothetical benefits are often exaggerated. At the very least, there is no "direct" choice to be made, just as there was not in the case of Stephen stealing Professor Noggins's books.

Even some animal protectionists have been seduced by variations of this argument. For example,

Peter Singer accepts that questions about benefit are often hypothetical, but he still maintains that "if one, or even a dozen animals had to suffer experiments in order to save thousands, [he] would think it right and in accordance with equal consideration of interests that they should do so."[14] This is what Singer should say, of course, since he is a "preference utilitarian." By the same standard, of course, it would also be right to sacrifice even a dozen innocent humans to save hundreds of others. But the fallacy in the argument lies in perpetuating the fantasy that there is a direct choice (at least in the case of animals) to be made. It is evident, for instance, that in the many examples provided earlier in this report (in section 1.1, "The Scale of the Problem"), no such direct or immediate choice was involved.

The APC also maintains that the principle that we should not deliberately cause suffering to innocent sentients "does not seem to rule out experiments on animals provided that they are anaesthetised."[15] Although it is true that some experiments may not cause significant pain or suffering (although they have the potential to; otherwise, they would not need to be licensed), only a small minority are conducted completely under general anesthetic. For example, in the United Kingdom, the percentage of experiments done completely under general anesthesia from which the animal is not permitted to wake up (i.e., he or she is killed before waking up) is only 3 percent.[16]

Even when experiments do not intentionally involve pain or suffering, it does not follow, of course, that they do not in fact involve pain or suffering. Consider the experience of dental work even under anesthetic. Although some or all of the direct pain may be ameliorated (at least for a period of time), it does not follow that the whole experience is not sufficiently traumatic to cause suffering. When one considers further how (as is often claimed) animals live closer to their emotions, then experiences such as fear, foreboding, anxiety, terror, and stress seem inevitable. And thus, simply eliminating physical pain does not address the full moral implications of these experiments. Moreover, the outcome of anesthesia is always in doubt.

But even allowing for the fact that a very small number of animals may be completely anesthetized (and accepting that this is to some degree a distraction because the APC argues for the justifiability of many experiments that do cause suffering), the argument misses the point that the issue of harm or suffering is not confined to the issue of the experiments themselves. As already indicated, the capture, breeding, transport, handling, and killing of sentients also cause harm or suffering or both. Consider, for example, the thousands of NHPs who are "wild-caught" for laboratories and who experience considerable suffering in the process (see the related discussion later in this report, in section 1.8, "Undercover Investigations"). The point about anesthesia makes the error of presuming that the only way animals can suffer is by feeling pain. Even if we do not consider the pain that deliverance of the anesthesia often causes, most animals used in experimentation have desires in addition to avoiding pain, the frustration of which presents a harm to these animals. Animals generally prefer mobility to lack of mobility, a rich environment to a barren one, and opportunities to express their natural instincts involving companionship and play. When they are made unwilling subjects in animal experiments, these desires are irrevocably thwarted, resulting in suffering.

The Issue of Necessity

We now turn more directly to the question of "necessity." The word is widely used in literature that seeks to defend animal testing. For example, in an article republished at *AnimalResearch.Info*, Sir John Vane writes that "the only way to be confident that a new medicine is likely to be safe and effective is to understand how that medicine behaves in a living system. That understanding can only be obtained from animal studies."[17] Alzheimer's Research UK, in its booklet *Why Research using Animals Can Help Defeat Dementia*, claims that "research using animals continues to be vital in the ongoing search for treatment that can slow or stop the disease process."[18] Again, the British Pharmacological Society states that "the use of animals in drug discovery is an essential component of this research."[19] The organization Understanding Animal Research goes further and suggests that "mainstream medical and scientific organisations and leading scientists all agree that animal research is essential for medical progress."[20] In the light of our subsequent discussion of necessity, to be presented

shortly, and specifically the admissions by the APC, we can only regard these statements as overblown and tendentious.

One example of how the contemporary debate is conducted can be seen in the ethical discussion contained in the SCHOL report. The report extends to eighty-one pages, but only one half-page (five paragraphs) is devoted to ethics.

It is worth examining these paragraphs in full:

2.1   There is no doubt that the issues raised by the remit of the Select Committee, besides being practical, are also moral or ethical. They centre on the question of how human beings should treat other animals. Moral beliefs and sentiment differ about the answer to this question.

2.2   There are those who, following a suggestion by Jeremy Bentham in the late 18th century, hold that all creatures capable of suffering are on an equal footing with human beings, regardless of "the number of the legs, the villosity of the skin, or the termination of the os sacrum." These people hold that being sentient confers a moral right on animals that they should not be used by human beings for research whose purpose is mainly to benefit humans. Some activists are prepared to uphold this view by violence.

2.3   More commonly, there are those who hold that the whole institution of morality, society and law is founded on the belief that human beings are unique amongst animals. Humans are therefore morally entitled to use animals, whether in the laboratory, the farmyard or the house, for their own purposes. And this belief is sometimes combined with a further belief that there is a moral imperative for human beings to develop medical and veterinary science for the relief of suffering, among both humans and other animals. This moral imperative permits the use in research laboratories of animals, whose suffering must be weighed against the ultimate relief of suffering towards which research is directed. This is encapsulated in the weighing of harms and benefits (the "cost/benefit" assessment) in the 1986 Act.

2.4 The belief that human beings have the moral right, and in some contexts the moral imperative, to use animals in research, does not entail that animals may be bred and kept for human purposes with total disregard for their suffering. The deliberate or negligent causing of suffering to another, whether human or animal, is a moral vice, cruelty, which is sometimes a crime. Therefore we have a moral duty to avoid or minimise animal suffering wherever possible.

2.5 The unanimous view of the Select Committee is that it is morally acceptable for human beings to use other animals, but that it is morally wrong to cause them "unnecessary" or "avoidable" suffering.[21]

Let us examine the first paragraph. We are told that the remit of the SCHOL is to consider the ethical aspects, yet the committee's very characterization of varying moral positions is oddly phrased to say the least: "Moral beliefs and sentiment differ about the answer to this question." This way of characterizing the ethical dimension implies that what is at stake is only people's moral "beliefs" or their moral "sentiments." The idea that ethics requires disciplined, rigorous analysis based on defensible propositions seems to have eluded the Lords. Instead of moral reasoning, we are to engage with "beliefs" and "sentiments."

The second paragraph states that those who follow Jeremy Bentham hold that animals capable of suffering are on an "equal footing" with human beings. But that is not the case. Singer's position (following Bentham and J. S. Mill) is that there should be "equal consideration of interests," but that does not mean that *all* interests should be treated equally or counted equally. Indeed, as shown previously, Singer does not oppose all experiments on animals. Taking suffering into account does not require positing an "equal footing" of all interests. Humans, for example, will have certain interests (e.g., participation in a parliamentary democracy) that other sentient beings will not and vice versa.

The second paragraph continues, "These people hold that being sentient confers a moral right on animals that they should not be used by human beings for research whose purpose is mainly to benefit humans. Some activists are prepared to uphold this view by violence." And in a footnote to the first sentence, SCHOL says, "This is the view taken by philosophers such as Peter Singer."[22] But of course, as we have shown, that is not Singer's view since he accepts the legitimacy of some experimentation (and he is also antiviolence in virtually all conceivable cases). Moreover, the view that sentiency incurs "a moral right" on sentients also misreads Singer. He does not believe that animals have moral rights as such, although this language is sometimes used by him as a shorthand. "These people" to whom SCHOL refers in the same line implicitly include Bentham himself, yet as a utilitarian like Singer, Bentham does not believe in moral rights and elsewhere even talks of rights as "nonsense upon stilts."[23]

As noted, the second paragraph ends by saying, "Some activists are prepared to uphold this view by violence." Who these "some" are is nowhere defined, and the statement's relevance to this part of SCHOL's report is unclear, unless it is an attempt at guilt by association. Although it is true that a tiny minority of animal activists have resorted to illegality, even violence, in defense of animals, it does not follow that these activists necessarily follow Bentham's argument (or rather, SCHOL's misunderstanding of it) or that Bentham's argument requires violent protest.

The third paragraph begins, "More commonly, there are those who hold that the whole institution of morality, society and law is founded on the belief that human beings are unique among animals. Humans are therefore morally entitled to use animals, whether in the laboratory, the farmyard or the house, for their own purposes." Leaving aside the grandiose claim that the "whole institution" (or, more accurately, institutions) of "morality, society and law" depends upon human "uniqueness," it is worth pondering what human uniqueness may mean or entail. All animals are unique in their own way; they may excel in aspects, such as speed, flight, language, physique, and so forth, that put humans to shame. In that sense, humans too are unique in possessing certain abilities and characteristics that not all animals share. But human uniqueness, no more significant than any other animal's uniqueness, does not by itself constitute an argument for using or not using other species.

When the paragraph continues—"Humans are *therefore* morally entitled to use animals, whether in the laboratory, the farmyard or the house, for their own purposes" (our emphasis)—we are confronted by a non sequitur. It simply does not follow that because humans are unique, they have the moral right to exploit other animals. That there are differences within and between species cannot be doubted. But the issue to be confronted is whether any of these differences are morally relevant, and without demonstrating how human uniqueness is morally relevant, the attempted argument collapses.

SCHOL continues: "And this belief is sometimes combined with a further belief that there is a moral imperative for human beings to develop medical and veterinary science for the relief of suffering, among both humans and other animals. This moral imperative permits the use in research laboratories of animals, whose suffering must be weighed against the ultimate relief of suffering towards which research is directed." Again we are dealing with "beliefs" rather than arguments as such. Beliefs are stated, but reasons for them are not given, let alone assessed. To make the point more emphatically, people have all kinds of beliefs about all kinds of things, but the question is which beliefs are better justified. Morality does not get settled by an opinion poll, as if we can tell the shape of the Earth by taking a poll. Precisely why human uniqueness should involve this "moral imperative" is not at all clear, and no reasons are given for it.

The report concludes the paragraph with this: "This moral imperative permits the use in research laboratories of animals, whose suffering must be weighed against the ultimate relief of suffering towards which research is directed. This is encapsulated in the weighing of harms and benefits (the 'cost/benefit' assessment) in the 1986 Act." But it does not follow—even if there is a "moral imperative" to relieve suffering—that the deliberate infliction of pain, death, or suffering upon other sentients is justified to achieve this aim. Indeed, it is generally acknowledged that acts matter more than omissions and that "it is worse to cause a harm than to fail to prevent one."[24] Neither does it follow that we can meet this "imperative" only by means of a cost-benefit assessment in which the suffering of individual sentients is weighed against whatever relief (if such there be) may come from such research. The necessary reasoning is not supplied that would enable us to consider such a position. This appears to be a conclusion without any serious attempt to analyze the ethical underpinnings of its support.

One way of grasping the arbitrariness of the judgment is to ask why human subjects should not also be included in the cost-benefit assessment. If, as we are told, there is a moral imperative to relieve suffering through research (and such research will be effective), why should humans not themselves also be subjected to experimentation, especially since the results from such experimentation would undoubtedly be greater? This is not a rhetorical question. We know that experimentation on human subjects, including prisoners of war, orphaned children, people of color, and serving soldiers, took place during the twentieth century. Defended by arguments similar to the argument now adopted by SCHOL, all these experiments were seen as necessary to the acquisition of useful knowledge.

The reply may come that humans are unique and therefore should not be used in scientific research. But leaving aside the uniqueness of not just humans but all species, it simply does not follow that our special endowments (if such they be) justify the infliction of suffering on other sentients. Indeed, an argument could be properly run in the opposite direction—namely, that because humans are unique (especially in a moral sense), they should agree to sacrifice themselves to achieve useful knowledge, rather than inflict suffering on others who are morally blameless.

And here, of course, we reach another rub: the assumption throughout the SCHOL report is that it is a morally simple or straightforward matter to justify the infliction of suffering on animals as a means to some greater good (however hypothetical). But as we have already indicated, although humans can agree to sacrifice themselves for a putative greater good, it is impossible for animals to do so. Animals are incapable of giving or withholding consent. Recognition of this point makes the infliction of suffering on animals not easier but harder (if not impossible) to justify. As Tom Regan rightly comments, "risks are not morally transferable to those who do not voluntarily choose to take them in the way this defense assumes."[25] Animals do not sacrifice themselves; we sacrifice them.

SCHOL concludes its section on ethics in this way: "The unanimous view of the Select Committee is that it is morally acceptable for human beings to use other animals, but that it is morally wrong to cause them 'unnecessary' or 'avoidable' suffering."[26] But this appeal to necessity begs questions and raises a number of problems.

The first issue is the problem of establishing necessity. Many pro-animal research documents speak freely of animal use being "necessary," but they seldom offer any definition of the term. In ethical terms, showing that something is necessary requires more than a simple appeal to what is customary, desirable, or even beneficial. Human wants or pleasures do not by themselves constitute moral necessity. By definition, necessity is an urgent and unavoidable requirement; the need has to be dictated by some compulsion or coercion that makes any other act impossible. When the concept is defined in this way, we can see immediately that only the weakest possible meaning of the word can reasonably apply in the case of animal experimentation. Far from being in a situation of having no choice or having to make a direct choice, or being coerced beyond our will, when humans choose to experiment, it is a voluntary act of will.

To be fair, even those who support experiments understand this point. "If there is a weakness in the case for animal experimentation within the terms laid down by the [1986 UK] Act, it lies in the difficulty of demonstrating necessity," argues the APC review in a remarkably candid confession.[27] The subsequent comments are no less so and are worth reproducing in full:

> The challenge, indeed the requirement of the Act, is to demonstrate in any given case that there is no alternative to animal experimentation of the kind proposed—that the desired and desirable objective cannot be achieved in any other way. If this were interpreted as the requirement to show that the desired result could not be achieved in any other way, then it would be very difficult indeed to demonstrate. In principle, and with enough changes assumed, any number of desirable results *might* be achieved. It is usually, and more plausibly however, interpreted as a requirement to show that the desired result *is not likely* to be achieved in any other way. But this means—"is not likely, given present circumstances." It is therefore open to opponents of experimentation to argue that present circumstances should be changed so as to make it more likely.[28]

The admissions here are telling. We are told that "it would be very difficult indeed to demonstrate" any necessity for animal experiments. We are further told that the best case that can be managed is that the desired result "*is not likely* to be achieved in any other way." However one characterizes these admissions, it should be clear that animal testing fails the test of necessity as understood ethically.[29] At the outset of its review, the APC argues that "it is evident that procedures that inflict injury on animals for reasons other than their own good require robust defence."[30] That being so, we have to conclude that the APC has simply failed to provide such a defense.

Another way of looking at this is to consider an actual experiment, which concerned diagnostic tests for tuberculosis. One hundred sixty subjects were selected, and tuberculin was injected into their eyes, skin, and muscles. Reports of the experiments detail the moans from the subjects, who were unable to sleep because of the pain in their eyes. "They kept their little hands pressed over their eyes, unable to sleep from the sensations they had to undergo."[31]

The subjects were not animals, however. They were human children. All were under the age of eight, and all but twenty-six were from St. Vincent's Catholic Orphanage in Philadelphia. The experiments were performed in 1908 as part of a series of clinical trials in Philadelphia, New York, and Baltimore to test the value of tuberculin as a possible cure for tuberculosis.[32]

The vast majority of people would regard such experiments on children as morally objectionable. In support of this view, they might point to various factors such as the innocence of the children, their defenselessness, their inability to consent, their inability to comprehend what was happening, and the obligation of the orphanage to protect orphaned children, not to mention the suffering the children had to undergo. But the question is, how can we logically oppose such tests on children without also opposing similar tests on other sentient animals? To be consistent in our moral reasoning, we must evaluate actions that harm all sentient creatures, not just human ones.

It is worth pointing out that however gruesome these tests might appear, they were performed with a high moral purpose. The aim of the experiments—to find a cure for tuberculosis (then an invariably fatal disease)—was surely laudable. And did they achieve useful results? Almost certainly the experiments yielded some scientific knowledge, even knowledge that could not have been (at the time) obtained elsewhere (indeed, more useful knowledge than from experimenting on animals of a different species). Despite that, most people would argue that it is wrong to use innocent children as means to an end, even if the results may prove beneficial. Even if there were gains, most would regard them as "ill-gotten."[33]

But consider this: the moral factors that might be deployed in defense of the children are almost identical to the moral factors that can be deployed in defense of animals also subjected to experiments. Animals too can suffer. Animals too cannot give or withhold consent. Animals too cannot represent themselves. Animals too are morally innocent or blameless. Animals too have difficulty comprehending what is happening to them or why. And animals are also vulnerable. Given this common set of factors, it is as difficult to justify experimentation on animals as it is to justify experimentation on young children.

Put another way, there are differences between animals and orphans, but they are not *morally relevant* differences. Examples of morally irrelevant differences include skin color, sexual orientation, and upbringing. No one could rationally justify differential moral treatment on the basis of such obviously morally irrelevant differences. So we must also add to the list another difference: species. That an individual is a member of another sentient species cannot by itself logically justify inferior moral treatment of that individual. The point is unassailable, and its logic is accepted even by those who support experimentation on animals. Philosopher R. G. Frey, for example, writes that "we cannot, with the appeal to benefit, justify (painful) animal experiments without justifying (painful) human experiments."[34]

Your Dog or Your Child

And yet the idea that experimentation involves us in a *direct* choice between human and animal welfare—the "your dog or your child" argument—still dominates public debate and is found even in supposedly authoritative documents, including, for example, the Weatherall report. In order to provide a moral basis

for defending such experiments, the report offers "the hospital fire thought experiment."[35] The scenario runs as follows:

> Suppose a major teaching hospital is on fire. As well as the full range of medical specialities treating patients of different ages (with differing life expectancies, quality of life and many other distinguishing features), the hospital also contains other life forms: visitors, health professionals, an animal house (including nonhuman primates), a maternity and assisted reproductive technology unit with stored embryos and gametes, and—inevitably—the hospital pet cat. For the very fastidious there are also live plants on many of the window ledges and live bacteria and viruses, both in vitro and in the bodies of patients and staff. How are we to prioritise rescue for all these different life forms with differing needs and capacities? And more precisely, how can we work out morally defensible priorities for rescue?[36]

What can we learn from this "thought experiment"? The Weatherall report thinks that all is plain sailing: "The 'hospital fire' thought experiment shows that *without knowing (or needing to know) the theoretical basis or ethical justification*, almost all humans intuitively make important distinctions about the moral importance of different living things."[37] But this line obfuscates the issue. The issue is not how some or even most people would respond "intuitively" to a given situation, but rather whether such responses are rationally supportable. Referring to what we may do "without knowing (or needing to know) the theoretical basis or ethical justification"—arguing that we can know what is right without rational argument—is problematic. Although moral intuitions have an important place in ethics as a starting point, they do not by themselves constitute a rational assessment or even an argument. As R. M. Hare indicates, there needs to be a second order of inquiry and scrutiny following such moral intuitions.[38] After all, many "intuited" that slavery was morally permissible at one time.

The Weatherall report maintains that two conclusions can be drawn from the "intuitive" decision by the majority of people in the scenario. The first is this:

1. Humans generally, and almost universally, accord a lower priority to all animals than they accord to any humans (which means, inter

alia, that they believe it right to save humans before animals).[39]

But this conclusion does not follow at all. All that follows from the hospital fire scenario (if the results are to be believed) is that humans will *in the given situation* respond in that way. The scenario is by definition a limited crisis situation in which one has to make a direct choice. But to philosophize from that one situation, in which most people may choose to save fellow human beings, to a supposed duty to choose humans beings in a wide range of normative situations, where there is no direct choice to be made, is logically fallacious. Thus, the report fails to distinguish between normal and crisis situations. What may happen in a crisis situation, where there is absolutely no alternative but to choose between competing claims, does not settle the issue of what is normally correct. For example, most people would probably save a member of their own family before someone else's family member, but it does not follow that it is therefore justifiable to experiment on someone else's child to save one's own. Again, consider a scenario in which an animal hospital is on fire, where one has to choose between the animals one can save. A person who keeps Siamese cats may well seek to save her own cat and other Siamese cats, but the fact that the person in this scenario makes that decision in that circumstance does not by itself imply that other cats are inferior or deserve inferior moral treatment.[40]

The second moral conclusion, according to the Weatherall report, is as follows:

> 2. Humans think it is morally required to sacrifice the lives of animals to save human life (*consistency then requires that they should do so—other things being equal—in medical research, as well as in hospital fires*). Humans do not always make these distinctions based on species prejudice, i.e. in favour of members of our own species, but based on an analysis or theory about what justifies such distinctions, which is race, gender and species neutral.[41]

Much is wrong with this paragraph as an example of moral reasoning. In the first place, the language of the argument has changed, and therefore so too has the nature of the putative argument. What was previously described as an "intuition" has now hardened into a supposed moral requirement. Although the report may see this requirement as a corollary of our intuitions about the "fire" scenario, no moral reasoning has been adduced to make it so. Second, the use of the word "sacrifice"—insofar as it implies (as it usually does) a voluntary act of the individual—is inappropriate. Animals do not sacrifice themselves; they are coerced, rather obviously against their will and their own best interests. Third, the parenthetical clause is deeply muddled: "consistency then requires that they should do so—other things being equal—in medical research, as well as in hospital fires." It does not follow that having done one thing in a crisis situation, we should do the same in another, entirely different circumstance. A variety of factors may come into play. And neither—and this is the central point—should it follow that what we do in a crisis situation should become what is known as "normative." The report again tries to obfuscate the issue by use of the words "other things being equal," as if the cases of a hospital fire and medical research are identical. But they are not, precisely because things are *not* equal. In the case of the hospital fire, one's choices are both direct and necessarily limited. That is not the case in animal research, where one faces no such direct choice. Indeed, in all such cases, one is not weighing two direct claims, but weighing an actual harm against only a hypothetical good. There is no urgency, crisis, or direct choice involved. Moreover, in the fire situation, one is not deliberately causing harm to those one does not rescue.

This latter point is accepted even by those who endorse animal experiments. It is worth repeating the judgment of the APC report: "in animal research we are rarely, if ever, presented with the stark situation in which we can save the life of a child by taking the life of an animal. Invariably other options and choices intervene. Hence, it is perfectly coherent to oppose animal experiments, by arguing that other options and choices are possible, but save the child if we are faced with a stark choice."[42]

The second line of the Weatherall report's second moral conclusion is as follows: "Humans do not always make these distinctions based on species prejudice, i.e. in favour of members of our own species, but based on an analysis or theory about what justifies such distinctions, which is race, gender and species neutral."[43] If such distinctions are not made simply on the basis of "species prejudice" (despite the apparent reliance on a crisis situation in which simple "intuitions" are appealed to) and instead rely on "an analysis or theory about what justifies such distinctions,"[44] all we can say is that we are not provided with that analysis or theory. The appeal here and throughout is to the uniqueness of humans, but without the necessary supporting argument to justify differential moral treatment of other sentient beings. Moreover, the assertion that such a theory is "species neutral" is simply that: an assertion. Again, we are not provided with any evidence or argument that would enable us to make this conclusion. It is the special pleading, the reliance on selected crisis situations, and the lack of cogent argumentation that makes the Weatherall report unpersuasive as a moral defense of experiments on animals.

Before we move to the next section, it is worth pondering another perspective. In the reports we have been considering, much has been made of the "uniqueness" of human beings. But it is worth asking, even if uniqueness is accepted, what this "uniqueness" entails. Chief among the distinguishing human capacities is the capacity for moral agency, the ability to distinguish between right and wrong and be morally responsible for our actions. But if it is true that we uniquely have this capacity, the usual argument should be turned on its head. It is precisely *because* we have such a moral capacity that we could and arguably should behave in a morally sensitive way to other sentient beings: it is our very capacity to act altruistically, to be generous and unselfish, that is the most important of all human potentialities. From this, it follows that humans should extend moral solicitude not only to fellow humans but also to all other beings capable of pain and suffering. Our perception of our own well-being should not be the only criterion on which we base our relations with the animal world. We are the species uniquely capable of seeing that other sentient species have their own interests and can be harmed in similar ways.

We are struck by the narrow definition of human benefit and welfare indicated by the reports we have considered. The APC report details at length the system of cost-benefit analyses, which it would like to see engaged in a thorough licensing system. But none of the criteria includes the possibility that it may not be in humanity's own interest to inflict suffering on fellow sentients. Are humans really benefited from inflicting injury on animals? At least it is a question worth asking, and it is noticeable in the roster of proposed criteria that this question is not even on the agenda.[45] It has been shown that animal abuse can harm us through, for example, desensitization, loss of empathy, habituation, and denial.[46] The idea that there are no debit consequences for human beings should therefore be jettisoned.

Notes

1. APC, *Review of Cost-Benefit Assessment*.

2. House of Lords, *Select Committee*.

3. Weatherall et al., *Use of Non-Human Primates*.

4. The APC has now been replaced by the Animals in Science Committee (ASC) under the amendments to the Animals (Scientific Procedures) Act that took effect in January 2013 following EU Directive 2010/63. The functions of the ASC are set out in the new section 20, subsection 2, which like its predecessor says that "in its consideration of any matter the Committee shall have regard both to the legitimate requirements of science and industry and to the protection of animals against avoidable suffering and unnecessary use in scientific procedures." Home Office, *Animals (Scientific Procedures) Act 1986 Amendment Regulations 2012* (London, 2012), accessed February 6, 2015, https://www.gov.uk/government/uploads/system/uploads/attachment_data/file/265691/Animals__Scientific_Procedures__Act_1986.pdf.

5. APC, *Review of Cost-Benefit Assessment*, 9–10.

6. John Paul II, *Veritatis Splendor: Encyclical Letter* (London: Catholic Truth Society, 1993), 115.

7. Ibid., 122, para. 80.

8. Ibid., 124, para. 81.

9. Regan, *The Case for Animal Rights*, 305ff, 307ff.

10. A. Linzey, *Why Animal Suffering Matters*, 106.

11. APC, *Review of Cost-Benefit Assessment*, emphasis added.

12. Ibid., 15.

13. S. Lederer, *Subjected to Science: Human Experimentation in America before the Second World War* (Baltimore, MD: Johns Hopkins University Press, 1995), 101, capitals in original. Lederer's much-overlooked thesis is that "the moral issues raised by experimenting on human beings were most intently pursued by the men and women committed to the protection of laboratory animals." Lederer, *Subjected to Science*, xiii–xiv.

14. P. Singer, *Practical Ethics* (Cambridge: Cambridge University Press, 1979), 58.

15. APC, *Review of Cost-Benefit Assessment*, 10.

16. Home Office, *Annual Statistics of Scientific Procedures on Living Animals Great Britain 2013* (London, 2013).

17. J. Vane, "Animal Research and Medical Progress," *AnimalResearch.Info* (1996), accessed January 3, 2015, http://www.animalresearch.info/en/medical-advances/articles-lectures/animal-research-and-medical-progress/.

18. Alzheimer's Research UK, *Why Research using Animals Can Help Defeat Dementia*, accessed January 3, 2015, http://www.alzheimersresearchuk.org/siteFiles/resources/documents/ALZ_Animalbooklet_FINALSINGLEST.pdf.

19. British Pharmacological Society, "Why Do We Use Animals in Scientific Research?" (2013), accessed January 3, 2015, http://www.bps.ac.uk/details/pageContent/855663/Why_do_we_use_animals_in_research.html?cat=bps12aae254a00.

20. Understanding Animal Research, "Human Health," accessed January 3, 2015, http://www.understandinganimal-research.org.uk/why/human-health/.

21. House of Lords, *Select Committee*, 15. In the report, this last paragraph is in bold.

22. Ibid., 15n40.

23. P. Schofield, C. Pease-Watkin, and C. Blamires, *The Collected Works of Jeremy Bentham: Rights, Representation, and Reform: Nonsense upon Stilts and Other Writings on the French Revolution* (Oxford: Oxford University Press, 2002).

24. H. LaFollette, "Animal Experimentation in Biomedical Research," in *The Oxford Handbook of Animal Ethics*, ed. T. L. Beauchamp and R. G. Frey (Oxford: Oxford University Press, 2011), 814.

25. Regan, *Case for Animal Rights*, 377.

26. House of Lords, *Select Committee*.

27. APC, *Review of Cost-Benefit Assessment*.

28. Ibid., 15, emphases in original.

29. The point is made even more starkly in the cover letter from APC chair professor Michael Banner to the Home Office minister commending the review. He writes, "While we conclude that *some* uses of animals *may* yield scientific knowledge, we argue that this does *not* settle the question of justification." APC, *Review of Cost-Benefit Assessment*, 1, our emphases.

30. APC, *Review of Cost-Benefit Assessment*, 8–9.

31. Lederer, *Subjected to Science*, 80.

32. Ibid., 80–81.

33. Regan, *Case for Animal Rights*, 393.

34. R. G. Frey, *Rights, Killing and Suffering* (Oxford: Basil Blackwell, 1983), 115. Frey also writes, "The case for anti-vivisectionism, I think, is far stronger than most people allow." Ibid.

35. Weatherall et al., *Use of Non-Human Primates*, 124.

36. Ibid., 124.

37. Ibid., our emphases.

38. R. M. Hare, *Moral Thinking: Its Levels, Method, and Point* (Oxford: Oxford University Press, 1981).

39. Weatherall et al., *Use of Non-Human Primates*, 124–25.

40. Not only is the conclusion flawed, but so actually is the scenario. We are reliably informed by firefighters that in such cases "you just get whoever you can (including animals) as fast as one can." The idea that one can rationally plan in the event of such an extreme crisis is fanciful, and indeed, thought experiments tend to be fanciful; that is why they are conducted in thought and not in reality.

41. Weatherall et al., *Use of Non-Human Primates*, 125, our emphasis.

42. APC, *Review of Cost-Benefit Assessment*, 15.

43. Weatherall et al., *Use of Non-Human Primates*, 125.

44. Ibid.

45. APC, *Review of Cost-Benefit Assessment*, 84–86.

46. A. Linzey, *Link*, 6–8.

The Problem of Institutionalization

IN THE LIGHT OF the foregoing discussion, the question might not unnaturally be asked: if the scientific and ethical case against animal experimentation is so strong, why does it continue as a legitimized social and moral practice?

This leads us to considering the phenomenon of institutionalization. Institutionalization may be defined as the process by which approval of certain practices is entrenched or embodied within organizations, social systems, and societies. By living in a society, we are automatically members of various institutions, whether they be families, schools, colleges, trade unions, political parties, businesses, religious bodies, universities, or corporations. Such institutions can have positive benefits in terms of enabling social cohesion, providing emotional and psychological support, and not least of all, enabling employment and job security. They help regulate social and commercial life and can help individuals find fulfillment.

But there is a downside to institutions—principally the way they can become self-perpetuating and resistant to reform. Hence, once institutionalized, a practice is seen as the norm of the organization, and only considerable upheaval or radical challenge will lead to fundamental change.

This focus on the institutionalization of animal experiments reveals how values, norms, and institutions are so closely intertwined that speciesist attitudes are tolerated and developed because, ideologically, they are seen as a given in spite of their arbitrary nature.

Speciesism, a term coined by Richard Ryder in 1974, may be defined as the "*arbitrary* favouring of one species' interests over the interests of others."[1] Many activists and scholars have compared speciesism to racism and sexism,[2] but unlike racism and sexism, speciesism has been little recognized, let alone sufficiently criticized. Indeed, speciesism is institutionalized in social life.

There are five principal aspects of institutionalization that should be noted.

Legislation

The criminal law consolidates institutionalized animal exploitation by tolerating the practices that take place in a range of institutions, such as research laboratories.[3] Many of the painful practices that are performed upon living animals in experiments would violate anticruelty laws, and such institutionalized practices account for the majority of the violence executed against animals.[4]

As we have seen, approximately 115.3 million animals annually are bred and used worldwide for the biomedical industry for experiments, and such experiments cover a range of painful and life-threatening procedures, including induction of tumors, strokes, brain damage, and spinal injuries, injection or force-feeding of toxic substances, and implantation of devices in the body, many of which are done with inadequate or even no pain relief. Animals are

UNIVERSITY OF WINCHESTER

LIBRARY

also frequently subjected to repeated stressful and even frightening behavioral tests, restriction of body movement and social interaction, and withdrawal of items essential for life such as food and water. Although most of us would define such actions as cruel, and these actions would defy existing laws if inflicted on companion animals, they are perfectly legal when conducted for the purposes of research. Along with intensive rearing regimes, these biomedical practices in conjunction with the law represent the most systematically organized abuse of animals.[5] In this way, the criminal law can be seen as a major structural and historical mechanism consolidating institutionalized animal exploitation.[6]

Institutional or Establishment Thinking

Second, institutionalization is also consolidated by institutional or establishment thinking. Institutionalized animal exploitation is an aspect of the established paradigm of research that sustains what the philosopher Jacques Derrida has called "the worst kinds of violence, that is, the purely instrumental, industrial, chemico-genetic treatment of living beings."[7] This paradigm is grounded in the idea that the scientific community knows what the world is like[8] and usually accepts as a matter of course that animal subjects can be used for experimental purposes. Issues that we have previously mentioned tend to be overlooked—for example, the problems with using animals as "models" for human beings, the harmful consequences for humans of using animal "models," and the ethical issues associated with using animals as resources.[9] Here the point can be understood in terms of contradictions: Animals are used in scientific research because they are deemed "similar" to human beings; ethical consideration, however, cannot be extended to them because they are "different." With regard to the use of animals as resources, the harmful consequences for animals should be paramount. As Paola Cavalieri points out, however, "the view that vivisected animals did not suffer offered a good [ethical] escape route" for those who advocated the use of animals in research.[10]

Those who sanction and carry out animal experiments view animals as tools and thus as means to an end.[11] Specifically, scientific developments in the field of genetics mean that we are seeing increasing numbers of GM animals from a growing range of species being used for increasingly diverse purposes in animal experiments. For example, in 2012 in the United Kingdom, the number of experiments using GM animals increased by 22 percent from the figure for 2011,[12] and again in 2013, it increased by another 6 percent.[13] There is an evident intellectual conformity to the established paradigm about animal experiments. Furthermore, there is a moral conformity to the established paradigm about the ethical issues associated with using animal subjects in experiments. This conformity is lucidly described by Dr. Donald Barnes, a former principal investigator at the US Air Force School of Aerospace Medicine. Barnes was in charge of irradiation experiments with the Primate Equilibrium Platform at Brooks Air Force Base but was dismissed for raising the question of ethics. Barnes says,

> I represented a classic example of what I choose to call "conditioned ethical blindness." My entire life had consisted of being rewarded for using animals, treating them as sources of human improvement or amusement. . . . During my sixteen years in the laboratory, the morality and ethics of using laboratory animals were never broached in either formal or informal meetings prior to my raising the issues during the waning days of my tenure as a vivisector.[14]

Animal experiments take place within the context of policies that are designed to regulate, or at least (theoretically) give guidance on how to reduce, the suffering of animals. These guidelines on animal suffering institutionalize what Robert Garner calls the "moral orthodoxy" of utilitarianism, in which humans are viewed as being justified in choosing to sacrifice the interests of animals in the event of any apparent conflict of interests with humans.[15] Many countries seek to regulate human-induced animal suffering by means of "protection" legislation or directives that are designed to reduce the suffering of some animals who are used for experimental purposes. The status of the measures varies along a spectrum of mandatory to voluntary. Animals included under the auspices of such measures vary among countries. As we have seen, the biomedical industry in the United

States successfully lobbied to prevent the majority of animals used in experimentation (mice, rats, fish, reptiles, and birds) from being included as animals under the Animal Welfare Act, the only national law covering the use of animals in experiments. On the other hand, in the EU, birds and fish are covered by "protection" directives. The measures seek to reduce pain, suffering, distress, or lasting harm to protected animals. In some parts of the world, such as the EU, such directives are based on the principle of the "Three Rs": replacement, reduction, and refinement. These are the guiding principles, first advanced by W. M. S. Russell and R. L. Burch in 1959, in an attempt to reduce the use of animals in testing. However, 2013 was the fourth consecutive year in which the number of experiments in the United Kingdom was actually higher than when the Animals (Scientific Procedures) Act 1986 came into force. The principle of the Three Rs extends to the quality of life of those animals used in research since it lays down minimum standards for housing and care.[16] Despite these measures, the institutionalization of experiments using animal subjects remains intact because the focus is on improving the perceived welfare of animals rather than on whether animal experiments should take place at all.

Experiments that use animal subjects are deemed to be beneficial to the health and well-being of humans and to animals as well. This is in the context of the medicalization of human conditions, where the improvement of human life through diagnosis, prevention, and treatment is a central objective. In biomedical research, partiality to human interests is obligatory[17] and is institutionalized in the form of legislation that requires all new biomedical products be tested on animals, where there is no immediate alternative, before they can be trialed on humans. This is an expensive business for researchers and thus involves considerable investment.

Public and Private Funding

Third, animal experiments are institutionalized through public and private funding. The pharmaceutical industry is a heavy investor in such research. For example, in 2010 the pharmaceutical industry in the EU invested twenty-seven billion euros in research

and development.[18] Experimenting with animal subjects is big business. The supply of animal subjects for such procedures makes a great deal of money for private firms. The total annualized sales of Charles River Laboratories (a supplier of animals and equipment for experiments) were reported to exceed US$1.2 billion in 2007.[19] There is a great deal of money to be made by the pharmaceutical industry as well. For example, in 2009 in the United Kingdom alone, the pharmaceutical industry generated £7 billion in trade surplus.[20] Enormous profits are made from existing drugs, and the medicalization of an increasing range of human conditions means that pharmaceutical companies can and do charge high prices for an increasing range of drugs.[21] Large pharmaceutical companies in the United States spend a lot of time and money seeking to influence federal government policy. According to the Center for Responsive Politics, pharmaceutical companies in the United States spent over $49 million on lobbying in 2013 alone.[22]

Thus, one primary obstacle facing researchers who might otherwise be disinclined to use animals in research is the fact that funding and regulatory bodies expect to see certain traditionally used methodologies, rather than "new" or emerging methodologies, or methodologies that funders have not yet seen operationalized. To receive funding, researchers might believe that they must experiment on animal "models," for if they do not, then they risk not being funded, which can have professional and personal consequences. As such, a legitimizing authority must signify acceptance of and approval for non-animal methods, so that researchers can reasonably expect to have their projects funded when their proposed methodology does not involve animals. Regulatory bodies perpetuate the cycle of animal experimentation by mandating that animals be used to test all new drug product candidates and by their tendency to hold a higher bar for accepting non-animal methods than animal experiments.

The Partiality of the Media

Fourth, there is the partiality of the media in reporting and covering issues relating to animals. Animal issues are often ignored, trivialized, or misrepresented.

Despite the fact that there is increasing public concern about the use of animals in experiments,[23] most media reporting and commentary favors the established view that using animals for human purposes is justifiable. Public understanding about animal experimentation is usually gained through media reports about breakthroughs in diagnosis and treatments of a range of feared human diseases. The reports are largely positive or uncritical.[24] A recent study has demonstrated that media reports tend to be overhyped and that this positive spin often originates from the researchers and their institutions.[25] In contrast, media reporting about animal advocates is often negative and critical. Steve Baker observes what he calls a "growing hysteria" in the media about the dangers of "animal rights activism."[26] Although the more recent ecological agenda has resulted in elements of the news media wishing to portray a concern for the environment (associated with a compassion for animals and worries about abuse and, most usually, species extinction), still the news media seek to convey the message that concern for animals is an extreme position to take.[27] Thus, the established nature of animal experimentation remains largely unquestioned.

Allied to this is the problem of secrecy. Much of the work that is undertaken in such research is done in secret. This lack of transparency has been of public concern. The Home Office in the United Kingdom has announced a consultation on transparency designed to keep the public informed about animal experimentation.[28] But the critical point remains that without adequate knowledge, the extent and nature of the use of animals in laboratories remain largely hidden.[29]

The Distorting Power of Language

Fifth, it is worth noting the power of language and the way in which it informs and consolidates our view of the use of animals in research. To put it most simply, language use constructs our understanding of the world, giving particular meanings and creating representations of reality.[30] These depictions of reality may be described as discourses, and embedded in them are ideological understandings of the world. Fairclough describes discourse as a "practice of not just representing the world, but of signifying the world, constituting and constructing the world

in meaning,"[31] and Gee explains the importance of ideologies where "theories ground beliefs and beliefs lead to actions."[32]

The Truth and Reconciliation Commission of South Africa indicated the power of ideologies to subvert and nullify the moral compass of individuals: "Ideologies in these sorts of combinations provide the means and grounds for people to act violently and yet, ironically, believe they are acting in terms of worthy, noble and morally righteous principles."[33]

However, discourses about the world, and the ideologies of these discourses, may not be apparent to their users. Dominant discourses can simply over time become "truth"—obvious, uncontested common sense.[34] As Bourdieu notes, this produces the "recognition of legitimacy through the misrecognition of arbitrariness."[35]

All of this is to say that language plays a critical role in framing the practice of, and the debate around, animal experimentation. Not only does science—and in particular experimentation—have its own form of language use, but on a societal level, the discourses construct various understandings of animal research as a practice and of its concomitant justifications. Noam Chomsky has pioneered critical awareness of how "thought control" operates within institutions, preventing us from being as critical of our own institutions as we are of others.[36]

The language used in animal experimentation obscures, justifies, exonerates, and minimizes what actually takes place in laboratories. Living sentient beings are linguistically transformed into "research animals," "systems," and "models," such as "surgically altered models, cardiovascular disease models and preconditioned models."[37] One company offers a "Retinal Degeneration and Neuroprotection Model," explaining, "We now offer a blue light exposure model that induces retinal damage and cell death."[38] In other words, the company offers a way of blinding captive sentient nonhumans. In another example, "naives" is a term used by the experimenters for marmosets who will have their brains damaged at some point in the future.[39]

Although animals may be subjected to what humans would describe as excruciatingly painful and distressing procedures, they are rarely said to be "hurt" or to "suffer."[40] They are "stressed" by such things as being given electric shocks, being put into cold water, being injected with chemicals, being placed in an oven, having their day and night cycles disrupted, or being used in the "forced swim test," otherwise known as the "behavioural despair test."[41] Death is obscured by descriptions such as "culled," "discarded," "terminated," "sacrificed," and "house-cleaning taking place."[42] They even use the word "humane" to describe the treatment of the animals in their care, a practice that has been criticized as a totally inappropriate use of the word as defined.[43]

The words used to describe many animals in general discourse carry the underlying implication that the inherent purpose of these sentient beings' lives is serving humans.[44] These "purposes" are deeply anthropocentric, and this is seen vividly in experimentation discourse, where individuals are given such labels as "laboratory animals," "lab rats," "lab monkeys," and so on, with the very term "guinea pig" being synonymous with being used for experiments. The implication is that experiments on "laboratory animals" simply involve using animals for their inherent purpose.

Psychological distance from events is another significant factor. Traditional scientific language is written as agentless, so nobody commits any violent act in lab testing. Electrodes are inserted, formalin is injected, arteries are tied off, holes are drilled in skulls, and mice are enucleated, all in the passive voice, with no human performing the actions. Animals are not blinded by anyone, but an ocular end point is reached. In addition, not all observations are recorded in reports of experiments, but only a selection of those deemed of interest to the experimenter and readers. This results in an edited and sanitized version of what has taken place. The struggling, cries, bleeding, repetitive behavior, moans, agitation, anxiety, pain, fear, depression, and vomiting from animals may be deemed of no relevance to the researcher and thus be linguistically expunged from reality.

Even in cases where such events are described, they are likely to be minimized and obscured by use of linguistic strategies. Dunayer notes that if an animal cries in pain, the animal may be described as exhibiting "vocalisation responses"; infants who are separated from their mothers may show "cognitive and affective responses to separation."[45] It is even at times

implied that animals are willing partners in experiments, as in "twelve sheep *donated* 45 per cent of their blood; six others *donated* at least 80 per cent"; "crab-eating macaques *took part* in experiments where they were deprived of water and had parts of their brains removed."[46]

Halliday and Matthiessen make these observations about science from a linguistic perspective: "The language of science, though forward-looking in its origins, has become increasingly anti-democratic: its arcane grammatical metaphor sets apart those who understand it and shields them from those who do not. It is elitist also in another sense, in that its grammar constantly proclaims the uniqueness of the human species."[47]

Work on moral disengagement recognizes that people can act in ways that are totally against their own moral and ethical beliefs, if certain facilitating conditions are present.[48] Some of these conditions are clearly present in the language of animal testing.

In popular as well as specialist texts, individuals or groups opposed to animal tests are often positioned as being opposed to "progress," and this inhibition of progress, it is claimed, will inevitably result in the loss of many human lives. A discourse closely interwoven with this one is the claim that the only way to have reached this point in human knowledge is to have experimented on animals. These discourses construct a continuous opposition of identities between "scientists" and "antivivisectionists," with the implicit understanding that those who oppose animal tests cannot be scientists and do not understand the work and its importance. The researchers are portrayed as a knowledgeable elite with specialist understanding of what is needed in order to do the best for society. The discourses assert that it is simply a lack of understanding that leads people to oppose animal experimentation and that if they really understood what happens and why it happens, people would not oppose the practice.

These erroneous identity constructions may go even further, where those opposed to animal experimentation are portrayed, at least by association, as "violent extremists" or "terrorists," whereas those who practice and fund animal use are never portrayed as supporting or causing harm of any kind. For example, in a *Nature* editorial regarding "animal activism" and its effects, "Animal Rights and Wrongs,"[49] there is much discussion of violence with phrases such as "physical attacks," "campaigns of harassment," "fire bombings," "violent activist behaviour," "vandalism," "lingering fear," "corrosive animal rights extremism," "tide of violent activity," "bully and blackmail," "terrorize researchers," and so on—fourteen such phrases in an editorial of only 765 words—but no mention of any harm carried out by researchers. Despite admitting that any violence against researchers worldwide is extremely rare and that the editorial applies only to "extremists," the article subtly implicates those who oppose experimentation while at the same time exonerating those who practice it.

The aforementioned factors indicate how problematic it is to conduct a rational public discussion of the moral issue and why researchers are inevitably resistant to change. When established medical authorities say in unison that animal experiments are essential to human health, it is often highly problematic for researchers in institutes to raise questions that they know will cause discomfort at best and censure at worst. There is no conspiracy of silence as such. Rather, the situation is more prosaic: establishment figures do not welcome the opening of questions that they have decided are already settled.

That institutionalization results in intellectual and moral stagnation is implicitly recognized by the APC report itself:

> Researchers and regulators, as well as others involved with the implementation of the [1986] Act, should not rest with the *status quo*, but should subject their cost-benefit judgements to an on-going and detailed critical evaluation. *This will involve engaging in creative and imaginative thinking*, so as to identify strategies and targets that can avoid or reduce animal suffering, maximise the benefits of studies in which animals are used, and so help to diminish the moral conflicts that are inherent—and, most people believe, regrettable—in the use of animals in research.[50]

The point is also echoed in the BMJ:

> The culture within research is shifting, and animal research is no longer as immune from challenge or criticism as it once was. Nonetheless, although science is more self-critical, in practice it can be

difficult to achieve change because stakeholders (governments, funders, universities, allied research industries, and researchers) may all have interests, not infrequently financial, in continuing to do things as they have always been done.[51]

But the question that must be asked is this: given the massive investment—moral, intellectual, and financial—in the practice of animal experimentation, and thus its widespread institutionalization within research institutes, how likely, even feasible, is it that "creative and imaginative thinking" will take place? Moreover, we should question the applicability of a "cost-benefit" (i.e., basically consequentialist) methodology to animal experimentation. The very idea conceives of animals as commodities, as resources that exist for human use, and not as ends in themselves.

It is difficult to avoid the conclusion that animal experimentation represents the institutionalization of a preethical view of animals. In some ways, we should not be surprised at that. Animal experiments emerged at a time when the dominant ethical paradigm was itself unenlightened, representing a largely or wholly instrumentalist view of animals. Scientific practice has yet to respond fully to the emerging ethical sensitivity to animals, which has been pioneered and has gained a measure of social acceptance especially during the last fifty years.

But the recognition of the problem of institutionalization also represents a moral opportunity. If animal experimentation represents the institutionalization of a preethical view of animals, then we have to ask whether it is possible to institutionalize research carried out in accordance with a fully ethical perspective. G. R. Dunstan writes of how the moralist, "having seen his vision, or arrived at his position by moral reasoning, must weave his insight into the fabric of society by creating an institution in which to embody it."[52] Institutionalization has received comparatively little attention in ethical theory, and it is now urgent that this question be raised in relation to our treatment of animals.

What, then, would the institutionalization of an ethical perspective on animal experimentation look like? Animal organizations have already made the first steps by founding and funding institutes dedicated to humane research. The value of these first steps should not be minimized. These organizations enable scientists to apply for grants to pursue non-animal research and also provide an opportunity for people to donate to research projects that do not harm animals. These admirable endeavors need to be supplemented by others equally pioneering and adventurous. Authoritative scientific journals dedicated to humane research need to be established—journals that refuse, as a matter of principle, to publish research that has involved the use of animals. In addition, there is a need for new academic posts—indeed, new university departments—given over to the instruction of researchers in non-animal methods and the dissemination of alternatives. We need to show universities and institutes of higher education worldwide that non-animal research can also attract major funding and research grants to rival those made by pharmaceuticals and existing pro-animal research bodies.

Moreover, instead of trying to uncritically defend existing animal research, universities especially should adopt a new ethical outlook that opposes such research in principle or, at the very least, facilitates full ethical discussion about the research taking place in their institutions and enables conscientious objections by staff and students in departments where animal research is undertaken. Doubtless, these changes will happen gradually, but with sufficient resources from animal organizations, the public, and governments (who often pay lip service to the need for alternatives), they can happen.

Notes

1. A. Linzey and P. Waldau, "Speciesism," in *Dictionary of Ethics, Theology, and Society*, ed. P. B. Clarke and A. Linzey (London: Routledge, 1996), 788, our emphasis.

2. See, for example, D. Nibert, *Animal Rights/Human Rights: Entanglement of Oppression and Liberation* (Plymouth, UK: Rowman and Littlefield, 2002).

3. C. P. Flynn, "A Sociological Analysis of Animal Abuse," in *The International Handbook on Animal Abuse and Cruelty: Theory, Research and Application*, ed. F. R. Ascione (West Lafayette, IN: Purdue University Press, 2008), 155–74.

4. Beirne, "For a Nonspeciesist Criminology."

5. T. Benton, "Rights and Justice on a Shared Planet: More Rights or New Relations?" *Theoretical Criminology* 2, no. 2 (1998): 149–75.

6. Beirne, "For a Nonspeciesist Criminology."

7. J. Derrida, "Violence against Animals," in *For What Tomorrow . . . a Dialogue*, ed. J. Derrida and E. Roudinesco, trans. J. Fort (Stanford, CA: Stanford University Press, 2004), 62–76; K. Peggs and B. Smart, "Nonhuman Animal Suffering: Critical Pedagogy and Practical Animal Ethics," *Society and Animals* (forthcoming).

8. T. S. Kuhn, *The Structure of Scientific Revolutions*, 15th anniv. ed. (Chicago: University of Chicago Press, 2012).

9. A. Knight, "Weighing the Costs and Benefits of Animal Experiments," *Altex Proceedings of the 8th World Congress on Alternatives and Animal Use in the Life Sciences, Montreal 2011* (Altex Proceedings, 2012), 289–94.

10. P. Cavalieri, "The Animal Debate: A Reexamination," in *In Defense of Animals: The Second Wave*, ed. P. Singer (Malden, MA: Blackwell, 2006), 59.

11. M. Midgley, *The Myths We Live By* (London: Routledge, 2004).

12. Home Office, *Annual Statistics of Scientific Procedures on Living Animals Great Britain 2012* (London, 2012).

13. Home Office, *Annual Statistics . . . 2013*.

14. Quoted in P. Singer, *Animal Liberation: A New Ethics for Our Treatment of Animals* (Toronto, Canada: Harper Perennial Modern Classics, 2009), 71.

15. R. Garner, *Animal Ethics* (Cambridge, UK: Polity, 2005).

16. European Parliament, *Directive 2010/63/EU*.

17. J. Welchman, "Xenografting, Species Loyalty, and Human Solidarity," *Journal of Social Philosophy* 4, no. 2 (2003): 244–55.

18. Association of the British Pharmaceutical Industry, *Animals and Medicines Research: Animal Research for the Discovery and Development of New Medicines* (London, 2011), 5, accessed May 9, 2014, http://www.abpi.org.uk/our-work/library/medical-disease/Documents/animals-medicines-research.pdf.

19. *Online Investor*, "Company Spotlight—Charles River Laboratories (NYSE: CRL)" (2008), accessed May 9, 2014, http://www.theonlineinvestor.com/orphans/articles/charles_river_laboratories.html.

20. Association of the British Pharmaceutical Industry, *Animals and Medicines Research*, 5.

21. B. Goldacre, *Bad Pharma: How Medicine Is Broken, and How We Can Fix It* (London: Fourth Estate, 2012).

22. Center for Responsive Politics, "Pharmaceuticals/Health Products: Long-Term Contribution Trends," accessed May 9, 2014, http://www.opensecrets.org/industries/totals.php?cycle=2014&ind=H04.

23. European Commission, *Eurobarometer Science*; J. Wilke and L. Saad, "Older Americans' Moral Attitudes Changing," *Gallup Politics* (2013), accessed August 11, 2014, http://www.gallup.com/poll/162881/older-americans-moral-attitudes-changing.aspx.

24. C. Molloy, *Popular Media and Animals* (Basingstoke, UK: Palgrave Macmillan, 2011).

25. P. Sumner, S. Vivian-Griffiths, J. Boivin, A. Williams,

C. A. Venetis, A. Davies, J. Ogden, et al., "The Association between Exaggeration in Health Related Science News and Academic Press Releases: Retrospective Observational Study," *British Medical Journal* 349 (2014): g7015.

26. S. Baker, *Picturing the Beast: Animals, Identity, and Representation* (Urbana: University of Illinois Press, 1993), 196.

27. Ibid., 206.

28. Home Office, *Consultation on the Review of Section 24 of the Animals (Scientific Procedures) Act 1986* (London, 2014).

29. J. Creamer, "Freedom of Information," in A. Linzey, *Global Guide*, 186–87.

30. M. Jorgensen and L. Phillips, *Discourse Analysis as Theory and Method* (London: Sage, 2002).

31. N. Fairclough, *Discourse and Social Change* (Cambridge: Polity Press, 1992), 64.

32. J. P. Gee, *Social Linguistics and Literacies: Ideology in Discourses*, 2nd ed. (London: Routledge, 1996), 21.

33. Truth and Reconciliation Commission, *Final Report of the Truth and Reconciliation Committee*, vol. 5, 297, accessed November 6, 2007, http://www.doj.gov.za/trc/report/finalreport/TRC%20VOLUME%205.pdf.

34. N. Fairclough, *Language and Power*, 2nd ed. (Harlow, UK: Pearson Education, 2001).

35. Quoted in ibid., 76.

36. N. Chomsky, *Chronicles of Dissent: Interviews with David Barsamian* (Monroe, ME: Common Courage, 1992), 11ff; N. Chomsky, *Understanding Power: The Indispensable Chomsky*, ed. P. R. Mitchell and J. Schoeffel (London: Vintage, 2003).

37. Charles River Laboratories, "Basic Research," accessed June 23, 2014, http://www.criver.com/products-services/basic-research.

38. Charles River Laboratories, "Ocular Toxicology," accessed June 23, 2014, http://www.criver.com/products-services/safety-assessment/toxicology/ocular-toxicology.

39. M. Bagot, "Inside Monkey Testing Centre Where Marmosets Are Given Brain Damage to Help Treat Parkinson's," *Daily Mirror*, May 28, 2014, http://www.mirror.co.uk/news/uk-news/see-inside-monkey-testing-centre-3618664#ixzz34DnWrccv.

40. J. Dunayer, *Animal Equality: Language and Liberation* (Derwood, MD: Ryce, 2001).

41. Ibid.

42. Ibid.

43. F. D. McMillan, "What Dictionary Are Animal Researchers Using?" *Journal of Animal Ethics* 2, no. 1 (2012): 1–5.

44. L. R. Mitchell, "Nonhumans and the Ideology of Purpose," *Anthrozoos* 25, no. 4 (2012): 491–502.

45. Dunayer, *Animal Equality*, 108.

46. Ibid., 118, 119, emphases added.

47. M. A. K. Halliday and C. Matthiessen, *An Introduction to Functional Grammar*, 3rd ed. (London: Hodder Arnold, 2004), 225.

48. A. Bandura, "Moral Disengagement in the Perpetration of Inhumanities," *Personality and Social Psychology Review* 3 (1999): 193–209, accessed November 27, 2014, http://www.uky.edu/~eushe2/Bandura/Bandura1999PSPR.pdf; A. Bandura, "Selective Moral Disengagement in the Exercise of Moral Agency," *Journal of Moral Education* 31, no. 2 (2002): 101–19, accessed November 27, 2014, https://historicalunderbelly.files.wordpress.com/2009/11/bandura_moraldisengagement1.pdf.

49. "Animal Rights and Wrongs" (editorial), *Nature* 470 (2011): 435, accessed February 24, 2011, http://www.nature.com/nature/journal/v470/n7335/full/470435a.html.

50. APC, *Review of Cost-Benefit Assessment*, 79, our emphases.

51. Pound, Bracken, and Bliss, "Is Animal Research Sufficiently Evidence Based?"

52. G. R. Dunstan, *The Artifice of Ethics* (London: SCM, 1974), 4.

The Failure of Control

DESPITE THE FOREGOING ISSUES, there remain many people who believe that the best, perhaps the only, way of securing the protection of animals in laboratories is through more legal controls and better regulations. Although we do not deny that some legal restrictions—for example, the move against cosmetic testing on animals and testing for household products—are to be welcomed,[1] we have to question whether many of the even well-meaning controls are effective in terms of preventing suffering. In this section, we examine five examples of attempts at control: inspection, licensing, supervised self-regulation, the Three Rs, and care and ethics committees. To avoid the charge that we are selecting the worst examples, we mainly focus on the United Kingdom, which, as we have noted, purportedly provides the most protection for animals.

Inspection

The first issue of questionable effectiveness concerns the inspection of experiments and compliance with regulations in the United Kingdom. To monitor compliance with the provisions of the Animals (Scientific Procedures) Act (ASPA), the inspectorate of the Animals in Science Regulation Unit (ASRU, formerly the Animals Scientific Procedures Inspectorate) is required to visit establishments to ensure compliance with the terms of the license issued. In the event of any breach of license conditions, the in-spectorate should report to and advise the secretary of state (also known as the Home Secretary) on the action to be taken. Since 2006 there has been a steady but noticeable decline in the number of inspections carried out and, conversely, a steady but noticeable increase in the number of infractions noted.[2] This statistical anomaly aside, it might appear—when we consider the figures in isolation—that the system of inspection works fairly well: year after year, the inspectors unearth (or are informed of) around thirty violations of license conditions, and in all cases, some form of action is taken against the license holders.[3] A more critical analysis of the inspectorate's own reports, on the other hand, reveals that the ASRU must institutionalize a working definition of welfare that is at odds with normal practice.

When dealing with violations, the inspectorate classifies infractions as falling between Category A (least serious) and Category D (most serious). According to the most recent available data, in 2011 and 2012, there were twenty-eight Category A infringements (fifteen in 2011 and thirteen in 2012), twenty-one Category B infringements (eleven in 2011 and ten in 2012), nine Category C infringements (six in 2011 and three in 2012), and one Category D infringement (in 2011). Insofar as Category A infringements are concerned, it is clear that these are deemed so minor as to be almost trivial: these cases, according to ASRU guidelines, are those that are characterized, inter alia, as having "no animal welfare implications" and are typically dealt with as requiring "no further action" beyond noting and recording the infraction.[4] When the (albeit scant) reports of what happened in these cases of Category A infringements are compared against the Home Office's categorization, a particularly telling picture emerges of exactly what the Home Office inspectorate's view of "no animal welfare implications" actually means. For instance, the "unexpected" exceeding of a severity band assessment—from moderate to substantial—did not, according to the inspectors, result in *any* animal welfare implications[5] despite the fact that a moderate level of suffering was at the time deemed to include those "protocols that have the potential to cause greater suffering but include controls which minimise severity," and a substantial level of suffering was "a major departure from the animal's usual state of health or well-being" according to the Home Office's own classifications.[6] Nor, according to the ASRU, were there *any* animal welfare implications resulting from "animals being left in a scanner overnight" (presumably without any of the most basic and mandatory requirements of welfare, such as food, water, and bedding).[7]

When Category B infringements are considered along the same lines—that is, the categorization of compromised animal well-being compared to what actually happened—a similar picture emerges. Category B violations are those that are "not sufficiently serious for referral for prosecution, revocation of licences or withdrawal of a certificate to be considered" and are characterized as having "animal welfare implications that do not necessarily involve avoidable or unnecessary pain, suffering, distress or lasting harm."[8] When there are, in the opinion of the inspectorate, "serious animal welfare implications involving avoidable pain, suffering, distress or lasting harm," these should be classified as Category C or D. Hence, it is clear that the inspectorate did not consider that the deaths of 474 fish, over a period of twenty-four to forty-eight hours, as a result of being kept in "water inappropriate to their needs," necessarily resulted in any "avoidable or unnecessary pain, suffering, distress or lasting harm." Likewise, it was not necessarily the case that lasting harm or unnecessary suffering was felt by the two rats "inadvertently left in an unattended procedure room without access to water from Friday to Sunday" or by the eleven mice who died

when the severity limit imposed by the license was unexpectedly exceeded or by the three rats who died after being left in a "warming box to prepare them for a procedure" and being promptly forgotten about.[9]

Similarly, according to Home Office classifications, no lasting harm was done to the mouse abandoned to die unattended over the course of a weekend following an ectopic heart transplant, and no avoidable suffering was felt by the five rats who, because of an "oversight" by the project license holder, were not given any pain relief for two weeks following spinal surgery.[10] In all of the afore-cited examples, the inspectorate was content that only a Category B infringement ("not necessarily involving avoidable pain, suffering, distress or lasting harm") had taken place.

The point to be made here is that in the context of scientific procedures, the regulators have their own definition of welfare, and this definition appears to rule out individual instances of suffering as relevant factors. How else would it be possible to state, as the Home Office inspectorate did, that the preceding accounts involve "animal welfare implications that do not necessarily involve avoidable or unnecessary pain, suffering, distress or lasting harm," unless one were to ascribe a meaning to "avoidable or unnecessary pain, suffering, distress or lasting harm" that does not include individual animal suffering?

This interpretation of "welfare" might be understandable if there was no statutory guidance determining the manner in which animals should be cared for and housed before, during, and after a procedure. But of course, there is statutory guidance in the form of the ASPA. Although the ASPA underwent significant changes in January 2013 to incorporate the EU's Directive 2010/63, the incidents referred to previously should be considered under the version of the act in force at the time of these incidents.

For any project (i.e., series of individual procedures and protocols) to be authorized, a license must be issued by the secretary of state. In her determination of whether the project is justified, the secretary of state must first engage in the cost-benefit analysis referred to earlier in this report. Second, she is to confirm that all establishments using animals for scientific purposes ensure that minimum levels of welfare and pre- and post-procedure care are adhered to, so as to avoid what Russell and Burch called the "contingent inhumanity" of imperfect husbandry by which suffering is inflicted upon an animal "as an incidental and inadvertent by-product . . . of the procedure, which is not necessary for its success."[11]

Consequently, numerous provisions are found in ASPA regulating all aspects of the experimental "process." For instance, subject to the exercise of the Home Secretary's discretion,[12] all experimentation must take place in a designated "scientific procedure establishment."[13] Under the terms of any license granted, all establishments should have "a person to be responsible for the day-to-day care of the protected animals" who should be specified,[14] and a veterinary surgeon or "other suitably qualified person" should be on hand (but not necessarily full-time).[15] Furthermore, a number of additional safeguards were added to the original text of the act through amendments to the regulations in 1998. In particular, section 10 requires that persons charged with the day-to-day care of animals be suitably trained and sufficient in number,[16] that the accommodation be fit for the purpose of satisfying the captive animals' basic health and well-being requirements, and that arrangements be in place to prevent, detect, and expeditiously eliminate avoidable pain or distress.[17] So that the Home Secretary is informed of whether the conditions in any establishment are "appropriate," section 10(6C) requires that regard be paid, during any licensing application, to the provisions of Annex II of the 1986 directive.[18]

Although it is clear that the Home Secretary must give "appropriate" consideration to Annex II, it is not entirely clear in all cases how much weight the Home Secretary should afford to an individual establishment's ability to comply with Annex II.[19] The annex itself, however, clarifies: the object of the annex is to "help authorities, institutions and individuals in their pursuit of the aims of the Directive"[20] but to go no further than simply acting as "recommendations to be used with discretion, designed as guidance to the practices and standards which all concerned should conscientiously strive to achieve."[21] Although regard is paid to Annex II during the license application stage, the Home Office *Code of Practice for the Housing and Care of Animals Used in Scientific Procedures* (1989), which largely replicates the principles contained within Annex II, governs the ongoing aspects of an-imal welfare.[22] Under section 21 of the ASPA, these codes of practice are given a degree of legal force by virtue of s.21(4), which states that a breach of the code by any licensee "shall not of itself render that person liable to criminal or civil proceedings but—(a) any such code shall be admissible in evidence in any such proceedings, and (b) if any of its provisions appears to the court conducting the proceedings to be relevant to any question arising in the proceedings it shall be taken into account in determining that question."

As the analysis of ASRU practice has revealed, however, the "nuts and bolts" safeguards are not, in themselves, sufficient to guarantee that individual animals do not succumb to those "incidental and inadvertent" harms that Russell and Burch warned against back in 1959. This may be precisely the point, however. Those persons charged with the implementation and enforcement of the 1986 act (in its pre-2012 incarnation) clearly did not view harms against the individual animals referred to previously as serious enough to warrant any significant censure, and for this there are two possible reasons.

First, the individual inspectors themselves might be insensible to the issue of animal suffering. Second, and most likely, the parameters of suffering at an institutional level rule out, on the basis of some quasi-utilitarian aggregation, instances of individual suffering as constituting a violation of the rules. It is, as most ethicists are aware, fairly easy to override or undervalue the suffering of individuals when looking at the aggregation of harms. However, even taking this into consideration, we still find no justification for how the deaths of 474 fish over a period of twenty-four to forty-eight hours did not constitute avoidable harm. The question then becomes, of course, if the deaths of 474 fish over a period of twenty-four to forty-eight hours did not constitute avoidable harm, then how many fish must die in water inappropriate to their needs for the utility calculus to be offended? And if two mice left in a procedure room without access to water for three days were deemed an insufficient number to warrant a finding of unnecessary harm, how many dehydrated and starved mice does it take to tip the scales? And if the regulators thought that no actionable harm was caused to the five rats left without pain relief for two weeks following spinal surgery, would they be compelled into action by a similar fate befalling ten rats or one hundred or ten thousand? If, as we have argued, animals have moral weight beyond their utility, then their individual suffering must be taken into account when inspections occur. Clearly, the inspection process, as the first step in the enforcement of regulations in the United Kingdom, is flawed.

Licensing

We now turn to the issue of licensing. As we have seen, all experiments performed in the United Kingdom require a license. Unfortunately, however, the level of institutional ambivalence to individual animals, as shown in the preceding discussion, is not confined only to the inspectorate. In one of the few cases brought before the courts to determine whether the actions of a laboratory constituted a breach of the license conditions imposed by ASPA and, consequently, required remedial or punitive action to be taken by the Home Secretary, the court demonstrated that, for the judiciary, harms done to individual animals do not matter.

In *Secretary of State for the Home Department v. BUAV* (2008), the plaintiff animal protection organization made numerous complaints to the Home Secretary about, inter alia, breaches of the conditions of three project licenses granted to the Cambridge University Department of Experimental Psychology. This particular laboratory was conducting experiments, as per the conditions of its license, on marmosets for the purpose of furthering "research into the functioning of the human brain and illnesses affecting it" (such as Parkinson's disease, Huntington's disease, and strokes). To this end, the marmosets were subjected to numerous invasive surgical procedures designed to induce strokes or to damage the brain.[23] The claimants alleged—on the basis of an undercover investigation—that the laboratory had committed numerous breaches of the conditions of its license. The claimants reported their findings to the Home Office, and an investigation was carried out by the Scientific Procedures Inspectorate. Upon receipt of the inspectorate's report, the Home Secretary decided that no action should be taken against the license holders. The British Union for the Abolition of Vivisection (BUAV) sought a judicial review of Home Office decisions.

The substance of the BUAV's complaints was two-fold. First, there had been a miscalculation of the severity limits during the license application and grant stage: none of the licensed protocols in any project would, said the university in its applications, exceed a "moderate" severity limit. The evidence brought by the BUAV, the organization claimed, showed that in any sensible view, certain procedures exceeded this limit and caused such foreseen adverse consequences that the only means by which this suffering could be alleviated was by killing the animals involved. Hence, said the BUAV, a severity limit of "substantial" should have been assigned to these protocols. Although the issue is an important one because severity is a key element in the cost-benefit test and, as was recognized by the court of appeal, is one that raises fundamental questions about the extent to which and when "death as an endpoint" (i.e., killing) can curtail suffering, it is to the second aspect of the BUAV case—dismissed rather disparagingly by the court as raising "no important point of law . . . nor any factual matter of enduring relevance"—to which we now turn.[24]

According to the BUAV's complaint, there had been numerous breaches of the conditions imposed by the license related to housing and aftercare provisions found under section 10(6B) of the ASPA. Specifically, said the BUAV, the facility could not evidence adequate overnight care for postoperative animals, and this absence of care caused unnecessary harm to, and the eventual deaths of, a number of marmosets.[25] Although the court did agree with the BUAV's submission that in order to demonstrate compliance with section 10(6B), proper records *should* have been kept, the salient aspect of this particular case was whether the inspector was entitled to reach the conclusion that the aftercare arrangements were adequate on the basis of the interviews conducted with staff (when they knew they were being investigated) and his own observations during the postinvestigation inspection. On this matter the court found that the inspector was entitled to reach such a conclusion because neither the ASPA nor its guidance prescribed any particular method of record-keeping; hence, the alleged system of "positive reporting"—whereby notes are made on the record of care only when there is "something of substance to say"—employed at the facility at night (but not during the day) was not inappropriate.[26] Crucially for present purposes, however, Lord Justice May (hereafter "May LJ") went on to say that even if the record-keeping at the facility was not a model of best practice, the inspector's general conclusion that the laboratory was well-run was "not vitiated by reference to a relatively small number of individual animals."[27] There are a number of issues stemming from May LJ's assertion in support of the inspector's conclusion that the Cambridge facility was generally well-run, despite the number of failings of individual care.

First, May LJ clearly was not concerned with individual animals because, for him, the cost-benefit analysis was an aggregative and cumulative process, and because "animal harm" under this aggregative assessment becomes actionable and illegitimate harm only when a certain (presumably numerical) threshold is surpassed, the "small number of individual animals" referred to in the BUAV case was an insufficient number to warrant action. (In fact, the number of marmosets adversely affected by the absence of overnight staff cover was not small, and the legal test for care arrangements, in any event, is one of reasonable foreseeability of harm, not whether the harm actually occurred.)

Second, although it was not explicitly expressed as such in the BUAV case, it would not be unreasonable to infer from the facts that the benefit obtained by the Cambridge facility from operating a suboptimum system of after-hours care was the avoidance of the costs and inconvenience of employing additional nighttime staff. Although this might not offend the ASPA on the basis that the ASPA simply requires that "sufficient staff" be employed, the use of the word "sufficient" in the ASPA is simply an example of a qualitatively valueless definition that might permit any factors, such as economic expediency and convenience, to be taken into consideration. In this sense, the ASPA—or an interpretation that allows expediency and convenience to become relevant considerations—is very much at odds with the principles underpinning the constraints imposed on scientific procedures that use animals: as this present study has previously shown, the decision to utilize animals in scientific experimentation can be justified only when it is *necessary* to do so. Consequently, it would be a perverse situation if causing harm to animals during the experiments themselves could be justified only in the absence of

an alternative, but causing harm during the pre- and postprocedure phases could be legitimized when it was financially convenient to do so.

Finally, one can reasonably assume that May LJ held the belief that if failings in care standards had occurred (and he would not be drawn into making any robust and unequivocal pronouncements on this matter), then this could be excused on the basis that "mistakes happen." The objection to this latter justification is that failings in care standards in institutions and establishments that are obliged, by law, to put in place procedures, systems, and safeguards to prevent these precise failings are not mistakes or unfortunate lapses: instead they are breaches of the precise duty imposed on the laboratory. As the preceding sections have demonstrated, although the precise housing and care provisions of the ASPA are found in the nonbinding *Code of Practice*, the bottom-line requirements—that those entities undertaking harmful scientific practices upon living animals take such measures as are required to prevent harms to the animals that are not deemed immediately relevant to and contingent upon the experiments themselves—are a precondition of the granting of any license. To brush aside, as May LJ did, the evident failings of the Cambridge facility on the spurious grounds that the ASPA does not explicitly specify that a certain process of record-keeping be established, or that a minimum number of supervised and trained staff be on duty at night, is to make a mockery of the principles that underpin the act. Ultimately, it is unsustainable to argue that to comply with the law, research establishments do not have to provide staff out-of-hours when it is both foreseeable and foreseen (by licenses) that an animal may require attention at that time to minimize suffering (including by euthanasia). It is inconceivable that human patients would not have access to such care, bearing in mind that patients are usually able to call for assistance.

A further simple but vital point about licensing systems needs to be made. Although licensing may give the appearance of control, almost the reverse is the case. Licensing by its very nature authorizes, empowers, and legitimates licensees. Perhaps the best example of this is the attempt by the UK government to introduce a licensing system for hunting with dogs. In the context of trying to secure some middle ground between self-regulation and abolition, which might appease anti-hunting members of Parliament (MPs), the government proposed a licensing scheme (not wholly dissimilar to that utilized for animal experiments) that would allow hunting to continue. The licensing system was to operate according to two principles—one of "cruelty" and the other of "utility" (again not wholly dissimilar to the cost-benefit analysis utilized for animal experiments). We now know that the then prime minister, Tony Blair, most reluctantly agreed to abolitionist legislation when it became clear that Labour MPs saw through this contrivance and voted against it.[28]

As one commentator made clear,

> registration and licensing would have given hunting a legal authority, which it never had before. Licensing, by definition, empowers or authorises what was not previously authorised. It would have legitimised, institutionalised, and, therefore, helped to perpetuate hunting. Registered hunting is worse than a fudge; the bill would have provided hunting with full legal protection and helped to make it immune from fundamental criticism.[29]

Licensing, then, creates a false sense of legitimacy and in effect reduces control over those carrying out animal experiments. It empowers and authorizes licensees by institutionalizing the practice itself.

It should also be noted that the people regulating animal research are not impartial, since they are often former animal researchers. According to the annual Home Office inspectorate reports, "all inspectors are registered veterinary or medical practitioners who have first-hand experience of biomedical research and possess higher scientific or clinical postgraduate qualifications."[30] In practice this means that the vast majority are previous animal researchers or veterinarians who have been responsible for laboratories using animals and indeed that this is the Home Office's preference.

Supervised Self-Regulation

In 2013 the EU Cosmetics Regulation prohibited both the testing of cosmetics on animals and the marketing of any products in the EU that had been tested on animals. Although this legislative move is certainly encouraging, animal testing in other contexts un-

fortunately continues. The method of "supervised self-regulation" places the onus on industry to identify and manage risks, resulting in conflicts of interest, and once again illustrates the failure to control animal experimentation. Placing trust in an industry that is necessarily driven and guided by self-interest creates more barriers to monitoring compliance and fails to increase alternatives to animal testing.

Any EU company wanting to manufacture, import, or sell products containing chemicals (paint, furniture, and clothing, to name a few) must demonstrate that the products will not harm human health or the environment. The EU regulation REACH (Regulation for Registration, Evaluation, Authorisation, and Restriction of Chemicals) governs the use and safety of chemicals in the EU, and in assessing the hazardous nature of any proposed substance, the regulation aims to reduce the use of animals in tests.

When large quantities of chemical substances are manufactured and imported in the EU, companies must submit proof to the European Chemicals Agency (ECHA) that they have managed risks associated with those substances. In effect, this means that the companies must submit dossiers detailing the substances they propose to use, the possible risks that may be involved, and the different ways that the company plans to deal with those risks. This may involve, for example, a proposal to test the toxicity of the chemical on animals. The legislation itself states that duplicate animal tests must be avoided and testing on vertebrate animals can be undertaken only as a last resort. For some animal tests, if there is no other prior data in relation to the chemical, then the manufacturer puts forward a testing proposal (for substances marketed at one hundred tons or above), which is assessed by ECHA and member state authorities "to check that the proposed test is likely to produce reliable and adequate data."[31]

In an effort to demonstrate transparency and promote information sharing, ECHA publishes testing proposals involving vertebrate animals on its website. Members of the public and organizations are then encouraged to provide "scientifically valid" data on the proposed chemical or substance.

The REACH framework basically shifts the responsibility for testing new chemicals—and therefore public safety—to the manufacturer or importer.

This method of regulation whereby risk management processes are mandated can be described as "supervised self-regulation." This form of regulation places considerable trust in the industry to honestly identify and manage risks. One major disadvantage of this form of regulation is that if the company being regulated knows more about the risks than the regulator, it is difficult for the regulator to monitor compliance. This in turn poses a significant threat to the public interest.[32]

In its publication *Guidance in a Nutshell: Registration*, ECHA states,

> REACH . . . is based on the principle that it is for manufacturers, importers and downstream users to ensure that they manufacture, place on the market or use such substances that do not adversely affect human health or the environment. The responsibility for the management of the risks of substances lies therefore with the natural or legal persons that manufacture, import, place on the market or use these substances in the context of their professional activities.[33]

In practice, this means that the decisions about which risks may be present and how these risks should be managed are left to the manufacturers. Therefore, if a manufacturer identifies a potential public health risk, and an animal experiment is proposed, the proposal is unlikely to be denied because the trust is placed in the regulated company to decide the appropriate risk management measure. Similarly misguided is the onus placed on other organizations and the public to volunteer information in relation to the substance. Information being voluntarily submitted by other organizations is highly unlikely since these manufacturers may be in competition with one another. It is also unlikely that members of the public will have the means, or the necessary incentive, to produce "scientifically valid" information to ECHA. In fact, a recent review of the process confirmed these assertions.[34]

Not only is this supervised self-regulatory model unsafe for consumers and the environment, since it relies on manufacturers to be accurate and honest about potential risks; it also does not align with REACH's aim to increase alternatives to testing on animals. Therefore, although there is a complex apparatus of control at work in the EU in relation to the introduction of new chemicals, in practice the regulatory framework falls short of achieving its goals.

The inevitable place of self-regulation, even within a formal regulatory framework, is emphasized by the APC report to which we referred earlier. The report argues that "it is important to realise that researchers themselves bear the responsibility for carrying out cost-benefit assessments of their work, including critical evaluation of the need for animal studies at all."[35]

The APC report also emphasizes the issue of comprehensibility:

> It is important that the information provided by the researchers really addresses costs and benefits in an accessible and meaningful manner, and clearly communicates the researchers' own assessments of the balance of likely benefit over harm. . . . We recommend that the project licence application form be designed so as to encourage more adequate, easy-to-understand and pertinent descriptions of costs and benefits and the relations between the two.[36]

Two things are notable here. First, if it is the responsibility of researchers to critically evaluate the need for animal studies and to carry out cost-benefit assessments of their own work, this gives rise to a conflict of interest. Although the regulators have the final say and should carry out their own evaluation, it is all too easy for researchers to assign weights to costs and benefits that are in their own favor. Second, and related, is the extraordinary way in which researchers are themselves envisaged to be both scientists and ethicists—even though they may have little or no training for the latter role. Of course, we may hope that scientists will be conscientious and diligent in keeping abreast of ethics literature, but that is separate from possessing ethical expertise in the form of assessing moral harms and benefits and being aware of challenges to performing utilitarian calculations, for example. Also, ethicists are knowledgeable of other ethical views that may be critically relevant to the assessment of animal studies. What is particularly disconcerting is that in the light of what is subsequently approved (by local ethical review committees and the Home Office itself)—that is, the subsequent lack of rejection of projects by the Home Office—it seems clear that the initial assessment by the researcher pretty much holds sway.

We shall address the issues of ethical committees shortly, but the point that needs to be made here is that it is very difficult even for scientists in one field to adequately judge the value of work in another—hence the right, but also revealing, emphasis on comprehensibility: making such project licenses "easy-to-understand." What happens, one wonders, when they are not easy to understand? Are the licenses simply waved through on the basis of trusting the researcher involved? Authorities in one field often rely on authorities in another, and so scientists should work closely with ethicists to ensure moral accountability and more effective control at the level of self-regulation.

The Three Rs

Within the member states of the EU, these guiding principles underpinning the use of animals in scientific research are found in Directive 2010/63. Having entered into force across all member states in January 2013, Directive 2010/63 does not simply replace and update the technical provisions of how and when animals can be used for scientific purposes enunciated in Directive 86/609. Instead, Directive 2010/63 represents—at its idealistic best—a move by the European Commission to fundamentally readdress the issue of animals and scientific procedures.

The previous regime was, at its heart, a tool by which scientific procedure establishments were subject to regulation simply to avoid a race to the bottom of standards; without a common set of minimum standards imposed across all European laboratories, unscrupulous undertakings would simply opt for the state with the least rigorous legislative regime, creating a significant (and uncompetitive) distortion of the market. Hence, Directive 86/609 strove to compel some form of minimum standards, not because these standards had any direct bearing on any pain and suffering felt by the animal subjects of scientific procedures, but because poor standards in one particular country could have the effect of creating an uneven playing field across the EU.

Directive 2010/63 does, of course, maintain the need to ensure that the competition within the EU remains healthy and viable across all member states, but its purpose has gone beyond this limited goal to ensure that some form of animal protection is a central tenet of the legislation, rather than a fortuitous by-product of avoiding the race to the bottom. This much is clear from both the language of the preamble (which sets out the operating principles, context, and justification for the legislation but has no binding legal effect in and of itself) and the articles of the directive itself (which set out the manner in which these principles should be put into effect by the member states).

In terms of the former, two highly significant points deserve attention here. First, there is the declaratory statement in the preamble that Directive 2010/63 represents "an important step towards achieving the final goal of full replacement of procedures on live animals for scientific and educational purposes as soon as it is scientifically possible to do so."[37] Clearly, the significance of this statement should not be overplayed: it neither pledges to end the use of animals in scientific procedures within any particular time frame nor binds any particular member states to any obligations to bring about an end to the use of animals. What this statement does do, however, is explicitly acknowledge that the use of animals in scientific experiments cannot and must not remain the norm for scientific advancement.

Second, of further significance regarding the aspiration of "full replacement" is the basis for the assertion: Directive 2010/63 recognizes that animals are sentient creatures with intrinsic—and not simply instrumental—value and that the use of animals for human purposes is a matter of serious public concern.

Quasi-prohibition (or rather the rhetoric of it) is at the heart of Directive 2010/63, and the first R of the Three Rs—replacement—is the first principle to be applied by the competent authorities of all member states: "Member States shall ensure that, wherever possible, a scientifically satisfactory method or testing strategy, not entailing the use of live animals, shall be used instead of a procedure."[38] Although this remains only a quasi-prohibition because of the use of the phrase "wherever possible," with its infinite possibilities for creative avoidance, the fact remains that the first thing specified by the first enjoining article of the directive is that there is a prohibition on animal testing unless a case can be made to justify the use of animal test subjects. When a case can be made for the granting of a license to conduct regulated procedures on animals, then—as one might naturally expect—the hierarchy of the Three Rs is to be strictly implemented: experimenters must seek to use the least number of animals possible (reduction) and use techniques involving the least degree of pain and harm (refinement). But it is not clear whether reduction or refinement wins when they clash.

Obviously, Directive 2010/63 is a highly detailed document, and because of its very nature (a directive of the EU, not a directly applicable regulation), it requires transposition into the laws of each member state by means of domestic legislation. Hence, it would be impossible to offer any detailed description of how each and every one of the principles found in the directive is applied in the twenty-eight member states of the EU. Directive 2010/63, therefore, when reduced to its simplest possible form, represents a significant regulation that underpins the direction of the laws of twenty-eight states, representing the collective values of over five hundred million people: a statement that scientific procedures involving the use of animals are implicitly undesirable and should be curtailed.

But the failure of this rhetoric to be actualized once again emphasizes the problem of failure to control because in practice there are few measurable ways in which this directive is being implemented. In order to adhere to the spirit and purpose of the directive, resources and expertise should be directed toward ensuring replacements for the use of animals in experiments—with non-animal alternatives becoming the norm—but this is clearly not the case. Alternatives are more often than not the Cinderella of the scientific world: underfunded and under-regarded, often with much tougher standards for acceptance than the equivalent animal tests. Unless and until a proportion of the huge amount of funding that is devoted to animal research is made available to pioneering non-animal research, there can be little hope of meeting the directive's rhetoric with reality.

Care and Ethics Committees

Many research institutes in the United Kingdom and the United States have care committees or local ethical review processes. Important questions are raised in relation to these committees: Are they reliable and trustworthy? And are they effective in policing animal experiments? As we have previously noted, there is often a significant conflict of interest for committee members in their advisory roles.

In the United States, the FDA is a federal regulatory agency within the US Department of Health and Human Services. The FDA is responsible for protecting public health and regulates the use and safety of human and veterinary drugs, biological products, medical devices, food supply, cosmetics, and products that emit radiation.

As such, the FDA has wide scope in setting the animal testing agenda in the United States. In relation to cosmetics, for example, the FDA does not specifically require manufacturers to test on animals. Instead, it advises companies to "employ whatever testing is appropriate and effective for substantiating the safety of their products."[39] Therefore, although the FDA does not specifically require testing to be undertaken on animals in relation to cosmetics, in effect its stance does nothing to discourage companies from testing cosmetics on animals.

An institutional animal care and use committee (IACUC) is required by US law to be established by institutions that use animals in research, to oversee the care and use of animals in those institutions. The IACUCs have broad responsibilities, and not all IACUC members have expertise in animal care. More troublesome is the fact that members might have conflicts of interest or bias. For example, some IACUCs are composed of a majority of researchers who use animals in research versus researchers who do not. Also, IACUCs oversee work of colleagues, and members of those committees might be hesitant to professionally criticize the work undertaken by professional peers whom they have to see day in and day out.

Since their conception in 1985, IACUCs have overseen animal use at institutions receiving federal grants. Although brought in as a response to public concerns about the treatment of animals in research, IACUCs were not specifically instructed to perform even elementary cost-benefit analyses of animal research protocols. Instead, IACUCs have, by and large, limited themselves to advisory or technical roles.

This disinclination to adopt a broader ethical approach to the role of IACUCs may be a result of the

UNIVERSITY OF WINCHESTER
LIBRARY

composition of the committees.[40] A recent study found that at twenty-one of the top twenty-five research institutions funded by the National Institutes of Health, an average of 67 percent of IACUC members were animal researchers, and 15 percent were veterinarians, many of whom conducted animal research. The study also found that 93 percent of IACUC chairpersons were animal researchers.[41] The disinclination to evaluate the ethical dimension of using animals in research is evident in a comprehensive study that found that 98 percent of in-house protocols were approved by IACUCs.[42]

Obviously, IACUCs would benefit from greater diversity on their committees to avoid groupthink.[43] Psychological studies have demonstrated that bias is prevalent in everyone and that we are twice as likely to seek information that fits our current worldview as we are to consider opposing views.[44] This is especially relevant when we consider that around 80 percent of members of IACUCs are engaged in animal experiments and that like-minded groups of people are more likely to reinforce their own biases than challenge them.[45]

Similar issues arise with the establishment and functioning of ethical review processes (ERPs) in the United Kingdom. Although the APC advises that ERPs should comprise a range of persons, including "lay people and people outside the establishment—all of whom can bring a 'fresh eye' to the issues raised by the work,"[46] it does not mandate that professional ethicists be counted among their number. This has to be a serious omission. Having one or two token ethicists would not by itself meet the ethical seriousness of the projects being considered, but when the majority of members are scientists (with no required expertise in moral deliberation) and no ethicists are involved, ERPs can hardly be judged to be *ethical* reviews in the first place. Yes, they may be scientific reviews (depending upon the range and expertise of the members), but they can hardly be called ethical ones.

Moreover, the APC itself notes that a Home Office review of ERPs commented that "some [scientists] still seem unwilling to allow their science to be challenged within the ERP, and are sometimes reluctant to offer a sustainable justification of proposed work."[47]

This means that even within the existing system in which some independency may be allowed, there is clearly a resistance to engage ethically with challenge or criticism. This is likely due to conflicts of interest and the problems with "supervised self-regulation," as discussed previously. It could also be due, in part, to lingering beliefs that science and ethics are to be kept separate as much as possible, from a mistaken perception of ethics as "subjective" and in opposition to science as "objective." Requiring animal ethicists to be members of such committees would not only make the reviews more objective in terms of reducing conflicts of interest but would also do much to overcome misconceptions about the relationship between science and morality.

A recent journal article by a previous chair of an animal care committee in South Africa provides a thoroughgoing critique of the operations of such committees and how they undervalue animal life. In particular she argues,

> Another way in which harms suffered by animals used for experiments are undervalued is illustrated by the fact that researchers who violate experimental protocols are not usually seriously reprimanded; there is great reluctance on the part of AECs [animal ethics committees]—on which animal researchers and technicians serve—to take experimenters to task.[48]

It seems abundantly clear that care committees do not normally provide a rigorous evaluation of proposals from an ethical perspective, nor do they feel obliged to utilize the services of animal ethicists on their committees. Care and ERP committees are fundamentally flawed in not addressing the ethical issue at stake in animal research. We do not currently have figures for the number of projects rejected by such committees or for what reasons. The danger is that such committees provide camouflage for unethical practices while creating an illusion of control over them.

Conclusion

We have discussed the principal forms of control, where controls exist, and have found them wanting. The IACUCs in the United States are so utterly lacking in independency that they do not provide a rigorous evaluation of proposals from an ethical point of view. Even within the UK system (frequently held up as a best-practice model), we find the inspection process flawed, the licensing system insufficient to prevent (and act upon) serious breaches, and ERPs insufficiently independent and reluctant to change. The Three Rs principles, which are endorsed by the EU and to which lip service is paid by governments (and which might have provided some impetus to change), are in practice massively underfunded and undervalued, so that alternatives are the Cinderella of scientific research.

Notes

1. M. Thew, "Cruelty-Free Labeling," in A. Linzey, *Global Guide*, 284–85; M. Thew, "Product Testing," in A. Linzey, *Global Guide*, 191–92.

2. Animals in Science Regulation Unit (ASRU), *Annual Report* (Home Office, 2011), 29–32; ASRU, *Annual Report* (Home Office, 2012), 35–38.

3. ASRU, *Annual Report* (2011), 29; ASRU, *Annual Report* (2012), 35. Over half of all breaches of licensing conditions are incidents of "self-reporting" by the license holders themselves. In these circumstances, the inspectorate's role becomes one of advising the Home Secretary of appropriate action to be taken.

4. ASRU, *Annual Report* (2011), 27; ASRU, *Annual Report* (2012), 33.

5. ASRU, *Annual Report* (2011), 11; ASRU, *Annual Report* (2012), 13–14.

6. Home Office, *Guidance on the Operation of the Animals (Scientific Procedures) Act 1986*, HC321, March 23, 2000 (London: Stationery Office, 2000), para. 5.42, accessed September 26, 2014, https://www.gov.uk/government/uploads/system/uploads/attachment_data/file/228542/0321.pdf. This guidance has been superseded under the new ASPA. There is no equivalent definition.

7. ASRU, *Annual Report* (2011), 11.

8. Ibid., 28; ASRU, *Annual Report* (2012), 33.

9. ASRU, *Annual Report* (2011), 11–13.

10. ASRU, *Annual Report* (2012), 14–15.

11. W. M. S. Russell and R. L. Burch, *The Principles of Humane Experimental Technique* (London: Methuen, 1959), 54.

12. Animals (Scientific Procedures) Act 1986, s.6(2), London, accessed September 26, 2014, http://www.legislation.gov.uk/ukpga/1986/14/contents.

13. Ibid., s.6(1).

14. Ibid., s.6(5)(a).

15. Ibid., s.6(5)(b).

16. Ibid., s.10(5A), s.10(6B).

17. Ibid., s.10(6B)(a–e). These provisions correlate almost exactly with those listed in article 5 of the then parent directive of 1986, Directive 86/609/EEC.

18. European Commission, *Council Directive 86/609/EEC of 24 November 1986 on the Approximation of Laws, Regulations, and Administrative Provisions of the Member States regarding the Protection of Animals Used for Experimental and Other Scientific Purposes* (1986).

19. "The conditions of a certificate issued under section 6 or 7 [those pertaining to breeding and supply establishments] shall include such conditions relating to the general care and accommodation of protected animals . . . as the Secretary of State considers appropriate." Animals (Scientific Procedures) Act 1986, s.10(6B).

20. European Commission, *Council Directive*, Annex II, introduction, para. 4.

21. Ibid., para. 6.

22. Substantial changes have been made to ASPA, effective from January 2013, to bring it in line with Directive 2010/63, which replaces Directive 86/609. It is yet unclear what benefit, if any, the new regulations will provide. But we discuss the previous directive in order to highlight the deficiencies.

23. *Secretary of State for the Home Department v. the Queen on the Application of Campaign to End All Animal Experiments (Trading as the British Union for the Abolition of Vivisection)*, Court of Appeal (Civil Division), April 23, 2008, EWCA Civ 417, para. 20.

24. Ibid., para. 75.

25. Ibid., para. 77.

26. Ibid., para. 76.

27. Ibid., paras. 77; 76; 80.

28. T. Blair, *A Journey* (London: Hutchinson, 2010), 304ff.

29. A. Linzey, *Why Animal Suffering Matters*, 92.

30. Home Office, *Animals in Science Regulation Unit: Annual Report 2013* (London, 2014).

31. European Chemicals Agency (ECHA), "What about Animal Testing?" accessed May 9, 2014, http://echa.europa.eu/chemicals-in-our-life/animal-testing-under-reach.

32. A. Freiberg, *The Tools of Regulation* (New South Wales, Australia: Federation Press, 2010), 36.

33. European Chemicals Agency (ECHA), *Guidance in a Nutshell: Registration*, accessed January 3, 2015, http://echa.europa.eu/documents/10162/13632/nutshell_guidance_registration_en.pdf.

34. K. Taylor, W. Stengel, C. Casalegno, and D. Andrew, "Food for Thought: Experiences of the REACH Testing Proposals System to Reduce Animal Testing," *Altex* 31, no. 2 (2014): 107–28.

35. APC, *Review of Cost-Benefit Assessment*, 65.

36. Ibid., 65–66.

37. European Parliament, *Directive 2010/63/EU*, 34.

38. Ibid., 39.

39. US Food and Drug Administration, "Animal Testing and Cosmetics," 2006, accessed January 3, 2015, http://www.fda.gov/cosmetics/scienceresearch/producttesting/ucm072268.htm.

40. L. A. Hansen, "Institution Animal Care and Use Committees Need Greater Ethical Diversity," *Journal of Medical Ethics* 39, no. 3 (2013): 188–90.

41. L. A. Hansen, J. R. Goodman, and A. Chanda, "Analysis of Animal Research Ethics Committee Membership at American Institutions," *Animals* 2, no. 1 (2012): 68–75.

42. S. Plous and H. Herzog, "Reliability of Protocol Reviews for Animal Research," *Science* 293 (2001): 608–9.

43. Hansen, "Institution Animal Care."

44. E. Pronin, T. Gilovich, and L. Ross, "Objectivity in the Eye of the Beholder: Divergent Perceptions of Bias in Self versus Others," *Psychological Review* 111, no. 3 (2004): 781–99; M. Heffernan, *Willful Blindness: Why We Ignore the Obvious at Our Peril* (New York: Walker, 2011); W. Hart, D. Albarracín, A. H. Eagly, I. Brechan, M. Lindberg, K. Lee, and L. Merrill, "Feeling Validated versus Being Correct: A Meta-Analysis of Selective Exposure to Information," *Psychological Bulletin* 135 (2009): 555–88; T. Pyszcynski, J. Greenberg, and K. Holt, "Maintaining Consistency between Self-Serving Beliefs and Available Data: A Bias in Information Evaluation," *Personality and Social Psychology Bulletin* 11 (1985): 179–90.

45. A. Tesser and S. Rosen, "Similarity of Objective Fate as a Determinant of the Reluctance to Transmit Unpleasant Information: The MUM Effect," *Journal of Personality and Social Psychology* 23 (1972): 46–53; C. R. Sunstein, *Going to Extremes: How Like Minds Unite and Divide* (Oxford: Oxford University Press, 2009).

46. APC, *Review of Cost-Benefit Assessment*, 69.

47. Ibid., 69–70.

48. E. Galgut, "Raising the Bar in the Justification of Animal Research," *Journal of Animal Ethics* 5, no. 1 (2015): 5–19.

1.8

Undercover Investigations

AT THE BEGINNING of our report, we indicated the limited nature of legislation (or even absence of law) regulating experimentation worldwide (see section 1.1). In the preceding section, we showed the lack of control, or failure of control, exercised in practice. In this section, we examine the issue of noncompliance. It is important to note that at least three things are required for improvement through regulation. First, there need to be laws and statutory guidelines to supplement those laws. Second, there needs to be adequate enforcement (including adequate and independent inspection). And third, there has to be compliance.

The issue of compliance is as important as the other two factors. Without compliance, regulations can have no impact at all. It is, therefore, especially serious that animal organizations have uncovered significant evidence of noncompliance over the past twenty years or so. In this section, we examine six such examples—one relating to international trade and five others in UK laboratories. Various animal organizations have employed undercover investigations, but here we focus on those conducted by the BUAV. We are grateful to the BUAV for providing the results of their investigations.

International Trade in Primates (1991)

In 1991 the BUAV followed the chain of supply for NHPs from Asia, Mauritius, and the Caribbean to research laboratories in the United Kingdom, Europe, and the United States.[1] An undercover worker was placed at Shamrock, a major UK facility for importing and holding NHPs, and Hazleton, a UK contract testing laboratory, while other investigators traveled to the main exporting countries to infiltrate the trapping network. Footage revealed the extensive suffering inflicted on monkeys during their capture, caging, transportation, holding at Shamrock, and eventual death in the laboratory.

Shamrock Ltd. was established in 1954 to supply free-living (otherwise known as "wild-caught") rhesus monkeys for research. Shamrock subsequently became one of the largest suppliers of NHPs for research within Europe, supplying many species of NHPs, including the most popular for research: rhesus macaques, long-tailed macaques, vervets, and baboons. Demands from laboratories for a continuous cheap supply of NHPs meant that the majority of NHPs, those traded internationally as well as those imported into the United Kingdom, were taken from their natural environment, since captive-bred macaques cost three times more.

The findings of this 1992 BUAV investigation included the following:

- The suffering endured by monkeys during trapping and transportation often resulted in high mortality rates. As many as eight out of every ten monkeys who were captured died before reaching the laboratory.

- There were appalling conditions at holding centers in source countries—for example, monkeys kept in cramped and overcrowded cages.
- Suffering and losses were inflicted on monkeys traveling as cargo on passenger airlines to destinations around the world.
- As many as 20 percent further deaths followed the arrival of the monkeys in the United Kingdom, due to illnesses such as enteritis and pneumonia. Others were killed because of their poor condition or deformity.
- Between 1988 and 1991, 3,220 macaques were imported into the United Kingdom by Shamrock; 611 of these subsequently died. In some cases the mortality rates were higher. For example, out of a shipment of fifty monkeys who were imported from one country, seventeen were dead within three months, and twenty-seven were dead within six months.
- At Shamrock, NHPs were kept in inadequate conditions (in barren cages and individually housed with no stimulation or exercise), resulting in abnormal behavior including circling, rocking, and self-mutilation.
- The suffering and distress experienced by the NHPs were increased by the general attitude and behavior of staff at Shamrock, including rough handling. NHPs were captured by nets and hauled to the ground, causing distress and injury, including cuts, bruises, and even loss of teeth.
- Experiments at Hazleton involved NHPs held in restraint "chairs" while forced to inhale toxic substances via a mask secured to their head. The monkeys would often scream and struggle while placed in these "chairs."
- At Hazleton, monkeys were slapped about the body by staff and were shaken and prodded while restrained. One monkey was called "Rape" because she screamed frequently.

These findings led to the following outcomes:

- There was a subsequent international move away from the trapping of monkeys for research. In the United Kingdom alone, following BUAV's "Paradise Lost" investigation, only 5 percent of monkeys imported during 1993 were taken from their natural environment. In 1990 it had been 77 percent.

- In 1995 the UK government announced a ban on the use of trapped monkeys in research unless there was "exceptional and specific justification." It also introduced a system whereby overseas suppliers of NHPs had to be inspected and approved before being given permission to import monkeys for research (this system has recently been abandoned).
- In 1994 Indonesia and the Philippines announced restrictions on the NHP trade and a ban on the export of trapped monkeys, although monkeys could continue to be trapped in the wild to establish or replenish breeding programs.
- A Home Office inquiry into Shamrock accepted the main criticisms made by the BUAV—namely, that management had failed to care for the NHPs, that staff were incompetent in care and handled animals inappropriately and insensitively, and that the conditions in which the animals were kept were inadequate. In 1993 Shamrock announced a ban on the import of free-living monkeys. A few years later, in 2000, the facility closed down.

Wickham Research Laboratory (1992)

In 1992 the BUAV carried out an investigation at Wickham Laboratories in the United Kingdom.[2] At this facility, rabbits, mice, and guinea pigs were subjected to a range of tests, including skin irritancy, toxicity (poisoning), and pyrogenicity studies for "quality control" (the routine batch testing of established drugs, medical devices, and solutions used in intravenous infusions). Products tested at Wickham were for a variety of UK and foreign chemical and pharmaceutical firms. Wickham also carried out batch testing on mice using the LD50 (lethal dose 50 percent) test for a product containing botulinum toxin (commonly known as botox).

During this investigation it was found that animal tests were being carried out at Wickham (for which the Home Office had granted licenses) despite these tests no longer being required by UK or European regulations.

Unprofessional scientific practice was also uncovered. Laboratory staff were told to weigh bags of mouse food rather than actual mice, to save time.

This was a clear breach of the Home Office license conditions and could lead to distorted test results. Other findings that breached the Home Office's *Code of Practice for the Housing and Care of Animals Used in Scientific Procedures* included rabbit cages poorly maintained—many had bars missing—and no bedding provided for the animals. As a result, many rabbits suffered from sore feet and abscesses, and others were found dead in their cages. Many animals were gassed in a CO_2 chamber that had a broken dial, making it impossible to assess the right dose of CO_2 to ensure rapid and humane killing. At one point the cylinder ran out and was not replaced for weeks, which meant that staff were left to break the necks of hundreds of mice at a time.

The BUAV called on the Home Office to withdraw Wickham's license to carry out experiments. The BUAV also believed an independent review of the whole operation of the 1986 Animals (Scientific Procedures) Act was needed.

These findings led to the following outcome:

- The Home Office conducted its own investigation, and on June 22, 1993, it released a statement announcing weaknesses that had been discovered and the actions Wickham Laboratories would need to take. It found Wickham to have poor local management, resulting in lax attitudes, and poor practices among staff. These included a readiness to falsify data on occasions. The investigation claimed to have found one case of unnecessary animal use. It was found that some aspects of the technical training were unsatisfactory, and the initial training was poorly structured. It was also found that the system lacked formal assessment of competence before unsupervised tasks were allocated to new employees.

The following actions were taken or directed:

- Wickham had to replace the person who had held day-to-day responsibility for running the animal house, and that person's license to use animals was revoked.
- A former license holder was warned that any future application for a personal license would be subjected to close scrutiny.
- A number of other staff members were sent letters warning them about their future conduct.
- Wickham was ordered to make acceptable improvements to training arrangements and operational procedures. It was directed that Wickham have a formal training scheme for all animal unit staff.
- Wickham's standard operating procedures relating to the care, husbandry, and euthanasia of animals were to be revised to the satisfaction of the inspectorate.

Harlan UK (1998–99)

In 1998–99 a ten-month undercover investigation was carried out by the BUAV at the Harlan UK Leicestershire site.[3] This site bred dogs (and other animals) for the research industry and was also contracted to look after animals in use by other institutions. The investigation revealed a lack of care for the dogs, as well as numerous breaches of government guidelines.

Harlan was founded in 1931 and is a major international company with locations all over the world. The Harlan UK Group consists of breeding establishments that sell to laboratories across the world. Harlan UK breeds a number of species of animals (including beagles, rabbits, guinea pigs, gerbils, hamsters, rats, and mice) and more than 225 stocks and strains of animals, including hybrid, mutant, transgenic, and surgically altered animals. Some facilities require only blood serum, plasma products, or organs; Harlan bleeds and kills these animals (including dogs) to the facilities' requirements.

During the investigation, breaches were found in the minimum standards of housing and care as stated in the Home Office's *Code of Practice for the Housing and Care of Animals in Designated Breeding and Supplying Establishments*, and the BUAV called for Harlan UK's certificate of designation to be withdrawn. The Animals (Scientific Procedures) Act 1986 (in force at the time) stated that "a certificate of designation is granted only to those establishments which meet the required standards of husbandry and care."

Key breaches uncovered by the BUAV included the following:

- Harlan failed to fully recognize the special requirements of breeding animals.

- The breeding females and stud dogs received little human contact or stimulation and no exercise.
- All dogs, including whelping females, were kept in bare pens, with no bedding other than a handful of sawdust as substrate.
- Other breaches included failure to adhere to minimum space requirements; failure to provide adequate staff training; failure to provide sufficient staff; failure to check the well-being of animals at least once daily; poor hygiene; moldy food-hoppers; mice in the units; and temperatures outside the recommended range.

The investigation also discovered loopholes in the government regulation of animal experimentation. Dogs at Harlan were overbred, causing the production of animals "surplus to requirements." These healthy "surplus" dogs were regularly killed, including some who were only a few months old. Between January 1998 and April 1999, the BUAV estimated that at least 250 dogs were killed who were considered "surplus to requirements." The government does not require breeding establishments to provide statistics to show how many "surplus" or breeding dogs are killed. Therefore, the public is not provided with accurate information as to how many dogs are held by the research industry each year. A second loophole in the government's regulations highlighted by the BUAV was that dogs at Harlan UK were often killed for blood serum and plasma. Yet again, the government does not require breeders to supply statistics on the number of animals killed for tissue, blood, or organs.

The BUAV was dissatisfied with the Home Office's response to the investigation and stated that the Home Office had failed to enforce legislation against animal cruelty and to properly investigate once breaches of legislation had been made.

The resulting report by the Home Office inspectorate generally praised the welfare conditions within the facility and rejected several of the BUAV's allegations. However, the BUAV argued that a closer reading of the report showed that many of the allegations had actually been accepted. The BUAV also accused the Home Office inspectorate of seeking to denigrate the BUAV investigator at every opportunity.

The APC, the government's advisory body, stated, "Many members felt that the report sought to exonerate Harlan-Hillcrest, with the risk of creating the impression that the conditions which prevailed there were deemed acceptable by the Inspectorate."[4]

Cambridge University (2002)

The BUAV carried out an investigation into the use of marmosets in neurological research at Cambridge University.[5] The NHPs were used for a mixture of basic research (including research to find out more about the brain) and applied research that was aimed at trying to develop a marmoset "model" for human illnesses such as stroke and Parkinson's disease. Hundreds of monkeys spent their entire lives in barren cages and were deliberately brain-damaged.

The research included the following:

- The monkeys were "trained" to carry out behavioral and cognitive tasks, before undergoing major surgery to have brain damage inflicted. Following the brain damage, they were then forced to repeat the tasks.
- Water deprivation and/or food restrictions were used to force the monkeys to carry out the tasks required of them (they were deprived of water for twenty-two out of every twenty-four hours, with intermittent respite, for months on end).
- In tests where monkeys were used as "models" for Parkinson's disease, they were shut into tiny Perspex boxes for up to one hour at a time, to see how often they would rotate (an effect of the brain damage). They were also given injections of amphetamine or apomorphine, which made them rotate faster or in the opposite direction.

All the experiments included the deliberate infliction of brain damage by cutting or sucking out parts of the brain or by injecting toxins. The postoperative effects of the brain surgery included pain, distress, bleeding from head wounds, fits, vomiting, tremors, swelling and bruising, loss in body temperature, failure to eat or drink, abnormal body movements such as head twisting and body rotation, the loss of use of one arm or the whole side of the animal's body, loss of balance, and visual disturbances. The long-term effects of the brain damage included physical disabilities, learning and memory impairment, weight loss, and lack of self-care.

Further concerns raised by the BUAV included the following:

- Hundreds of marmosets were kept in small, barren cages with little stimulation or enrichment.
- Just one technician had the responsibility of caring for approximately five hundred marmosets.
- Hand-rearing was not part of the husbandry routine, which meant that some "excess" newborn monkeys were left to die or were killed if they were not thriving.
- Monkeys who were experiencing the effects of significant brain damage were left unattended overnight for up to sixteen hours immediately following surgery.
- Several monkeys were killed on "welfare grounds" or were found dead after the brain surgery.

Yet despite this level of suffering inflicted on the marmosets, the Home Office had categorized the experiments as "moderate" rather than "substantial." If the experiments had been classed as causing "substantial" suffering, the APC would have had to scrutinize them before any licenses were granted, if they were granted at all.[6]

These findings led to the following outcomes:

- The BUAV called for an inquiry that was independent of the Home Office. However, in the face of a promise made to Parliament by a Home Office minister after the APC's criticism following the Harlan investigation, the Home Office inspectorate carried out its own investigation. The Home Office report dismissed, misrepresented, or completely ignored the BUAV's allegations; levels of animal suffering were also seriously downplayed. Even clear breaches of project licenses that involved additional animal suffering beyond that allowed in the licenses were dismissed as "a few minor infringements of a technical nature."
- With the information obtained during their investigation and in the light of the subse-

quent review, the BUAV applied to the United Kingdom's high court for permission to seek a judicial review of the legality of the Home Office's application of the law in the Cambridge case and of the wider implementation of animal experiments legislation. The BUAV was successful on the assessment of Cambridge severity limits (overruled in the court of appeal) and lost on the care arrangements issue. The courts acknowledged that the Home Office had been unlawful in approaching its own guidance about how to assess severity. A legal discussion of the findings is provided in section 1.7.

Wickham Research Laboratory (2009)

A second BUAV investigation took place at Wickham Laboratories in Hampshire in 2009.[7] The BUAV found yet again that the laboratory was testing substances on animals for which no test was required or where there was a valid alternative. Some of these tests were pyrogenicity tests during which rabbits were injected with a substance and forcibly restrained by their necks in stocks for hours at a time. Individual rabbits were then routinely reused in the test. The BUAV also uncovered more details of the LD50 tests being conducted on a massive scale to check batches of the highly toxic botulinum toxin product.

The key findings included the following:

- Animals were kept in small, virtually barren cages that failed to meet their behavioral and social needs.
- Some animals were being used in tests that were no longer required by national and international regulations.
- The LD50 test for botulinum toxin product, also seen during the 1992 investigation, was still being conducted. However, since that time, a valid test-tube alternative to the test (the SNAP-25 assay) had been developed. The BUAV argued that under UK law, this test should be used because it had been validated by no less than an official UK government laboratory and had been used by that laboratory since 1999 for the same purpose. Inexplicably, the UK Home Office was not insisting on this test ten years later.

- Despite a UK and EU ban on the use of animals for cosmetic testing, there appeared to be a loophole in the law that allowed animals to continue to be used in tests for the botulinum toxin product that, although licensed for medical use, could very well end up being used—quite legally—for cosmetic purposes (as botox).

The BUAV was particularly concerned with the suffering and death of what amounted to hundreds of mice every week in the LD50 test. Researchers injected botulinum toxin into the abdomen of the mice and then periodically observed the animals to see how many died. The mice would become increasingly paralyzed, eventually gasping for breath and suffocating to death; no pain relief was provided for the mice.

As a token consideration with respect to animal welfare, staff were supposed to observe the mice and identify those who were judged unlikely to survive until the next check. This was a completely inadequate way of controlling suffering, but in any event, using the company's own data, the BUAV discovered that this so-called humane end point was a sham because far more of the mice in question died an agonizing death than were directly killed.

Most mice in the higher-dose categories died during the test. Those considered unlikely to survive until the next check were taken out into the corridor and crudely killed on the floor by staff, who broke their necks with a ballpoint pen. New members of the staff who had never killed mice before were expected to practice breaking necks with a ballpoint pen on live mice. However, during this training, staff sometimes broke the backs of mice rather than their necks. Even experienced staff had problems and caused back injuries.

These findings led to the following outcome:

- The Home Office set up a semi-independent inquiry and in 2010 released its report on Wickham Laboratories, which found breaches in animal testing licenses issued to the company. The report substantiated many of the BUAV's findings.

The key findings of the Home Office report included the following:[8]

- Too many mice in the LD50 tests were being "found dead" rather than being "humanely" killed by staff—in breach of the institution's license to monitor the animals regularly.
- Staff incompetence in the way mice were killed led to their suffering, including the practice of neck-breaking with a pen on the corridor floor.
- Key staff did not carry out their legal responsibilities under the ASPA, including the named veterinary surgeon, who did not ensure the welfare of rabbits.
- Staff training in the monitoring and killing of animals was poor.

One of the companies commissioning tests on rabbits at Wickham moved to non-animal alternatives, and the UK Veterinary Medicines Directorate launched a review into the use of rabbits for pyrogenicity testing. This review found that twenty-six veterinary drugs were still being tested on animals when there was no longer any scientific need. The review prompted a change in the licenses for these drugs, sparing an estimated thirty-eight thousand animals.[9]

The following actions were taken or directed:

- The Home Office immediately ordered the staff to stop killing the mice on the floor.
- A number of other staff members received letters warning them about their future conduct.
- Wickham Laboratories was ordered to make acceptable improvements to its formal training arrangements and operational procedures.
- Improvements had to be made to the monitoring during the LD50 tests. The Home Office investigation following the BUAV's investigation found that 80 to 100 percent of mice in the relevant groups were in fact dying from the botox.
- The Home Office report acknowledged that there was a potential conflict of interest with the named veterinary surgeon (NVS) responsible for animal welfare, who was also a major company shareholder. The NVS subsequently stood down, and the Home Office introduced new guidance aimed at preventing such conflicts.

Despite the preceding findings, the BUAV was disappointed that the Home Office had failed to properly investigate whether the drugs tested at Wickham Laboratories necessitated animal tests, in particular whether such tests were required by national and international regulators. Following a judicial review brought by the BUAV after this investigation, the Home Office agreed that, with quality control testing, it had to make sure before an animal test for a particular substance took place that there were no available alternatives. New guidance was issued to inspectors.

The Home Office initially strongly denied that it had any responsibility to ensure that the botox was not actually used for cosmetics. However, following the judicial review, the Home Secretary, Theresa May, conceded that she did have the responsibility to make sure that the end use of the botox was not for cosmetic purposes. However, all the signs indicate that the Home Office has done nothing to enforce the condition, with the result that the tests appear to be continuing at Wickham.

Imperial College, London (2012)

During an undercover investigation in 2012,[10] the BUAV documented a catalog of shortcomings and wrongdoing by Imperial College staff and researchers that caused more distress and suffering to the animals (rats and mice) in their care than was allowed in the experiments. Findings included breaches in and lack of knowledge of UK Home Office project licenses, a failure to provide adequate anesthesia and pain relief, incompetence and neglect, and disturbing methods used to kill animals.

The key concerns raised by the BUAV investigation included the following:

- There was underestimation of the degree of suffering in project licenses. Experimental protocols were given a "moderate" limit even when the anticipated adverse effects clearly called for a "substantial" classification of the research. One research project involved kidney transplantation, a major procedure by any standard. Some rats had both their kidneys removed via abdominal surgery and were left with just one transplanted kidney. The subsequent Home Office review said that senior inspectors not involved in the original clas-

sifications were asked to review them. There was "agreement that some procedures may not have been classified as of sufficiently high severity."[11]

- Poor monitoring of animals resulted in suffering and breaches of humane "end points" (the point at which further suffering must not take place). In one case, where mice were found to be in a distressed state on a Monday morning, a senior technician stated, "I am so disgusted. Those poor mice," and "If the Home Office was in, we would have been screwed if they saw those mice."

- Researchers lacked knowledge of the severity limits of their project licenses and the humane "end points" they were supposed to apply. When asked about the severity limits on their licenses, many researchers did not know. One said, "So do I get to call a friend?" Not knowing the severity levels and "end points" could result in animals being subjected to even more pain and suffering than permitted.

- The investigation found poor application of the methods used for killing animals, leading to unnecessary suffering, and the controversial use of a guillotine to carry out live decapitation.

- Poor surgical and other procedures resulted in animal deaths and suffering. One researcher, for example, raised concerns about the competence of a colleague: "I think you should keep an eye on [name withheld] because he makes many mistakes."

- Unsupervised researchers, with little experience, were anesthetizing and carrying out surgery on animals. One researcher who was anesthetizing a rat to re-staple a surgery wound admitted, "I've never done this before," and "I only came down here for the first time yesterday, so I haven't even seen these rats before."

- Researchers failed to provide adequate anesthesia and analgesics. There were several occasions when animals appeared to be inadequately anesthetized, as a consequence of inadequate monitoring or use of inappropriate anesthesia or deliberately due to fears about losses of animals during surgery. One researcher who did not want to wait for hours for a rat to recover from anesthesia on a Friday afternoon stated, "But I won't give it a full dose. As long as there is enough for it to be not fully under but, you know, not feeling too much pain."

- Pop music was played at high levels throughout the facility, adding to animals' distress. The music was even played during surgery itself, while animals were recovering, and during killing.

These findings led to the following outcomes:

- The Home Office announced it would carry out an investigation, and Imperial College immediately commissioned its own inquiry. A report was then published in December 2013. The inquiry subsequently known as "the Brown Report" was carried out by professor Steve Brown, director of the Medical Research Council's Mammalian Genetics Unit. The report concluded that Imperial College "did not have in place adequate operational, leadership, management, training, supervisory and ethical review systems."[12] Other findings from the review included the following:

In terms of operational structures and standards, communication and working practices, as well as the mechanisms for reporting animal welfare concerns, we found that there was considerable room for improvement and the introduction of significant changes. These would have a substantive impact upon animal welfare. . . .

We recommend an increase in staffing levels that will allow the increased involvement of animal care staff with *in vivo* research programmes . . . and ensure greater independent overview of animal welfare out of hours and at weekends. . . .

We found that the provision of training, supervision and competency assessment was *ad hoc*, and that there was little evidence of effective mechanisms for sharing information and best practice across staff. . . . We recommend a significant increase in resource for training and competency assessment.[13]

The university's Animal Welfare and Ethical Review Body—which is responsible for reviewing animal use—was found to be "not fit for purpose" and in need of "wholesale reform."[14] Additionally, professor Brown commented in the press release for the report, "While our focus has been on Imperial College, the

committee's recommendations should serve as a useful framework for other institutions to review their policies and practices."[15]

The Animals in Science Committee (ASC), the government advisory body, published its own report in July 2014 based on the findings of the Home Office investigation at Imperial College and the Brown Report. This report found that Imperial College had breached its establishment license and concluded that there was "a systematic pattern of infringements, of which the ASC notes that at least two involved tangible welfare costs."[16] The ASC report recommended that "the Minister should consider whether he can continue to have confidence in the current ELH [establishment license holder] at ICL [Imperial College London] retaining this role."[17]

The ASC report concluded that

the regime at ICL clearly fell short of the standard required by the Animals (Scientific Procedures) Act 1986. The HOI investigation [Home Office investigation at Imperial College] identified a pattern of infringements that reflected underlying systematic failings. . . . In particular, failings of culture and communications impeded the promotion of best practice and the 3Rs, whilst NACWOs [named animal care and welfare officers] and biomedical staff were insufficiently involved in procedures and post-procedure recovery. This was symptomatic of a deeper failure of leadership, giving rise to, and in turn compounded by, an inadequately resourced Biomedical Services senior management team.[18]

In 2014 the current establishment license holder at Imperial College stepped down from holding that responsibility, effective immediately, at the insistence of the minister.

Conclusion

Some may argue that because some of the egregious practices that were brought to light were, to some degree, subsequently rectified, this shows how the system of regulation is effective. We cannot share that view. The point to grasp is that these abuses were brought to light only by undercover investigations. Without those investigations, the abuses almost certainly never would have been discovered, nor would remedial measures have been taken. And this is the even more pertinent point: these abuses happened *despite* the panoply of regulation in the United Kingdom, including detailed laws, the licensing system, the inspectorate, the ERPs, and the national advisory committee (APC/ASC). What these examples demonstrate is that even despite all these regulations, animals are not protected against egregious suffering in the United Kingdom, even in leading academic institutions that have a reputation for scientific excellence.

Another consideration also gives us pause. Often we are told that animals in laboratories are treated with scrupulous care and that every attempt is made by researchers and technicians to avoid animal suffering. For example, we are assured of the following: "There is a consensus in the scientific community that accepts a moral imperative to fulfil the principle of humane experimental technique expounded upon by Russell and Burch, the 3Rs. In practice, conscientious researchers make every effort to observe the spirit of legislation."[19]

But in the light of these undercover revelations, another interpretation presents itself—namely, that although some researchers may be conscientious in the discharge of their responsibilities, the prevailing institutional ethos is such that harm to "laboratory animals" is counted as a small thing in comparison with the research work undertaken. Without accusing any researchers of callousness, we suggest that the predominant ethos—where animals are used for human ends—in laboratories works against the highest possible standards. As such, standards can only, at best, mitigate the suffering that can lawfully be inflicted on animals.

The ineluctable conclusion is not just that there were failures in the many examples cited, but that such failures are endemic in a system in which animals are seen and used as "laboratory tools." Animal experimentation is not adequately policed even by the supposedly highest standards of care and the greatest degree of regulation.

Notes

1. British Union for the Abolition of Vivisection (BUAV), *Briefing Paper on the Primate Trade, Role of Shamrock (Great Britain) Ltd. and Hazleton UK* (1992).

2. BUAV, "A BUAV Investigation at Wickham Research Laboratories" (unpublished report, 1993).

3. BUAV, "A BUAV Investigation at Harlan UK" (unpublished report, 1999).

4. APC, *Report of the Animal Procedures Committee for 2003* (Home Office, 2004), 47.

5. BUAV, "A BUAV Investigation into Marmoset Neuroscience Research at Cambridge University" (unpublished report, 2002).

6. The findings of the BUAV investigation were launched with an in-depth political news item on BBC Two's *Newsnight*. The focus of *Newsnight* was the BUAV's concerns about the Home Office licensing system—that the Home Office had been misleading the public about the reality of animal suffering in laboratories, downplaying it by labeling such invasive research as "moderate" rather than "substantial." The *Newsnight* reporter said, "Under the present licensing system, it seems that the true extent of suffering endured by laboratory animals is being systematically obscured." Hours before *Newsnight*, then prime minister Tony Blair had defended the university and the NHP research in what he called his "Science Matters" speech. He said that "the response of the government must be to encourage openness, transparency and honesty," and he claimed that Britain has "one of the world's strictest, most regulated regimes for animal experimentation." Blair went on to say, "Cambridge University intends to build a new centre for neurological research. Part of this would involve using primates to test potential cures for diseases like Alzheimer's and Parkinson's. But there is a chance the centre will not be built because of concerns about public safety dangers and unlawful protests. We cannot have vital work stifled simply because it is controversial." BBC Two, *Newsnight*, May 23, 2002, accessed February 10, 2015, http://news.bbc.co.uk/1/hi/programmes/newsnight/2005130.stm.

7. BUAV, "A BUAV Investigation at Wickham Research Laboratories" (unpublished report, 2009).

8. Animals Scientific Procedures Inspectorate, *A Review on the Issues and Concerns Raised in the Report, "The Ugly Truth—A BUAV Investigation at Wickham Laboratories"* (2010), accessed March 1, 2015, https://www.gov.uk/government/uploads/system/uploads/attachment_data/file/116820/wickham-laboratories.pdf.

9. BUAV, "BUAV Congratulates UK Veterinary Agency for Removing Obsolete Batch Animal Tests," *Politics.co.uk*, July 13, 2011, accessed March 1, 2015, http://www.politics.co.uk/opinion-formers/buav-british-union-for-the-abolition-of-vivisection/article/buav-congratulates-uk-veterinary-agency-for-removing-obsolet.

10. BUAV, "BUAV Report to the Home Office: Animal Experiments at Imperial College London" (unpublished report, 2013).

11. Home Office, *Report of ASRU Investigation into Compliance. Ref: A8(1)* (London, 2014).

12. Brown Committee, "The Brown Report: Independent Investigation into Animal Research at Imperial College London" (2013), 7, accessed January 4, 2015, http://brownreport.info/wp-content/uploads/2014/02/The-Brown-Report.pdf.

13. Ibid., 8–9, emphases in original.

14. Ibid., 14, 8.

15. Brown Committee, "Independent Investigation into Animal Research at Imperial College Published" (press release, 2013), accessed January 4, 2015, http://brownreport.info/wp-content/uploads/2014/02/Brownreportpressrelease.pdf.

16. Animals in Science Committee (ASC), *Lessons to Be Learnt, for Duty Holders and the Regulator, from Reviews and Investigations into Non-Compliance* (2014), 2, accessed January 4, 2015, https://www.gov.uk/government/uploads/system/uploads/attachment_data/file/326003/ASClessons-ToBeLearnt2Jul14.pdf.

17. Ibid., 5.

18. Ibid., 4.

19. F. Darling and K. P. Dolan, "Animals in Cancer Research," *AnimalResearch.Info* (2007), accessed January 3, 2015, http://www.animalresearch.info/en/medical-advances/articles-lectures/animals-cancer-research/.

1.9

Consideration of Counterarguments

WE NOW TURN TO a range of counterarguments used to defend animal research and respond to them.

Surely the answer to the lapses in control is better, more effective control.

We have already detailed the many practical considerations that should make us wary of relying on putative controls. Indeed, the whole notion of control is grounded in a systemic mischaracterization of the moral status of animals.

Isn't it better to leave these matters to scientists who know more than we do?

Scientists are often best equipped to answer factual questions about what sorts of experimentation are most likely to be effective. However, they are not best equipped to address the moral question of animal experimentation. Scientists are not experts on morality, and so on the topic of moral status, they have no particular expertise. Besides, there is a legitimate public interest in how animals are treated, not least of all because, inter alia, public money is used to fund scientific research.

Humans have been given "dominion" over animals, which means we can use them as we want.

Dominion in its original context in Genesis 1 certainly did *not* mean despotism or that humans could do as they please to animals. The biblical theology of the first creation saga in Genesis is that God created the world and all its plants and animals, who were blessed and given their own living space, and then humans were made in the image of God and given dominion. The ideas of *imago dei* and dominion need to be read together. God created a world, fashioned humans in the divine image, and then gave them responsibility to care for the world as God intended. Humans were the species commissioned to look after the earth and render an account to God. This is made explicit in Genesis 1:29, when having been made in the image and given dominion, humans are given a vegetarian diet. Herb-eating dominion can hardly be a license for tyranny. The attempt, therefore, to interpret dominion as meaning that "might is right" is a misreading of the first Genesis narrative. Not only is this the view of the original narrative; it is now the established view of biblical scholars.[1]

How can we consistently oppose animal experiments in a society that accepts the killing of animals for food?

We accept that the new ethical paradigm we have outlined will involve major changes to the way we treat animals, including those reared and killed for food. But we aver that there is still a distinction to be made between the two practices. Almost everyone who eats meat believes that animals may be killed but that this must be done "humanely." Whether it is possible to "humanely" raise and kill billions of animals for food, especially in intensive conditions, is, of course, disputable, but at least *in theory* such a distinction is maintained.

In animal experiments, however, suffering is endemic. In most cases, it is a question of deliberately and intentionally causing harm. This is not some accidental or incidental feature of experimentation; it is rather inherent in the practice. Even when procedures do not deliberately involve suffering, suffering nevertheless is entailed in the practices of capture, trade, transport, confinement, and manipulation that animal experimentation involves. Even if, therefore, our sole concern is for the suffering of animals rather than their death, it follows that animal experimentation warrants particular censure and requires special justification, if any is possible.

Are not those who oppose animal experiments guilty of intimidation, if not violence?

We do not support violence, arson, intimidation, or illegality. We believe that the tiny number of activists who are involved in such activities are engaged in morally self-contradictory behavior—self-contradictory because people who seek to justify such actions invariably appeal to the ends justifying the means, which is precisely the consequentialist rationale of researchers who use animals. Moreover, such tactics rob animal advocates of the moral high ground and are attempts (in democratic countries at least) to shortcut the system. But it should not be overlooked that research on animals regularly inflicts violence and suffering on millions of animals. Although there can be no consequentialist justification for violent protests, by the same standard we should also reject consequentialist justifications for inflicting violence on animals in research.

Cannot animal research be justified retrospectively in virtue of the advances in science during the last century?

No, and for many reasons. It is difficult to assess how much of the progress has been due to animal research, and it is even more difficult to claim that we could not have had at least as much progress if all the time, money, and resources had been put into different kinds of research. Most fundamentally, this assumes a certain conception of justification that we should reject—that is, consequentialist justification. Should

we torture innocent humans and place such scenes on TV if we know that this will drastically reduce the crime rate? Many would not be sanguine about this idea.

Is it not better that these experiments take place in Britain where there are some controls rather than in other countries where there are few, if any, controls in place?

Well, maybe it is "better" (though some of us are not confident about that), but that hardly addresses the main point against invasive animal research. It is a bit like saying we should torture the innocent human only in Britain because there the torture will last only one hour, whereas in some other country the torture will last two hours. Just as we ought not to torture innocent humans, we ought not to conduct invasive research on animals. If we abolished such testing, there would be no issue of "controls."

Did not the Nazi government ban experiments on animals?

Heinrich Himmler, in his notorious Posen Speech of 1943, made a direct connection between the Final Solution and the Third Reich's supposedly enlightened laws regarding animal welfare: "We shall never be rough or heartless where it is not necessary; that is clear. We Germans, who are the only people in the world who have a decent attitude to animals, will also adopt a decent attitude to these human animals, but it is a crime against our own blood to worry about them."[2]

In practice, the various animal welfare laws that were enacted under Nazi rule were not as comprehensive in their application as they were in their drafting. Experimentation on animals (as well as humans) continued, especially for military purposes. Despite his rhetoric, Himmler explicitly authorized experiments on animals.[3] It is also the case, as just shown, that the Nazi protection of animals was a tool to justify a rather different approach to human beings.[4] The simple claim, then, that the Nazis banned experiments on animals is untrue. More importantly, it is irrelevant. Just because someone espousing an evil ideology agrees with you on one issue does not mean you are wrong on that issue. It is always possible to find dubious fellow travelers on any issue.

Animals lack the cognitive sophistication to have a sense of self or of time, and thus they cannot experience the higher-order suffering that humans can experience. Animals can experience pain, but humans—because of their higher-level cognitive capacities—experience suffering on top of that, so humans have more overall experience of pain. It follows that experimenting on animals is not morally comparable to experimenting on humans: we do not harm animals to the extent that we would harm humans subjected to the same treatment.

The problem with this argument is that having higher-level cognitive capacities often serves to mitigate rather than increase one's overall experience of pain. Humans can, for instance, understand why they are experiencing pain and when it will cease in ways that beings without higher-level cognitive capacities cannot. Thus, in fact, pain may sometimes be worse for animals than for us. Sahar Akhtar writes,

> Beings with only a rudimentary sense of time and of self may be at the greatest disadvantage from pain. They may possess enough self- and time-awareness to suffer from the anticipation and memory of pain, but not enough to be able to discount pain, choose to refrain from focusing on pain, form expectations about the cessation of pain, or to consider other interests or times without pain.[5]

Are not people who oppose animal experiments obligated to forgo any benefits that might come from such experimentation or any products that have been tested on animals?

There is certainly a strong case for avoiding cosmetics and other consumer products that have been tested on animals (within a specified time frame) as a means of supporting cruelty-free products or as a way of registering a protest. The same may be said of some other products that may help jolt pharmaceutical companies into rethinking current testing regimes. Many animal organizations have sponsored and organized such boycotts. But it would be impossible to stop using each and every product that has, at some time or another, been tested on animals for the simple reason that every commercial (and not even only commercial) product has been tested, at some time or another, on animals. The range of usage of animals is so extensive—including, but not limited to, fire-extinguisher substances, dyes, paints,

hair sprays, weaponry, poisons, radiation, plastics, agrichemicals, and even vegetable and herbal products—that no one can live entirely free of products once tested on animals. The notorious LD50 poisoning test—designed to ascertain the dose at which 50 percent of the animals to whom a substance is given die—has been carried out using water, the very stuff of life.

It should also be mentioned that experiments on human subjects have also resulted in some gains. These human subjects have ranged from children to people of color, soldiers, prisoners of war, and the mentally challenged.[6] For example, after World War II, the US government granted immunity to Japanese scientists who had performed grisly experiments on foreigners and prisoners of war in exchange for their research data on human adaptability to the environment.[7] It is more than likely that, directly or indirectly, such experiments on a variety of subjects have contributed to an increase in scientific knowledge of which most of us are the beneficiaries.

It does not follow then, of course, that even if these gains are ill-gotten, we should not make use of them. Even Nazi experiments on Jewish people (allegedly) produced some useful results. It is pusillanimous, therefore, to suggest, as have some scientists, that those who oppose animal experiments should forswear all its conceivably useful results. Since we live in a society where almost all usable substances—from soybeans to plain water—have been tested on animals, any attempt to do this would be impossible.

Lord Winston has proposed that medical products should be labeled as "tested on animals." Do you agree?

We welcome attempts at transparency and full disclosure. But if this is not just a publicity ploy or a backdoor attempt to gain public acquiescence of animal experiments, then there needs to be *full* disclosure. People should be informed not only as to whether animals were used but also as to what kinds of animals, how much suffering they had to undergo, what conditions they were kept in, and whether such experiments actually helped or hindered progress. By definition, one could not include all those animals—the vast majority—whose use has not led to a therapeutic product.

Moreover, why stop at "medical" products? The whole gamut of commercially produced items, including household products, cosmetics, chemicals, weaponry, poisons, plastics, and the rest, should also be labeled. What logical grounds can there be for insisting that only some products be labeled and not others—unless, of course, the real purpose of the proposal is to co-opt unsuspecting (and largely unaware) patients into a moral acquiescence of the virtues of animal testing in the absence of proper evidence and discussion?[8]

Notes

1. G. A. Jónsson, *The Image of God: Genesis 1:26–28 in a Century of Old Testament Research* (Lund, Sweden: Almqvist and Wiksell, 1988). Cited and discussed in A. Linzey, *Why Animal Suffering Matters*, 28–29.

2. H. Himmler, "Audio Excerpts from the Speech Given by Heinrich Himmler to SS Group Leaders in Posen, Occupied Poland" (1943), *The History Place*, accessed September 29, 2014, http://www.historyplace.com/worldwar2/holocaust/h-posen.htm; P. Longerich, *Heinrich Himmler* (Oxford: Oxford University Press, 2013).

3. J. Delarue, *The History of the Gestapo*, trans. M. Savill (London: Macdonald, 1964), 262.

4. B. Sax, *Animals in the Third Reich: Pets, Scapegoats, and the Holocaust* (New York: Continuum, 2000).

5. S. Akhtar, "Animal Pain and Welfare: Can Pain Sometimes Be Worse for Them Than for Us?" in *The Oxford Handbook of Animal Ethics*, ed. T. L. Beauchamp and R. G. Frey (Oxford: Oxford University Press, 2011), 510.

6. M. H. Pappworth, *Human Guinea Pigs: Experimentation on Man* (London: Penguin, 1969).

7. R. Whymant, "The Brutal Truth about Japan," *London Guardian*, August 14, 1982.

8. Winston, *Hansard*, col. 623. Cited and discussed in A. Linzey and Cohn, "Wanted: Full Disclosure."

Summary and Conclusions

THE DELIBERATE AND ROUTINE abuse of innocent, sentient animals involving harm, pain, suffering, stressful confinement, manipulation, trade, and death should be unthinkable. Yet animal experimentation is just that: the "normalization of the unthinkable."[1] It is estimated that 115.3 million animals are used in experiments worldwide per annum (see section 1.1). In terms of harm, pain, suffering, and death, this constitutes one of the major moral issues of our time.

This normalization flies in the face of what is now known about the extent and range of how animals can be harmed. The issue of the complexity of animal awareness, especially animal sentience (defined as the capacity to experience pain and pleasure), cannot be ignored. Unlike our forebears, we now know, as reasonably as we can know of humans, that animals (notably, mammals, birds, and reptiles) experience not only pain but also shock, fear, foreboding, trauma, anxiety, stress, distress, anticipation, and terror to a greater or lesser extent than humans do. This is the conclusion of many scientific books and scientific papers in peer-reviewed scientific journals (see section 1.2).

This normalization is buttressed by an overconfidence in animal experiments as a scientific technique. The current debate has been given new impetus by the new scientific critiques, especially in relation to the unreliability of animal experiments, the unpredictability of laboratory environments, the discordance between human diseases and "animal models"

of disease, interspecies differences in physiology and genetic function, and the development of more predictive human-based testing. The upshot is that it is no longer accurate or reasonable (if it ever was) to say that the only moral choice is between experimenting on animals and giving up on scientific progress (see section 1.3).

This normalization is based on the discredited idea that animals are just tools for human use, means to human ends, fungible items, and commodities that can be treated and dispensed with as humans think fit. During the last forty years, there has been considerable growth in intellectual work on the ethical status of animals. This new work has challenged the ideas that (1) humans should always have absolute priority in our moral thinking (moral anthropocentrism), (2) animals exist for human beings, to serve their interests and wants (instrumentalism), and (3) humans should be distinguished and separated from other animals in terms of a binary "them" and "us" (dualism), in which animals are inevitably denigrated (see section 1.4).

This normalization is challenged by new moral thinking that centers around three positions: (1) Individual animals have worth in themselves. Sentient beings (beings capable of pleasure and pain) are not just things, objects, machines, or tools; they have their own interior life that deserves respect. This view extends to sentients as individuals, not just as collectivities or as part of a community. (2) Given the conceding of sentience, there can be no rational grounds for not taking animals' sentience into account or for excluding individual animals from the same basic moral consideration that we extend to individual human beings. And (3) it follows that causing harm to individual sentient beings (except when it is for their own good—for example, in a veterinary operation), if not absolutely wrong, minimally requires strong moral justification. Indeed, some would argue that such acts of harming innocent (i.e., morally blameless) sentients is absolutely wrong (see section 1.4).

This normalization is belied by rational factors that should commend animals as subjects of special moral solicitude: (1) Animals cannot give or withhold their consent. (2) They cannot represent or vocalize their own interests. (3) They cannot understand or rationalize their suffering. (4) They are morally innocent or blameless. (5) They are vulnerable and relatively defenseless. These considerations make justifying harm to animals (like harm to human infants) especially difficult (see section 1.4).

This normalization is based on flawed moral arguments. We have examined three authoritative reports:

1. The UK government's Animal Procedures Committee (APC) argues that even if inflicting suffering is an "intrinsic" wrong, it may not be an "absolute" wrong if it can "be shown to be the lesser of two wrongs that we have to choose between."[2] But that argument supposes what is in need of justification—namely, that there is a direct or immediate choice to be made, which is what the APC (elsewhere) acknowledges is extremely rare: "in animal research we are rarely, if ever, presented with the stark situation in which we can save the life of a child by taking the life of an animal" (see section 1.5).[3]

2. The House of Lords Select Committee argues, inter alia, that humans are "unique" and that "therefore" they can utilize animals in experiments.[4] But this is a non sequitur. What has to be shown is how humans are unique and how that justifies inferior moral treatment of animals (see section 1.5).

3. The Weatherall Committee argues, inter alia, that we are justified in experimenting on animals because, in the case of a hospital fire, we would "intuitively" choose to save the

human patients.[5] But the conclusion does not follow. All that follows (if the results are to be believed) is that humans will in the given situation respond in that way. The scenario is by definition a limited crisis situation in which one has to make a direct choice. But to philosophize from that one situation, in which most people may choose to save fellow human beings, to a supposed duty to choose human beings in a wide range of normative situations, where there is no direct choice to be made, is logically fallacious (see section 1.5).

This normalization is reinforced by the massive institutionalization of animal experiments through (1) legislation, (2) institutional and establishment thinking, (3) public and private funding, (4) the partiality of the media, and (5) the language of experimentation, which obscures, justifies, exonerates, and minimizes what actually takes place in laboratories (see section 1.6). The result of these factors is, inter alia, moral stagnation and resistance to change. We cannot avoid the conclusion that animal experimentation represents the institutionalization of a preethical view of animals.

This normalization is augmented by a range of regulations and controls, which in reality do very little to protect animals and indeed often do the reverse. We have shown how inspection is flawed, how licensing creates a false sense of legitimacy, how supervised self-regulation in the EU is inadequate, how the Three Rs are not enforced, and how care and ethics committees do not provide a rigorous evaluation of proposals from an ethical perspective and are fundamentally flawed in not addressing the basic ethical issue. The Three Rs, which are endorsed by the EU and to which lip service is paid by governments (and which might have provided some impetus to change), are in practice massively underfunded, so that alternatives are the Cinderella of scientific research. Even where controls exist, we find them wanting (see section 1.7). This is confirmed by disturbing evidence provided by undercover investigations (see section 1.8).

This normalization is justified by the oft-repeated assertion that human interest requires such experiments, but it has to be questioned whether humans are ever benefited by the abuse of animals. Humans can be harmed by abuse of animals—for example, by desensitization, loss of empathy, habituation, and denial. We now know that there is a strong link between animal abuse and violence to human beings (see section 1.2). Also, the new scientific evidence must make us challenge the claim of utility, since we now know that many experiments have provided misleading or erroneous results (see section 1.3). In addition, the very logic that would justify experiments on animals also justifies the practice in relation to humans, and of course, prisoners of war, people of color, Jewish people, and children, among others, have been made subject to experimentation (see sections 1.4 and 1.5).

This normalizing of the unthinkable needs to be de-normalized and de-institutionalized. Ethical re-search techniques need to be fully institutionalized, and there should be a massive switch of funding to non-animal replacement techniques as a matter of urgency.

Notes

1. L. Peattie, "Normalizing the Unthinkable," *Bulletin of Atomic Scientists* (1984): 32–36.
2. APC, *Review of Cost-Benefit Assessment.*
3. Ibid.
4. House of Lords, *Select Committee.*
5. Weatherall et al., *Use of Non-Human Primates.*

Bibliography

Adam, C. L., P. Findlay, R. Aitken, J. Milne, and J. Wallace. "In Vivo Changes in Central and Peripheral Insulin Sensitivity in a Large Animal Model of Obesity." *Journal of Endocrinology* 153, no. 7 (2012): 3147–57.

Akhtar, A. *Animals and Public Health: Why Treating Animals Better Is Critical to Human Welfare.* Basingstoke, UK: Palgrave Macmillan, 2012.

———. "The Need to Include Animal Protection in Public Health Policies." *Journal of Public Health Policy* 34, no. 4 (2013): 549–59.

Akhtar, A., J. J. Pippin, and C. B. Sandusky. "Animal Models in Spinal Cord Injury: A Review." *Reviews in the Neurosciences* 19, no. 1 (2008): 47–60.

Akhtar, S. "Animal Pain and Welfare: Can Pain Sometimes Be Worse for Them Than for Us?" In *The Oxford Handbook of Animal Ethics*, edited by T. L. Beauchamp and R. G. Frey, 494–518. Oxford: Oxford University Press, 2011.

Allen, A. "Of Mice and Men: The Problems with Animal Testing." *Slate*, June 1, 2006. Accessed May 13, 2014. http://www.slate.com/articles/health_and_science/medical_examiner/2006/06/of_mice_or_men.html.

Alzheimer's Research UK. *Why Research Using Animals Can Help Defeat Dementia.* Accessed January 3, 2015. http://www.alzheimersresearchuk.org/siteFiles/resources/documents/ALZ_Animalbooklet_FINALSINGLEST.pdf.

Animal Procedures Committee (APC). *Report of the Animal Procedures Committee for 2003.* Home Office, 2004.

———. *Review of Cost-Benefit Assessment in the Use of Animals in Research.* 2003. Accessed September 29, 2014. https://www.gov.uk/government/uploads/system/uploads/attachment_data/file/119027/cost-benefit-assessment.pdf.

"Animal Rights and Wrongs." Editorial. *Nature* 470 (2011): 435. Accessed February 24, 2011. http://www.nature.com/nature/journal/v470/n7335/full/470435a.html.

Animals in Science Committee (ASC). *Lessons to Be Learnt, for Duty Holders and the Regulator, from Reviews and Investigations into Non-Compliance.* 2014. Accessed January 4, 2015. https://www.gov.uk/government/uploads/system/uploads/attachment_data/file/326003/ASClessonsToBeLearnt2Jul14.pdf.

Animals in Science Regulation Unit (ASRU). *Annual Report.* Home Office, 2011.

———. *Annual Report.* Home Office, 2012.

Animals (Scientific Procedures) Act 1986. London. Accessed September 26, 2014. http://www.legislation.gov.uk/ukpga/1986/14/contents.

Animals Scientific Procedures Inspectorate. *A Review on the Issues and Concerns Raised in the Report, "The Ugly Truth—A BUAV Investigation at Wickham Laboratories."* 2010. Accessed March 1, 2015. https://www.gov.uk/government/uploads/system/uploads/attachment_data/file/116820/wickham-laboratories.pdf.

Aquinas, T. *Summa contra Gentiles.* In *Basic Writings of Saint Thomas Aquinas.* Vol. 2. Translated by A. C. Pegis. New York: Random House, 1945.

———. *Summa Theologiae.* Edited by the English Dominican Fathers. New York: Benzinger Brothers, 1918.

Archibald, K., and R. Coleman. "How Human Biology Can Prevent Drug Deaths." *New Scientist* 2895 (2012). Accessed November 27, 2014. http://www.newscientist.com/article/mg21628950.200-how-human-biology-can-prevent-drug-deaths.html#.VHcTvzGsWSp.

Aristotle. "Nicomachean Ethics." In *The Works of Aristotle.* Translated by W. D. Ross. London: Oxford University Press, 1915.

———. *The Politics.* Translated by T. A. Sinclair. London: Penguin, 1985.

Ascione, F. R., and P. Arkow, eds. *Child Abuse, Domestic Violence, and Animal Abuse.* West Lafayette, IN: Purdue University Press, 1999.

Association of the British Pharmaceutical Industry. *Animals and Medicines Research: Animal Research for the Discovery and Development of New Medicines.* London, 2011. Accessed May 9, 2014. http://www.abpi.org.uk/our-work/library/medical-disease/Documents/animals-medicines-research.pdf.

Attarwala, H. "TGN1412: From Discovery to Disaster." *Journal of Young Pharmacists* 2, no. 3 (2010): 332–36.

Badawy, A. B. A., S. Bano, and A. Steptoe. "Tryptophan in Alcoholism Treatment I: Kynurenine Metabolites Inhibit the Rat Liver Mitochondrial Low Km Aldehyde Dehydrogenase Activity, Elevate Blood Acetaldehyde Concentration and Induce Aversion to Alcohol." *Alcohol and Alcoholism* 46, no. 6 (2011): 651–60.

Bagot, M. "Inside Monkey Testing Centre Where Marmosets Are Given Brain Damage to Help Treat Parkinson's." *Daily Mirror*, May 28, 2014. http://www.mirror.co.uk/news/uk-news/see-inside-monkey-testing-centre-3618664#ixzz34DnWrccv.

Bailey, J. "An Assessment of the Role of Chimpanzees in AIDS Vaccine Research." *Alternatives to Laboratory Animals* 36, no. 4 (2008): 381–428.

Bailey, J., M. Thew, and M. Balls. "An Analysis of the Use of Animal Models in Predicting Human Toxicology and Drug Safety." *Alternatives to Laboratory Animals* 42, no. 3 (2014): 181–99.

———. "An Analysis of the Use of Dogs in Predicting Human Toxicology and Drug Safety." *Alternatives to Laboratory Animals* 41, no. 5 (2013): 335–50.

Baker, S. *Picturing the Beast: Animals, Identity, and Representation.* Chicago: University of Illinois Press, 1993.

Balcombe, J. P., N. D. Barnard, and C. Sandusky. "Laboratory Routines Cause Animal Stress." *Contemporary Topics in Laboratory Animal Science* 43 (2004): 42–51.

Baldwin, A., and M. Bekoff. "Too Stressed to Work." *New Scientist* 194 (2007): 24.

Bandura, A. "Moral Disengagement in the Perpetration of Inhumanities." *Personality and Social Psychology Review* 3 (1999): 193–209. Accessed November 27, 2014. http://www.uky.edu/~eushe2/Bandura/Bandura1999PSPR.pdf.

———. "Selective Moral Disengagement in the Exercise of Moral Agency." *Journal of Moral Education* 31, no. 2 (2002): 101–19. Accessed November 27, 2014. https://historicalunderbelly.files.wordpress.com/2009/11/bandura_moraldisengagement1.pdf.

Banner, M. "Ethics, Society and Policy: A Way Forward." In *Animal Biotechnology and Ethics*, edited by A. Holland and A. Johnson, 325–29. London: Chapman and Hall, 1998.

BBC Two. *Newsnight*, May 23, 2002. Accessed February 10, 2015. http://news.bbc.co.uk/1/hi/programmes/newsnight/2005130.stm.

Beirne, P. "For a Nonspeciesist Criminology: Animal Abuse as an Object of Study." *Criminology* 37, no. 1 (1999): 117–47.

Benton, T. "Rights and Justice on a Shared Planet: More Rights or New Relations?" *Theoretical Criminology* 2, no. 2 (1998): 149–75.

Bernstein, M. *On Moral Considerability: An Essay on Who Morally Matters.* Oxford: Oxford University Press, 1998.

———. *Without a Tear: Our Tragic Relationship with Animals.* Chicago: University of Illinois Press, 2004.

Blair, T. *A Journey.* London: Hutchinson, 2010.

British Heart Foundation. *Animals and Heart Research.* Leaflet. 2010.

British Pharmacological Society. "Why Do We Use Animals in Scientific Research?" 2013. Accessed January 3, 2015. http://www.bps.ac.uk/details/pageContent/855663/Why_do_we_use_animals_in_research.html?cat=bps12aae254a00.

British Union for the Abolition of Vivisection (BUAV). *Briefing Paper on the Primate Trade, Role of Shamrock* (Great Britain) Ltd., and Hazleton UK. 1992.

———. "BUAV Congratulates UK Veterinary Agency for Removing Obsolete Batch Animal Tests." *Politics.co.uk*, July 13, 2011. Accessed March 1, 2015. http://www.politics.co.uk/opinion-formers/buav-british-union-for-the-abolition-of-vivisection/article/buav-congratulates-uk-veterinary-agency-for-removing-obsolet.

———. "A BUAV Investigation at Harlan UK." Unpublished report, 1999.

———. "A BUAV Investigation at Wickham Research Laboratories." Unpublished report, 1993.

———. "A BUAV Investigation at Wickham Research Laboratories." Unpublished report, 2009.

———. "A BUAV Investigation into Marmoset Neuroscience Research at Cambridge University." Unpublished report, 2002.

———. "BUAV Report to the Home Office: Animal Experiments at Imperial College London." Unpublished report, 2013.

Brown Committee. "The Brown Report: Independent Investigation into Animal Research at Imperial College London." 2013. Accessed January 4, 2015. http://brownreport.info/wp-content/uploads/2014/02/The-Brown-Report.pdf.

———. "Independent Investigation into Animal Research at Imperial College Published." Press release, 2013. Accessed January 4, 2015. http://brownreport.info/wp-content/uploads/2014/02/Brownreportpressrelease.pdf.

Bruins, M. J., M. A. M. Vente-Spreeuwenberg, C. H. Smits, and L. G. J. Frenken. "Black Tea Reduces Diarrhoea Prevalence but Decreases Growth Performance in Enterotoxigenic Escherichia Coli-Infected Post-Weaning Piglets." *Journal of Animal Physiology and Animal Nutrition* 95, no. 3 (2011): 388–98.

Brydges, N. M., L. Hall, R. Nicolson, M. C. Holmes, and J. Hall. "The Effects of Juvenile Stress on Anxiety, Cognitive Bias, and Decision Making in Adulthood: A Rat Model." *PLoS One* 7, no. 10 (2012): e48143.

Carruthers, P. "Animal Mentality: Its Character, Extent, and Moral Significance." In *The Oxford Handbook of Animal Ethics*, edited by T. L. Beauchamp and R. G. Frey, 373–406. Oxford: Oxford University Press, 2011.

———. "Brute Experience." *Journal of Philosophy* 86, no. 5 (1989): 258–69.

Cavalieri, P. "The Animal Debate: A Reexamination." In *In Defense of Animals: The Second Wave*, edited by P. Singer, 54–68. Malden, MA: Blackwell, 2006.

Center for Responsive Politics. "Pharmaceuticals/Health Products: Long-Term Contribution Trends." Accessed May 9, 2014. http://www.opensecrets.org/industries/totals.php?cycle=2014&ind=H04.

Charles River Laboratories. "Basic Research." Accessed June 23, 2014. http://www.criver.com/products-services/basic-research.

———. "Ocular Toxicology." Accessed June 23, 2014. http://www.criver.com/products-services/safety-assessment/toxicology/ocular-toxicology.

Cherednichenko, G., R. Zhang, R. A. Bannister, V. Timofeyev, N. Li, E. B. Fritsch, W. Feng, et al. "Triclosan Impairs Excitation-Contraction Coupling and Ca^{2+} Dynamics in Striated Muscle." *Proceedings of the National Academy of Sciences* 109, no. 35 (2012): 14158–63.

Chomsky, N. *Chronicles of Dissent: Interviews with David Barsamian.* Monroe, ME: Common Courage, 1992.

———. *Understanding Power: The Indispensable Chomsky.* Edited by P. R. Mitchell and J. Schoeffel. London: Vintage, 2003.

Clemedson, C., E. McFarlane-Abdulla, M. Andersson, F. A. Barile, M. C. Calleja, C. Chesne, R. Clothier, et al. "MEIC Evaluation of Acute Systemic Toxicity; Part II: In Vitro Results from 68 Toxicity Assays Used to Test the First 30 Reference Chemicals and a Comparative Cytotoxicity Analysis." *Alternatives to Laboratory Animals* 24, Suppl. 1 (1996): 273–311.

Clemedson, C. E., F. A. Barile, C. Chesne, M. Cottin, M. Curren, B. Eckwall, M. Ferro, et al. "MEIC Evaluation of Acute Systemic Toxicity. Part VII. Prediction of Human Toxicity by Results from Testing of the First 30 Reference Chemicals with 27 Further In Vitro Assay." *Alternatives to Laboratory Animals* 28 (2000): 161–200.

Coates, P. J., M. V. Appleyard, K. Murray, C. Ackland, J. Gardner, D. C. Brown, D. J. Adamson, et al. "Differential Contextual Responses of Normal Human Breast Epithelium to Ionizing Radiation in a Mouse Xenograft Model." *Cancer Research* 70, no. 23 (2010): 9808–15.

Cohen, B. J., and F. M. Loew. "Laboratory Animal Medicine: Historical Perspectives." In *Laboratory Animal Medicine*, edited by J. G. Fox, B. J. Cohen, and F. M. Loew, 1–18. New York: Academic Press, 1984.

Creamer, J. "Freedom of Information." In A. Linzey, *Global Guide,* 186–87. Chicago: University of Illinois Press, 2013.

Curry, S. H. "Why Have So Many Drugs with Stellar Results in Laboratory Stroke Models Failed in Clinical Trials? A Theory Based on Allometric Relationships." *Annals of the New York Academy of Sciences* 993 (2003): 69–74.

Darling, F., and K. P. Dolan. "Animals in Cancer Research." *AnimalResearch.Info,* 2007. Accessed January 3, 2015. http://www.animalresearch.info/en/medical-advances/articles-lectures/animals-cancer-research/.

Darwin, C. *The Expression of the Emotions in Man and Animals.* London: John Murray, 1872. Accessed August 11, 2014. http://darwin-online.org.uk/content/frameset?itemID=F1142&viewtype=side&pageseq=1.

DeGrazia, D. *Taking Animals Seriously: Mental Life and Moral Status.* Cambridge: Cambridge University Press, 1996.

Delarue, J. *The History of the Gestapo.* Translated by M. Savill. London: Macdonald, 1964.

Derrida, J. "The Animal That Therefore I Am (More to Follow)." In *Animal Philosophy: Essential Readings in Continental Thought,* edited by P. Atterton and M. Calarco, 113–28. London: Continuum, 2004.

———. "Violence against Animals." In *For What Tomorrow . . . a Dialogue,* edited by J. Derrida and E. Roudinesco, 62–76. Translated by J. Fort. Stanford, CA: Stanford University Press, 2004.

Dirnagl, U. "Bench to Bedside: The Quest for Quality in Experimental Stroke Research." *Journal of Cerebral Blood Flow and Metabolism* 26 (2006): 1465–78.

Dolan, S., M. D. Gunn, C. Crossan, and A. M. Nolan. "Activation of Metabotropic Glutamate Receptor 7 in Spinal Cord Inhibits Pain and Hyperalgesia in a Novel Formalin Model in Sheep." *Behavioural Pharmacology* 22 (2011): 582–88.

Dorri, M., S. Shahrabi, and A. Navabazam. "Comparing the Effects of Chlorhexidine and Persica on Alveolar Bone Healing following Tooth Extraction in Rats: A Randomised Controlled Trial." *Clinical Oral Investigation* 16, no. 1 (2010): 25–31.

Dunayer, J. *Animal Equality: Language and Liberation.* Derwood, MD: Ryce, 2001.

Duncker, S. C., D. Philippe, C. Martin-Paschoud, M. Moser, A. Mercenier, and S. Nutten. "*Nigella sativa* (Black Cumin) Seed Extract Alleviates Symptoms of Allergic Diarrhoea in Mice, Involving Opioid Receptors." *PLoS One* 7, no. 6 (2012): e39841.

Dunstan, G. R. *The Artifice of Ethics.* London: SCM, 1974.

European Chemicals Agency (ECHA). *Guidance in a Nutshell: Registration.* 2013. Accessed January 3, 2015. http://echa.europa.eu/documents/10162/13632/nutshell_guidance_registration_en.pdf.

———. "What about Animal Testing?" Accessed May 9, 2014. http://echa.europa.eu/chemicals-in-our-life/animal-testing-under-reach.

European Commission. *Council Directive 86/609/EEC of 24 November 1986 on the Approximation of Laws, Regulations, and Administrative Provisions of the Member States regarding the Protection of Animals Used for Experimental and Other Scientific Purposes.* 1986.

———. *Eurobarometer Science and Technology Report.* 2010. Accessed May 9, 2014. http://ec.europa.eu/public_opinion/archives/ebs/ebs_340_en.pdf.

———. *Glossary of Terms and Guidelines for Statistical Tables by Member States.* XI/411/97. 1997.

European Parliament. *Directive 2010/63/EU of the European Parliament and of the Council of 22 September 2010 on the Protection of Animals Used for Scientific Purposes.* 2010. Accessed January 3, 2015. http://eur-lex.europa.eu/legal-content/EN/TXT/PDF/?uri=CELEX:32010L0063&from=EN.

Fairclough, N. *Discourse and Social Change.* Cambridge: Polity Press, 1992.

UNIVERSITY OF WINCHESTER
LIBRARY

———. *Language and Power.* 2nd ed. Harlow, UK: Pearson Education, 2001.

Flynn, C. P. "Examining the Links between Animal Abuse and Human Violence." *Crime, Law, and Social Change* (Special issue: Animal Abuse and Criminology) 55 (2011): 453–68.

———. "A Sociological Analysis of Animal Abuse." In *The International Handbook on Animal Abuse and Cruelty: Theory, Research and Application*, edited by F. R. Ascione, 155–74. West Lafayette, IN: Purdue University Press, 2008.

Freiberg, A. *The Tools of Regulation.* New South Wales, Australia: Federation Press, 2010.

Frey, R. G. *Rights, Killing, and Suffering.* Oxford: Basil Blackwell, 1983.

Gaffney, J. "The Relevance of Animal Experimentation to Roman Catholic Methodology." In *Animal Sacrifices: Religious Perspectives on the Use of Animals in Science*, edited by T. Regan. Philadelphia, PA: Temple University Press, 1986.

Galgut, E. "Raising the Bar in the Justification of Animal Research." *Journal of Animal Ethics* 5, no. 1 (2015): 5–19.

Garner, J., S. Watts, C. Parry, J. Bird, G. Cooper, and E. Kirkman. "Prolonged Permissive Hypotensive Resuscitation Is Associated with Poor Outcome in Primary Blast Injury with Controlled Haemorrhage." *Annals of Surgery* 251, no. 6 (2010): 1131–39.

Garner, J. P. "Stereotypies and Other Abnormal Repetitive Behaviors: Potential Impact on Validity, Reliability, and Replicability of Scientific Outcomes." *Institute for Laboratory Animal Research Journal* 46, no. 2 (2005): 106–17.

Garner, R. *Animal Ethics.* Cambridge, UK: Polity, 2005.

Garrett, J. R. "The Ethics of Animal Research: An Overview of the Debate." In *The Ethics of Animal Research: Exploring the Controversy*, edited by J. R. Garrett. Cambridge, MA: MIT Press, 2012.

Gee, J. P. *Social Linguistics and Literacies: Ideology in Discourses.* 2nd ed. London: Routledge, 1996.

Ghooi, R. B. "The Nuremberg Code—A Critique." *Perspectives on Clinical Research* 2, no. 2 (2011): 72–76.

Godlee, F. "How Predictive and Productive Is Animal Research?" *British Medical Journal* 348, no. 3719 (2014).

Goldacre, B. *Bad Pharma: How Medicine Is Broken, and How We Can Fix It.* London: Fourth Estate, 2012.

Gombay, A. *Descartes.* Oxford: Blackwell, 2007.

Goodman, J. R., B. A. Casey, and E. Cherry. "Mounting Opposition to Vivisection." *Contexts* 11, no. 2 (2012): 68–69.

Grodin, M. A., and L. H. Glantz. *Children as Research Subjects: Science, Ethics and Law.* Oxford: Oxford University Press, 1994.

Gross, D. M. "Defending the Humanities with Charles Darwin's *The Expression of the Emotions in Man and Animals* (1872)." *Critical Inquiry* 37 (2010): 34–59. Accessed August 11, 2014. http://iicas.ucsd.edu/_files/conferences/science-emotions/abstracts/Gross_abstract.pdf.

Guerrini, A. "Natural History, Natural Philosophy, and Animals, 1600–1800." In *A Cultural History of Animals in the Age of Enlightenment*, edited by M. Senior, 121–44. Oxford: Berg, 2007.

Gullone, E. *Animal Cruelty, Antisocial Behaviour, and Aggression: More Than a Link.* Basingstoke, UK: Palgrave Macmillan, 2012.

Haldane, E. S., and G. R. T. Ross, eds. *Discourse on Method in Philosophical Works of Descartes.* London: Cambridge University Press, 1950.

Halliday, M. A. K., and C. Matthiessen. *An Introduction to Functional Grammar.* 3rd ed. London: Hodder Arnold, 2004.

Hampton, T. "Targeted Cancer Therapies Lagging: Better Trial Design Could Boost Success Rate." *Journal of the American Medical Association* 296, no. 16 (2006): 1951–52.

Hanke, T. "Lessons from TGN1412." *The Lancet* 368, no. 9547 (2006): 1569–70.

Hansen, L. A. "Institution Animal Care and Use Committees Need Greater Ethical Diversity." *Journal of Medical Ethics* 39, no. 3 (2013): 188–90.

Hansen, L. A., J. R. Goodman, and A. Chanda. "Analysis of Animal Research Ethics Committee Membership at American Institutions." *Animals* 2, no. 1 (2012): 68–75.

Hare, R. M. *Moral Thinking: Its Levels, Method, and Point.* Oxford: Oxford University Press, 1981.

Hart, P. C., C. L. Bergner, B. D. Dufour, A. N. Smolinsky, R. J. Egan, J. L. LaPorte, and A. V. Kalueff. "Analysis of Abnormal Repetitive Behaviors in Experimental Animal Models." In *Translational Neuroscience in Animal Research: Advancement, Challenges, and Research Ethics*, edited by J. E. Warnik and A. V. Kalueff, 71–82. New York: Nova Science, 2009.

Hart, W., D. Albarracín, A. H. Eagly, I. Brechan, M. Lindberg, K. Lee, and L. Merrill. "Feeling Validated versus Being Correct: A Meta-Analysis of Selective Exposure to Information." *Psychological Bulletin* 135 (2009): 555–88.

Health Research Extension Act of 1985. Public Law 99–158. Accessed May 9, 2014. http://grants.nih.gov/grants/olaw/references/hrea1985.htm.

Heffernan, M. *Willful Blindness: Why We Ignore the Obvious at Our Peril.* New York: Walker, 2011.

Himmler, H. "Audio Excerpts from the Speech Given by Heinrich Himmler to SS Group Leaders in Posen, Occupied Poland." 1943. *The History Place.* Accessed September 29, 2014. http://www.historyplace.com/worldwar2/holocaust/h-posen.htm.

Hobbes, T. "De Cive [1642]." In *The English Works of Thomas Hobbes of Malmesbury.* Vol. 2. Edited by W. Molesworth. London: John Bohn, 1841.

Hoggan, G. Letter. *Morning Post*, February 2, 1875.

Home Office. *Animals in Science Regulation Unit: Annual Report 2013.* London, 2014.

———. *Animals (Scientific Procedures) Act 1986 Amendment Regulations 2012.* London, 2012. Accessed February 6, 2015. https://www.gov.uk/government/uploads/system/uploads/attachment_data/file/265691/Animals_Scientific_Procedures_Act_1986.pdf.

———. *Annual Statistics of Scientific Procedures on Living Animals Great Britain 2012.* London, 2012.

———. *Annual Statistics of Scientific Procedures on Living Animals Great Britain 2013.* London, 2013.

———. *Code of Practice for the Housing and Care of Animals Used in Scientific Procedures.* London, 1989.

———. *Consultation on the Review of Section 24 of the Animals (Scientific Procedures) Act 1986.* London, 2014.

———. *Guidance on the Operation of the Animals (Scientific Procedures) Act 1986.* HC321. March 23, 2000. London: Stationery Office. Accessed September 26, 2014. https://www.gov.uk/government/uploads/system/uploads/attachment_data/file/228542/0321.pdf.

———. *Report of ASRU Investigation into Compliance.* Ref: A8(1). London, 2014.

Horrobin, D. F. "Modern Biomedical Research: An Internally Self-Consistent Universe with Little Contact with Medical Reality?" *Nature Reviews Drug Discovery* 2 (2003): 151–54.

House of Lords. *Select Committee on Animals in Scientific Procedures, Volume 1—Report.* London, 2002. Accessed September 29, 2014. http://www.publications.parliament.uk/pa/ld200102/ldselect/ldanimal/150/150.pdf.

Hume, D. *Enquiry concerning the Principles of Morals.* Edited by L. A. Selby-Brigge. Oxford: Clarendon Press, 1902. Originally published in 1751.

Hunt, P. A., C. Lawson, M. Gieske, B. Murdoch, H. Smith, A. Marre, T. Hassold, and C. A. VandeVoort. "Bisphenol A Alters Early Oogenesis and Follicle Formation in the Fetal Ovary of the Rhesus Monkey." *Proceedings of the National Academy of Sciences* 109, no. 43 (2012): 17525–30.

Hursthouse, R. "Virtue Ethics and the Treatment of Animals." In *The Oxford Handbook of Animal Ethics*, edited by T. L. Beauchamp and R. G. Frey, 119–43. Oxford: Oxford University Press, 2011.

Hussain, W., P. M. Patel, R. Chowdury, C. Cabo, E. J. Ciaccio, M. J. Lab, H. S. Duffy, A. L. Wit, and N. S. Peters. "The Renin-Angiotensin System Mediates the Effects of Stretch on Conduction Velocity, Connexin43 Expression, and Redistribution in Intact Ventricle." *Journal of Cardiovascular Electrophysiology* 21, no. 11 (2010): 1276–83.

Irving, D. N. "Need to Know: Nuremberg Code, Declaration of Helsinki, Belmont Report, OHRP." *Life Issues*, June 27, 2013. Accessed November 7, 2014. http://www.lifeissues.net/writers/irv/irv_214needtoknow.html.

John Paul II. *Veritatis Splendor: Encyclical Letter.* London: Catholic Truth Society, 1993.

Jónsson, G. A. *The Image of God: Genesis 1:26–28 in a Century of Old Testament Research.* Lund, Sweden: Almqvist and Wiksell, 1988.

Jorgensen, M., and L. Phillips. *Discourse Analysis as Theory and Method.* London: Sage, 2002.

Kamberov, Y. G., S. Wang, J. Tan, P. Gerbault, A. Wark, L. Tan, Y. Yang, et al. "Modelling Recent Human Evolution in Mice by Expression of a Selected EDAR Variant." *Cell* 152 (2013): 691–702.

Kant, I. *Lectures on Ethics: Duties towards Animals and Other Spirits.* Translated by L. Infield. New York: Harper and Row, 1963.

———. *Metaphysics of Morals.* Translated by J. Ladd. New York: Bobbs-Merrill, 1965.

Kean, H. *Animal Rights: Political and Social Change in Britain since 1800.* London: Reaktion Books, 1998.

Knight, A. *The Costs and Benefits of Animal Experiments.* Basingstoke, UK: Palgrave Macmillan, 2011.

———. "Weighing the Costs and Benefits of Animal Experiments." In *Altex Proceedings of the 8th World Congress on Alternatives and Animal Use in the Life Sciences, Montreal 2011,* 289–94. Altex Proceedings, 2012.

Korsgaard, C. "Interacting with Animals: A Kantian Account." *The Oxford Handbook of Animal Ethics*, edited by T. L. Beauchamp and R. G. Frey, 91–118. Oxford: Oxford University Press, 2011.

Kuhn, T. S. *The Structure of Scientific Revolutions.* 15th anniv. ed. Chicago: University of Chicago Press, 2012.

Kurth, T. B., F. Dell'Accio, V. Crouch, A. Augello, P. T. Sharpe, and C. De Bari. "Functional Mesenchymal Stem Cell Niches in Adult Mouse Knee Joint Synovium in Vivo." *Arthritis and Rheumatology* 63, no. 5 (2011): 1289–1300.

LaFollette, H. "Animal Experimentation in Biomedical Research." In *The Oxford Handbook of Animal Ethics*, edited by T. L. Beauchamp and R. G. Frey, 796–825. Oxford: Oxford University Press, 2011.

LaFollette, H., and N. Shanks. "Animal Models in Biomedical Research: Some Epistemological Worries." *Public Affairs Quarterly* 7 (1993): 113–30.

———. *Brute Science: Dilemmas of Animal Experimentation.* London: Routledge, 1996.

Lansbury, C. *The Old Brown Dog: Women, Workers, and Vivisection in Edwardian England.* Madison: University of Wisconsin Press, 1985.

Lederer, S. *Subjected to Science: Human Experimentation in America before the Second World War.* Baltimore, MD: Johns Hopkins University Press, 1995.

Ledford, H. "Flaws Found in Mouse Model of Diabetes." *Nature,* May 28, 2009. Accessed May 13, 2014. http://www.nature.com/news/2009/090528/full/news.2009.523.html.

Lenz, W. "Thalidomide and Congenital Anomalies." *The Lancet* 279, no. 7219 (1962): 45–46.

Lewis, C. S. *Vivisection.* Boston: New England Anti-Vivisection Society, 1947.

Lewis, D. Y., and R. R. Brett. "Activity-Based Anorexia in C57/BL6 Mice: Effects of the Phytocannaboid, Delta-9-Tetrahydrocannabinol (THC) and the Anandamide Analogue, OMDM-2." *European Neuropsychopharmacology* 20 (2010): 622–31.

Linzey, A. *Animal Theology.* London: SCM Press, 1994.

———. *Creatures of the Same God: Explorations in Animal Theology.* Winchester, UK: Winchester University Press, 2007.

———, ed. *The Global Guide to Animal Protection.* Chicago: University of Illinois Press, 2013.

———, ed. *The Link between Animal Abuse and Human Violence.* Brighton, UK: Sussex Academic Press, 2009.

———. *Why Animal Suffering Matters: Philosophy, Theology, and Practical Ethics.* Oxford: Oxford University Press, 2009.

Linzey, A., and D. Yamamoto. *Animals on the Agenda: Questions about Animals for Theology and Ethics.* London: SCM Press, 1998.

Linzey, A., and P. B. Clarke. *Animal Rights: A Historical Anthology.* New York: Columbia University Press, 2004.

Linzey, A., and P. N. Cohn. "Wanted: Full Disclosure." Editorial. *Journal of Animal Ethics* 2, no. 2 (2012): v–vii.

Linzey, A., and P. Waldau. "Speciesism." In *Dictionary of Ethics, Theology, and Society,* edited by P. B. Clarke and A. Linzey, 788–92. London: Routledge, 1996.

Linzey, C. "Animals in Catholic Thought: A New Sensitivity?" In *The Animals in Us: We in Animals,* edited by S. Wróbel, 187–202. Frankfurt, Germany: Peter Lang, 2014.

Lockwood, R., and A. W. Church. "An FBI Perspective on Animal Cruelty: Alan C. Brantley Interviewed by Randall Lockwood and Ann W. Church." In *The Link between Animal Abuse and Human Violence,* edited by A. Linzey, 223–27. Brighton, UK: Sussex Academic Press, 2009.

Longerich, P. *Heinrich Himmler.* Oxford: Oxford University Press, 2013.

Lutz, C., A. Well, and M. Novak. "Stereotypic and Self-Injurious Behavior in Rhesus Macaques: A Survey and Retrospective Analysis of Environment and Early Experience." *American Journal of Primatology* 60, no. 1 (2003): 1–15.

MacKenzie, C. "The Importance of Relational Autonomy and Capabilities for an Ethics of Vulnerability." In *Vulnerability: New Essays in Ethics and Feminist Philosophy,* edited by C. MacKenzie, W. Rogers, and S. Dodds, 33–59. Oxford: Oxford University Press, 2014.

Mahaffy, J. P. *Descartes.* London: Blackwood, 1901.

Mason, P. *The Brown Dog Affair: The Story of a Monument That Divided the Nation.* London: Two Sevens, 1997.

MatTek Corporation. Reports presented at the annual Society of Toxicology meeting in Seattle, March 16–20, 2008. Accessed July 20, 2008. http://www.mattek.com.

Mayor, S. "Researchers Refine In Vitro Test That Will Reduce Risk of 'First in Humans' Drug Trial." *British Medical Journal* 337 (2008): 3016.

McBride, W. G. "Thalidomide and Congenital Abnormalities." Letter. *The Lancet* 278, no. 7216 (1961): 1358.

McMillan, F. D. "What Dictionary Are Animal Researchers Using?" *Journal of Animal Ethics* 2, no. 1 (2012): 1–5.

Midgley, M. *The Myths We Live By.* London: Routledge, 2004.

Mitchell, L. R. "Nonhumans and the Ideology of Purpose." *Anthrozoos* 25, no. 4 (2012): 491–502.

Mogil, J. S., S. G. Wilson, K. Bon, S. E. Lee, K. Chung, P. Raber, J. O. Pieper, et al. "Heritability of Nociception I: Responses of 11 Inbred Mouse Strains on 12 Measures of Nociception." *Pain* 80, no. 1–2 (1999): 67–82.

Molloy, C. *Popular Media and Animals.* Basingstoke, UK: Palgrave Macmillan, 2011.

Morgan, K. N., and C. T. Tromborg. "Sources of Stress in Captivity." *Applied Animal Behaviour Science* 102, no. 3–4 (2007): 262–302.

Moss, S. *Birds Britannia: Why the British Fell in Love with Birds.* London: Collins, 2011.

Mumford, H., C. J. Docx, M. E. Price, A. C. Green, J. E. H. Tattersall, and S. J. Armstrong. "Human Plasma-Derived BuChE as a Stoichiometric Bioscavenger for Treatment of Nerve Agent Poisoning." *Chemico-Biological Interactions* 203, no. 1 (2013): 160–66.

National Commission for the Protection of Human Subjects of Biomedical and Behavioural Research. *The Belmont Report: Ethical Principles and Guidelines for the Protection of Human Subjects of Research.* US Department of Health and Human Services, 1979. Accessed November 27, 2014. http://www.hhs.gov/ohrp/humansubjects/guidance/belmont.html.

Nelson, S. L. "The Connection between Animal Abuse and Family Violence: A Selected Annotated Bibliography." *Animal Law Review* 17, no. 2 (2011): 369–414.

Nibert, D. *Animal Rights/Human Rights: Entanglement of Oppression and Liberation.* Plymouth, UK: Rowman and Littlefield, 2002.

Niu, Y., B. Shen, Y. Cui, Y. Chen, J. Wang, L. Wang, Y. Kang, et al. "Generation of Gene-Modified Cynomolgus Monkey via Cas9/RNA-Mediated Gene Targeting in One-Cell Embryos." *Cell* 156, no. 4 (2014): 836–43.

Nuffield Council on Bioethics. *The Ethics of Research involving Animals,* 2005. Accessed May 13, 2014. http://nuffieldbioethics.org/wp-content/uploads/The-ethics-of-research-involving-animals-full-report.pdf.

"Nuremberg Code, The." Accessed January 2, 2015. http://www.hhs.gov/ohrp/archive/nurcode.html. Originally published in *Trials of War Criminals before the Nuremberg Military Tribunals under Control Council Law No. 10,* vol. 2, 181–82. Washington, DC: US Government Printing Office, 1949.

Omoe, H. "Recent Trends in Animal Experimentation in Japan: On the Revision and Implementation of the Law for the Humane Treatment and Management of Animals." *Quarterly Review* 21 (2006): 13–31.

Online Investor. "Company Spotlight—Charles River Laboratories (NYSE: CRL)." 2008. Accessed May 9, 2014. http://www.theonlineinvestor.com/orphans/articles/charles_river_laboratories.html.

Oram, M. W. "Visual Stimulation Decorrelates Neuronal Activity." *Journal of Neurophysiology* 105 (2011): 942–57.

Palazzini, P., ed. *Dictionary of Moral Theology.* London: Burns and Oates, 1962.

Palfreyman, M. G., V. Charles, and J. Blander. "The Importance of Using Human-Based Models in Gene and Drug Discovery." *Drug Discovery World,* 2002. Accessed May 13, 2014. http://www.ddw-online.com/fall-2002/p148472-the-importance-of-using-human-based-models-in-gene-and-drug-discovery.html.

Pappworth, M. H. *Human Guinea Pigs: Experimentation on Man.* London: Penguin, 1969.

Passingham, R. E. "The Need for Research on Non-Human Primates in Cognitive Neuroscience." *AnimalResearch.Info,*

2006. Accessed January 3, 2015. http://www.animalresearch. info/en/medical-advances/articles-lectures/the-need-research-non-human-primates-cognitive-neuroscience/.

Peattie, L. "Normalizing the Unthinkable." *Bulletin of Atomic Scientists* (1984): 32–36.

Peggs, K. *Experiments, Animal Bodies, and Human Values.* London: Routledge, 2017.

Peggs, K., and B. Smart. "Nonhuman Animal Suffering: Critical Pedagogy and Practical Animal Ethics." In *Society and Animals* (forthcoming).

Perel, P., I. Roberts, E. Sena, P. Wheble, C. Briscoe, P. Sandercock, M. Macleod, L. E. Mignini, P. Jayaram, and K. S. Khan. "Comparison of Treatment Effects between Animal Experiments and Clinical Trials: Systematic Review." *British Medical Journal* 334, no. 7586 (2007): 197.

Pippin, J. "Animal Research in Medical Sciences: Seeking a Convergence of Science, Medicine, and Animal Law." *South Texas Law Review* 54 (2013): 469–511.

Plous, S., and H. Herzog. "Reliability of Protocol Reviews for Animal Research." *Science* 293 (2001): 608–9.

Pope, A. "Of Cruelty to Animals." In *A Hundred English Essays*, edited by R. Vallance. London: Thomas Nelson, 1950.

Pound, P., M. B. Bracken, and S. D. Bliss. "Is Animal Research Sufficiently Evidence Based to Be a Cornerstone of Biomedical Research?" *British Medical Journal* 348, no. 3387 (2014).

Preece, R. *Awe for the Tiger, Love for the Lamb: A Chronicle of Sensibility to Animals.* Vancouver, Canada: University of British Columbia Press, 2002.

Pronin, E., T. Gilovich, and L. Ross. "Objectivity in the Eye of the Beholder: Divergent Perceptions of Bias in Self versus Others." *Psychological Review* 111, no. 3 (2004): 781–99.

Pyszcynski, T., J. Greenberg, and K. Holt. "Maintaining Consistency between Self-Serving Beliefs and Available Data: A Bias in Information Evaluation." *Personality and Social Psychology Bulletin* 11 (1985): 179–90.

Raven, C. *The Creator Spirit.* London: Longmans, 1927.

Rawls, J. *A Theory of Justice.* Oxford: Oxford University Press, 1972.

Regan, T. *The Case for Animal Rights.* London: Routledge and Kegan Paul, 1983.

Rollin, B. E. *The Unheeded Cry: Animal Consciousness, Animal Pain, and Science.* Oxford: Oxford University Press, 1990.

Rowlands, M. *Animal Rights: A Philosophical Defence.* 2nd rev. ed. Basingstoke, UK: Palgrave Macmillan, 1998.

———. *Animal Rights: Moral Theory and Practice.* Basingstoke, UK: Palgrave Macmillan, 2009.

———. *Animals like Us.* London: Verso, 2002.

———. *Can Animals Be Moral?* Oxford: Oxford University Press, 2012.

Royal Society. *Use of Genetically Modified Animals.* London, 2001. Accessed September 29, 2014. https://royalsociety.org/~/media/Royal_Society_Content/policy/publications/2001/10026.pdf.

Russell, W. M. S., and R. L. Burch. *The Principles of Humane Experimental Technique.* London: Methuen, 1959.

Ryder, R. D. *Victims of Science: The Use of Animals in Research.* Rev. ed. London: National Anti-Vivisection Society, 1983.

Sax, B. *Animals in the Third Reich: Pets, Scapegoats, and the Holocaust.* New York: Continuum, 2000.

Scerri, C., C. A. Stewart, D. J. K. Balfour, and K. C. Breen. "Nicotine Modifies In Vivo and In Vitro Rat Hippocampal Amyloid Precursor Protein Processing in Young but Not Old Rats." *Neuroscience Letters* 514, no. 1 (2012): 22–26.

Schofield, P., C. Pease-Watkin, and C. Blamires. *The Collected Works of Jeremy Bentham: Rights, Representation, and Reform: Nonsense upon Stilts and Other Writings on the French Revolution.* Oxford: Oxford University Press, 2002.

Schweitzer, A. *Civilisation and Ethics.* Translated by C. T. Campion. London: Allen and Unwin, 1923.

Secretary of State for the Home Department v. the Queen on the Application of Campaign to End All Animal Experiments (Trading as the British Union for the Abolition of Vivisection). Court of Appeal (Civil Division). April 23, 2008. EWCA Civ 417.

Sena, E. S., B. van der Worp, D. Howells, and M. Macleod. "How Can We Improve the Pre-Clinical Development of Drugs for Stroke?" *Trends in Neurosciences* 30 (2007): 433–39.

Séralini, G. E., E. Clair, R. Mesnage, S. Gress, N. Defarge, M. Malatesta, D. Hennequin, and J. Spiroux de Vendômois. "Long-Term Toxicity of a Roundup Herbicide and a Roundup-Tolerant Genetically Modified Maize." *Food and Chemical Toxicology* 50, no. 11 (2012): 4221–31.

Shao, A., A. Broadmeadow, G. Goddard, E. Bejar, and V. Frankos. "Safety of Purified Decolorized (Low Anthraquinone) Whole Leaf Aloe Vera (L) Burm. F. Juice in a 3-Month Drinking Water Toxicity Study in F344 Rats." *Food and Chemical Toxicology* 57 (2013): 21–31.

Singer, P. *Animal Liberation: A New Ethics for Our Treatment of Animals.* Toronto, Canada: Harper Perennial Modern Classics, 2009.

———. *Practical Ethics.* Cambridge: Cambridge University Press, 1979.

Smith, J. A., and K. M. Boyd, eds. *Lives in the Balance: The Ethics of Using Animals in Biomedical Research.* Oxford: Oxford University Press, 1991.

Spencer, C. M., O. Alekseyenko, S. M. Hamilton, A. M. Thomas, E. Serysheva, L. A. Yuva-Paylor, and R. Paylor. "Modifying Behavioral Phenotypes in Fmr1KO Mice: Genetic Background Differences Reveal Autistic-Like Responses." *Autism Research* 4, no. 1 (2011): 40–56.

Sumner, P., S. Vivian-Griffiths, J. Boivin, A. Williams, C. A. Venetis, A. Davies, J. Ogden, et al. "The Association between Exaggeration in Health Related Science News and Academic Press Releases: Retrospective Observational Study." *British Medical Journal* 349 (2014): g7015.

Sunstein, C. R. *Going to Extremes: How Like Minds Unite and Divide.* Oxford: Oxford University Press, 2009.

Taylor, K., N. Gordon, G. Langley, and W. Higgins. "Estimates for Worldwide Laboratory Animal Use in 2005." *Alternatives to Laboratory Animals* 36 (2008): 327–42.

Taylor, K., W. Stengel, C. Casalegno, and D. Andrew. "Food for Thought: Experiences of the REACH Testing Proposals System to Reduce Animal Testing." *Altex* 31, no. 2 (2014): 107–28.

Tesser, A., and S. Rosen. "Similarity of Objective Fate as a Determinant of the Reluctance to Transmit Unpleasant Information: The MUM Effect." *Journal of Personality and Social Psychology* 23 (1972): 46–53.

Thew, M. "Cruelty-Free Labeling." In A. Linzey, *Global Guide*, 284–85. Chicago: University of Illinois Press, 2013.

———. "Product Testing." In A. Linzey, *Global Guide*, 191–92. Chicago: University of Illinois Press, 2013.

Truth and Reconciliation Commission. *Final Report of the Truth and Reconciliation Committee*, 1998. Vol. 5. Accessed November 6, 2007. http://www.doj.gov.za/trc/report/finalreport/ TRC%20VOLUME%205.pdf.

Understanding Animal Research. "Human Health." Accessed January 3, 2015. http://www.understandinganimalresearch. org.uk/why/human-health/.

US Food and Drug Administration. "Animal Testing and Cosmetics." 2006. Accessed January 3, 2015. http://www.fda.gov/ cosmetics/scienceresearch/producttesting/ucm072268.htm.

———. *Innovation or Stagnation: Challenge and Opportunity on the Critical Path to New Medical Products*. 2004. Accessed January 2, 2015. http://www.fda.gov/ScienceResearch/SpecialTop-ics/CriticalPathInitiative/CriticalPathOpportunitiesReports/ ucm077262.htm.

van der Worp, H. B., D. W. Howells, E. S. Sena, M. J. Porritt, S. Rewell, V. O'Collins, and M. R. Macleod. "Can Animal Models of Disease Reliably Inform Human Studies?" *PLoS Medicine* 7, no. 3 (2010): e1000245.

Vane, J. "Animal Research and Medical Progress." *AnimalResearch.Info*, 1996. Accessed January 3, 2015. http://www.an-imalresearch.info/en/medical-advances/articles-lectures/an-imal-research-and-medical-progress/.

Vorobyov, V., J. C. F. Kwok, J. W. Fawcett, and F. Sengpiel. "Effects of Digesting Chondroitin Sulphate Proteoglycans on Plasticity in Cat Primary Visual Cortex." *Journal of Neuroscience* 33, no. 1 (2013): 234–43.

Voskoglou-Nomikos, T., J. L. Pater, and L. Seymour. "Clinical Predictive Value of the *In Vitro* Cell Line, Human Xenograft, and Mouse Allograft Preclinical Cancer Models." *Clinical Cancer Research* 9, no. 11 (2003): 4227–39.

Waite, T. *Taken on Trust*. London: Hodder and Stoughton, 1993.

Weatherall, D., et al. *The Use of Non-Human Primates in Research*. 2006. Accessed September 29, 2014. https://royalsociety.org/~/ media/Royal_Society_Content/policy/publications/2006/ Weatherall-Report.pdf.

Welchman, J. "Xenografting, Species Loyalty, and Human Solidarity." *Journal of Social Philosophy* 4, no. 2 (2003): 244–55.

Westacott, E. *A Century of Vivisection and Anti-Vivisection: A Study of Their Effect upon Science, Medicine, and Human Life during the Past Hundred Years*. Ashingdon, UK: C. W. Daniel, 1949.

Whymant, R. "The Brutal Truth about Japan." *London Guardian*, August 14, 1982.

Wiebers, D. O., H. P. Adams, and J. P. Whisnant. "Animal Models of Stroke: Are They Relevant to Human Disease?" *Stroke* 21 (1990): 1–3.

Wilke, J., and L. Saad. "Older Americans' Moral Attitudes Changing." *Gallup Politics*. 2013. Accessed August 11, 2014. http:// www.gallup.com/poll/162881/older-americans-moral-atti-tudes-changing.aspx.

Winston, R. *Hansard*, House of Lords, October 24, 2011. Column 623. Accessed January 2, 2015. http://www.publica-tions.parliament.uk/pa/ld201011/ldhansrd/text/111024-0002. htm#11102443000399.

World Medical Association. "Declaration of Helsinki—Ethical Principles for Medical Research involving Human Subjects." 2013. Accessed November 7, 2014. http://www.wma.net/en/ 30publications/10policies/b3/.

PART 2

THE SUPPORTING ESSAYS

Animal Experimentation in Classical Antiquity

Simon Pulleyn

THIS ESSAY IS ABOUT invasive interventions practiced on animals in classical antiquity. The word "animals" is to be understood throughout to refer to nonhuman animals. By "experiment," people usually mean some procedure that has been designed to test a hypothesis or at the very least to discover how a system works.[1] Nowadays the term "animal experimentation" very often means pharmaceutical testing; in antiquity, there is relatively little evidence for this.[2] Most of what the sources describe involves the vivisection of live animals or the dissection of dead ones purposely killed for anatomical investigation. That is the subject of the present discussion.

Experiment and Observation

One may know things about animal behavior and physiology without having performed an experiment directly. One might, for example, simply have observed what happens to an animal who is injured. Greek poets knew all sorts of things about how animals killed each other.[3] This is not the result of experimentation and lies outside the scope of this discussion.

One might also assert a thing because one has conjectured that it is so without seeing the need for experimental confirmation. For example, Anaxagoras's theory that foods[4] such as bread must contain the elements of the human tissues that they sustain (called by Aristotle "homoeomeria"[5]) was not readily amenable to experimental proof. Lucretius summarily dismissed this with the observation that one does not see any blood in a loaf of bread.[6] Here, however, we are concerned with people who did design and perform experiments that were reported in their own writings or those of others.

The Hippocratic Corpus

The Hippocratic writers are certainly not ignorant of anatomical matters, but the topic is neither systematically pursued nor their chief concern.[7] They are stronger on observation and therapeutics. That said, in the *De Morbo Sacro*, there is a description of the brain of a goat who dies with epilepsy: "ἢν διακόψῃς τὴν κεφαλὴν, εὑρήσεις τὸν ἐγκέφαλον ὑγρὸν ἐόντα καὶ ὕδρωπος περίπλεων καὶ κακὸν ὄζοντα" (If you cut open the head, you will find the brain to be watery and full of dropsy and foul-smelling).[8] It is unclear from the context whether this is about opening the head of a goat who is still alive, thereby bringing about the animal's death, or opening the head of one who has happened to drop dead and was known to be epileptic.

But there is an unambiguous example of vivisection in the *De Corde*:

ἢν γάρ τις κυάνῳ ἢ μίλτῳ φορύξας ὕδωρ δοίη δεδιψηκότι πάνυ πιεῖν, μάλιστα δὲ συΐ, τὸ γὰρ κτῆνος οὐκ ἔστιν ἐπιμελὲς οὐδὲ φιλόκαλον, ἔπειτα δὲ εἰ ἔτι πίνοντος ἀνατέμνοις τὸν λαίμον, εὕροις ἂν τοῦτον κεχρωσμένον τῷ ποτῷ· ἀλλ᾽ οὐ παντὸς ἀνδρὸς ἡ χειρουργία.

(For if one were to mix up water with blue or red dye and give it to drink to [a creature] that is very thirsty, especially to a pig—for this animal is neither careful nor elegant—and if you were then to cut its throat while still drinking, you would find this [the throat] colored by the drink. But surgery [literally, handwork] is not for every man.)[9]

It is striking that the writer makes value judgments about the work. First, we hear that this sort of "handwork" is not for everyone ("χειρουργία" means no more than handwork and is the etymon for "surgery," via Latin "chirurgia"). One might assume that he means that only the most accomplished operator will succeed. But we might recall that the Hippocratic Oath appears to put surgery on a separate—and lower—level from medicine, the physician being required to swear that he will not cut into his patients but will hand that work over to ἐργάται (workers).[10] In Greek, these are not usually persons of high status.[11] Second, the pig is said to be especially suited for the experiment precisely because the pig is neither ἐπιμελές (careful)[12] nor φιλόκαλον (elegant). There is an implicit moral judgment here—the animal almost selects herself and deserves her fate because she lacks the faculty of discerning what is beautiful and behaves without decorum.

Aristotle

Aristotle's *Historia Animalium* (Enquiry into animals) was effectively the foundation of modern zoology, seeking to establish the known phenomena concerning animals and to posit the reasons behind them. Concerning anatomy, Aristotle says, "ἄγνωστα γάρ ἐστι μάλιστα τὰ τῶν ἀνθρώπων, ὥστε δεῖ πρὸς τὰ τῶν ἄλλων μόρια ζῴων ἀνάγοντας σκοπεῖν, οἷς ἔχει παραπλησίαν τὴν φύσιν" (Human [inward parts] are in particular unknown, so that it is necessary by reference to the parts of other animals to see to which [human parts] they are similar in nature).[13]

The son of a doctor, Aristotle was naturally interested in humans as one kind of animal. He suggests here that because people at the time did not know about the internal parts of human beings, it was necessary to look to those animals who were similar in nature to humans. Two points emerge from this. First, we may conclude that the dissection of the human cadaver was unknown in Aristotle's day; otherwise, he would not recommend recourse to animals.[14] The second is the apparently unexamined assertion that one may learn about human anatomy by looking at animals who are "similar."

There is also the problem that, in examining a dead animal, one might draw mistaken conclusions as to how the creature functioned in life: "ἐν μὲν γὰρ τοῖς τεθνεῶσι τῶν ζῴων ἄδηλος ἡ φύσις τῶν κυριωτάτων φλεβῶν διὰ τὸ συμπίπτειν εὐθὺς ἐξιόντος τοῦ αἵματος μάλιστα ταύτας" (In dead animals, the nature of the chief arteries is obscure because as the blood leaves them, they immediately collapse).[15] What he is describing is what modern anatomists call negative pressure. In a dead human or animal, some blood is sucked back into the heart from blood vessels so that they appear to be empty when opened.[16]

This being so, Aristotle suggests that the best recourse might sometimes be to humans who happen to be unusually emaciated: "οἱ δ ἐν τοῖς λελεπτυσμένοις σφόδρα ἀνθρώποις ἐκ τῶν τότε ἔξωθεν φαινομένων τὰς ἀρχὰς τῶν φλεβῶν διώρισαν" (Others have distinguished the origins of the arteries from things externally visible in the bodies of extremely emaciated human beings).[17] He similarly recommends studying emaciated animals rather than dead ones: "χαλέπης δ᾽ οὔσης, ὥσπερ εἴρηται πρότερον, τῆς θεωρίας ἐν μόνοις τοῖς ἀποπεπνιγμένοις τῶν ζῴων προλεπτυνθεῖσιν ἔστιν ἱκανῶς καταμαθεῖν" (Since it is, as has been said before, difficult to look solely at animals that have been strangled, it is sufficient to draw conclusions from animals that have been emaciated beforehand).[18]

We note that the reference to animals who have been emaciated involves a verb in the aorist passive (προλεπτυνθεῖσιν). He does not mean animals who simply happen to be thin, but animals who have been deliberately made thin beforehand (προ-) by having their food withheld. There is a contrast here with the passage concerning emaciated humans who just happen to be thin rather than having been made so.[19]

Aristotle also describes experiments involving the deliberate maiming of various kinds of animals. In the case of millipedes, for example, he notes that they can still move about even if one injures one of their legs:

ὅσα δὲ πολύποδά ἐστιν, οἷον αἱ σκολόπενδραι, τούτοις δυνατὸν μὲν καὶ ἀπὸ περιττῶν ποδῶν πορείαν γίνεσθαι, καθάπερ φαίνεται ποιούμενα καὶ νῦν, ἄν τις αὐτῶν ἕνα πηρώσῃ τῶν ποδῶν, διὰ τὸ τὴν τῶν ἀναστοίχων ποδῶν κολόβωσιν ἰᾶσθαι τῷ λοίπῳ πλήθει τῶν ἐφ᾽ ἑκάτερα ποδῶν.

(As for animals with many feet, such as the millipedes, it is possible for these to make their way by reason of their abundance of legs, as they plainly actually do, if someone maims one of their legs, because the mutilation of the legs on one side is cured by the remaining multitude of corresponding legs on the other side.)[20]

We cannot really tell from the words "ἄν τις" (if someone) whether Aristotle or one of his assistants performed this almost childish act of mutilation or whether it was just a well-known phenomenon.

This raises a broader question about Aristotle's use of experiments in general. Francis Bacon famously said that the ancients scarcely ever experimented;[21] he conceded that Aristotle does refer to experiments but accuses him of twisting the evidence to fit his own views.[22] This emerges in an interesting way from Aristotle's description of the blinding of immature birds: "καὶ διὰ τοῦτο τῶν χελιδόνων ἐάν τις ἐκκεντήσῃ τὰ ὄμματα πάλιν ὑγιάζονται· γιγνομένων γὰρ ἀλλ᾽ οὐ γεγεννημένων φθείρονται, διόπερ φύονται καὶ βλαστάνουσιν ἐξ ἀρχῆς" (Thus if one puts out the eyes of swallows, they recover again. They [the eyes][23] suffer the injury when they are in the process of becoming and are not yet fully formed and so they come into being and grow afresh).[24]

Once again, the reference to the operator is concealed behind the words "ἐάν τις" (if somebody). We thus cannot be sure of the source of this assertion. But what is plain is that it is untrue. Swallows do not regain their sight if blinded in the early stage of their lives after hatching.[25] Thus, Aristotle is either lying about an experimental result or retelling a story that he has not himself verified.

Some of Aristotle's other references to anatomy leave the reader unclear about whether he is referring to information procured by examining dead animals or by vivisection. In the *Historia Animalium* he refers to the apex of the heart and says, "εἰς τὸ πρόσθεν ἔχει ἡ καρδία τὸ ὀξύ· λάθοι δ᾽ ἂν πολλάκις διὰ τὸ μεταπίπτειν διαιρουμένων" (The pointed end of the heart points forward—but it might frequently escape one's notice because of some movement while dissection is being carried out).[26]

This detail looks more like the result of personal experience often repeated—the word "πολλάκις" suggests the observation of someone who has seen all of this before. But it is possible that Aristotle is taking this over from some other source. Whatever be the truth of this, one cannot deny that this suggests a tradition of sustained inquiry, whether or not by Aristotle himself.

What we do not get from these texts is any discussion of whether and how it might be justifiable to experiment on animals. To some extent, of course, one might assume that a society that thinks it legitimate to kill animals for sacrifice to the gods and for food, which are in fact overlapping categories, is unlikely to think it immoral to kill them in order to promote science.

In his other works, Aristotle does tend to say that the mental faculties of animals are inferior to those of humans. He says that animals have no λόγος (reason), λογοσμός (calculation), διάνοια (thought), or νοῦς (mind).[27] This denial of various mental faculties might be conjectured to lie beneath the license to experiment that Aristotle and others felt that they enjoyed. Alternatively, and more probably, one might conclude that people experimented on animals because they could, without feeling the need to invoke the further justification of philosophers. We will return to this later.

Galen

Galen, writing in Greek under the Roman Empire toward the end of the first century AD, gives us the most sustained and detailed descriptions of dissection and vivisection. He recommends that preferably one ought to study skeletons in the medical schools of Alexandria. Failing that, one might have the good fortune to be present when a river opens a grave and carries away the body. The student who is not fortunate enough to see any of these things will need to have recourse to animals:

σὺ δέ, εἰ μήδε τοιοῦτον μήδεν εὐτύχησας θεάσασθαι, πίθηκον οὖν ἀνατεμών, ἐπ᾽ αὐτοῦ κατανόησον ἕκαστον τῶν ὀστῶν ἀκριβῶς ἀφελὼν τὰς σάρκας. ἔκλεξαι δὲ εἰς τοῦτο τῶν πιθήκων τοὺς ὁμοιοτάτους ἀνθρώπωι.

(But you, if you are not even fortunate enough to be able to look at something like this, well then cut up an ape and in it study each of the bones when you have carefully removed the flesh. For this purpose, select those of the apes most similar to man.)[28]

The use of animals is for Galen a pis aller for the student who is unfortunate enough not to have human cadavers to study. This is similar to what we found in Aristotle. A modern medical student might not be quick to suppose that one could learn human anatomy from an ape.

Galen's tone is not only professional but moralistic:

ἐπιμελῶς δὲ χρὴ πάντα πράττειν τὸν γυμνάζόμενον ἐν ταῖς ἀνατομαῖς, ἄχρι τοῦ καὶ ἀποδέρειν αὐτόν. εὐθὺς οὖν ὀκτὼ μῦς ἠγνόησαν οἱ πρὸ ἐμοῦ, πιστεύσαντες ἄλλοις ἐκδέρειν τοὺς πιθήκους, ὥσπερ κἀγὼ κατ᾿ ἀρχάς.

(The person who is practicing in anatomy must do everything with care, including skinning the animal himself. Those before me overlooked eight muscles, because they trusted others with skinning the apes, as I also did in the beginning.)[29]

He stresses working carefully ("ἐπιμελῶς" is the first word in the sentence). This is a theme that recurs in Galen.[30] It also reminds us of the Hippocratic reference to the suitability of the pig to having his or her throat cut because the animal is a careless and inelegant drinker.[31] The student is referred to as one who is going through a program of training (γυμναζόμενον), the verb being from the same root as "gymnasium." The student is effectively being put through his paces. There is also the interesting comment that Galen himself learned from his own carelessness at the outset of his professional career. The use of "κἀγὼ" implies "even I"—even the master made mistakes at the outset. Animal experimentation is plainly by this stage an established part of the curriculum.

We reach a particular moral low point when Galen is discussing how to kill apes for dissection: "καὶ λαβὼν αὐτὸν ἐν ὕδατι πεπνιγμένον οὕτως, ὡς εἴωθα πράττειν, ὑπὲρ τοῦ μηδὲν θλασθῆναι τῶν ἐν τῷ τραχήλῳ μορίων" (So I took it [the ape] once it had been drowned in water, as I usually do, so that none

of the structures in the neck is crushed).[32] The clear implication of this is that the alternative to drowning the ape was strangling it. One imagines that both strangulation and drowning caused great distress to the apes who were killed and must have involved considerable physical violence. There is behind this advice the notion that strangulation had been tried quite often before people realized that it was counterproductive because it destroyed structures in the neck that the anatomists wished to investigate. One also shudders at the words "ὡς εἴωθα πράττειν" (as I usually do): The clear indication is that these drownings are a regular business in Galen's laboratory—the sort of thing that would today be commended with the Orwellian term "best practice."

This passage concerning the exposure of the heart in a living creature is particularly revealing:

ἔτι δὲ τῆς γυμνουμένης καρδίας ἀπαθεῖς φυλάττειν πρόκειταί σοι τὰς ἐνεργείας ἁπάσας, ὥσπερ οὖν καὶ φυλάττονται. καὶ γὰρ ἀναπνέον ὡσαύτως καὶ κεκραγὸς φαίνεται τὸ ζῷον, καὶ εἰ λύσαις δὲ τῶν συνδέσμων αὐτὸ, τρέχον, ὡς ἔμπροσθεν ἔτρεχε. εἰ δὲ καὶ περιλάβοις ἔτι δέσμοις τὸ τραῦμα, καὶ τρόφην ὄψει προσφερόμενον, ἢν πεινῆσαν τύχῃ, καὶ πῖνον, ἢν διψήσῃ.

(While the heart is still exposed, your task is to preserve all the faculties unimpaired—as in fact they are. So the animal manifestly breathes and cries out and, if you loose it from its bonds, runs around as it used to before. And if you compress the wound with ligatures, it will be seen taking food, if it happens to be hungry, and drinking, if it is thirsty.)[33]

First, the use of the word "τραῦμα" (wound) makes it clear that Galen is in no doubt that the animals are being injured. It is noteworthy that the same term is used in human surgery—but the difference is that humans have the capacity to consent. Second, there is something unspeakable about the notion of closing the animal's chest and watching him run about, cry out (doubtless in pain), and feed and drink—as though nothing were wrong. Third, it is the task (πρόκειταί σοι)[34] of the anatomist to keep the animal's various faculties unharmed—not for the animal's sake but because the experiment requires further procedures after the heart has been exposed.[35]

But once these further steps have been completed, says Galen, "καταφρονήσεις γε νῦν τῆς αἱμορραγίας αὐτῶν· οὐ γάρ σοι πρόκειται νῦν ζῶν φυλάττειν τὸ ζῷον" (You must now pay no regard to their haemorrhaging; it is no longer your task to keep the animal alive).[36] The choice of the word "καταφρονήσεις" (pay no regard) imports a pejorative tone. It normally denotes despising something, or at least viewing something as beneath one. It is revealingly harsh in this context when the animal is bleeding to death. But the operator is to have no regard for this. The phrase "οὐ . . . σοι πρόκειται" (It is not your task) (which we have seen before)[37] indicates that the student has his appointed task and is not to forget this.

The shedding of blood recurs in another context when Galen recommends practicing one's technique on a dead animal so that, when experimenting upon a live one, the procedure may be performed as bloodlessly as possible:

γυμνασθῆναί σε βούλομαι πρότερον ἐπὶ τεθνεῶτος τοῦ ζῴου γνωρίζειν ἀκριβῶς ἑκάστου τῶν λεχθησομένων τὴν θέσιν, ἵν᾽ ἐπὶ ζῶντος ὅτι τάχιστα γυμνοῦν αὐτὰ δυνήθῃ ἀναιμωτί, καθόσον οἷόν τε.

(I want you to practice beforehand on a dead animal so that you may be precisely acquainted with the position of each of the parts so that in the living animal you may expose each as quickly as possible, so far as is feasible, without loss of blood.)[38]

Given what we have already seen, we may surmise here, too, that the counsel to avoid loss of blood has nothing to do with the welfare of the animal but is for the convenience of the operator. The animal needs to survive until all the procedures have been completed.

In the passage concerning the exposure of the heart, Galen goes on to comment on the experience of the animal. It is asserted that an animal is "δυσπαθέστερον"[39] (less easily affected by pain) than a human being. This is no more than a bald assertion: animals are less given to pain because that is how it seemed to Galen. We need not suppose that Galen is appealing to previous writing concerning the impassibility of animal souls. At any rate, there is nothing about the attested distribution of the word "δυσπαθής" (impassive) to suggest that it belonged specifically in philosophical discussions about ani-

mals.[40] It is also urged that the animal is in any event an ἄλογον ζῷον (irrational being).[41] This apparently technical language might at first blush appear to be an appeal to earlier tradition, most notably Aristotle, concerning animals' lack of reason. On the other hand, it appears that the word was more or less a synonym for animals and was perhaps no more philosophical in tenor than "brute" in older registers of English.[42] There is perhaps a justification wrapped up in the use of the word but only at the general level that animals are "dumb" and "not like us."

We also find in Galen's exposition of his procedures an element of showmanship that seems to us to sit ill with laboratory science. He speaks about "τὰς ἐγχειρήσεις, ἃς ἤδη τεθέανται πολλοὶ πολλάκις, ἐνεργεῖν δ᾽ οὐδ᾽ ὀλίγοι δύνανται" (experiments that many have already often seen, but which very few are able to perform).[43] The verb "τεθέανται" is perhaps better translated "watched" than "seen." It is from "θεάομαι" and belongs with the noun "θέατρον." If we ask why it is that we speak of anatomy theaters and operating theaters, the custom is clearly old. One might say that this is a small hook on which to hang the argument that Galen was a sort of theatrical master of ceremonies, laying out shows for an audience of spectators. But there are other texts that cannot be ignored. He seems to have been particularly proud of an experiment involving the ligation of nerves in the living animal:

κέκραγε γὰρ οὕτω παιόμενον, εἶτ᾽ ἐξαίφνης ἄφωνον γινόμενον ἐπὶ τῷ σφιγχθῆναι τοῖς λίνοις τὰ νεῦρα τοὺς θεατὰς ἐκπλήττει. θαυμαστὸν γὰρ εἶναι δοκεῖ, νεύρων βροχισθέντων, ἀπολλύσθαι τὴν φωνήν.

(For the animal cries out when it is struck but then suddenly becomes voiceless when the nerves are ligated with cords and astounds the onlookers. For it seems to be astonishing that the voice should be destroyed when nerves are tied off.)[44]

The persons observing the procedure are θεαταί, the same as persons in a theater watching a play. This spectacle will ἐκπλήττω them—a strong verb, glossed by Henry George Liddell and Robert Scott as "drive out of one's senses by a sudden shock, amaze, astound."[45] We might note that Galen himself refers to the *sudden* contrast between phonation and silence with the adverb "ἐξαίφνης." This sudden reversal might remind one of the Aristotelian notion of περιπέτεια,[46] the sort of staggering and sudden reversal of fortune that is integral to tragic theater.[47] Galen also explicitly refers to the spectacle as seeming θαυμαστόν—amazing. This, too, is typical of theater and is commonly used to describe περιπέτειαι (reversals of fortune).[48]

So Galen is impresario and thaumaturge.[49] The same kind of callousness that we find in his disregard for the animals who are the objects of his spectacles is found in the onlookers: "ἐθεάσασθε γοῦν ἐκεῖνο τὸ ζῷον ἐπὶ τῇ τοῦ νωτιαίου τομῇ, κατ᾽ ἀρχὴν τοῦ μεταφρένου γενομένη, πεσὸν μὲν αὐτίκα καὶ πλάγιον κείμενον, ἄφωνον δὲ ὑπάρχον" (You saw that animal when the cut was made in the spine, at the beginning of the back, how it fell down at once and lay on its side and remained dumb).[50] Galen severed the spine of a living animal, and the animal fell to the ground. We picture the young men looking on at the spectacle to see what would happen next. Everyone is complicit in the act, but nobody sees it as such.

The notion of spectacle can sometimes rebound unfavorably even on the master. Thus, for example, Galen appears to have learned the hard way that apes were not always a good subject for experiment: "ἐφ᾽ ὑῶν δὲ μάλιστα πάντα τὰ τοιαῦτα δεικνύντα με ἐθεάσασθε πολλάκις ἰδίᾳ τε καὶ δημοσίᾳ, διὰ τὸ μήτε πλέον ἔχειν τι πίθηκον ἐν ταῖς τοιαύταις ἀνατομαῖς, εἰδεχθές τ᾽ εἶναι τὸ θέαμα" (You have often watched me demonstrating such things in pigs but in private and in public, since in anatomical procedures such as this an ape brings no advantage and the spectacle is hateful to look at).[51]

Several points arise here. First, it is once again the peculiar fate of the pig that she recommends herself for vivisection. We have already seen that the pig is most useful for experiments involving vocalization because she squeals so loudly. We also recollect the pig's usefulness as a careless drinker of whatever colored liquid was put before her in the experiment where the Hippocratic writer would go on to cut the pig's throat while she was yet drinking. Now we read that the pig is useful because the spectacle of her suffering is less hateful for the onlooker than that of an ape. Galen does not say here why this is so, but we might conjecture that it has to do with the fact that the

ape has a more human face, and his grimaces might be more disturbing to the operator and audience.

Of course, Galen would not be likely to say that the spectacle of the ape is hateful unless he had himself been involved in it. In that part of the work whose Greek text is lost but that survives in Arabic translation, he is even more explicit:

I say, then that for this purpose you must procure a pig or a goat, in order to combine the two requirements. In the first place, you avoid seeing the unpleasing expression of the ape when it is being vivisected. The other reason is that the animal on which the dissection takes place should cry out with a really loud voice—a thing one does not find with apes.[52]

There is, of course, something that moves our pity in the ape bearing his torment with relatively little vocalization—something viewed by Galen as a mere operational inconvenience. The hatefulness of experimenting on apes does not appear to make Galen pause to ask whether there is anything amiss with the procedure. Indeed, he elsewhere emphasizes the need to be pitiless when operating.

Looking again at the Arabic translation, we find the following:

But as for what concerns the vivisection itself, it should proceed on both animals in the same fashion. That is to say, every cut that you impose should travel in a straight line, just as it travels in the dead animal, and the cut should without pity or compassion penetrate into the deep tissues in order that within a single stroke you may lay free and uncover the skull of the animal.[53]

We have seen that Galen appears to take the view that animals do not feel pain—either at all or at least certainly not to the same degree as humans do. And yet we have also seen that he noticed the grimaces of apes enough to suggest avoiding them. Can it seriously not have crossed his mind that they were suffering? Certainly, all his advice tends toward the importance of students having good technique, putting on an impressive show, and cutting without pity.

This last point is interesting. In nothing that Galen does is there the slightest hint of guilt. When he says that animals do not suffer as humans do, there is little sense that this is a philosophical position in the sense that he is relying on Aristotle or some such authority. One might suppose that he is relying on his own experience as an operator. But here again, one wonders whether he can truly believe this given that he notes the grimaces of apes when they are subjected to the knife. It is hard not to conclude that Galen and others who vivisected animals were not really looking for philosophical or scientific justification for their actions. The figures we have looked at, from Hippocrates to Galen, are separated by seven hundred years in time and hundreds of miles in distance. Athens of the fifth century BC was not the same as Rome in the late second century AD. And yet in all these worlds, the business of animal sacrifice was central. Animals were killed on a daily basis for food, of course, but all of this was intimately bound up with the sacrificial system.[54] In such a world, one can see how one might think that people thought of animals as simply there to be killed for vivisection as for sacrifice "because they could."[55]

Notes

1. Heinrich von Staden takes the view that Hellenistic investigators were not so much in the business of framing hypotheses of general application as in the business of seeing what might work in a given case and reasoning from that to similar ones. H. von Staden, "Experiment and Experience in Hellenistic Medicine," *Bulletin of the Institute of Classical Studies* 22 (1975): 192. G. E. R. Lloyd, on the other hand, shows how some experiments are designed to prove or disprove definite hypotheses. G. E. R. Lloyd, *Methods and Problems in Greek Science* (Cambridge: Cambridge University Press, 1991), 92.

2. M. D. Grmek and G. Gourevitch, "Les expériences pharmacologiques dans l'antiquité," *Archives Internationales d'Histoire des Sciences* 35 (1985): 3–27.

3. See, for example, Homer, *Iliad* 5.159–65.

4. G. S. Kirk, J. E. Raven, and M. Schofield, *The Pre-Socratic Philosophers* (Cambridge: Cambridge University Press, 1983), 375.

5. Aristotle, *De Caelo* 302a28; Aristotle, *Physica* 187a23.

6. Lucretius, *De Rerum Natura* 1.830, 859–66, esp. 880–96.

7. E. D. Phillips, *Greek Medicine* (London: Thames and Hudson, 1973), 41–48.

8. Hippocrates, *De Morbo Sacro* 11.10–12.

9. Hippocrates, *De Corde* 2.5–8.

10. Hippocrates, *Oath*, lines 23–4.

11. The term "ἐργάται" can be used for farmers (Hdt. 4.109; Dem. 35.32) or a working ox (Archil. 35 in M. L. West, *Iambi et Elegi Graeci ante Alexandrum Cantiti*, 2nd. ed. (Oxford: Oxford University Press, 1989) or even worker wasps (Arist. HA 627.b.32). The use of the term to describe judges (Lycophron, *Alexandra* 128) is most likely a metaphor and not a likely indication that the word describes persons of higher status.

12. We shall see later that the carelessness of the pig in drinking is contrasted with the carefulness required of a student practicing anatomy (Galen, *De anat. admin.* 2.230.17–2.231.1; 2.232.13–16).

13. Aristotle, *Historia Animalium* 494.b.22–3.

14. This is not the place for a systematic discussion of the history of morbid anatomy in antiquity. It is enough to say that it more or less began in Alexandria in the Ptolemaic period. The interested reader may consult Lloyd, *Methods and Problems*, 164–93, and J. Longrigg, "Anatomy in Alexandria in the Third Century BC," *British Journal for the History of Science* 21 (1988): 455–88.

15. Aristotle, *Historia Animalium* 511.b.14–16.

16. C. R. S. Harris, *The Heart and the Vascular System in Ancient Greek Medicine: From Alcmaeon to Galen* (Oxford: Oxford University Press, 1973), 8:92–93.

17. Aristotle, *Historia Animalium* 511.b.20–23.

18. Ibid., 513.a.12–14.

19. In the perfect tense, as here, the middle and passive voices are morphologically identical. It is, however, reasonable to assume that this verb is middle rather than passive: the reference is far more likely to be to people who have become emaciated than those subjected to deliberate starvation.

20. Aristotle, . . . *De Incessu Animalium* 708.b.4–9.

21. "*Vix unum experimentum adduci potest*" (scarcely one experiment can be cited), Francis Bacon and Thomas Fowler, *Bacon's Novum Organum*, 2nd ed. (Oxford: Clarendon Press, 1889), 1.73. Sambursky likewise says, "With very few exceptions, the Ancient Greeks throughout a period of eight hundred years made no attempt at systematic experimentation." S. Sambursky, *The Physical World of the Greeks* (London: Routledge, 1956), 2. The words "with very few exceptions" are cautious, but then so arguably are Bacon's "*vix unum.*"

22. Bacon and Fowler, *Novum Organum* 1.63: "*experientiam ad sua placita tortam circumducit et captivam*" (He twists experience to what pleases him and leads it about as a captive).

23. The references to "they" here are to the eyes and not the swallows. The word for "eyes" is in the neuter plural and would usually take a singular verb in Greek. The verbs here are, however, in the plural. The only plural noun refers to the swallows. But it is quite clear from the context that it is the eyes that grow back and not the birds themselves.

24. Aristotle, *De Generatione Animalium* 774.b.31–34.

25. Dr. A. H. W. Bates of University College London, personal communication. I understand that an eye that is damaged at the embryonic stage can repair itself to some extent but not if totally destroyed. There is no suggestion that this is what is meant here.

26. Aristotle, *Historia Animalium* 496.a.10–11ff.

27. Aristotle, *De Anima* 428.a.22; *De Anima* 415.a.7–8; 434.a.5–11; *De Partibus Animalium* 641.b.7; *De Anima* 404.b.4–6; 414.b.18–19.

28. Galen, *De anat. admin.* 2.222.2–6. The same idea surfaces at 2.224.11–12: if one cannot procure human specimens, then one must study the parts of those animals "παραπλησίων ἀνθρώπῳ" (similar to mankind).

29. Ibid., 2.230.17–2.231–3.

30. Ibid., 2.232.15.

31. Hippocrates, *De Corde* 2.5.

32. Galen, *De anat. admin.* 2.233.7.

33. Ibid., 2.631.9–15.

34. Compare ibid., 2.640.1.

35. Galen, *De anat. admin.* 2.631.9–15; compare πρόκειταί σοι in ibid., 2.640.1; 2.636–38.

36. Ibid., 2.640.1.

37. Ibid., 2.631.10; 2.640.1 (without the negative but with the same prescriptive force).

38. Ibid., 2.662.9–12.

39. Ibid., 2.631.9.

40. The term "δυσπαθής" is found in Plutarch referring to numbness to pain in old men and to women not feeling the cold (*Moralia* 625b7; 651c8 in G. Bernardakis, *Plutarchi Chaeronensis Moralia* [Leipzig: Teubner 1888–96]); Lucian uses it to refer to human bodies being toughened by exercise (*Anacharsis* 24). There is an exception in its use by the second-century AD Stoic Hierocles to refer to animals (*Elements* 2.19–20 in Ilaria Ramelli and David Konstan, *Hierocles the Stoic: Elements of Ethics, Fragments, and Excerpts* [Atlanta: Society for Biblical Literature, 2009]).

41. Galen, *De anat. admin.* 2.631.9.

42. Democritus 68 [55] B.164.D–K; Xenophon, *Hieron* 7.3. In the *Septuagint*, the word was regularly used for animals, with no real sense that a philosophical tradition was being invoked—it was just a standard piece of paronomasia (LXX 4 Ma 14.14; LXX Sap. 11.15); this was likewise the case in the New Testament at 2 Ep Petr 1.12.

43. Galen, *De anat. admin.* 2.665.4–5.

44. Ibid., 2.669.6–10.

45. Henry George Liddell and Robert Scott, *A Greek-English Lexicon*, ed. H. S. Jones, 9th ed. (Oxford: Clarendon, 1940), 517.

46. Aristotle, *Poet.* 1452.a.22.

47. Aristotle, *Rhet.* 1371.b.10, refers to these changes of fortune as amazing in the same way as narrow escapes from danger.

48. Ibid., 1371.b.10–11; Diodorus Siculus, *Historiae* 8.10.3.

49. This topic has been explored at length by Maud Gleeson, "Shock and Awe: The Performance Dimension of Galen's Anatomy Demonstrations," in *Galen and the World of Knowledge*, ed. C. Gill, T. Whitmarsh, and J. Wilkins (Cambridge: Cambridge University Press, 2010), 85–114.

50. Galen, *De anat. admin.* 2.677.16–678.1.

51. Ibid., 2.690.10.

52. W. L. H. Duckworth, *Galen on Anatomical Procedures: The Later Books*, ed. M. C. Lyons and B. Towers (Cambridge: Cambridge University Press, 1962), 18.

53. Ibid., 19.

54. K. Latte, *Römische Religionsgeschichte*, 2nd ed. (Munich: C. H. Beck, 1976), 379–93; M. Beard, J. North, and S. Price, *Religions of Rome* (Cambridge: Cambridge University Press, 1998), 148ff. For parallels in the Greek world, see R. Parker, *On Greek Religion* (Ithaca: Cornell University Press, 2011), 124–70.

55. We do not know what became of the remains of the unhappy animals vivisected by Galen. One imagines that most Romans did not want to eat a Barbary ape. But the pig was a common victim for Galen and was also a common victim in Roman sacrifices. One wonders whether vivisected pigs were ever eaten after death.

Bibliography

Aland, K., M. Black, C. Martini, B. Metzger, and A. Wikgren, eds. *Novum Testamentum Graece*. 26th ed. Stuttgart: Deutsche Bibelstiftung, 1981.

Aristotle. *Ars Rhetorica*. Edited by W. D. Ross. Oxford: Clarendon, 1959.

———. *De Anima*. Edited by W. D. Ross. Oxford: Clarendon, 1961.

———. *De Animalium Motione et de Animalium Incessu*. Edited by W. Jaeger. Leipzig: Teubner, 1913.

———. *De Caelo*. Edited by D. J. Allan. Oxford: Clarendon, 1936.

———. *De Generatione Animalium*. Edited by H. J. Drossaart Lulofs. Oxford: Clarendon, 1936.

———. *De Partibus Animalium*. Edited by B. Langkavel. Leipzig: Teubner, 1868.

———. *Historia Animalium*. Edited by L. Dittmeyer. Leipzig: Teubner, 1907.

———. *Physica*. Edited by W. D. Ross. Oxford: Clarendon, 1977.

Bacon, Francis, and Thomas Fowler. *Bacon's Novum Organum*. 2nd ed. Oxford: Clarendon Press, 1889.

Beard, M., J. North, and S. Price. *Religions of Rome*. Cambridge: Cambridge University Press, 1998.

Bernardakis, G. *Plutarchi Chaeronensis Moralia*. Leipzig: Teubner, 1888–96.

Demosthenes. *Orationes*. Edited by W. Rennie. Vol. 2. Pt. 2. Oxford: Clarendon, 1936.

Diels, H. *Die Fragmente der Vorsokratiker*. Edited by W. Kranz. Vol. 2. Zurich: Weidmann, 1989.

Diodorus Siculus. *Historiae*. Edited by L. Dindorf and F. Vogel. Vol. 2. Leipzig: Teubner, 1890.

Duckworth, W. L. H. *Galen on Anatomical Procedures: The Later Books*. Edited by M. C. Lyons and B. Towers. Cambridge: Cambridge University Press, 1962.

Galen. *De Anatomicis Administrationibus*. Edited by I. Garofalo. Milan: Biblioteca Universale Rizzoli, 1991.

Gleeson, M. "Shock and Awe: The Performance Dimension of Galen's Anatomy Demonstrations." In *Galen and the World of*

Knowledge, edited by C. Gill, T. Whitmarsh, and J. Wilkins, 85–114. Cambridge: Cambridge University Press, 2010.

Grmek, M. D., and G. Gourevitch. "Les expériences pharmacologiques dans l'antiquité." *Archives Internationales d'Histoire des Sciences* 35 (1985): 3–27.

Harris, C. R. S. *The Heart and the Vascular System in Ancient Greek Medicine: From Alcmaeon to Galen*. Oxford: Oxford University Press, 1973.

Herodotus. *Historiae*. Edited by C. Hude. Vol. 1. 3rd ed. Oxford: Clarendon, 1927.

Hippocrates. *Oeuvres Complètes*. Edited by É. Littré. Paris: Baillière, 1839–61.

Homer. *Iliad*. Edited by M. L. West. Stuttgart: Teubner, 1998.

Kirk, G. S., J. E. Raven, and M. Schofield. *The Pre-Socratic Philosophers*. Cambridge: Cambridge University Press, 1983.

Latte, K. *Römische Religionsgeschichte*. 2nd ed. Munich: C. H. Beck, 1976.

Liddell, H. G., and R. Scott. *A Greek-English Lexicon*. Edited by H. S. Jones. 9th ed. Oxford: Clarendon, 1940.

Lloyd, G. E. R. "Experiment in Early Greek Philosophy and Medicine." In *Methods and Problems in Greek Science*, 70–99. Cambridge: Cambridge University Press, 1991.

Longrigg, J. "Anatomy in Alexandria in the Third Century BC." *British Journal for the History of Science* 21 (1988): 455–88.

Lucian. *Opera*. Edited by C. Jacobitz. Vol. 3. Leipzig: Teubner, 1904.

Lucretius. *De Rerum Natura*. Edited by C. Bailey. 2nd ed. Oxford: Clarendon, 1921.

Lycophron. *Alexandra*. Edited by S. Hornblower. Oxford: Oxford University Press, 2015.

Parker, R. *On Greek Religion*. Ithaca: Cornell University Press, 2011.

Phillips, E. D. *Greek Medicine*. London: Thames and Hudson, 1973.

Rahlfs, A., ed. *Septuaginta*. 2 vols. 9th ed. Stuttgart: Deutsch Bibelstiftung, 1935.

Ramelli, Ilaria, and David Konstan. *Hierocles the Stoic: Elements of Ethics, Fragments, and Excerpts*. Atlanta: Society for Biblical Literature, 2009.

Sambursky, S. *The Physical World of the Greeks*. London: Routledge, 1956.

Staden, H. von. "Experiment and Experience in Hellenistic Medicine." *Bulletin of the Institute of Classical Studies* 22 (1975): 178–99.

West, M. L. *Iambi et Elegi Graeci ante Alexandrum Cantiti*. 2nd. ed. Oxford: Oxford University Press, 1989.

Xenopohon. *Opera Omnia*. Edited by E. C. Marchant. Vol. 5. Oxford: Clarendon, 1920.

UNIVERSITY OF WINCHESTER
LIBRARY

Gender and the Animal Experiments Controversy in Nineteenth-Century America

Robyn Hederman

IN MARCH 1909 the *New York Times* reported, "Passion for Animals Really a Disease: Its Name Is Zoophil-Psychosis, Dr. Dana Says, and It Attacks Morbid Lovers of Pets." This headline referred to an article published in the *Medical Record* by the neurologist Charles L. Dana, who diagnosed a "heightened concern for animals to be a form of mental illness." After the disease develops, "the individual becomes the victim of a psychosis and a source of distress to self and friends, or demoralization to family and of serious social injustice."[1] Advocates of animal experimentation embraced zoophil-psychosis to pathologize antivivisectionists. The *New York Times* concluded that women were especially susceptible to the affliction, "which like the historic hysterias, 'phobias' and fanaticisms of history, is apt to sweep over whole communities."[2]

Gender was a powerful component of the nineteenth-century vivisection controversy in the United States. The nineteenth-century battle over animal experimentation reflects changing attitudes toward middle-class social practices, the education of children, and the role of women in the public sphere. By situating this debate within nineteenth-century social history, we gain insight into the goals of antivivisectionists and the scientific and medical community's campaign to discredit them. This essay suggests that the medical profession's visceral opposition was not merely a reaction to the challenge against animal experimentation but also exemplified the gender conflicts of the era.

The women involved in the early antivivisectionist movement were rooted in the nineteenth-century concept of "true womanhood." The True Woman's cherished values were religion, purity, deference, and domesticity. Domesticity adopted the conventions of gentility and Christian religion.[3] In *Pets in America: A History*, Katherine C. Grier makes the connection between nineteenth-century domesticity and the domestic ethic of kindness to animals. Grier explains that the humane treatment of animals became a symbol of bourgeois gentility. A mother's most important role in the home was to influence her children to be guided by good moral principles and to create self-disciplined adults. Mothers instructed their children to be kind to animals, believing that children would learn to express compassionate sentiments outside the family.[4]

In her book *Disorderly Conduct*, the historian Carroll Smith-Rosenberg describes the arrival of the "New Woman" in the late nineteenth century. Smith-Rosenberg explains that women who had raised money and had worked in the field hospitals during the Civil War continued their work after the war. These women became convinced that they could use their innate feminine values to solve the social evils of their society. They transformed the values of the True Woman to fit their new priorities. They became the "conscience and the housekeepers of America."[5] Women accented their roles as "guardians of private and public morality" and extended their proper spheres of influence through benevolence work.[6] Estelle Freedman, in her article "Separatism as Strategy," describes the nineteenth-century reform organizations as examples of "female institution building." Freedman claims that the creation of a separate, public sphere mobilized women to obtain political power in society.[7] Yet, as the True Woman emerged into the New Woman, she challenged her traditional role in society.[8]

Caroline White and the American Anti-Vivisection Society

The antivivisection movement obtained the support of American women by embracing these ideas and cultural values. Caroline Earle White was raised in an atmosphere of reform by a Quaker father who was a strong abolitionist. In 1883 White established the first antivivisection organization in the United States, the American Anti-Vivisection Society (AAVS). In 1867 White was one of the founders of the Pennsylvania Society for the Prevention of Cruelty to Animals (SPCA). Being a woman, however, she was prevented from serving on the board of directors. White later became president of the Women's Branch of the Pennsylvania SPCA (WSPCA), in which capacity she confronted the vivisection controversy.[9]

In 1869 White received permission from the city of Philadelphia to create a temporary pound for animals. The physician S. Weir Mitchell notified White in 1870 that he requested an order "enabling [him] to select from dogs before they are killed by [the pound's] agents, as such are needed for [his] studies."[10] When White refused, Mitchell appealed to the male companion organization. When White's decision was supported by the SPCA, Mayor Daniel Fox and the Philadelphia City Council passed an ordinance authorizing the society to round up dogs for its shelter. The medical profession derided the Women's Branch in the *Medical Times*, claiming that the cause of prevention of cruelty to animals had failed when "a number of women conceived the idea that a female branch was desirable."[11]

This confrontation strengthened White's resolve against vivisection. On a trip to London, White met with the British antivivisectionist Frances Power Cobbe, whom White described as "the apostle of anti-vivisection." At one meeting, Cobbe suggested,

"Why don't you form an anti-vivisection society? There is not one in all the United States, and I think it is a disgrace to the country."[12]

White and Mary F. Lovell formed the AAVS at a meeting of the Women's Branch of the Pennsylvania SPCA in 1883.[13] Although the original members of the executive committee consisted of an even number of men and women, the AAVS soon became a women's society.

Initially, the organization's purpose was to regulate vivisection because it hoped to receive cooperation from the medical community. When no cooperation was forthcoming, the society passed a resolution to declare itself in favor of total abolition.[14] Many physicians left the organization after the society adopted the policy of abolition, leaving women to fill the open positions. By 1895 the executive committee was composed of three men and seventeen women.[15] Although the official policy of the AAVS became total abolition, White was pragmatic and supported several approaches in her activism.[16]

White did not fully embrace Cobbe's views of feminism.[17] Yet, she did cast antivivisection as a women's issue. Emphasizing the True Woman's values of piety and service, White characterized the issue of antivivisection as an issue for Christian women and mothers. The AAVS members believed that "as Christians and mothers their goal was to uplift society, not to champion women's rights as individuals."[18] In the 1890s they imputed that practicing vivisection was sinful and therefore anathema to Christian living.[19]

The AAVS reached larger audiences as a result of its connection with the Women's Christian Temperance Union (WCTU) under the leadership of Frances Willard. Willard's "Do everything" policy attracted women of all persuasions, and it became a place where women could find a forum for reform.[20] The antivivisection movement became connected with the WCTU in the 1890s. Both movements accepted the premise that women were responsible for preserving the moral fiber of society.

Lovell became the national director of the Department of Mercy for the WCTU. The Department of Mercy was devoted to the prevention of cruelty to animals and was associated with the growing antivivisection movement in Britain and the United States. The Department of Mercy reached out to schools to teach children the importance of kindness to animals. Sydney H. Coleman, in *Humane Society Leaders in America*, notes that Lovell considered humane education to be "the real antidote to war and to all other cruelty and crime."[21]

The antivivisection movement emphasized the negative effects on students who watched or participated in vivisection. The antivivisectionists were troubled by the callous effect animal experimentation had on male students and what antivivisectionists perceived to be the students' already cruel tendencies. Lovell warned that the "mania for torture" would cause schoolboys to become incapable of mercy, and the kindness taught by mothers would be undone.[22] Although the AAVS did believe girls were less susceptible to violent tendencies, AAVS members were disturbed to learn that Bryn Mawr and Wellesley Colleges practiced vivisection at their institutions.[23]

The AAVS joined the National Council of Women (NCW) in 1894.[24] In February 1895, White and Lovell addressed the NCW's convention about the need for women to be concerned about vivisection. White presented a paper, "Is Vivisection Morally Justifiable?" Lovell suggested in her presentation, "The Worst Thing in the World," that physicians who practiced vivisection lacked feelings of mercy and respect for delicacy, and she questioned whether they were suitable to treat women patients.[25] Lovell denounced the cruelty of vivisection as the deadliest sin and cautioned the audience not to make Earth "a hell to God's innocent creatures."[26]

White was involved in several legislative battles, and she attempted to bring criminal charges against physicians who were involved in animal experimentation. In 1890 the WSPCA arrested two vivisectionists for cruelty and neglect. The WSPCA unsuccessfully brought criminal charges against Dr. Benjamin Shimwell, claiming that he had performed a cruel surgical procedure on a dog. Later that year, Professor William E. Ashton was arrested for a misdemeanor under the Pennsylvania anticruelty statute. The charges included his alleged failure to provide food or water after performing surgical experiments. The WSPCA ultimately declined to prosecute Professor Ashton after the medical community vowed to support him. Even though both prosecutions failed, White justified her actions by asserting that the unsuccessful prosecution of Eugene Magnan in England had led to the enactment of the 1876 Cruelty to Animals Act.[27]

In 1914 Dr. Joshua Sweet, assistant professor of surgical research at the University of Pennsylvania, and five other professors were indicted under the state cruelty statute. Sweet received the first jury trial in the United States for criminal charges arising from animal experimentation.[28] The Sweet trial was based on the kennel keeper's testimony that the dogs under his control were not properly housed or fed after the experiments. The testimony further revealed that the dogs' wounds were not treated or bandaged properly. Another witness claimed that the dogs suffered intense pain. The jury was deadlocked after forty-six hours of deliberation, and Sweet and his colleagues were not retried. Nonetheless, the medical profession was unsettled by Judge Amafee Bregy's charge to the jury defining cruelty. Judge Bregy charged that "the law says that any person who is guilty of wanton and cruel torture of an animal shall be guilty of a crime. The law does not say they shall not be guilty if they do so for a scientific purpose. Scientific purpose does not excuse cruelty."[29] After this trial, the medical profession initiated campaigns across the country to change the cruelty laws to exclude animal experimentation.[30]

The Medical Profession

The American Medical Association, the New York State Medical Society, and other state and county medical societies fought a relentless battle to destroy the antivivisection movement. They were joined by a majority of veterinarians and scientists, who helped promote the benefits of animal experimentation. It is beyond the scope of this essay to sufficiently address the numerous campaigns initiated by the medical profession or to fully develop their reasons to prevent the movement from gaining support. Yet, historians have suggested that this fight was ignited by the medical profession's desire to elevate its status in American society. Physicians believed that they could achieve greater prestige by adapting the European model of medical education, where animal research was the core component of education.[31]

Paul Starr, in his *Social Transformation of American Medicine*, asserts that late nineteenth-century doctors suffered from status anxiety. Manuals designating the proper conduct of physicians warned that overfamiliarity with patients would result in a lack of deference. D. W. Cathell, author of *The Physician Himself*, noted that the physician may encounter "many presumptuous patients or his keen friend" who would question the doctor about his course of treatment.[32]

Although the use of disparaging terms to describe antivivisection agitation was common, the language became vituperative when it pertained to women. Does this reaction toward women antivivisectionists also reflect late nineteenth-century scientific assumptions about the mental and physical capabilities of women? Several historians have addressed the nineteenth-century medical treatment of women.[33] In her essay "Gender and Medical Treatment in Nineteenth-Century America," Regina Morantz-Sanchez notes that as traditional religious beliefs declined in the late nineteenth century, society looked to the medical community to define "traditional definitions of femininity which limited women's social role to domesticity."[34] Popular medical books emphasized women's deficient nature and their inability to cope outside the domestic sphere.[35] According to Ann Douglas Wood, popular medical books proposed that "ladies get sick because they are unfeminine—in other words, sexually aggressive, intellectually ambitious, and defective in proper womanly submission and selfishness." Many physicians proposed that women's medical problems resulted from their lack of femininity and that these women could restore their health by returning to housework and childbearing.[36]

Within this social context, the medical establishment criticized women antivivisectionists as unnatural because they did not fulfill their womanly duties.[37] One physician commented that "in this howl about our dumb friends, there is a mighty feminine appeal, especially to those women unfortunate to have no children."[38] The charge of hysteria was prevalent. One medical journal described the antivivisectionists as having "surrendered themselves to a morbid sentimentality little short of fanaticism."[39] Hysteria was a peculiarly female disease characterized by moral weakness, lack of willpower, and what physician S. Weir Mitchell claimed occurred in women who lacked "rational endurance" and who had lost their power of "self-rule." Smith-Rosenberg points out that nineteenth-century medical literature described the hysterical female as a "child-woman" who was highly impressionable and had strong dependency needs and a weak ego.[40]

Hysteria and Zoophil-Psychosis

Federal and state legislation to regulate or prohibit vivisection was introduced in the early twentieth century. Some of this legislation was in response to the Rockefeller Institute, which was founded in New York State as an institution dedicated to animal research. The Davis-Lee Bill to restrict vivisection was introduced into the 1908–9 New York State legislative session. Although the bill was initially favored by the New York Senate Judiciary Committee, its support diminished after Diana Belais of the New York Anti-Vivisection Society introduced a competing bill.[41] Press coverage took a more offensive tone. An article discussing the challenge to the Rockefeller Institute described the antivivisectionists as "ignorant scrub women [who] set themselves up as authorities on scientific work."[42]

During these legislative battles, New York neurologist Dana published an article in the *Medical Record*, diagnosing a psychological disease called "zoophil-psychosis." Zoophil-psychosis was described as an excessive concern for animals. Dana was a strong advocate of vivisection. He hoped that animal experimentation could validate neurology in a time when the emergence of Freudian psychology to explain mental illness threatened to undermine its theories.[43] Dana accused the zoophilists of caring nothing for human suffering and predicted that those suffering from zoophil-psychosis could develop more "psychopathic states."[44] Zoophil-psychosis was said to affect both sexes, yet Dana claimed that women were particularly susceptible to the disease because "the nervous system of women is naturally less stable and less under volitional control."[45]

The claim that the antivivisectionists were unstable was now supported by a distinct diagnosis.[46] The historian Craig Buettinger claims that the charge had become so common by 1914 that the physiologist Frederic S. Lee proposed that "the antivivisection mania" be "recognized as a well-developed form of mental disease."[47] Critics of antivivisection pointed out that few of the activists had children. The critics claimed that the affliction usually appeared "after the usual age of parenthood and in many instances can be explained as replacing the normal 'psychoses' which we call maternal love."[48] In James Peter Warbasse's *Conquest of Disease through Animal Experimentation*, the doctor observed that zoophil-psychosis cases usually afflicted "antivivisectionists" and "kindred cults," where "these cases display a sympathy for suffering in animals while they show decidedly less concern for human suffering." Warbasse referred to an unnamed German scientist who had "divided women into two classes—the mother-type and the prostitute type. Women displaying a fondness for fondling dogs, [the German scientist] explicitly explains, do not belong to the mother type."[49]

Conclusion

A study of the early vivisection debate provides insight into the medical and scientific attitudes about the nature of women, while revealing society's reaction to women's changing roles. White was able to harness the values of "the cult of true womanhood," to motivate American women to organize against animal experimentation. In her 1913 speech before the International Anti-Vivisection and Animal Protection Congress, White spoke of conscience and asked,

> When it comes to the last hour of your life, do you not think if reasoning faculties are spared to you, that it will be a great consolation to feel that you always protected the poor, the helpless and unfortunate, and that you exercised a particular care toward those animals who, unable to tell you of their sufferings and miseries, could only by an imploring look beseech your assistance?[50]

The women involved in the early antivivisection movement transposed the cherished values of the True Woman to extend their moral influence to cure what they believed to be evil in society. Studying the vivisection controversy unveils how the medical profession dealt with women's changing roles in society, and it demonstrates social and cultural tensions in the late nineteenth and early twentieth centuries.

In Elizabeth Stuart Phelps's 1904 novel *Trixy*, Miriam Lauriet speaks to these tensions while dealing with her suitor, the medical researcher Olin Steele.

She confronts him after recovering her spaniel Caro and her friend's dog Trixy from the lab where he works. Steele justifies his experimentation on Caro by asserting that Lauriet takes a "very feminine view of the circumstances." Lauriet decides that she can never marry Steele because she cannot see "how any true woman can take a vivisector's hand."[51]

Notes

1. Charles L. Dana, "The Zoophil-Psychosis: A Modern Malady," *Medical Record* 75, no. 10 (March 1909): 381–83.

2. "Passion for Animals Really a Disease," *New York Times*, March 18, 1909.

3. Several sources provide a detailed analysis of domesticity: Barbara Welter, "The Cult of True Womanhood: 1820–1860," in *Dimity Convictions: The American Woman in the Nineteenth Century* (Athens: Ohio University Press, 1976), 21–41; Nancy F. Cott, *The Bonds of Womanhood: "Woman's Sphere" in New England, 1780–1835* (New Haven: Yale University Press, 1977); Barbara Leslie Epstein, *The Politics of Domesticity: Women, Evangelism, and Temperance in Nineteenth-Century America* (Middletown, CT: Wesleyan University Press, 1981); Lori Ginzberg, *Women and the Work of Benevolence: Morality, Politics, and Class in the Nineteenth-Century United States* (New Haven, CT: Yale University Press, 1990).

4. Katherine C. Grier, *Pets in America: A History* (Orlando, FL: Harvest Book, 2006), 164, 166; Katherine C. Grier, "Childhood Socialization and Companion Animals: United States, 1820–1870," *Society and Animals* 7, no. 2 (1999): 95–96, 100. See also Ruth H. Bloch, "American Feminine Ideals in Transition: The Rise of the Moral Mother, 1785–1815," *Feminist Studies* 4, no. 2 (June 1978): 113–14.

5. Carroll Smith-Rosenberg, "Bourgeois Discourse and the Progressive Era," in *Disorderly Conduct: Visions of Gender in Victorian America* (New York: Oxford University Press, 1985), 173–77; Welter, "Cult of True Womanhood," 41. The New Woman emerged in the 1880s and 1890s. The New Woman was considered confident and independent. Smith-Rosenberg describes these women as physicians, educational reformers, writers, and those involved in the settlement movement. See Smith-Rosenberg, "Bourgeois Discourse," 176–77.

6. Epstein, *Politics of Domesticity*, 1–9.

7. Estelle Freedman, "Separatism as Strategy: Female Institution Building and American Feminism, 1870–1930," *Feminist Studies* (Fall 1979): 513, 517.

8. See Smith-Rosenberg, "Bourgeois Discourse," 176; Welter, "Cult of True Womanhood," 41.

9. The Women's Pennsylvania Society for the Prevention of Cruelty to Animals was separately incorporated in 1897. Sydney H. Coleman, *Humane Society Leaders in America, with a Sketch of the Early History of the Humane Movement in England* (Albany, NY: American Humane Association, 1924), 180.

10. Bernard Oreste Unti, "The Quality of Mercy: Organized Animal Protection in the United States, 1866–1930," PhD diss., Department of History, American University, 2002, 334–35. S. Weir Mitchell was an expert on neurology and the inventor of the rest cure for neurasthenics and invalid women. He was most notably referenced in Charlotte Perkins Gilman's short story "The Yellow Wallpaper" (1892). Gilman later said that she sent a copy of the story to the physician who had so nearly driven her mad. Charlotte Perkins Gilman, *The Yellow Wallpaper*, ed. Dale M. Bauer, Bedford Cultural Editions, (Boston: Bedford/St. Martin's, 1998), 41–58, 348–49.

11. Unti, "Quality of Mercy," 338.

12. Caroline Earle White, "The History of the Antivivisection Movement," *Proceedings of the International Anti-Vivisection and Animal Protection Congress* (New York: Tudor, 1914), 25, 28.

13. Coleman, *Humane Society Leaders,* 203–8.

14. White, "History of the Anti-Vivisection Movement," 28–31; see also Albert Leffingwell, *An Ethical Problem* (New Haven, CT: C. P. Farrell, 1914), 216–17.

15. Craig Buettinger, "Women and Antivivisection in Late Nineteenth-Century America," *Journal of Social History* 30, no. 4 (1997): 859. Buettinger cites the AAVS annual reports for the period from 1883 to 1895.

16. Unti, "Quality of Mercy," 339.

17. See Buettinger, "Women and Antivivisection," 859. For an analysis of British antivivisection and feminism, see Coral Lansbury, *The Old Brown Dog: Women, Workers, and Vivisection in Edwardian England* (Madison: University of Wisconsin Press, 1985); Coral Lansbury, "Gynaecology, Pornography, and the Antivivisection Movement," *Victorian Studies* 28, no. 3 (1985): 413–37; Hilda Keen, "'The Smooth Cool Men of Science': The Feminist and Socialist Response to Vivisection," *History Workshop Journal* 40 (1995): 16–38. Yet, Susan E. Lederer notes that the theme of feminism and sexual surgery was not completely ignored by American writers. Susan E. Lederer, *Subjected to Science: Human Experimentation in America before the Second World War* (Baltimore: Johns Hopkins University Press, 1995), 38; Susan E. Lederer, "The Controversy over Animal Experimentation in America, 1880–1914," in *Vivisection in Historical Perspective*, ed. Nicolaas A. Rupke (London: Croom Helm, 1987), 236–58. See Elizabeth Stuart Phelps, *Though Life Us Do Part* (Boston: Houghton, Mifflin, 1908); Elizabeth Stuart Phelps, *Trixy* (Boston: Houghton, Mifflin, 1904).

18. Buettinger, "Women and Antivivisection," 863.

19. Ibid.

20. Ruth Bordin, *Women and Temperance: The Quest for Power and Liberty, 1873–1900* (Philadelphia: Temple University Press, 1981), 97. Frances Willard was the president of the WCTU from 1879 until her death in 1898. She reshaped the organization with her "Do everything" policy. The "Do everything" campaign aimed at solving specific societal problems, such as poverty, prison reform, and humane education.

Bordin notes that it provided a way for all women to relate to the movement. By 1883 only three of the twenty departments dealt with promoting temperance. See also Ruth Bordin, *Frances Willard: A Biography* (Chapel Hill: University of North Carolina Press, 1986), 129–30.

21. Coleman, *Humane Society Leaders,* 186.

22. Buettinger, "Women and Antivivisection," 864.

23. AAVS Minute Book 1889–1900, 119–27, quoted in ibid.

24. The NCW was a coalition of major women's reform movements of the time. It originated in 1888 when the National Women's Suffrage Association (NWSA) invited a number of women's reform groups to the fortieth-anniversary commemoration of Seneca Falls. Yet, suffrage was not a priority of the NCW.

25. Buettinger, "Women and Antivivisection," 864–65; "Women Talk about Dress: Long Skirts and Corsets Condemned by National Council," *New York Times*, February 28, 1895, 13.

26. Buettinger, "Women and Antivivisection," 863; "National Council of Women: Sessions in February and March, 1895, in Washington," *New York Times*, October 25, 1894, 3; "The Progressive Women," *New York Times*, February 19, 1895, 16; "Women Discuss Cruelty," *New York Times,* February 24, 1895, 3.

27. Unti, "Quality of Mercy," 341; "Law for Doctor's Dogs," *Philadelphia Press*, June 24, 1890. For more on Eugene Magnan, see Richard French, *Antivivisection and Medical Science in Victorian Society* (Princeton: Princeton University Press, 1975), 55–62, 80–81.

28. "News of the Week," *Medical Record* 85, no. 17 (April 25, 1914): 758; "Tell of Sufferings of Vivisected Dogs; Witnesses Testify against Dr. Joshua Sweet of the University of Pennsylvania," *New York Times*, April 16, 1914.

29. "News of the Week"; "Judge's Decision Hits Vivisection," *New York Tribune*, April 18, 1914; "Cruelty Case Jury Unable to Agree," *New York Times*, April 19, 1914; "The Trial of the Doctors," *New York Times*, April 18, 1914; "The Law as She Is Read," *New York Times*, April 21, 2014.

30. Section 10 of the New York cruelty statute of 1867 included a specific exclusion for "properly conducted scientific experiments or investigations." See An Act for the More Effectual Prevention of Cruelty to Animals N.Y. Rev. ch. 375, §§1–10 (1867) in David Favre and Vivien Tsang, "The Development of Anti-Cruelty Laws during the 1800s," *Detroit College of Law Review* (Spring 1993): 1–35, appendix A: The 1867 New York Anti-Cruelty Law. See also Animal Welfare Institute (AWI), *Animals and Their Legal Rights: A Survey of American Laws from 1641 to 1990* (Washington, DC: AWI, 1990), 5.

31. Mary L. Westermann-Cicio, "Of Mice and Medical Men: The Medical Profession's Response to the Vivisection Controversy at the Turn of the Century," PhD diss., Department of History, State University of New York at Stony Brook, 2001, 137. On the history of medicine in the United States, see Paul Starr, *The Social Transformation of American Medicine: The*

Rise of a Sovereign Profession and the Making of a Vast Industry (New York: Basic Books, 1982).

32. Quoted in Starr, *Social Transformation*, 85–88, 88.

33. Ann Douglas Wood, "'The Fashionable Diseases': Women's Complaints and Their Treatment in Nineteenth-Century America," in *Women and Health in America: Historical Readings*, ed. Judith Walzer Leavitt (Madison: University of Wisconsin Press, 1984), 222–38; Carroll Smith-Rosenberg and Charles Rosenberg, "The Female Animal: Medical and Biological Views of Women and Her Role in Nineteenth-Century America," in Judith Walzer Leavitt, ed., *Women and Health in America: Historical Readings* (Madison: University of Wisconsin Press, 1984), 12–37; Carroll Smith-Rosenberg, "The Hysterical Woman: Sex Roles and Role Conflict in Nineteenth-Century America," in *Disorderly Conduct: Visions of Gender in Victorian America* (New York: Oxford University Press, 1985), 197–216; Diane Price Herndl, *Figuring Feminine Illness in American Fiction and Culture, 1840–1940* (Chapel Hill: University of North Carolina Press, 1993). For a full discussion of the subject of the medical profession's attitude toward women in the nineteenth century, see Cynthia E. Russet, *Sexual Science: The Victorian Construction of Womanhood* (Cambridge, MA: Harvard University Press, 1989).

34. Regina Morantz-Sanchez, *Sympathy and Science: Women Physicians in American Medicine* (New York: Oxford University Press, 1985), 205.

35. See, for example, Edward H. Clarke, *Sex in Education, or, a Fair Chance for Girls* (Boston: J. R. Osgood, 1873). Dr. Clarke of Harvard proposed that young women of the 1870s were ill because they were destroying their wombs and childbearing abilities by pursuing a course of higher education.

36. Wood, "Fashionable Diseases," 226–27.

37. Ibid., 227; Smith-Rosenberg and Rosenberg, "Female Animal," 19.

38. Walter B. Cannon, "Medical Control of Vivisection," *North American Review* 191 (1910): 814.

39. "Philadelphia," *The British Medical Journal* 1, no. 2049 (April 7, 1900): 879.

40. Smith-Rosenberg, "Hysterical Woman," 211–12. The term "hysteria" is derived from the Greek and means "uterus." It was thought to be a disorder of women, caused by alterations in the womb. Ilza Veith, *Hysteria: The History of a Disease* (Chicago: University of Chicago Press, 1965), 1.

41. Unti, "Quality of Mercy," 636–41; Leffingwell, *Ethical Problem*, 218–19; Walter B. Cannon, *Antivivisection Legislation: Its History, Aims, and Menace* (Chicago: American Medical Association, 1913), 4–6.

42. Westermann-Cicio, "Of Mice and Medical Men," 148.

43. Dana, "Zoophil-Psychosis," 381–83; Craig Buettinger, "Antivivisection and the Charge of Zoophil-Psychosis in the Early Twentieth Century," *Historian* 55, no. 2 (1993): 277–88. In the late nineteenth century, neurologists proposed that "nervous exhaustion, or neurasthenia, manifested itself in a plethora of physical and mental woes." Buettinger, "Antivivisection," 279.

44. Dana, "Zoophil-Psychosis," 381–83. See Charles L. Dana, *The Text-Book of Nervous Diseases: For the Use of Students and Practitioners of Medicine*, 8th ed. (New York: William Wood, 1915), 509.

45. Charles L. Dana, "Neurasthenia," *Post-Graduate* 6 (1890–91); 26, quoted in Francis G. Gosling, *Before Freud: Neurasthenia and the American Medical Community, 1870–1910* (Urbana: University of Illinois Press, 1987), 103–4.

46. Dana, "Zoophil-Psychosis," 381–83; Buettinger, "Antivivisection," 277–88. By the 1890s, the neurologists were focused upon mental disturbances, such as depression and anxiety, and believed that the physical problems were imaginary. See Gosling, *Before Freud*, 81.

47. Buettinger, "Antivivisection," 285; "Passion for Animals Really a Disease," *New York Times*, March 18, 1909; "Topic of the Time," *New York Times*, March 9, 1909.

48. "Explains Methods of Medical Experiment: Prof. Murlin of Cornell," *New York Times*, February 10, 1911; "The Zoophil-Psychosis," *New York Times*, July 11, 1909.

49. James Peter Warbasse, *The Conquest of Disease through Animal Experimentation* (New York: D. Appleton, 1910), 158–61; William W. Keen, *The Influence of Antivivisection on Character*, 2nd ed. (Chicago: American Medical Association, 1920).

50. White, "History," 34.

51. Phelps, *Trixy*, 218, 274.

Bibliography

Bloch, Ruth H. "American Feminine Ideals in Transition: The Rise of the Moral Mother, 1785–1815." *Feminist Studies* 4, no. 2 (June 1978): 101–26.

Bordin, Ruth. *Frances Willard: A Biography*. Chapel Hill: University of North Carolina Press, 1986.

———. *Women and Temperance: The Quest for Power and Liberty, 1873–1900*. Philadelphia: Temple University Press, 1981.

Buettinger, Craig. "Antivivisection and the Charge of Zoophil-Psychosis in the Early Twentieth Century." *Historian* 55, no. 2 (1993): 277–88.

———. "Women and Antivivisection in Late Nineteenth-Century America." *Journal of Social History* 30, no. 4 (1997): 857–70.

Cannon, Walter B. *Antivivisection Legislation: Its History, Aims, and Menace*. Chicago: American Medical Association, 1913.

———. "Medical Control of Vivisection." *North American Review* 191 (1910): 814.

Clarke, Edward H. *Sex in Education, or, a Fair Chance for Girls*. Boston: J. R. Osgood, 1873.

Coleman, Sydney H. *Humane Society Leaders in America, with a Sketch of the Early History of the Humane Movement in England*. Albany: American Humane Association, 1924.

Cott, Nancy F. *The Bonds of Womanhood: "Women's Sphere" in New England, 1780–1835*. New Haven: Yale University Press, 1977.

Dana, Charles L. *The Text-Book of Nervous Diseases: For the Use of Students and Practitioners of Medicine.* 8th ed. New York: William Wood, 1915.

———. "The Zoophil-Psychosis: A Modern Malady." *Medical Record* 75, no. 10 (March 1909): 381–83.

Epstein, Barbara Leslie. *The Politics of Domesticity: Women, Evangelism, and Temperance in Nineteenth-Century America.* Middletown, CT: Wesleyan University Press, 1981.

Favre, David, and Vivien Tsang. "The Development of Anti-Cruelty Laws during the 1800s." Appendix A: The 1867 New York Anti-Cruelty Law. *Detroit College of Law Review* (Spring 1993): 1–35.

Freedman, Estelle. "Separatism as Strategy: Female Institution Building and American Feminism, 1870–1930." *Feminist Studies* (Fall 1979): 512–29.

French, Richard D. *Antivivisection and Medical Science in Victorian Society.* Princeton: Princeton University Press, 1975.

Gilman, Charlotte Perkins. *The Yellow Wallpaper.* Edited by Dale M. Bauer. Bedford Cultural Editions. Boston: Bedford/St. Martin's, 1998.

Ginzberg, Lori. *Women and the Work of Benevolence: Morality, Politics, and Class in the Nineteenth-Century United States.* New Haven: Yale University Press, 1990.

Gosling, F. G. *Neurasthenia and the American Medical Community, 1870–1910.* Urbana: University of Illinois Press, 1987.

Grier, Katherine C. "Childhood Socialization and Companion Animals: United States, 1820–1870." *Society and Animals* 7, no. 2 (1999): 95–120.

———. *Pets in America: A History.* Orlando, FL: Harvest Book, 2006.

Herndl, Diane Price. *Figuring Feminine Illness in American Fiction and Culture, 1840–1940.* Chapel Hill: University of North Carolina Press, 1993.

Keen, Hilda. "'The Smooth Cool Men of Science': The Feminist and Socialist Response to Vivisection." *History Workshop Journal* 40 (1995): 16–38.

Keen, William W. *The Influence of Antivivisection on Character.* 2nd ed. Chicago: American Medical Association, 1920.

Lansbury, Coral. "Gynaecology, Pornography, and the Antivivisection Movement." *Victorian Studies* 28, no. 3 (1985): 413–37.

———. *The Old Brown Dog: Women, Workers, and Vivisection in Edwardian England.* Madison: University of Wisconsin Press, 1985.

Leavitt, Judith Walzer, ed. *Women and Health in America: Historical Readings.* Madison: University of Wisconsin Press, 1984.

Lederer, Susan E. "The Controversy over Animal Experimentation in America, 1880–1914." In *Vivisection in Historical Perspective*, edited by Nicolaas A. Rupke, 236–58. London: Croom Helm, 1987.

———. *Subjected to Science: Human Experimentation in America before the Second World War.* Baltimore: Johns Hopkins University Press, 1995.

Leffingwell, Albert. *An Ethical Problem.* New Haven, CT: C. P. Farrell, 1914.

Morantz-Sanchez, Regina. *Sympathy and Science: Women Physicians in American Medicine.* New York: Oxford University Press, 1985.

"News of the Week." *Medical Record* 85, no. 17 (April 25, 1914): 758.

Phelps, Elizabeth Stuart. *Though Life Us Do Part.* Boston: Houghton, Mifflin, 1908.

———. *Trixy.* Boston: Houghton, Mifflin, 1904.

"Philadelphia." *The British Medical Journal* 1, no. 2049 (April 7, 1900): 879.

Russet, Cynthia E. *Sexual Science: The Victorian Construction of Womanhood.* Cambridge, MA: Harvard University Press, 1989.

Smith-Rosenberg, Carroll. "Bourgeois Discourse and the Progressive Era." In *Disorderly Conduct: Visions of Gender in Victorian America*, 167–81. New York: Oxford University Press, 1985.

———. "The Hysterical Woman: Sex Roles and Role Conflict in Nineteenth-Century America." In *Disorderly Conduct: Visions of Gender in Victorian America*, 197–216. New York: Oxford University Press, 1985.

Smith-Rosenberg, Carroll, and Charles Rosenberg. "The Female Animal: Medical and Biological Views of Women and Her Role in Nineteenth-Century America." In *Women and Health in America: Historical Readings*, edited by Judith Walzer Leavitt, 12–27. Madison: University of Wisconsin Press, 1984.

Starr, Paul. *The Social Transformation of American Medicine: The Rise of a Sovereign Profession and the Making of a Vast Industry.* New York: Basic Books, 1982.

Unti, Bernard Oreste. "The Quality of Mercy: Organized Animal Protection in the United States, 1866–1930." PhD diss., Department of History, American University, 2002.

Veith, Ilza. *Hysteria: The History of a Disease.* Chicago: University of Chicago Press, 1965.

Warbasse, James Peter. *The Conquest of Disease through Animal Experimentation.* New York: D. Appleton, 1910.

Welter, Barbara. "The Cult of True Womanhood: 1820–1860." In *Dimity Convictions: The American Woman in the Nineteenth Century*, 21–41. Athens: Ohio University Press, 1976.

Westermann-Cicio, Mary L. "Of Mice and Medical Men: The Medical Profession's Response to the Vivisection Controversy at the Turn of the Century." PhD diss., Department of History, State University of New York at Stony Brook, 2001.

White, Caroline Earle. "The History of the Antivivisection Movement." *Proceedings of the International Anti-Vivisection and Animal Protection Congress*, 25–35. New York: Tudor Press, 1914.

Wood, Ann Douglas. "'The Fashionable Diseases': Women's Complaints and Their Treatment in Nineteenth-Century America." In *Women and Health in America: Historical Readings*, edited by Judith Walzer Leavitt, 222–38. Madison: University of Wisconsin Press, 1984.

Is "Necessity" a Useful Concept in Animal Research Ethics?

John Rossi and Samual A. Garner

THE CURRENT STATE of animal research ethics is marked by a deep political divide. On the one hand, the past forty years have witnessed the development of a substantial academic literature around animals' moral standing and the ethics of animal use, including the use of animals in scientific research. One recent estimate holds that over fifteen hundred scholarly books have been published on animal welfare and ethics,[1] and the number of journal articles surely ranks in the thousands. Much if not most of this scholarly literature has been critical of the status quo of animal use in research.[2] Under this status quo, at least 115 million animals (and quite possibly many more) are used in research each year worldwide,[3] often in highly invasive ways, and are typically killed at the termination of the experiment. Critics of the ethics of animal research have questioned the degree to which it has produced important medical advances. They have argued that harms to animals in research are not being sufficiently minimized, that alternatives to animal use in research are not being sought aggressively enough, and that animals' moral standing is such that much (and perhaps even all) invasive research would not be ethically justified even if it did produce important medical advances.[4]

On the other hand, the scientific and regulatory communities have yet to seriously engage these ethical criticisms. Regulations regarding animal research, though incrementally changing, are generally still very permissive worldwide. This is certainly true of the United States.[5] Although the philosophical literature on animal ethics is quite sizable, articles relating to the ethics of animal research only rarely appear in scientific journals, with scientists seldom publishing on the issue in other forums. When such articles from the scientific community do appear, they tend to be short, tend not to substantively engage ethical criticisms and arguments relevant to animal research, and are all too often highly inflammatory.[6] Instead, the dominant framing for animal research ethics within the scientific and regulatory communities continues to be one of "necessity."

The concept of necessity features in animal research at two levels. At the first and broader level, representatives of the biomedical community commonly assert that animal research is generally "necessary" as an institutionalized practice (or that animal research is "essential" or "required," which amounts to the same thing). For example, the *U.S. Government Principles for the Utilization and Care of Vertebrate Animals Used in Testing, Research, and Training* states that "the development of knowledge necessary for the improvement of the health and well-being of humans as well as other animals requires *in vivo* experimentation with a wide variety of animal species."[7] Similarly, the American College of Laboratory Animal Medicine, an accrediting body for veterinary specialists in laboratory animal medicine, asserts that "humane experimentation involving animals is necessary to provide knowledge vital to preserve and improve health and quality of life for man and animals."[8] The California Biomedical Research Association has an entire "fact sheet" titled "Why Are Animals Necessary in Biomedical Research?"[9] Many other articles and editorials authored by scientists echo these claims of necessity.[10] Such broad claims seem intended to support and justify the commonplace use of animals in research, as opposed to viewing such animal use as an exceptional or rare (though perhaps still justifiable) practice.

At a second and more specific level, the concept of necessity figures into the regulation of individual animal experiments. In this essay we focus on the United States' regulations. US regulations require that before animals may be used in research, investigators and committees reviewing animal research (institutional animal care and use committees, or IACUCs) must determine that animal-based methods are necessary for answering the scientific question and that non–animal-based methods would not suffice. If this question is answered in the affirmative for an experiment, then (in conjunction with other criteria laid out below) an IACUC cannot prohibit the use of animals on the grounds that harms to them are excessive or are not proportional to the anticipated benefits of the experiment.[11] Once the decision has been made to use animals in an experiment, investigators are required to use anesthesia and analgesia for procedures potentially causing pain or distress. However, anesthesia and/or analgesia might be withheld if the investigator believes this to be "scientifically necessary" to the achievement of the experimental objectives.[12] Similarly, the *Guide for the Care and Use of Laboratory Animals*, which amplifies the requirements of the *U.S. Public Health Service Policy on Humane Care and Use of Laboratory Animals*, mandates social housing for nonhuman primates but allows exceptions "if it is necessary to house animals singly—for example, when justified for experimental purposes."[13]

The concept of necessity has also been invoked concerning the use of specific species of animals in research. For example, in 2011 the Institute of Medicine authored a report, *Chimpanzees in Biomedical and Behavioral Research: Assessing the Necessity*, in which the authors take up the question of whether the continued use of chimpanzees in such research is "necessary for research discoveries and to deter-

mine the safety and efficacy of new prevention or treatment strategies" (for the record, the answer was mostly "no").[14] And under US regulations, investigators are required to consider the "3Rs" of refinement and replacement of animal use, as well as reduction of the number of animals used in research.[15] One refinement strategy is to use species of animals that are cognitively and affectively less advanced than the species originally proposed (e.g., replacing rats with zebrafish), on the assumption that such a replacement will lessen the harm experienced by the animals. However, as with other points in the US regulations, the necessity of a particular species to experimental objectives trumps other ethical considerations: if it is determined that a more advanced species is necessary to the achievement of the experimental objectives, then the IACUC must allow for this choice.

Despite the centrality of the concept of necessity in the biomedical community's regulation of and rhetoric about animal research, there appears to be very little philosophical work exploring this concept or responding to scientists' and regulators' claims that animal research is necessary.[16] This omission is particularly curious in light of the now-large philosophical literature on animal ethics. It might be the case that scholars writing about animal ethics believe that philosophical work to date has implicitly addressed such claims of necessity. Indeed, much previous work in animal ethics is relevant to this issue of necessity. However, ethics is an extended dialogue, and progress in this dialogue is facilitated when one party responds directly to the claims of another. Such a direct response is also important since the scientific community has not generally taken steps to embrace philosophical work in animal ethics and since some scientists seem to understand the idea of "scientific necessity" as trumping ethical criticisms of animal research.[17] Further, formally exploring the concept of necessity in animal research leads us to reflect on some seldom-asked ethical questions, such as the obligatoriness of achieving medical progress and the role that justice plays in constraining allowable harms to animals in pursuing such progress. In the remainder of this essay, we clarify what claims of necessity might mean in the context of animal research and whether such claims can sufficiently justify research that harms animals. Our goal is not simply to address the question of whether harmful animal research is morally justified (though we believe that much of it isn't) but, rather, to consider whether the concept of necessity is informative or adequate in thinking about such justification.

On the Nature of "Necessity"

We begin by clarifying the sense of "necessity" at issue, since this term has multiple meanings in both ordinary language and philosophy. Without getting into philosophical technicalities, we can note that animal research is not necessary in the metaphysical sense that it *must* be done or is impossible not to do. Should we wish to, we could halt harmful animal research—there might be consequences to doing so, but we could do it. Instead, and as the preceding discussion suggests, the kind of necessity at issue appears to be "instrumental" or "means-end" necessity, which denotes the idea that if we wish to accomplish a certain goal (end), then we must engage in animal research to achieve this goal.[18] Typically, the goal or end in question is the development of new ways to prevent, treat, or cure disease. The advancement of knowledge is also sometimes considered a goal of biomedical research, but this knowledge is most often thought to have value because it might eventually lead to the development of new therapies.[19]

A pure claim of instrumental necessity entails no ethical conclusions. To say that a particular end requires a certain means to achieve it does not entail that the end is in the first place valuable or desirable, that the end has a particular level of value attached to it, or that the end justifies the means. Thus, if persons or organizations asserting the necessity of animal research intend only for these claims to be pure means-end claims, then such claims perform no work when it comes to the ethical justification of animal research.

However, documents discussing the necessity of animal research are typically normative and not merely descriptive, since claims of necessity almost always seem intended to ethically justify animal research.[20] Thus, the implicit moral claim under consideration in this essay amounts to the following: *If we want to achieve medical progress, then it is necessary for us to perform animal research, and because animal research is necessary in this instrumental sense, it is permissible (or even obligatory) in a moral sense.* We'll refer to this as the "necessity principle." This necessity principle represents an explicit articulation of what defenders of animal research seem to have in mind when they assert its necessity. Although assertions of the necessity of animal research sometimes describe this as "scientific necessity," as this principle makes clear, most such assertions are also ethical in nature.

The necessity principle employs the notion of "restricted necessity": "restricted necessity takes the end as given—that is, not subject to evaluation—and asks only whether the course of action suggested is an indispensable means to that end."[21] At the institutional level, "the end taken as given" is the end of medical progress. However, as will be discussed in this essay, the concept of "medical progress" is ambiguous and requires specification. As a result, the necessity principle just introduced also requires specification, since it makes the ethical acceptability of animal research dependent on the research's contributions to medical progress. A strict version of the necessity principle might allow only for research that has a high chance of contributing to medical progress, research that contributes to particularly important kinds of medical progress, or both.

Having said this, assertions of the necessity of animal research usually seem intended to defend not just the general practice of animal research but also more specifically the status quo of animal research under the current regulations. Support for this conclusion comes from the fact that materials defending the necessity of animal research often speak favorably of current regulations (whether in the United States, the United Kingdom, or elsewhere) and imply or state outright that such regulations offer substantial protections to animals, protections that ensure the justifiability of what research gets conducted.[22] And in the United States at least, the current regulations governing animal experiments also employ the notion of restricted necessity. As already discussed, these regulations do

> not ask IACUCs to balance animal suffering against the scientific merit or promise of any given exper-

iment. Instead, [they ask] IACUCs to ensure only that any given protocol has scientific merit and that any animal suffering the protocol induces is strictly necessary to that science. The result is that any study that will advance science, even in a very small way, can be used to justify tremendous amounts of animal suffering, as long as the suffering is necessary to the advance.[23]

Just the same, the choice of species used and the decision to use animals in the first place are both subordinated to the specific aims of the experiment. To the extent that commentators asserting the necessity of animal research desire to support this status quo, the intended version of the necessity principle appears to be a permissive one. Some scientists defending the necessity of animal research are explicit on this point: "an experiment that uses animals would be justifiable if it is done in such a way that causes minimal pain to the animals involved and if all possible alternative methods have been explored" (i.e., if animal use and any pain caused therein are instrumentally necessary to answering the scientific question at hand).[24]

Because the necessity principle incorporates an ethical judgment, its defensibility depends on whether it offers sufficient ethical justification for harmful animal research. This can be determined by assessing the necessity principle against leading accounts of our moral obligations to animals and against the requirements of an adequate ethical justification more generally. We discuss this issue in the following section. Some of the criticisms we levy against the necessity principle are based on its logic and thus apply to any version of it, whereas others are directed against the permissive version introduced here, which we believe to be the intended version in most cases. In the discussion that follows, it will be helpful to keep in mind that the necessity principle does not stand alone but, rather, rests on a few key assumptions. One of these is the scientific assumption that animal research is effective in achieving the end of medical progress. The necessity principle also rests on two ethical assumptions—namely, that similar research conducted on human beings would be unethical and that conducting such research on animals is *not* unethical. These assumptions will be examined in more detail in the following discussion.

Does the Necessity Principle Offer Sufficient Ethical Justification?

The necessity principle introduced previously in this essay holds that harmful animal research is morally justified because it is instrumentally necessary to the achievement of medical progress. However, from a logical perspective, no plausible moral theory would license a harm to some individual(s) simply because that harm is instrumentally necessary to the achievement of a benefit, even if the benefit in question is important and otherwise worthy of pursuit.[25] Two examples will be provided here, though the point generalizes to other theories as well.[26] First, consider utilitarianism, which in its classical formulation holds that the right action is the action that best maximizes benefits over harms among all possible courses of action. As soon as this theory is spelled out, we can appreciate that its logic is very different from the necessity principle: the necessity principle asks only whether animal research is a necessary means to some benefit, whereas utilitarianism requires us to examine the importance of the benefit and the magnitude of the costs, licensing harms only to the extent that they are part of a welfare-maximizing (or harm-minimizing) scheme.

Deontological (i.e., duty- or rule-based) ethical theories are even stricter, since according to such theories individuals deserve moral protections (e.g., as enshrined in rights) that cannot be eroded to serve the general welfare, except perhaps in situations of emergency that cannot be likened to animal research.[27] Our current approach to regulating human research is deontological in nature. Though research with human beings is instrumentally necessary for generating knowledge and improvements to human health, we have set strict limits on allowable harms to human participants in research. This is especially true for humans who, like nonhuman animals, cannot provide authentic consent. For example, in the United States allowable risk and harm in human pediatric research is limited to "minimal risk" or a minor increment over this, where "minimal risk" is defined as that not exceeding the risk of daily life activities or routine physical or psychological examinations.[28]

It might be objected that the preceding point applies only to human-human morality and not to animal research ethics and that the instrumental necessity of animal research to achieving medical progress *does* justify animal use. This could be because animals have a lower moral standing than humans or because animals have no direct moral standing at all. In the former view, it might be asserted that although "one may attend to animal interests, human interests always take precedence."[29] Thus, the argument goes, although animals should not be caused avoidable or gratuitous harm in research, any harms to animals that are *unavoidable* in the pursuit of the experimental objectives can be justified as long as these objectives are intended to contribute in some way to medical progress. However, this objection fails for a number of reasons. In the first place, almost all contemporary philosophers writing about animal ethics agree that nonhuman animals have *some* direct moral standing, and so the necessity principle cannot be vindicated on the grounds that animals' interests do not matter morally. Further, such a position would be even more permissive than the necessity principle under consideration and therefore would not support even the limited "humane care and use" paradigm currently regnant under US regulations.[30] Thus, defenders of the necessity principle have reason to reject no-status views as well.

Assuming that nonhuman animals have some direct moral standing, the question then becomes "How much?" An increasing number of scholars have argued that animals deserve equal moral consideration (EC) to humans, meaning that animals' interests deserve the same amount of moral protection that we grant to humans' comparable interests—and furthermore that animals' interests cannot be morally "discounted."[31] EC views are typically defended by way of negative argument: having established that animals have moral standing, we ask whether there are any good reasons to think that their interests deserve less moral consideration than human interests, and it turns out to be the case that all candidate reasons are indefensible. The idea that species per se should determine moral considerability has been roundly criticized as both arbitrary and question-begging (why not family or genus, for example?), and few if any contemporary philosophers espouse this view.

If instead it is held that animals deserve less moral consideration than humans on the basis that animals are not self-aware beings possessed of sophisticated rational agency, then this argument also has the consequence that infants, senile persons, and mentally disabled persons deserve less moral consideration than "fully rational" humans.[32] Most persons will not want to accept this conclusion. However, upholding this "rational agency" argument for morally discounting animals' interests while also finding a defensible way to include nonrational humans in the sphere of individuals deserving of full moral standing is dubious.[33] Additionally, appeals to "moral community" are sometimes used to justify granting lesser moral consideration to animals, the idea being that we have special obligations to other humans with whom we have certain relationships (e.g., children). However, although this might be true, such obligations are invariably positive in nature and do not justify our harming other humans with whom we do not have such relationships.[34] Thus, it is unclear why this argument should justify harmful animal research.

If animals deserve EC, then the necessity principle clearly fails to justify harmful animal research, in either its strict or its permissive versions. A utilitarian view incorporating EC (some would say this is definitional to utilitarianism) would have to weigh animals' interests equally to humans' interests in the calculus of benefits and harms. As we have already seen, this is both different from and more demanding than the necessity principle. If we retain the deontological approach to research ethics that we employ for humans and also accept EC for animals, then the necessity principle fails here, too: the level of protection that we should grant to animals in research would, in this view, be more or less equivalent to the level of protection that we grant to humans in research, with the result being that most current animal research would be halted.[35]

The necessity principle also fails to provide sufficient justification for harming animals if we conclude that animals deserve unequal moral consideration (UC), meaning that animals' interests deserve some moral consideration but less than that given to humans' interests. This is certainly true of the permissive version of the principle and is most likely true of stricter versions of the principle as well. The most plausible version of a UC view, the sliding-scale view, holds that moral considerability is a function of the prudential value of a life—that is, the richness of a life to the individual living it. At the top of the hierarchy stand humans, who deserve full moral consideration. As one moves "down" the phylogenetic scale, animals of progressively lesser cognitive, affective, and social complexity are granted progressively lesser moral consideration.[36] According to the sliding-scale view, the permissibility of harming an animal depends on (at least) three criteria: the degree of harm involved; the animal's place on the sliding scale, which will determine how much moral weight we give to this harm; and the significance of the human interest that is being advanced by harming the animal. Again we can see that harms to animals cannot be justified in this view merely because they are instrumentally necessary to the production of some benefit.

It is possible that a restrictive version of the necessity principle might share some similarities with the sliding-scale UC view, since such a restrictive version might appeal to the magnitude and probability of benefit in licensing harmful animal research. Even here, though, costs to animals do not seem to be part of the equation, and if the necessity principle is amended to include considerations of costs to animals, the probability and magnitude of possible benefit, and the moral status of the animals in question, then it can no longer really be regarded as a necessity-based justification of animal research. Instead, such a view seems to have turned into a UC-based account.

The preceding discussion highlights a second problem with the necessity principle, particularly in its permissive form: apart from its logical deficiencies in justifying harm, the substantive level of protection it offers to animals in research falls well short of any reasonable account of our moral obligations to animals. According to the permissive version of the necessity principle, any harm to animals in research, no matter how severe, can be justified as long as the harm is an unavoidable part of an experiment that is (reasonably) aimed at producing medical progress of some kind. There is no requirement that the benefit be great, that its realization be probable, or that the benefit exceed the costs. But as already discussed, a deontological view coupled with EC would result in the abolition of almost all harmful animal research, apart from that which imposes only the minimal level of harm also allowable in human pediatric research.

Utilitarian thinking has been used to both justify and criticize animal research, and admittedly there is more than a small amount of uncertainty in calculations of the costs and benefits of animal research.[37] Having said this, most scholars who write about utilitarianism and animals (and certainly the analyses we regard as most comprehensive) have argued that this theory would prohibit much animal research, both as a retrospective historical judgment and as a prospective judgment moving forward.[38] Even granting that animal research has produced important human benefits, its predictive value has historically been rather poor, with failures being far more numerous than successes. Further, some (perhaps even many) "successes" have been products that do not represent an important medical benefit (e.g., "me, too" drugs designed primarily to enrich industry). Weighed against this, harms to animals in research are both certain and massive. The sheer number of animals killed in research each year alone (more than a hundred million), coupled with the harm they experience while alive—a cost aggregated many times over—creates a welfare debit so large that even some very important new human therapies (e.g., an important new chemotherapeutic drug) developed periodically would arguably have a hard time outweighing the harms. If we are serious about justifying animal research on a utilitarian view, then we have our argumentative work cut out for us and cannot fall back upon proclamations that the benefits of such research are incalculably great and thus that no further analysis needs to be done.[39] And importantly, the requirement that medical benefits to humans or other animals outweigh the costs to animals used in research means that a truly utilitarian approach would be much more demanding than the necessity principle.

As for deontological views incorporating UC, these are relatively newer and have not received the same amount of scholarly attention as utilitarian or other EC-based views. However, our discussion of the sliding-scale view allows us to appreciate that it would likely prohibit invasive research on some species, such as chimpanzees or dolphins, because their mental sophistication grants them full or near-full moral standing.[40] And like utilitarianism, such a view would also substantially limit research with many other sentient animals, because harms to animals must be justified by a compensatory benefit and because some animals' moral standing would be sufficiently high as to grant their interests preferential weighting in a cost-benefit calculus. Some recent scholarship has gone even further and argued that even if animals are due lesser moral consideration than humans, harmful animal research will still be unjustified.[41]

The preceding criticisms apply to a lesser degree to the strict version of the necessity principle, but they apply nonetheless.

Is Medical Progress a Moral Imperative?

In the hope of circumventing objections on the basis of animals' moral status, a defender of the necessity principle might invoke the idea of unconditional, obligatory medical progress. Such a person might argue that medical progress in preventing, treating, or curing disease is of such high moral importance as to be an overriding goal that we are morally obligated to pursue, regardless of its costs to animals. Continued animal research would thus be "necessary" to meet this nonnegotiable goal. In fact, this seems to be the view of numerous scientists writing about animal research. For example, in a 2011 article, neuroscientist Dario L. Ringach asserts that "when scientists are confronted with the incredible suffering caused by disease on one hand and faced with our proven ability to challenge such maladies on the other, we feel a *moral imperative* to act."[42]

This idea of an unconditional obligation to pursue medical progress is intriguing and, to the best of our knowledge, has not been given much consideration in the philosophical literature on animal research. However, it runs up against a number of difficulties. First, the notion of an *unconditional* positive obligation presupposes the idea of a positive obligation more generally. Certainly, it is true that disease, debility, and early death are bad for individuals experiencing them and that such individuals, ceteris paribus, would be better off not having experienced such. Additionally, many persons would consider it morally praiseworthy to help others. But a praiseworthy action is not the same

thing as an obligatory action. Although many moral theories hold that we have positive obligations of assistance, some do not. Even assuming some positive obligations, the obligation to pursue medical progress might not rank among these. Thus, the claim of an *unconditional* obligation to pursue medical progress assumes this more general burden of proof.

Assuming this general burden of proof can be met, the idea of an *unconditional* positive obligation might be incoherent and thus indefensible. Any positive obligations we might plausibly be claimed to have seem conditional on the costs required to achieve them. In a utilitarian scheme, the extent of our positive obligations is dependent on what would maximize utility, a determination that must take into account costs and that is therefore conditional. In a nonconsequentialist moral outlook, if we can accomplish significant good for others without sacrificing anything of significant value to ourselves, then it seems more plausible prima facie that we have a positive obligation than if we must sacrifice something of significant moral value to achieve the same level of good. Again, this speaks to the conditionality of such obligations.

A third and related problem is that the notion of medical progress that we are considering is one that would entail significant costs to many individuals, mostly nonhuman animals. Supposed positive obligations (e.g., the provision of medical care to persons unable to afford it) sometimes involve redistributing resources (e.g., money) from one party to another and thus involve some measure of harm to the persons from whom we are taking the resources. However, there seems to be an important distinction to be drawn between harms that involve taking resources and physical or emotional harms. Although the former can certainly be controversial, even demanding theories of positive obligation hold that these obligations only apply to the extent that giving to others doesn't compromise our own most important interests. In contrast, our strictest negative obligations seem to be those that involve not imposing significant physical or emotional harms on others, as animal research certainly does. It seems conceptually problematic to recognize a positive obligation when doing so involves the violation of a strict negative obligation, especially since negative obligations are often thought to take priority over positive obligations. All of this is to say that the idea of an unconditional positive obligation is problematic.

What Is the Relevant Specification of "Medical Progress"?

Even if the idea of an unconditional positive obligation can be defended, we immediately encounter another problem, which is that "medical progress" is a vague notion requiring specification: it can accrue to varying degrees and at varying rates. What is the relevant degree of benefit, and how quickly must it be achieved? Determining this is important because the extent and harmfulness of animal research to be tolerated will plausibly depend on the degree and rapidity of human benefit that we are arguing is obligatory. If the relevant specification of "obligatory medical progress" were "as much progress as possible in the shortest amount of time," then we would expect such progress to require use of a comparatively greater number of animals and in comparatively more harmful research than if the relevant specification were "modest benefit achieved over a long time-course." For example, prohibiting some kinds of especially invasive research on cognitively advanced animals (e.g., nonhuman primates) might result in the loss of a particular kind of benefit for humans, or it might mean that the realization of this benefit would have to wait until alternative methods to live animals in research are further developed beyond where they are today. In choosing between different specifications of "medical progress," a value judgment will thus be required, with practical consequences for animals following from this value judgment.

Further, in order to avoid begging the question, some argument must be provided as to why a particular degree and particular rate of medical progress are the obligatory ones. It might be tempting to say "as much progress and as fast as is possible," but the amount of progress possible will depend to some degree on the extent of financial and social investment in animal research. If the relevant sense of progress is "maximal progress," then this would imply that we should divert public funding away from other areas and into animal research. Such other areas could in-

clude, but not be limited to, preventive public health efforts, universal health insurance, social disability programs, the defense budget, education, food aid, the arts and humanities, environmental protection and regulation, the police force, infrastructure, and others. It seems dubious that anyone would seriously argue that funding for all of these and other areas should be wholly diverted into animal research. Rather, individuals would likely argue that animal research should be funded "reasonably" and "in balance with" these other areas. However, if we assume that the current funding level of animal research is not the ideal funding level, then an additional conversation about public priorities in the allocation of limited financial resources will be necessary. Different persons will likely have different funding priorities, further complicating the discussion.

The point here is as much pragmatic as it is philosophical: most parties asserting the necessity of animal research do so without much elaboration of the claim. However, the fact that "medical progress" requires a value-laden specification detracts from the ability of necessity arguments (which implicitly rely on the concept of medical progress) to serve as a straightforward justification of the necessity of animal research. In order to adequately clarify the scope of such necessity arguments, much more would need to be said than typically is. Further, the preceding discussion casts additional doubt on the coherence of the idea of obligatory medical progress. If the specification of "obligatory medical progress" is reasonably constrained by the pursuit of other moral goods, then why should it not also be constrained by the welfare of the animals used in such research?

Finally, it is not clear what kind of satisfactory justification might be offered to explain what it is about a particular degree and rate of medical progress that, among many alternatives, makes it a moral good so important that its pursuit is an overriding requirement, regardless of cost. And if this degree of medical progress were achieved, would that satisfy defenders of animal research, or would they simply move the goalposts? If the latter, such a move would suggest that it is really animals' perceived lower moral standing rather than a putative level of obligatory medical progress that is underlying this defense.

Is Animal Research the Most Effective Means?

Let us assume for the sake of argument that the idea of "unconditionally obligatory medical progress" can be vindicated and furthermore that we can defensibly specify the obligatory amount and rate of medical progress. These concessions still do not vindicate the necessity principle because animal research is neither the only nor the most effective means of achieving such progress.

First, even if animal research were reasonably effective in predicting human responses, there would always be interspecies extrapolation required, and therefore human research would be a more effective means of achieving medical progress. Performing on humans the kind of invasive research that we now perform on animals would presumably allow us to achieve a greater degree of progress and achieve it more quickly.[43] At present we do not use humans in research that harms them significantly because we deem it unethical. However, in the argument presently considered, the obligation to achieve medical progress is *unconditional* and therefore trumps the normal stringency of our obligations not to harm others—and this would include humans. Therefore, such invasive human research not only should be allowed but also could be conceived of as obligatory because it is a more effective means to achieving medical progress than is animal research. Alternatively, the price of allowing obligations of nonmaleficence to constrain our use of humans in achieving medical progress is that it should constrain our use of animals, too. If it is replied that the amount of medical progress that is unconditionally obligatory just so happens to correspond to what can be achieved with animals but not the greater degree of progress that could be achieved with humans—well, that seems ad hoc and suspiciously convenient.

Second, despite strong claims from the scientific community about the historical benefits of animal research, the accuracy of animal models in predicting human responses has not been evaluated to a sufficient extent, and the lack of availability of certain kinds of data makes this evaluation especially challenging.[44] Based on what systematic reviews are available, the accuracy of animal research in predicting both human toxicity and the effectiveness of drugs appears to be far less than what we once assumed, sometimes being no better than chance.[45] Animal studies also frequently appear to be poorly designed from a methodological standpoint: they often have inadequate sample sizes, do not prespecify a hypothesis, do not include randomization or blinding, and may not use models or designs that adequately recapitulate the condition of the human disease or the timing and approach to treatment.[46] The predictive value of animal research might increase if its methodological rigor was increased, but this is uncertain. However, given the state of the evidence, it does seem that we lack good reason to make strong blanket statements about the effectiveness of animal research as a means to achieving the end of medical progress. This does not mean that animal research has never produced any or even many important medical benefits, only that overall, its failures are frequent enough to cast doubt on its general effectiveness in predicting human responses.

Third, even assuming their scientific validity, the putative necessity of animal models to medical progress must be viewed in light of the fact that animal research has been a required part of preclinical testing for decades and an integral part of scientific investigation for even longer. Other routes of investigation have rarely been explored, and financial investment into alternative methods has been very modest.[47] Even with such modest investment, some strides are being made, and it is possible that if significant financial investment into alternatives became commonplace, this entire discussion might soon become moot.

Finally, we should consider why medical progress might be thought a moral imperative in the first place. Presumably, the explanation would be that human welfare matters; that disease, debility, and early death significantly detract from human welfare; and that we have a moral obligation to do something about it. But this same reasoning might lead us to question whether the development of new medical therapies is the most efficient way to promote human welfare and to fight disease, as opposed to doing a better job of providing medical care, sanitation, and other basic goods to persons in need of them.[48] For example, according to the Food and Agricultural Organization of the United Nations, 805 million people are suffering from chronic undernourishment;[49] according to the

World Health Organization (WHO), 1.1 billion people do not have access to clean drinking water;[50] and the seventeen neglected tropical diseases prioritized by the WHO affect more than 1.4 billion people.[51] It is difficult to appreciate why developing new medical therapies would be an unconditional moral obligation when attending to these other ills is not. If addressing these other problems *is* an unconditional moral obligation, then limited resources might be better spent on other humanitarian causes and public health efforts rather than the diseases of affluence that occupy most of our scientific efforts.

Necessity, Justice, and the Lifeboat

Assuming that most of the other issues discussed here could be overcome, persons asserting an unconditional obligation to achieve medical progress might try to defend the necessity principle as follows. They might argue that although humans are indeed the best biological model for developing new ways to prevent, treat, and cure human diseases, we should adhere to a principle of "least harm" in pursuing medical progress, which simply means that we should try to achieve the required amount of medical progress with the least total harm possible. After all, they might argue, even though medical progress is an obligatory pursuit, this does not mean that harms to humans and animals occasioned in this pursuit lose all ethical salience. In turn, it might be argued that the way to achieve the obligatory amount of medical progress (which, let us recall, must be specified in a non–question-begging way, but let us overlook this for now) with the least total harm would be to shift as many of the risks and harms as is possible onto animals. The rationale here is that although humans and nonhuman animals might have some relevantly similar interests, such as an interest in avoiding suffering, our interests in avoiding death are not relevantly similar: humans lose more in dying than do nonhuman animals.[52] This being the case and because invasive research often results in the death of the subjects used, the course of action causing the least total harm would also be the course of action that makes animals bear as much of the risk and harm in research as is possible. Notably, if medical progress is indeed an unconditional moral imperative, then this argument might apply *even if* animals are due EC and have strong negative rights against being harmed—a strong right is not necessarily an indefeasible right.

There is precedent for this kind of thinking in animal ethics. Philosopher Tom Regan, a famous proponent of a very strong version of animal rights theory, has argued that most mammals and humans alike are "subjects of a life" who possess equal inherent value and an equal right not to be harmed for the benefit of others. Nonetheless, he has argued that in very limited scenarios—what he calls "prevention cases"—it might sometimes be morally permissible to sacrifice an animal life to save a human life, if all would otherwise perish. For example, in his famous "lifeboat case," four humans and a dog are in a lifeboat that can hold only four individuals. One individual must be thrown overboard, or else all five will drown, and Regan argues that it should be the dog who is thrown overboard because she will be harmed least by death; throwing the dog over is a way of minimizing unavoidable harm.[53] Similarly, it might be argued that shifting all of the risk and harm onto animal research subjects is a way of minimizing the unavoidable harm that must occur to achieve the medical progress that is our unconditional obligation.

This "least harm" argument is intriguing, but before considering it further, we should remind ourselves that it becomes relevant to our discussion of necessity only if we grant a series of argumentative assumptions and concessions that seem highly implausible. Still, even if we grant these concessions and assumptions, the argument from "least harm" remains problematic.

One immediate problem with this line of reasoning is that it would not always result in the sacrifice of animals over humans. Death will sometimes harm particular animals more than particular humans (e.g., it would harm a normal chimpanzee more than a person with very significant cognitive impairment), so the "least harm" approach to achieving medical progress would sometimes require the use of humans in invasive research instead of animals.[54] Further, although it is often assumed that the more cognitively and affectively advanced a creature is, the more the animal suffers in research, this may not be true in all respects. Bernard Rollin has argued, for example, that animals' inability to comprehend the nature of their suffering and see an end to it arguably can make this suffering even more acute than human suffering.[55] Additionally, we should keep in mind that because animal models imperfectly (even in the best-case scenario) predict human responses, a greater number of animals would be required in research to achieve a given amount of medical progress than would be required if humans were used, on account of false starts and misleading results. In order to say that the "least harm" approach favors using animals over humans, we would need not only to compare the kinds of harms experienced by the individuals used in research but also to multiply these harms by the number of individuals used. Whether the result favors the use of humans or nonhuman animals is unclear.

Another problem is that biomedical research is not really a lifeboat situation, despite superficial similarities. In the lifeboat scenario, all individuals in the boat would otherwise die, whereas in the case of animal research, we are deliberately and coercively placing animals in harm's way who would not otherwise have been there. Thus, the "sacrifice" of animals in research is not really a way of limiting *unavoidable* harm as much as it is a way of limiting *total* harm by making animals bear all of the costs of the good we are pursuing and thus shifting harm away from some parties and onto others. This explains why harmful research might violate animals' rights, whereas their sacrifice in the lifeboat scenario would not.[56] In the latter case, inaction would result in the animal's death, whereas in the former case it would not. Further, lifeboat scenarios are intended to apply to highly exceptional situations not approximating socially institutionalized activities. As Susan Finsen argues,

> In order to see why scientific research is fundamentally different from the lifeboat situation, we need to look beyond the coercion and risk factors, and indeed beyond the conditions . . . we have considered so far to constitute the lifeboat situation. While these features are necessary common features of lifeboat situations, I believe there is another important feature, namely, the exceptional nature of lifeboat situations. Getting caught in lifeboat situations is not a foreseeable problem, and it is not one that we are likely to institutionalize. Indeed, the foreseen and thus deliberate placing of individuals at risk might properly be compared to a terrorist activity, such as the taking of hostages

or the hijacking of an airplane. The individuals responsible for creating such situations are considered highly culpable, regardless of whether they wind up running the same risks as their victims. In other words, lifeboat situations are, by their nature, not deliberately devised public institutions. . . . Disease and death are not unforeseeable, but inevitable parts of life. Their foreseeability allows us to create institutions and rules for dealing with these situations. Their foreseeability creates the possibility, and even the obligation, to make sure that in handling these situations, we do not violate anyone's rights.[57]

If medical progress is an unconditional moral imperative, then (pro tanto) rights violations in research might be unavoidable. However, the preceding points of disanalogy between biomedical research and lifeboat situations mean that we must appeal to more than a principle of "least harm" in deciding the distribution of risk and harm. We believe that in this case, obligations to limit harm should be considered alongside justice-based obligations to distribute benefits and burdens fairly among all parties. Exactly what this comes to will depend on how we conceptualize animals' moral standing viz. humans. However, if nonhuman animals' interests deserve substantial moral consideration or equal moral consideration to humans' interests, then there seems to be something wrong with institutionalizing a practice that results in animals bearing most or all of the costs of research while we humans reap most of the benefits—even if this course of action were to limit total harm. Such a course of action does not seem consistent with viewing nonhuman animals as members of the moral community. Giving more attention to distributive justice would result in a more equitable distribution of risk and harm between human and nonhuman animals than would occur in the "least harm" approach and certainly a more equitable distribution than occurs under the status quo.

The requirement that we balance considerations of justice and nonmaleficence is also consistent with leading approaches to biomedical ethics, such as coherentism or principlism, which holds that the four principles of respect for autonomy, nonmaleficence, beneficence, and justice must be balanced against each other and no principle has strict priority in this balancing.[58] This requirement might also be justified, for example, through a Rawlsian approach to justice whereby we make decisions regarding the distribution of research risk behind a "veil of ignorance," including species.[59]

This conclusion squares with the idea that animals have independent moral value and are not merely resources for our use. We can observe that different groups of humans have differing capacities to be harmed in research, but neither our regulations nor our conceptions of justice allow one group of humans to bear all of the costs of research—in fact, the very same individuals who might be candidates for being "harmed less" by certain research procedures (e.g., cognitively impaired persons) are often given *more* protection under the regulations and not less. Moreover, if research on nonhuman animals were not possible—or were deemed to be ineffective—then we would have to achieve obligatory medical progress through the use of humans alone. But it is unclear why this fact would negate the considerations of justice just mentioned, and it seems likely that we would continue to prohibit the undue exploitation of select groups of humans for the gain of all. Since the best arguments indicate that sentient animals deserve significant and perhaps equal moral consideration, a similar conclusion would seem to apply to them as well as to humans.

Conclusion

Both scientific rhetoric and regulations governing animal research frequently appeal to the idea that harmful animal research is morally justified because such research is necessary to medical progress. Here we have explored this idea of "necessity," arguing that it is not simply a scientific determination but, rather, is conditional on ethical concerns. When philosophical arguments about animals' moral standing and the justification of harm are taken into account, the instrumental necessity of animal research to achieving a particular end does not automatically make the research defensible. In fact, according to the weight of philosophical scholarship, significant reforms to animal research practices are necessary worldwide. Thus, the "necessity principle," as we have termed it, justifies neither harmful animal research in the abstract

nor the regulatory status quo in reality. In response to such criticisms, it might be argued that pursuing medical progress is an unconditional moral imperative requiring animal research, but this argument founders for a number of reasons. The very idea of an unconditional obligation to secure medical progress might very well be incoherent, and significant philosophical problems arise when we try to specify what an obligatory level of medical progress might look like. Further, this account shifts the justification for harmful animal research away from animals' moral standing and toward an end goal of overriding value, but in this latter argument, exploiting humans would be a faster and more effective means to achieving the end of medical progress. It might also be more effective to shift resources away from biomedical research and toward other public health and socioeconomic reforms if our goal is to improve human well-being. Finally, even if we vindicate the idea of obligatory medical progress and the status of animal research as an effective means to achieve it, justice-based considerations would likely prevent us from shifting most of the risk and harm of such research onto animals.

Thus, we conclude that "necessity" is not a useful criterion to inform the ethics of animal research. Moving forward, the biomedical and regulatory communities would do well to abandon the rhetoric of necessity and address in more direct fashion the ethical arguments relevant to animal research.

Notes

1. Aysha Akhtar, *Animals and Public Health: Why Treating Animals Better Is Critical to Human Welfare* (New York: Palgrave Macmillan, 2012), 24.

2. David DeGrazia, "The Ethics of Animal Research: What Are the Prospects for Agreement?" *Cambridge Quarterly of Healthcare Ethics* 8 (1999): 23–34.

3. Katy Taylor, Nicky Gordon, Gill Langley, and Wendy Higgins, "Estimates for Worldwide Laboratory Animal Use in 2005," *ATLA* 36 (2008): 327–42.

4. Evelyn Pluhar, *Beyond Prejudice: The Moral Significance of Human and Nonhuman Animals* (Durham: Duke University Press, 1995); David DeGrazia, *Taking Animals Seriously: Mental Life and Moral Status* (New York: Cambridge University Press, 1996); David DeGrazia, *Animal Rights: A Very Short Introduction* (New York: Oxford University Press, 2002); Tzachi Zamir, *Ethics and the Beast: A Speciesist Argument for Animal Liberation* (Princeton: Princeton University Press, 2007); Peter Singer, *Animal Liberation* (New York: Harper-

UNIVERSITY OF WINCHESTER
LIBRARY

Collins, 2009); Tom Regan, *The Case for Animal Rights* (Los Angeles: University of California Press, 2004); Sue Donaldson and Will Kymlicka, *Zoopolis: A Political Theory of Animal Rights* (Oxford: Oxford University Press, 2011); Andrew Knight, *The Costs and Benefits of Animal Experiments* (New York: Palgrave Macmillan, 2011); Robert Bass, "Lives in the Balance: Utilitarianism and Animal Research," in *The Ethics of Animal Research: Exploring the Controversy*, ed. Jeremy Garrett (Cambridge, MA: MIT Press, 2012), 81–106; Bernard Rollin, "The Moral Status of Invasive Animal Research," *Hastings Center Special Report: Animal Research Ethics: Evolving Views and Practices*, November–December 2012, S4–6, http://animalresearch.thehastingscenter.org; Akhtar, *Animals and Public Health*.

5. See Larry Carbone, *What Animals Want: Expertise and Advocacy in Laboratory Animal Welfare Policy* (New York: Oxford University Press, 2004); Stephen Latham, "U.S. Law and Animal Experimentation: A Critical Primer," *Hastings Center Special Report: Animal Research Ethics: Evolving Views and Practices*, November–December 2012, S35–39, http://animalresearch.thehastingscenter.org.

6. Charles S. Nicoll and Sharon M. Russell, "Animal Rights, Animal Research, and Human Obligations," *Molecular and Cellular Neuroscience* 3, no. 4 (1992): 271–77, doi:10.1016/1044-7431(92)90023-u; Mark Matfield, "Animal Experimentation: The Continuing Debate," *Nature Reviews Drug Discovery* 1 (2002): 149–52; Greg Miller, "Animal Extremists Get Personal," *Science* 318 (2007): 1856–58; Frank Gannon, "Animal Rights, Human Wrongs?" *EMBO Reports* 8, no. 6 (2007): 519–20; Adrian Morrison, "Perverting History in the Service of 'Animal Rights,'" *Perspectives in Biology and Medicine* 45, no. 4 (2002): 606–19; Dario L. Ringach, "The Use of Nonhuman Animals in Biomedical Research," *American Journal of the Medical Sciences* 342, no. 4 (2011): 305–13, doi:10.1097/maj.0b013e31822a6c35; "Inhumane Treatment of Nonhuman Primate Researchers," *Nature Neuroscience* 18, no. 6 (2015): 787. For discussion, see also Nathan Nobis, "The Harmful, Nontherapeutic Use of Animals in Research Is Morally Wrong," *American Journal of the Medical Sciences* 342, no. 4 (2011): 297–304.

7. *U.S. Government Principles for the Utilization and Care of Vertebrate Animals Used in Testing, Research, and Training*, quoted in Institute for Laboratory Animal Research (ILAR), *Guide for the Care and Use of Laboratory Animals*, 8th ed. (Washington, DC: National Academies Press, 2011), 199.

8. American College of Laboratory Animal Medicine, "Position Statement on Animal Experimentation," accessed April 1, 2017, http://www.aclam.org/Content/files/files/Public/Active/position_animalexperimentation.pdf.

9. California Biomedical Research Association, "CBRA Fact Sheet: Why Are Animals Necessary in Biomedical Research?" accessed September 10, 2015, http://ca-biomed.org/csbr/pdf/fs-whynecessary.pdf.

10. Gannon, "Animal Rights, Human Wrongs?"; Ringach, "Use of Nonhuman Animals"; Colin Blakemore, "Should We Experiment on Animals? Yes," *London Telegraph*, October 28, 2008, accessed September 10, 2015, http://www.telegraph.co.uk/news/science/science-news/3353960/Should-we-experiment-on-animals-Yes.html.

11. US Laboratory Animal Welfare Act (AWA), 7 USC §2131–59 (2008); National Institutes of Health, Office of Laboratory Animal Welfare (NIH OLAW), *Public Health Service Policy on Humane Care and Use of Laboratory Animals* (Washington, DC: US Department of Health and Human Services, 2002) (includes PL 99-158 Health Research Extension Act, 1985).

12. US AWA §2143 (2008).

13. ILAR, *Guide*, 60; see also NIH OLAW, *Public Health Service Policy*.

14. Institute of Medicine, *Chimpanzees in Biomedical and Behavioral Research: Assessing the Necessity* (Washington, DC: National Academies Press, 2011), 1.

15. US AWA §2143 (2008); see also NIH OLAW, *Public Health Service Policy*, which relies on the AWA.

16. Two exceptions are Nobis, "Harmful, Nontherapeutic Use"; and Gary L. Francione, "The Use of Nonhuman Animals in Biomedical Research: Necessity and Justification," *Journal of Law, Medicine, and Ethics* (Summer 2007): 241–48.

17. See Gannon, "Animal Rights, Human Wrongs?"

18. After drafting this manuscript, we became aware that Nobis has also made this point. See Nobis, "Harmful, Nontherapeutic Use."

19. The question of whether knowledge is intrinsically valuable is one that we will not pursue in this essay, though it has received some attention in the philosophical literature. Suffice it to say that the arguments we elaborate in this discussion can be applied to the goals of medical progress and knowledge alike, as well as to any putative benefit of research.

20. The 2011 Institute of Medicine report is a possible exception to this, since its authors are careful to note that research with chimpanzees raises serious ethical issues and that "the chimpanzee's genetic proximity to humans and the resulting biological and behavioral characteristics . . . demand a greater justification for conducting research using this animal model" (Institute of Medicine, *Chimpanzees*, 2). Even here, though, one must be careful to pay attention to the implicit rhetorical force of necessity claims. It seems likely that if the report's authors had concluded that continued research with chimpanzees was scientifically necessary (again, they did not), then this conclusion would have been taken as a reason to continue current research uses of chimpanzees—if not by the report's authors, then certainly by some readers.

21. US Congress, Office of Technology Assessment, *Alternatives to Animal Use in Research, Testing, and Education* (Washington, DC: US Government Printing Office, 1986).

22. See, for example, American Physiological Society, "Who Makes Sure Research Animals Are Treated Well?" (2013), accessed September 10, 2015, http://www.animalresearchcures.org/treatedwell.htm.

23. Latham, "U.S. Law," S38. It should be noted that some commentators have argued that cost-benefit assessment (CBA) is permitted by the US regulations. (For example, see Michael D. Mann and Ernest D. Prentice, "Should IACUCs Review Scientific Merit of Animal Research Projects?" *Lab Animal* 33, no. 1 [2004]: 26–31.) However, such an interpretation of the US regulations is exceptional and constitutes a minority view. Further, in practice it seems to be the case that IACUCs seldom if ever employ CBA. However, beginning with the eighth edition of the ILAR's *Guide for the Care and Use of Laboratory Animals*, published in 2011, there appears to be a nascent movement afoot to introduce CBA to IACUC protocol review (see, e.g., Fara Moulvi, "Conducting a Risk/Benefit Evaluation for IACUC Proposals," *PRIM&R's Ampersand*, August 16, 2012, accessed September 10, 2015, http://primr.blogspot.com/2012/08/conducting-riskbenefit-evaluation-for.html). This interpretation is based on some (admittedly vague) language added to this newest edition of the guide (see Moulvi, "Conducting a Risk/Benefit Evaluation"). Because the *Guide* is not technically a regulation and only amplifies the existing regulations and because the existing regulations do not clearly mandate CBA (indeed, their language seems to contravene it in multiple places), the status of CBA in IACUC review moving forward is both unclear and evolving. The agencies responsible for authoring and/or enforcing the US regulations—the US Department of Agriculture (USDA) and National Institutes of Health (NIH)—have as yet not commented explicitly on this issue.

24. Gannon, "Animal Rights, Human Wrongs?" 520.

25. See also Nobis, "Harmful, Nontherapeutic Use."

26. For a discussion of virtue ethics and animal research that also upholds this point, see Garrett Merriam, "Virtue, Vice, and Vivisection," in *The Ethics of Animal Research: Exploring the Controversy*, ed. Jeremy Garrett (Cambridge, MA: MIT Press, 2012), 125–46.

27. An example here would be the quarantine and isolation of persons during a major infectious-disease pandemic. Cases of justifiable human rights infringements in order to serve the general welfare tend to be exceptional in nature and also involve harms that are much lesser in extent than those routinely imposed on animals in research.

28. US Department of Health and Human Services, "Protection of Human Subjects," 45 CFR 46 (2009), http://www.hhs.gov/ohrp/humansubjects/guidance/45cfr46.html.

29. Baruch Brody, "Defending Animal Research: An International Perspective," in *The Ethics of Animal Research: Exploring the Controversy*, ed. Jeremy Garrett (Cambridge, MA: MIT Press, 2012), 53–66. Brody labels the quoted view the "lexical priority" view, because although it acknowledges that nonhuman animals have *some* direct moral standing, it also holds that humans' interests always win out over animals' interests when the two conflict, even when the human interest at stake is modest and the animal interest significant. Hence, in this view, humans' interests have "lexical priority" over animals' interests. It should be noted that Brody merely describes this view as a reasonable approximation of the current US regulations and that he does not find it to be a plausible view.

30. See Brody, "Defending Animal Research."

31. See Pluhar, *Beyond Prejudice*; DeGrazia, *Taking Animals Seriously*; DeGrazia, *Animal Rights*; Regan, *Case for Animal Rights*; Singer, *Animal Liberation*; Donaldson and Kymlicka, *Zoopolis*.

32. See Pluhar, *Beyond Prejudice*; DeGrazia, *Taking Animals Seriously*; DeGrazia, *Animal Rights*; Regan, *Case for Animal Rights*; Singer, *Animal Liberation*; Donaldson and Kymlicka, *Zoopolis*.

33. DeGrazia, *Animal Rights*; Nathan Nobis, "Carl Cohen's 'Kind' Arguments for Animal Rights and against Human Rights," *Journal of Applied Philosophy* 21, no. 1 (2004): 43–59, doi:10.1111/j.0264-3758.2004.00262.x.

34. DeGrazia, *Animal Rights*; Steven F. Sapontzis, "On Justifying the Exploitation of Animals in Research," *Journal of Medicine and Philosophy* 13 (1988): 177–96.

35. DeGrazia, *Taking Animals Seriously*; DeGrazia, *Animal Rights*; Regan, *Case for Animal Rights*; John Rossi, "Is Equal Moral Consideration Really Compatible with Unequal Moral Status?" *Kennedy Institute of Ethics Journal* 20, no. 3 (2010): 251–76, doi:10.1353/ken.2010.0004.

36. DeGrazia, *Taking Animals Seriously*; DeGrazia, *Animal Rights*; David DeGrazia, "Moral Status as a Matter of Degree?" *Southern Journal of Philosophy* 46, no. 2 (2008): 181–98, doi:10.1111/j.2041-6962.2008.tb00075.x.

37. For a discussion of uncertainty in cost-benefit assessment, see Andrew Rowan, "Debating the Value of Animal Research," in *The Ethics of Animal Research: Exploring the Controversy*, ed. Jeremy Garrett (Cambridge, MA: MIT Press, 2012), 197–214.

38. See Knight, *Costs and Benefits*, and Bass, "Lives in the Balance," for discussion.

39. Such proclamations are common by defenders of animal research. For example, Ringach says the following: "The relevant question for the utilitarian is, has animal research so far, as a field, produced sufficiently important benefits as to be justified? I honestly believe that any person with basic knowledge of medical history must answer this question in the affirmative" ("Use of Nonhuman Animals," 311). Carl Cohen claims that "remarkable advances in medical science, achievements precious to human beings beyond calculation, but possible only through the use of animals in laboratory research, far outweigh the loss of animal lives entailed." See Carl Cohen, "In Defense of the Use of Animals," in Carl Cohen and Tom Regan, *The Animal Rights Debate* (Lanham, MD: Rowman and Littlefield, 2001), 85. These kinds of statements are dramatic but do little to vindicate the utilitarian case in favor of animal research.

40. See DeGrazia, *Taking Animals Seriously*, and DeGrazia, *Animal Rights*, for discussion.

41. Zamir, *Ethics and the Beast*.

42. Ringach, "Use of Nonhuman Animals," emphasis ours. For other articles containing language suggestive of this point, see Nicoll and Russell, "Animal Rights"; Carl Cohen, "The Case for the Use of Animals in Biomedical Research," *New England Journal of Medicine* 315, no. 14 (1986): 865–70; Speaking of Research, "This House Does Not Believe Animal Research Is a Moral Hazard," February 3, 2013, accessed September 10, 2015, http://speakingofresearch.com/2013/02/03/this-house-does-not-believe-animal-research-is-a-moral-hazard/.

43. See Sapontzis, "On Justifying the Exploitation"; Francione, "Use of Nonhuman Animals."

44. Robert A. J. Matthews, "Medical Progress Depends on Animal Models—Doesn't It?" *Journal of the Royal Society of Medicine* 101, no. 2 (2008): 95–98, doi:10.1258/jrsm.2007.070164.

45. Ibid.; Knight, *Costs and Benefits*; Pablo Perel, Ian Roberts, Emily Sena, Philipa Wheble, Catherine Briscoe, Peter Sandercock, Malcolm Macleod, Luciano E. Mignini, Pradeep Jayaram, and Khalid S. Khan, "Comparison of Treatment Effects between Animal Experiments and Clinical Trials: Systematic Review," *BMJ* 334, no. 7586 (2007): 197, doi:10.1136/bmj.39048.407928.be; Pandora Pound and Michael B. Bracken, "Is Animal Research Sufficiently Evidence Based to Be a Cornerstone of Biomedical Research?" *BMJ* 348 (2014): g3387, doi:10.1136/bmj.g3387.

46. Akhtar, *Animals and Public Health*; Carol Kilkenny, Nick Parsons, Ed Kadyszewski, Michael F. W. Festing, Innes C. Cuthill, Derek Fry, Jane Hutton, and Douglas G. Altman, "Survey of the Quality of Experimental Design, Statistical Analysis, and Reporting of Research using Animals," *PLoS ONE* 4, no. 11 (2009): doi:10.1371/journal.pone.0007824.

47. Akhtar, *Animals and Public Health*; Francione, "Use of Nonhuman Animals."

48. Charles K. Fink, "Animal Experimentation and the Argument from Limited Resources," *Between the Species*, (Spring 1991): 90–95; Francione, "Use of Nonhuman Animals."

49. United Nations Food and Agricultural Organization, *The State of Food Insecurity in the World (SOFI) 2014* (Rome: United Nations Food and Agricultural Organization, 2014), accessed September 9, 2015, http://www.fao.org/publications/sofi/2014/en/.

50. World Health Organization, "Health through Safe Drinking Water and Basic Sanitation," accessed September 9, 2015, http://www.who.int/water_sanitation_health/mdg1/en/.

51. World Health Organization, "Neglected Tropical Diseases," accessed April 1, 2017, http://www.who.int/neglected_diseases/diseases/en/.

52. For discussion, see DeGrazia, *Taking Animals Seriously*; DeGrazia, *Animal Rights*; DeGrazia, "Moral Status."

53. Regan, *Case for Animal Rights*, chap. 8.

54. Susan Finsen, "Sinking the Research Lifeboat," *Journal of Medicine and Philosophy* 13 (1988): 197–212.

55. Bernard Rollin, *The Unheeded Cry: Animal Consciousness, Animal Pain and Science* (New York: Oxford University Press, 1990).

56. Finsen, "Sinking the Research Lifeboat."

57. Ibid., 206.

58. Tom Beauchamp and James Childress, *Principles of Biomedical Ethics*, 7th ed. (New York: Cambridge University Press, 2009).

59. Mark Rowlands, "Contractarianism, Animals and Risk," in *The Ethics of Animal Research: Exploring the Controversy*, ed. Jeremy Garrett (Cambridge, MA: MIT Press, 2012), 148–66.

Bibliography

Akhtar, Aysha. *Animals and Public Health: Why Treating Animals Better Is Critical to Human Welfare*. New York: Palgrave Macmillan, 2012.

American College of Laboratory Animal Medicine. "Position Statement on Animal Experimentation." Accessed April 1, 2017. https://www.aclam.org/Content/files/files/Public/Active/position_animalexperimentation.pdf.

American Physiological Society. "Who Makes Sure Research Animals Are Treated Well?" 2013. Accessed September 10, 2015. http://www.animalresearchcures.org/treatedwell.htm.

Bass, Robert. "Lives in the Balance: Utilitarianism and Animal Research." In *The Ethics of Animal Research: Exploring the Controversy*, edited by Jeremy Garrett, 81–106. Cambridge, MA: MIT Press, 2012.

Beauchamp, Tom, and James Childress. *Principles of Biomedical Ethics*. 7th ed. New York: Cambridge University Press, 2009.

Brody, Baruch. "Defending Animal Research: An International Perspective." In *The Ethics of Animal Research: Exploring the Controversy*, edited by Jeremy Garrett, 53–66. Cambridge, MA: MIT Press, 2012.

California Biomedical Research Association. "CBRA Fact Sheet: Why Are Animals Necessary in Biomedical Research?" Accessed September 10, 2015. http://ca-biomed.org/csbr/pdf/fs-whynecessary.pdf.

Carbone, Larry. *What Animals Want: Expertise and Advocacy in Laboratory Animal Welfare Policy*. New York: Oxford University Press, 2004.

Cohen, Carl. "The Case for the Use of Animals in Biomedical Research." *New England Journal of Medicine* 315, no. 14 (1986): 865–70.

DeGrazia, David. *Animal Rights: A Very Short Introduction*. New York: Oxford University Press, 2002.

———. "The Ethics of Animal Research: What Are the Prospects for Agreement?" *Cambridge Quarterly of Healthcare Ethics* 8 (1999): 23–34.

———. "Moral Status as a Matter of Degree?" *Southern Journal of Philosophy* 46, no. 2 (2008): 181–98. doi:10.1111/j.2041-6962.2008.tb00075.x.

———. *Taking Animals Seriously: Mental Life and Moral Status*. New York: Cambridge University Press, 1996.

Donaldson, Sue, and Will Kymlicka. *Zoopolis: A Political Theory of Animal Rights*. Oxford: Oxford University Press, 2011.

Fink, Charles K. "Animal Experimentation and the Argument

from Limited Resources." *Between the Species* (Spring 1991): 90–95.

Finsen, Susan. "Sinking the Research Lifeboat." *Journal of Medicine and Philosophy* 13 (1988): 197–212.

Francione, Gary L. "The Use of Nonhuman Animals in Biomedical Research: Necessity and Justification." *Journal of Law, Medicine, and Ethics* (Summer 2007): 241–48.

Gannon, Frank. "Animal Rights, Human Wrongs?" *EMBO Reports* 8, no. 6 (2007): 519–20.

"Inhumane Treatment of Nonhuman Primate Researchers." *Nature Neuroscience* 18, no. 6 (2015): 787.

Institute for Laboratory Animal Research (ILAR). *Guide for the Care and Use of Laboratory Animals*. 8th ed. Washington, DC: National Academies Press, 2011.

Institute of Medicine. *Chimpanzees in Biomedical and Behavioral Research: Assessing the Necessity*. Washington, DC: National Academies Press, 2011.

Kilkenny, Carol, Nick Parsons, Ed Kadyszewski, Michael F. W. Festing, Innes C. Cuthill, Derek Fry, Jane Hutton, and Douglas G. Altman. "Survey of the Quality of Experimental Design, Statistical Analysis, and Reporting of Research using Animals." *PLoS ONE* 4, no. 11 (2009). doi:10.1371/journal.pone.0007824.

Knight, Andrew. *The Costs and Benefits of Animal Experiments*. New York: Palgrave Macmillan, 2011.

Latham, Stephen. "U.S. Law and Animal Experimentation: A Critical Primer." *Hastings Center Special Report: Animal Research Ethics: Evolving Views and Practices*, November–December 2012, S35–39. http://animalresearch.thehastingscenter.org.

Mann, Michael D., and Ernest D. Prentice. "Should IACUCs Review Scientific Merit of Animal Research Projects?" *Lab Animal* 33, no. 1 (2004): 26–31.

Matfield, Mark. "Animal Experimentation: The Continuing Debate." *Nature Reviews Drug Discovery* 1 (2002): 149–52.

Matthews, Robert A. J. "Medical Progress Depends on Animal Models—Doesn't It?" *Journal of the Royal Society of Medicine* 101, no. 2 (2008): 95–98. doi:10.1258/jrsm.2007.070164.

Merriam, Garrett. "Virtue, Vice, and Vivisection." In *The Ethics of Animal Research: Exploring the Controversy*, edited by Jeremy Garrett, 125–46. Cambridge, MA: MIT Press, 2012.

Miller, Greg. "Animal Extremists Get Personal." *Science* 318 (2007): 1856–58.

Morrison, Adrian. "Perverting History in the Service of 'Animal Rights.'" *Perspectives in Biology and Medicine* 45, no. 4 (2002): 606–19.

Moulvi, Fara. "Conducting a Risk/Benefit Evaluation for IACUC Proposals." *PRIM&R's Ampersand*. August 16, 2012. Accessed September 10, 2015. http://primr.blogspot.com/2012/08/conducting-riskbenefit-evaluation-for.html.

National Institutes of Health, Office of Laboratory Animal Welfare (NIH OLAW). *Public Health Service Policy on Humane Care and Use of Laboratory Animals*. Washington, DC: US Department of Health and Human Services, 2002. (Includes PL 99-158 Health Research Extension Act, 1985.)

Nicoll, Charles S., and Sharon M. Russell. "Animal Rights, Animal Research, and Human Obligations." *Molecular and Cellular Neuroscience* 3, no. 4 (1992): 271–77. doi:10.1016/1044-7431(92)90023-u.

Nobis, Nathan. "Carl Cohen's 'Kind' Arguments for Animal Rights and against Human Rights." *Journal of Applied Philosophy* 21, no. 1 (2004): 43–59. doi:10.1111/j.0264-3758.2004.00262.x.

———. "The Harmful, Nontherapeutic Use of Animals in Research Is Morally Wrong." *American Journal of the Medical Sciences* 342, no. 4 (2011): 297–304.

Perel, Pablo, Ian Roberts, Emily Sena, Philipa Wheble, Catherine Briscoe, Peter Sandercock, Malcolm Macleod, Luciano E. Mignini, Pradeep Jayaram, and Khalid S. Khan. "Comparison of Treatment Effects between Animal Experiments and Clinical Trials: Systematic Review." *BMJ* 334, no. 7586 (2007): 197. doi:10.1136/bmj.39048.407928.be.

Pluhar, Evelyn. *Beyond Prejudice: The Moral Significance of Human and Nonhuman Animals*. Durham: Duke University Press, 1995.

Pound, Pandora, and Michael B. Bracken. "Is Animal Research Sufficiently Evidence Based to Be a Cornerstone of Biomedical Research?" *BMJ* 348 (2014): g3387. doi:10.1136/bmj.g3387.

Regan, Tom. *The Case for Animal Rights*. Los Angeles: University of California Press, 2004. First published 1983.

Ringach, Dario L. "The Use of Nonhuman Animals in Biomedical Research." *American Journal of the Medical Sciences* 342, no. 4 (2011): 305–13. doi:10.1097/maj.0b013e31822a6c35.

Rollin, Bernard. "The Moral Status of Invasive Animal Research." *Hastings Center Special Report: Animal Research Ethics: Evolving Views and Practices*, November–December 2012, S4–6. http://animalresearch.thehastingscenter.org.

———. *The Unheeded Cry: Animal Consciousness, Animal Pain, and Science*. New York: Oxford University Press, 1990.

Rossi, John. "Is Equal Moral Consideration Really Compatible with Unequal Moral Status?" *Kennedy Institute of Ethics Journal* 20, no. 3 (2010): 251–76. doi:10.1353/ken.2010.0004.

Rowan, Andrew. "Debating the Value of Animal Research." In *The Ethics of Animal Research: Exploring the Controversy*, edited by Jeremy Garrett, 197–214. Cambridge, MA: MIT Press, 2012.

Rowlands, Mark. "Contractarianism, Animals and Risk." In *The Ethics of Animal Research: Exploring the Controversy*, edited by Jeremy Garrett, 148–66. Cambridge, MA: MIT Press, 2012.

Sapontzis, Steven F. "On Justifying the Exploitation of Animals in Research." *Journal of Medicine and Philosophy* 13 (1988): 177–96.

Singer, Peter. *Animal Liberation*. New York: HarperCollins, 2009. First published 1975.

Speaking of Research. "This House Does Not Believe Animal Research Is a Moral Hazard." February 3, 2013. Accessed September 10, 2015. http://speakingofresearch.com/2013/02/03/this-house-does-not-believe-animal-research-is-a-moral-hazard/.

Taylor, Katy, Nicky Gordon, Gill Langley, and Wendy Higgins. "Estimates for Worldwide Laboratory Animal Use in 2005." *ATLA* 36 (2008): 327–42.

United Nations Food and Agricultural Organization. *The State of Food Insecurity in the World (SOFI) 2014*. Rome: United Nations Food and Agricultural Organization, 2014. Accessed

September 9, 2015. http://www.fao.org/publications/sofi/2014/en/.

US Congress. Office of Technology Assessment. *Alternatives to Animal Use in Research, Testing, and Education*. Washington, DC: US Government Printing Office, 1986.

US Department of Health and Human Services. "Protection of Human Subjects." 45 CFR 46 (2009). http://www.hhs.gov/ohrp/humansubjects/guidance/45cfr46.html.

US Laboratory Animal Welfare Act (AWA). 7 USC 2131–59 (2008).

World Health Organization. "Drinking-Water." November 2016. http://www.who.int/mediacentre/factsheets/fs391/en/.

———. "Health through Safe Drinking Water and Basic Sanitation," accessed September 9, 2015, http://www.who.int/water_sanitation_health/mdg1/en/.

———. "Neglected Tropical Diseases." Accessed April 1, 2017. http://www.who.int/neglected_diseases/diseases/en/.

Zamir, Tzachi. *Ethics and the Beast: A Speciesist Argument for Animal Liberation*. Princeton: Princeton University Press, 2007.

Science Fiction and Science Fact
Ethics and Nonhuman Animal Experiments

Kay Peggs

EACH YEAR MILLIONS of nonhuman animal subjects are treated as objects whose value is assumed to lie in the uses to which they can be put for the health and well-being of humans. In this form of institutionalized exploitation, nonhuman animals are exposed to a range of procedures and experiments that would be considered the stuff of nightmares if they were imposed on humans. Such nightmarish scenarios are evidenced in science-fictional accounts that present terrifying future worlds where humans are used as experimental devices by machines, by beings from other planets, by humans who have been allocated hierarchical supremacy over experimental human subjects, and by nonhuman animals. These depictions say a great deal about human fears about the future. But these future visions that so terrify humans are the present-day realities for nonhuman animals who are used for experimental purposes.

Popular culture reveals a great deal about human societies,[1] and American science fiction explores a range of current social concerns, obsessions, and problems.[2] Science fiction is replete with human fears, and these fears take many forms.[3] In "The Measure of a Man," a much-discussed episode of the second season of *Star Trek: The Next Generation*, the audience is offered an insight into a disturbing world of highly sophisticated artificial intelligence. In this episode the autonomy and rights of a machine (which is humanlike in appearance and behavior) are put into question. The points made in this episode can be extrapolated to issues associated with the rights of humans,[4] but I go further and draw conclusions about the human exploitation of nonhuman animals. In this essay, through the lens of this episode, I explore the ethics of using nonhuman animals for experimental purposes.

The Measure of a Man

In "The Measure of a Man," the android Lieutenant Commander Data is the subject of a hearing to determine whether he is owned by the Star Trek Corporation.[5] This is significant because if the corporation owns him, he has no choice about his fate. Data is an android with an "emotion chip"; he serves as a second officer onboard the starship USS *Enterprise*. Both Data and the chip were created by scientist Dr. Noonien Soong. The hearing to determine Data's fate has been called by the ship's captain, Jean-Luc Picard, in response to Commander Bruce Maddox's (associate chair of robotics) appeal to allow him to dismantle Data. Maddox's reason: "So that I can learn from it and construct more."[6] Audience members are expected to be shocked because they have known Data since the start of the first season of *The Next Generation*. For the audience, Data is not an "it"; he is not a contraption. *He* is a person. He is a cherished character and is an essential member of the crew.

The decision about whether to dismantle Data is to be based on the assessment of whether he is sentient.

This is the focus from the start of the hearing, when Picard (a defender of Data's interests) asks Maddox, "Is it your contention that Lieutenant Commander Data is not a sentient being and therefore is not entitled to all the rights reserved for all life forms within this federation?" In response, Maddox offers clarification of what sentience is rooted in: "Intelligence. Self-awareness. Consciousness." It is beyond question, I think, that the audience is expected to believe that Data's intelligence, self-awareness, and consciousness have been revealed not just in previous episodes but also earlier in this specific episode. Just minutes before, in response to Picard's question to Data about whether he understands the purpose of the hearing, Data says that it has been called to determine "[my] rights and status," which will be decided on the basis of whether "I am a person or property." When asked what is at stake, he answers, "My right to choose. Perhaps my very life."

Unlike the audience and Picard, Maddox must be persuaded to question his own assumption that Data is not sentient. Picard takes the initiative. In response to Maddox's account of sentience, Picard asks the unexpected question, "Why am I sentient?" Maddox finds the question absurd, responding that it is obvious that he is. Not so for Picard, who seems much more reflexive in his considerations. He wants Maddox and Starfleet's judge advocate general Captain Phillipa Louvois, to reflect on their assumptions about sentience and rights. Picard warns that the decision made about Data—"this creation of our genius"—"will reveal the kind of a people we are. . . . It could significantly redefine the boundaries of personal liberty and freedom, expanding them for some and savagely curtailing them for others." He follows this with the question, "Are you prepared to condemn him and all who come after him to servitude and slavery?"

In a provocative response, Captain Louvois contemplates, "Does Data have a soul? I don't know that he has. I don't know that I have. But I have got to give him the freedom to explore that question himself." She rules that he has "the freedom to choose." Data formally tells Maddox that he refuses to be dismantled. The audience expends a sigh of relief.

Throughout the series, Lieutenant Commander Data offers an outsider's perspective on humankind.[7] Robert Scheerer, the director, described this episode as having "a great deal to say about man, humanity, what our problems in the world are today and hopefully what we can do about it in the future."[8] This view is echoed by Claudia Sonego, who declares that "the episode deals with the issue of human rights and freedom of human beings and sentient intelligence—everywhere it can be found—to control their own lives. In the process, they touched on topics such as slavery, human rights, the right of choice, freedom and even the global responsibility of human societies."[9] Yes, the episode does do that, and it facilitates a questioning of our treatment of those who are designated "Others," the nonhuman animals who are evaluated in relation to anthropocentric understandings of sentience, who have no choice, who are experimented upon and killed by the millions in research laboratories, so that—to use Commander Maddox's words almost to the letter—we can "learn from" them.

In this essay I consider the use of nonhuman animal subjects as they are constructed as legitimate resources for biomedical experiments. Research that uses nonhuman animals for experiments and testing is regarded to be a moral issue in a number of countries because at least some nonhuman animals are granted moral standing.[10] For example, in the European Union the use of nonhuman animal subjects for the testing of cosmetics is considered unwarranted and unethical and thus is illegal,[11] whereas the use of nonhuman animal subjects in biomedical experiments is considered warranted and ethical if it conforms to the legal requirements.[12] So in accordance with the moral orthodoxy, priority is given to human health–related medical science in terms of the legal position of nonhuman animals who have been conferred sentience. This priority is found, as well, in public attitudes; there is more public acceptance of experiments that use nonhuman animal subjects if the experiments have human-health objectives.[13] In this essay I seek to challenge the ethics of using nonhuman animals in biomedical science, and because this is given ethical primacy, I confront assumptions about the ethical legitimacy of the use of nonhuman animal subjects in any experiments.[14]

In the course of this discussion, I engage with some of the policies that are associated with nonhuman animal experiments for biomedical research. Rather than providing a comprehensive overview of the legal position, which would be impossible in the space available, I explore aspects of the legalized use of nonhuman animal subjects for experiments for the health benefits of humans. I do this because the law consolidates institutionalized nonhuman animal exploitation by authorizing the practices that take place in a range of institutions, such as research laboratories.[15] Many of the deaths of nonhuman animals and the painful practices that are performed upon their living bodies in experiments would violate anticruelty laws, yet these institutionalized deaths and practices account for the majority of the violence executed against animals.[16] I reflect on the legitimated suffering and deaths of nonhuman animal subjects, legitimated because the needs of nonhuman animals are viewed as being subordinate to the needs of humans in the context of biomedicine. Unlike the fictional android Lieutenant Commander Data, nonfictional nonhuman animals who are used in biomedical experiments have not been granted the freedom to choose; rather, the legal and moral framework upholds and underpins the exploitation, suffering, and death that are inflicted upon them.

Nonhuman Animals, Rights, and Moral Accountability

Returning to the previously quoted words of Lieutenant Commander Data, the audience is not surprised to hear that this machine is able to understand that the hearing has been called to determine his "rights and status" and to answer the question as to whether he is "a person or property."[17] The appearance as well as the behavior of a robot influences human interaction with it,[18] and Data presents attitudes and behavior with which the audience can identify. Despite his mechanized idiosyncrasies, which are often used to comedic effect, Data is virtually human to the audience. So the audience is ahead of the judge. How can the rights and status of the cherished humanlike Data be called into question? For the audience he is not property—he is a person. Undoubtedly, most members of the audience would come to the conclusion that, his being so like a human, he has rights. However, members of that same audience would, no doubt, be very surprised if they read Harriet Ritvo's book *The Animal Estate: The English and Other Creatures in the Victorian Age*, in which she suggests that in the earliest laws for which there

are records, nonhuman animals were accorded a legal status, and they had rights and responsibilities.[19] She maintains that in many countries nonhuman animals were considered to be responsible for their actions and could be sentenced to die for what were seen as their crimes.[20] In his early book on the subject, Edward Payson Evans catalogues court cases in which nonhuman animals, such as pigs, chickens, rats, mice, bees, and gnats, were cited as defendants in criminal court cases.[21] These trials happened throughout the world for more than one thousand years.[22] Although the earliest of the 191 prosecutions listed by Evans center on the punishments of exorcism or excommunication,[23] the later trials suggest that nonhuman animals were accorded the status of criminal subjects since they could be, and sometimes were, executed for crimes.[24] For example, Evans details a number of cases in which pigs were executed for infanticide.[25] Evans displays much disgust about the ill-treatment of nonhuman animals in these trials and subsequent executions and much contempt for the behavior of the humans involved.[26] He writes that the trials were based in "gross and brutal medieval conceptions" of justice that declined as more "refined and humanitarian modern conceptions of justice" emerged.[27] He saw the decline of such trials as a progressive step.[28]

Although, as Piers Beirne makes clear, there are deficiencies in Evans's analysis because medieval records were often poor and there are difficulties with understanding the trials,[29] Ritvo offers a thought-provoking perspective on the changes in the law that, in the context of this essay, resonates with the hearing that Data had to undergo. While acknowledging the cruel conditions that a present-day reader would see as accompanying the criminal prosecution of nonhuman animals, Ritvo suggests that the trials reveal a positive element in that, at that time, at least some nonhuman animals were not seen as merely the property of humans.[30] The cases that Evans refers to and that Ritvo recounts do not detract from the fact that the flesh of nonhuman animals was eaten, that their skins and fur were worn, and that they were subjected to experiments, but being viewed as responsible for their actions, nonhuman animals were regarded as morally accountable subjects and were sometimes treated accordingly.[31] Subsequent legislative changes rendered nonhuman animals the property of humans, which gave humans the responsibility for assessing the danger that nonhuman animals might pose to others or to the property of others, for which humans were required to take appropriate action in order to prevent instances of injury and damage.[32] Thus, the legal rights of nonhuman animals were wiped out.[33] Ritvo concludes that this change reflected "a fundamental shift in the relationship between humans and their fellow creatures, as a result of which people systematically appropriated power they had previously attributed to animals, and animals became significantly and primarily seen as the objects of human manipulation."[34] Notwithstanding a range of acts and directives that are designed to protect the welfare of nonhuman animals, that is, to regulate the treatment of nonhuman animals rather than outlaw their use,[35] in the present day the nonhuman animal subjects themselves are not seen as the victims of crimes. Rather, they are seen as the property of humans, who, as their designated "owners," are seen as the victims of crimes.

The property status and commodification of nonhuman animals are explicit in their use in biomedical experiments, the focus of this discussion. The motivation for the transformation of nonhuman animal beings into tools for biomedical experiments resonates with Maddox's reason for wanting to dismantle Data: "So that I can learn from it and construct more."[36] Tom Holder's reasoning is a clear example. He argues that "animal research has been and remains crucial to the development of modern medicine. The reasons for ongoing research are manifold from finding ways to treat cancer to understanding the mechanisms behind neurodegeneration to developing new vaccines against HIV/AIDS, malaria and other diseases."[37] The interests of the millions of nonhuman animals who are used in this way every year are not taken into account.

Nonhuman Animal Experiments, Animal Welfare, and the Law

Because there is no precise calculation of the number of nonhuman animal subjects who are used in experiments, we must turn to the estimated, conservative annual worldwide figure of 115.3 million living vertebrate nonhuman animals, a figure suggested by Katy Taylor and her colleagues.[38] The figure is an estimate because 79 percent of countries do not publish statistics.[39] The figure is conservative because many nonhuman animals are not included in the published figures. For example, the US Animal Welfare Act excludes nonhuman animals who are categorized as being "cold-blooded," such as reptiles and amphibians, and others, such as rats, mice, birds, and nonhuman animals who are used in agricultural experiments.[40] In consequence, for example, the figure published by the US Department of Agriculture, Animal and Plant Health Inspection Service, of around 1.13 million nonhuman animals used in experiments in the United States in the fiscal year 2010 underrates the number considerably,[41] especially when we recall that rats and mice make up the overwhelming majority of all laboratory subjects used in the United States.[42] Additionally, as Taylor et al. make clear, the statistics for most countries cover only vertebrate species of nonhuman animals (who are considered to feel pain);[43] there are many more invertebrates (and some vertebrates) who are not included in the statistics because they are not considered to be "animals" in terms of the legal requirements.[44]

Unlike the android Lieutenant Commander Data, whose fictional plight was broadcast to an audience of millions, the terrible reality that humans impose on millions of nonhuman animals is occluded by the progressive removal of living nonhuman animals from our everyday experiences.[45] Ted Benton reflects that "the largest-scale and most systematically organized abuses of nonhuman animals occur in intensive rearing regimes in agriculture and in research laboratories."[46] But what happens to nonhuman animals in these places is largely hidden from public view. In research laboratories the experiments that take place cover a range of painful and life-threatening procedures, and many of these practices are inflicted without anesthesia (for further discussion, see the report in part 1, the current volume). Various regulations relating to the welfare of nonhuman animals worldwide prohibit their abuse in experiments,[47] but many of the procedures and practices that occur in laboratories and beyond would violate anticruelty laws if they were not authorized.[48] Thus, the exploitation of nonhuman animals is institutionalized and socially acceptable in certain situations because an "anthropocentric distinction is made between animal abuse and animal use."[49] Not labeling these harms as abuses, because of the purported difference between the unlawful "unnecessary" suffering that is associated with human abuse and the lawful "necessary" suffering that is associated with human use, overlooks the interests of nonhuman animals in favor of the interests of humans.[50] The fictional android Data was able to use the legal hearing to his advantage because it provided legal redress to the prospect of his being used as a research tool. It is not so for the millions of nonhuman animal subjects who are used annually. As Beirne contends, the "criminal law is a major structural and historical mechanism in the consolidation of institutionalized animal abuse."[51] This is due to the assumption that justifiable nonhuman animal experiments can take place for the reason that there can be "'humane use' of animals by humans."[52]

Data's legal redress means that he has the right to his life. No matter how compassionate his dismantlement and no matter how useful the observation of his inner workings might have been for scientific research, these developments would not compensate for his forced demise. If audience members put themselves in his place, it seems likely that they would rather be granted the right to *choose* their fate than be *forced* to die compassionately. Nonhuman animals who are used in experiments are not given the right to choose or the right to their lives. Particular nonhuman animals are accorded welfare protection in some parts of the world, but this does not constitute the right not to be used in experiments. Welfare protection often centers on considerations regarding their social and housing needs, their food and drink requirements, and the amount of suffering that takes place during experiments and death. Ostensibly, welfare is monitored by professionals. For example, in the United Kingdom, veterinarians and named animal care and welfare officers (NACWOs) are employed to recognize and monitor the suffering of nonhuman animals in laboratories with a view to improving their welfare.[53] This approach to welfare supports the idea that their suffering must be weighed against the interests of humans and science.

In this regard Dan Lyons comments that the UK Animals (Scientific Procedures) Act 1986 appears to be "highly significant because it seemed to introduce a novel legal framework that represented a fundamental change, from 'animal use' to 'animal welfare,' in the way that animals' interests are considered."[54] Although some (e.g., the Royal Society for the Prevention of Cruelty to Animals [RSPCA] in the United Kingdom) argue that this approach to welfare is a move toward ending the exploitation of nonhuman animals in laboratories, others criticize the position for not seeking to bring to an immediate end nonhuman animal exploitation because the notion of welfare centers on effecting exploitation that is more bearable to the nonhuman animals and therefore more acceptable to humans.[55] Of course, only nonhuman animals whose pain is recognized and whose consequent suffering is deemed to be morally relevant are included in such legal frameworks; millions of nonhuman animals are not considered to be morally relevant in this way.[56]

Sentience, Suffering, and Moral Relevance

As we have seen, the question that is central to this episode of *The Next Generation* is whether the android Lieutenant Commander Data is sentient. For Data to be regarded as a person and thus be permitted to choose his fate, he must be considered sentient in the terms that Commander Maddox offers—that is, he must display "intelligence," "self-awareness," and "consciousness."[57] Maddox's interpretation of sentience seems to be rooted in the work of the seventeenth-century philosopher René Descartes, who believed that the universe is composed of two kinds of substances: the incorporeal mind (i.e., the mental substance of the mind) and the corporeal soul (i.e., the material substance of the body). He explains, "One is purely mechanical and corporeal and depends solely on the force of the spirits and the construction of our organs, and can be called the corporeal soul: the other is the incorporeal mind, the soul which I have defined as a thinking substance."[58] Because he perceived the mind to be "distinct from and superior to matter,"[59] Descartes's observations of human behavior and speech led him to conclude that only humans have minds. This quality is not shared by machines because, he said, machines act "not from understanding but from the disposition of their organs," which means that a machine "could never use words" in such a way that it could "give an appropriately meaningful answer to whatever is said in its presence."[60] Had Descartes been in control of proceedings in the episode of *The Next Generation*, he might have been confounded—Data seems to pass his language and behavior tests of being human.[61] Data's plight is fictional, but the possibility that forms of artificial intelligence might be regarded as persons in the future is being contemplated at present.[62] Machines could be developed that would also pass Descartes's assessment of being human.

Such assessments are based in being humanlike, so inevitably, they are anthropocentric. In so many ways the fictional android Data looks and sounds human, and he also seems to respond as a human would. The audience is urged to engage with his humanlikeness. In a different form such anthropocentric assessments are manifest in the nonfictional world of nonhuman animal experiments in at least two ways. First, nonhuman animals who are used in experiments are considered to be unlike humans; thus, they can be used, morally, as resources. But the appeal to human-nonhuman animal similarity is essential to claims about experiments' scientific veracity because in the absence of similarities such experiments would be considered futile. So differences are deemed to be sufficiently significant to permit such experiments on moral grounds, yet similarities are deemed to make these experiments scientifically valuable on human-benefit grounds. Carol Adams observes that this duplicitous "formula for knowledge" rests in the notions that "animals are not like us so we can . . . animals are like us so we conclude . . ."[63]

A second related way in which anthropocentric assessments are used comes in the form of comparisons that are made between particular nonhuman animals and humans in order to determine whether they have a right not to be used in experiments. This is evident in campaigns that have sought to grant personhood to specific nonhuman animals. Perhaps the most familiar is the Great Ape Project, which proposes a UN Declaration of the Rights of Great Apes that would confer basic legal rights on nonhuman great apes (bonobos, chimpanzees, gorillas, and orangutans).[64] Because nonhuman hominids are regarded as having cognitive abilities similar to those of humans, the campaign urges that they should be given the rights to their lives and be included as equals with humans in the moral community,[65] which would include the right not to be subjected to experiments. Bans and restrictions on the use of nonhuman hominids in experiments are already in place in a number of countries.[66] Although the release of any nonhuman animal from the subjection, suffering, and lack of self-determination that is fundamental to being used as a human resource is very welcome, the problems with centering only on those who are considered to have minds similar to humans' minds as a condition for not treating them as tools "reinforces and perpetuates an unjustifiable speciesist hierarchy."[67] The commodification and objectification of millions of other nonhuman animal subjects who are not seen as having humanlike minds persists.

Suffering, though not referred to by Commander Maddox, is often presented as the defining feature of sentience. For example, Peter Singer argues that "the limit of sentience (using the term is convenient, if not strictly accurate, shorthand for the capacity to suffer or experience enjoyment or happiness) is the only defensible boundary of concern for the interests of others."[68] Singer is drawing on Jeremy Bentham's well-known pronouncement that regarding the treatment of nonhuman animals, "The question is not, Can they reason? Can they talk? But Can they suffer?"[69] In appealing to the ability to suffer, Bentham is countering the Cartesian focus on the ability to reason (discussed previously). Bentham insists that pleasure and pain should provide the foundation for how humans treat other sentient beings.

This concern with suffering has led to a range of intersecting hierarchies, and the right not to suffer for nonhuman animals is weighed up against the interests of humans and science. John Dupre sees this as the legacy of Cartesian assumptions about the differences between humans and nonhuman animals.[70] Because Descartes understood nonhuman animals to have a mechanized existence, he is often credited with the idea that they do not suffer. Jacques Derrida differs in his view of Descartes's position. He suggests that Descartes did recognize that nonhuman animals can suffer but believed that their suffering was not morally relevant because he supposed that the suffering of nonhuman animals was experienced without thought.[71] Conversely, human suffering is morally relevant for Descartes because it is tied to the capacity for reason, which provides the basis for the moral consideration of suffering in humans.[72]

Whatever Descartes thought, and the dispute about that continues,[73] the legacy seems to be the same because even in the case of those nonhuman animals who are recognized as being able to suffer in terms that humans accept (and millions of nonhuman animals are not so recognized), their suffering is somehow viewed as less important than the suffering of humans,[74] and this is a function of notions of moral standing. All humans have moral standing and have *equal* moral standing, so every human can be morally wronged.[75] Not all nonhuman animals are recognized as having moral standing, and where moral standing is recognized, in terms of the current moral orthodoxy, nonhuman animals' moral standing can be overridden for what is considered the greater good of humans.[76] So in the event of a conflict of interest between nonhuman animals whose suffering is recognized and the suffering of humans (who are deemed to suffer more), in terms of notions of moral relevance, "we would be justified in choosing to sacrifice the interests of animals."[77] So if Cartesian scientists did think that all nonhuman animals are unable to suffer, Mark Rowlands warns that "in some respects we are much worse. . . . At least they thought that animals were incapable of suffering."[78]

Although Data's hearing rests in anthropocentric views of sentience, Data is given the benefit of any doubt; Captain Louvois admits that she does not know. What she does know is that Data has preferences. Humans know that nonhuman animals have preferences. As Derrida and Elisabeth Roudinesco make clear, "we cannot imagine that an animal doesn't suffer when [he or she] is subjected to laboratory experimentation."[79] Thus, as Gary Francione maintains,[80] we cannot morally justify using any sentient nonhuman animals under any circumstance. This is not to say that the notion of sentience is unproblematic. Ned Hettinger is concerned about the way that "sentiocentrism . . . extends moral concern beyond humans only to our closest cousins, the sentient animals, and denies direct moral concern to 99 percent of living beings on the planet."[81] If we are to retain the notion of sentience, we should go beyond anthropocentric conceptualizations. Francione argues

that subjective awareness and having preferences, desires, wants, and interests should be the key.[82] These interests do not have to be like human interests, and they might not be clear to us, but we should give the benefit of any doubt.

Concluding Remarks

Science fiction is replete with human fears about the future. A recurring theme is one in which the human species or groups of humans are used as resources in experiments. In these dystopian scenarios, humans are constructed as being—and are used as—objects. Their only value is extrinsic. Their personhood is denied. The hearing that is endured by Lieutenant Commander Data expresses some of these fears. Although Data is an android—a machine—his human-like appearance and behavior invite the audience to empathize with him in his plea to control his own future. He could be compelled to become an object in an experiment and be dismantled, or he could be granted the rights of a free human person—that is, the right to choose his own fate. He is granted the latter. Although in the present day there are humans and groups of humans who are subjected to appalling discrimination and oppression, in law all humans have equal moral standing.[83] Machines do not have moral standing, but the possibility that "super-intelligent" artificial intelligence might have moral standing in the future is being contemplated by scientists in the present day.[84]

The moral standing of nonhuman animals has been contemplated for hundreds of years, and since the 1970s, the sentience of nonhuman animals has been a topic of great interest to biologists.[85] Since then the number of nonhuman animal species that have been granted the status of being sentient has grown.[86] To be sure, this is grounded in anthropocentric understandings of what constitutes sentience, but even within the terms of this anthropocentric assessment, the number has grown. Yet still, these nonhuman animals are used by the millions every year in experiments. Indeed, the number of nonhuman animals who are used has grown as well.

Nonhuman animals are treated as objects whose value is assumed to lie in the uses to which they can be put for the health and well-being of humans, and this is enshrined in law. The legal system of the fictional future gave Data the right to a hearing, and the judge granted him the right to choose his future. However, the law is a major structural and historical mechanism for denying nonhuman animals the rights to their lives. The legal system permits humans to interact with nonhuman animals in terms of how useful they are to us "rather than as beings living for their own sake and with their own purposes."[87] The suffering they endure, the refusal of their right to choose, and the denial of their right to life are legitimated. But science fiction helps us to "reimagine our moral relations with animals."[88] In the present day we need to argue for a transformation that sees nonhuman animals as individual actors who are accorded moral and legal status, in which their preferences and desires are recognized, where they are not exposed to human-imposed suffering, and where their right to live is respected.

Notes

1. V. Alexander, *Sociology of the Arts: Exploring Fine and Popular Forms* (Oxford: Blackwell, 2003).

2. L. Geraghty, *American Science Fiction Film and Television* (London: Berg, 2009).

3. For example, see S. Schneider, *Science Fiction and Philosophy: From Time Travel to Superintelligence* (Chichester, UK: Wiley, Blackwell, 2009).

4. C. Sonego, "Italian Star Trek: The Measure of a Man," *Star Trek*, October 15, 2014, http://www.startrek.com/article/italian-star-trek-the-measure-of-a-man.

5. An android is a "sophisticated robot constructed on the model of a human being." R. Hanley, *Is Data Human? The Metaphysics of Star Trek* (New York: Basic Books, 1997), 42.

6. All quoted dialogue from the episode comes from R. Scheerer, dir., "The Measure of a Man," *Star Trek: The Next Generation*, season 2, episode 9, aired February 13, 1989.

7. L. Nemeck, *Star Trek: The Next Generation Companion* (New York: Pocket Books, 2003).

8. EW Staff, "'Next Generation': The Top 10 Episodes," *Entertainment Weekly*, September 19, 2007, http://www.ew.com/article/2007/09/20/star-trek-next-generation-top-10-episodes.

9. C. Sonego, "Italian Star Trek."

10. R. Garner, *Animal Ethics* (Cambridge: Polity, 2005).

11. European Parliament, "Regulation (EC) No 1223/2009 of the European Parliament and of the Council of 30 November 2009 on Cosmetic Products," *Official Journal of the European Union L* 342 (December 22, 2009): 59–208.

12. European Parliament, "Directive 2010/63/EU of the European Parliament and of the Council of 22 September 2010 on the Protection of Animals Used for Scientific Purposes," *Official Journal of the European Union L* 276 (October 20, 2010): 33–79.

13. K. Peggs, "Transgenic Animals, Biomedical Experiments, and 'Progress,'" *Journal of Animal Ethics* 3, no. 1 (2013): 41–56.

14. K. Peggs, "An Insufferable Business: Ethics, Nonhuman Animals, and Biomedical Experiments," *Animals* 5, no. 3 (2015): 624–42.

15. C. P. Flynn, "A Sociological Analysis of Animal Abuse," in *The International Handbook on Animal Abuse and Cruelty: Theory, Research, and Application*, ed. F. R. Ascione (West Lafayette, IN: Purdue University Press, 2008), 155–74.

16. P. Beirne, "For a Nonspeciesist Criminology: Animal Abuse as an Object of Study," *Criminology* 37, no. 1 (1999): 117–47.

17. Scheerer, "Measure of a Man."

18. T. S. Minato, "Development of an Android Robot for Studying Human-Robot Interaction," in *Innovations in Applied Artificial Intelligence: 17th International Conference on Industrial and Engineering Applications of Artificial Intelligence and Expert Systems, IEA/AIE 2004, Ottawa, Canada, May 17–20, 2004, Proceedings*, ed. B. Y. Orchard (Berlin: Springer, 2004), 424–34.

19. H. Ritvo, *The Animal Estate: The English and Other Creatures in the Victorian Age* (Cambridge, MA: Harvard University Press, 1987), 1.

20. Ibid.

21. E. P. Evans, *The Criminal Prosecution and Capital Punishment of Animals* (Clark, NJ: Lawbook Exchange, 2007), first published 1906.

22. N. C. Sweeney, "The Vanished Legal Rights of Animal Criminals," *Environmental Law and Management* 26 (2014): 24.

23. P. Beirne, "The Law Is an Ass: Reading E. P. Evans' The Medieval Prosecution and Capital Punishment of Animals," *Society and Animals* 2, no. 1 (1994): 32.

24. Ritvo, *Animal Estate*.

25. Evans, *Criminal Prosecution*, 143–44.

26. Beirne, "Law Is an Ass."

27. Evans, *Criminal Prosecution*, 256.

28. Beirne, "Law Is an Ass."

29. Ibid.

30. Ritvo, *Animal Estate*.

31. Ibid., 2.

32. Ibid.

33. Sweeney, "Vanished Legal Rights."

34. Ritvo, *Animal Estate*, 2.

35. G. L. Francione, *Animals as Persons: Essays on the Abolition of Animal Exploitation*, Critical Perspectives on Animals (New York: Columbia University Press, 2008).

36. Scheerer, "Measure of a Man."

37. T. Holder, "Standing Up for Science: The Antivivisection Movement and How to Stand Up to It," *EMBO Reports* 15, no. 6 (2014): 625–30.

38. K. Taylor, N. Gordon, G. Langley, and W. Higgins, "Estimates for Worldwide Animal Use in 2005," *Alternatives to Laboratory Animals* 36 (2008): 327.

39. Ibid.

40. A. Goldberg, "Use of Animals in Research: A Science-Society Controversy? The American Perspective: Animal Welfare Issues," *Altex: Alternatives to Animal Experimentation* 19, no. 3 (2002): 137–39.

41. US Department of Agriculture, *Annual Report Animal Usage by Fiscal Year* (2010), accessed January 19, 2014, https://www.aphis.usda.gov/animal_welfare/efoia/downloads/2010_Animals_Used_In_Research.pdf.

42. Goldberg, "Use of Animals."

43. Taylor et al., "Estimates."

44. For further discussion, see Peggs, "Insufferable Business."

45. J. Wolch and J. Emel, *Animal Geographies: Place, Politics, and Identity in the Nature-Culture Borderlands* (London: Verso, 1998), xi.

46. T. Benton, "Rights and Justice on a Shared Planet: More Rights or New Relations?" *Theoretical Criminology* 2, no. 2 (1998): 171.

47. G. Cazaux, "Labelling Animals: Non-Speciesist Criminology and Techniques to Identify Other Animals," in *Issues in Green Criminology: Confronting Harms against Environments, Humanity, and Other Animals*, ed. P. Beirne (Cullompton, UK: Willan, 2007), 87–113.

48. Beirne, "For a Nonspeciesist Criminology," 128.

49. P. Beirne, "Animal Rights, Animal Abuse, and Green Criminology," in *Issues in Green Criminology: Confronting Harms against Environments, Humanity, and Other Animals*, ed. P. Beirne (Cullompton, UK: Willan, 2007), 55; Cazaux, "Labelling Animals," 103.

50. Ibid.

51. Beirne, "For a Nonspeciesist Criminology," 129.

52. S. Donaldson and W. Kymlicka, *Zoopolis: A Political Theory of Animal Rights* (Oxford: Oxford University Press, 2011), 3.

53. K. Peggs and B. Smart, "Nonhuman Animal Suffering: Critical Pedagogy and Practical Animal Ethics," *Society and Animals*, no. 2 (2017).

54. D. Lyons, "Protecting Animals versus the Pursuit of Knowledge: The Evolution of the British Animal Research Policy Process," *Society and Animals* 19 (2011): 361.

55. See, for example, Francione, *Animals as Persons*.

56. Garner, *Animal Ethics*.

57. Scheerer, "Measure of a Man."

58. R. Descartes, "Animals Are Machines," in *Environmental Ethics: Divergence and Convergence*, ed. S. J. Armstrong (New York: McGraw-Hill, 1993), 284.

59. F. E. Sutcliffe, introduction to *Discourse on Method and Other Writings*, by R. Descartes (Middlesex, UK: Penguin, 1968), 19.

60. Quoted in J.-P. Séris, "Language and Machine in the Philosophy of Descartes," in *Essays on the Philosophy and Science of René Descartes*, ed. S. Voss (New York: Oxford University Press, 1993), 179.

61. Hanley, *Is Data Human?* 47.

62. For example, see N. Bostrom and E. Yudkowsky, "The Ethics of Artificial Intelligence," in *Cambridge Handbook of Artificial Intelligence*, ed. K. A. Frankish (New York: Cambridge University Press, 2014), 316–34.

63. C. Adams, *Neither Man nor Beast: Feminism and the Defense of Animals* (New York: Continuum, 1995), 52.

64. For example, see P. Singer and P. Cavalieri, *The Great Ape Project: Equality beyond Humanity* (London: Fourth Estate, 1993).

65. Ibid.

66. For example, see NEAVS, "International Bans," *Project R&R*, accessed November 6, 2015, http://www.releasechimps.org/laws/international-bans.

67. Francione, *Animals as Persons*, 20.

68. P. Singer, *Practical Ethics*, 3rd ed. (Cambridge: Cambridge University Press, 2011), 50.

69. J. Bentham, *An Introduction to the Principles of Morals and Legislation*, ed. J. H. Burns and H. L. A. Hart (London: Athlone, 1970), 283, first published 1789.

70. J. Dupre, "Human Kinds and Biological Kinds: Some Similarities and Differences," *Philosophy of Science* 71, no. 5 (2004): 892–900.

71. J. Derrida, *The Animal That Therefore I Am* (New York: Fordham University Press, 2008), 28.

72. Ibid., 28.

73. For example, see I. J. Duncan, "The Changing Concept of Animal Sentience," *Applied Animal Behaviour Science* 100 (2006): 11–19.

74. For discussion, see A. Linzey, *Why Animal Suffering Matters: Philosophy, Theology, and Practical Ethics* (Oxford: Oxford University Press, 2009).

75. J. Sytsma and E. Machery, "The Two Sources of Moral Standing," *Review of Philosophy and Psychology* 3, no. 3 (2012): 303–24.

76. Garner, *Animal Ethics*, 15.

77. Ibid., 23.

78. M. Rowlands, *Animals like Us* (London: Verso, 2002), 5.

79. J. Derrida and E. Roudinesco, *For What Tomorrow . . . a Dialogue*, trans. J. Fort (Stanford: Stanford University Press, 2004), 70.

80. Francione, *Animals as Persons*.

81. N. Hettinger, "Environmental Ethics," in *Encyclopedia of Animal Rights and Animal Welfare*, ed. M. Bekoff and C. Meaney, 2nd ed. (Santa Barbara, CA: Greenwood, 2010), 222.

82. Francione, *Animals as Persons*, 11.

83. R. J. Arneson, "What, if Anything, Renders All Humans Morally Equal?" in *Peter Singer and His Critics*, ed. D. Jamieson (Oxford: Blackwell, 1999), 103.

84. For example, see Bostrom and Yudkowsky, "Ethics of Artificial Intelligence."

85. Duncan, "Changing Concept," 11.

86. For example, in the European Union, most invertebrates are deemed to be incapable of suffering and thus are not subject to the welfare protections that are offered by the legislation. However, invertebrate species in the cyclostome and cephalopod categories have now been recognized, and thus they are granted the welfare protections that are offered to vertebrate species whose suffering has been recognized.

87. H. Pedersen, "Schools, Speciesism, and Hidden Curricula: The Role of Critical Pedagogy for Humane Education Futures," *Journal of Futures Studies* 8, no. 4 (2004): 2.

88. J. Clements, "How Science Fiction Helps Us Reimagine Our Moral Relations with Animals," *Journal of Animal Ethics* 5, no. 2 (2015): 181–88.

Bibliography

Adams, C. *Neither Man nor Beast: Feminism and the Defense of Animals*. New York: Continuum, 1995.

Alexander, V. *Sociology of the Arts: Exploring Fine and Popular Forms*. Oxford: Blackwell, 2003.

Arneson, R. J. "What, if Anything, Renders All Humans Morally Equal?" In *Peter Singer and His Critics*, edited by D. Jamieson, 103–28. Oxford: Blackwell, 1999.

Beirne, P. "Animal Rights, Animal Abuse, and Green Criminology." In *Issues in Green Criminology: Confronting Harms against Environments, Humanity, and Other Animals*, edited by P. Beirne, 55–86. Cullompton, UK: Willan, 2007.

———. "For a Nonspeciesist Criminology: Animal Abuse as an Object of Study." *Criminology* 37, no. 1 (1999): 117–47.

———. "The Law Is an Ass: Reading E. P. Evans' The Medieval Prosecution and Capital Punishment of Animals." *Society and Animals* 2, no. 1 (1994): 27–46.

Bentham, J. *An Introduction to the Principles of Morals and Legislation*. Edited by J. H. Burns and H. L. A. Hart. London: Athlone, 1970. First published 1789.

Benton, T. "Rights and Justice on a Shared Planet: More Rights or New Relations?" *Theoretical Criminology* 2, no. 2 (1998): 149–75.

Bostrom, N., and E. Yudkowsky. "The Ethics of Artificial Intelligence." In *Cambridge Handbook of Artificial Intelligence*, edited by K. A. Frankish, 316–34. New York: Cambridge University Press, 2014.

Cazaux, G. "Labelling Animals: Non-Speciesist Criminology and Techniques to Identify Other Animals." In *Issues in Green Criminology: Confronting Harms against Environments, Humanity, and Other Animals*, edited by P. Beirne, 87–113. Cullompton, UK: Willan, 2007.

Clements, J. "How Science Fiction Helps Us Reimagine Our Moral Relations with Animals." *Journal of Animal Ethics* 5, no. 2 (2015): 181–88.

Derrida, J. *The Animal That Therefore I Am*. New York: Fordham University Press, 2008.

Derrida, J., and E. Roudinesco. *For What Tomorrow . . . a Dialogue*. Translated by J. Fort. Stanford: Stanford University Press, 2004.

Descartes, R. "Animals Are Machines." In *Environmental Ethics: Divergence and Convergence*, edited by S. J. Armstrong, 281–85. New York: McGraw-Hill, 1993.

Donaldson, S., and W. Kymlicka. *Zoopolis: A Political Theory of Animal Rights*. Oxford: Oxford University Press, 2011.

Duncan, I. J. "The Changing Concept of Animal Sentience." *Applied Animal Behaviour Science* 100 (2006): 11–19.

Dupre, J. "Human Kinds and Biological Kinds: Some Similarities and Differences." *Philosophy of Science* 71, no. 5 (2004): 892–900.

European Parliament. "Directive 2010/63/EU of the European Parliament and of the Council of 22 September 2010 on the Protection of Animals Used for Scientific Purposes." *Official Journal of the European Union L* 276 (October 20, 2010): 33–79.

———. "Regulation (EC) No 1223/2009 of the European Parliament and of the Council of 30 November 2009 on Cosmetic Products." *Official Journal of the European Union L* 342 (December 22, 2009): 59–208.

Evans, E. P. *The Criminal Prosecution and Capital Punishment of Animals*. Clark, NJ: Lawbook Exchange, 2007. First published 1906.

EW Staff. "'Next Generation': The Top 10 Episodes." *Entertainment Weekly*, September 19, 2007. Accessed January 19, 2014. http://www.ew.com/article/2007/09/20/star-trek-next-generation-top-10-episodes.

Flynn, C. P. "A Sociological Analysis of Animal Abuse." In *The International Handbook on Animal Abuse and Cruelty: Theory, Research, and Application*, edited by F. R. Ascione, 155–74. West Lafayette, IN: Purdue University Press, 2008.

Francione, G. L. *Animals as Persons: Essays on the Abolition of Animal Exploitation*. Critical Perspectives on Animals. New York: Columbia University Press, 2008.

Garner, R. *Animal Ethics*. Cambridge: Polity, 2005.

Geraghty, L. *American Science Fiction Film and Television*. London: Berg, 2009.

Goldberg, A. "Use of Animals in Research: A Science-Society Controversy? The American Perspective: Animal Welfare Issues." *Altex: Alternatives to Animal Experimentation* 19, no. 3 (2002): 137–39.

Hanley, R. *Is Data Human? The Metaphysics of Star Trek*. New York: Basic Books, 1997.

Hettinger, N. "Environmental Ethics." In *Encyclopedia of Animal Rights and Animal Welfare*, edited by M. Bekoff, 221–23. 2nd ed. Santa Barbara, CA: Greenwood, 2010.

Holder, T. "Standing Up for Science: The Antivivisection Movement and How to Stand Up to It." *EMBO Reports* 15, no. 6 (2014): 625–30.

Linzey, A. *Why Animal Suffering Matters: Philosophy, Theology, and Practical Ethics*. Oxford: Oxford University Press, 2009.

Lyons, D. "Protecting Animals versus the Pursuit of Knowledge: The Evolution of the British Animal Research Policy Process." *Society and Animals* 19 (2011): 356–67.

Minato, T. S. "Development of an Android Robot for Studying Human-Robot Interaction." In *Innovations in Applied Artificial Intelligence: 17th International Conference on Industrial and*

Engineering Applications of Artificial Intelligence and Expert Systems, IEA/AIE 2004, Ottawa, Canada, May 17–20, 2004, Proceedings, edited by B. Y. Orchard, 424–34. Berlin: Springer, 2004.

NEAVS. "International Bans." *Project R&R*, 2017. Accessed November 6, 2015. http://www.releasechimps.org/laws/international-bans.

Nemeck, L. *Star Trek: The Next Generation Companion*. New York: Pocket Books, 2003.

Pedersen, H. "Schools, Speciesism, and Hidden Curricula: The Role of Critical Pedagogy for Humane Education Futures." *Journal of Futures Studies* 8, no. 4 (2004): 1–14.

Peggs, K. "An Insufferable Business: Ethics, Nonhuman Animals, and Biomedical Experiments." *Animals* 5, no. 3 (2015): 624–42.

———. "Transgenic Animals, Biomedical Experiments, and 'Progress.'" *Journal of Animal Ethics* 3, no. 1 (2013): 41–56.

Peggs, K., and B. Smart. "Nonhuman Animal Suffering: Critical Pedagogy and Practical Animal Ethics." *Society and Animals* 25, no. 2 (2017).

Ritvo, H. *The Animal Estate: The English and Other Creatures in the Victorian Age*. Cambridge, MA: Harvard University Press, 1987.

Rowlands, M. *Animals like Us*. London: Verso, 2002.

Scheerer, R., dir. "The Measure of a Man." *Star Trek: The Next Generation*, season 2, episode 9. Aired February 13, 1989.

Schneider, S. *Science Fiction and Philosophy: From Time Travel to Superintelligence*. Chichester, UK: Wiley, Blackwell, 2009.

Séris, J.-P. "Language and Machine in the Philosophy of Descartes." In *Essays on the Philosophy and Science of René Descartes*, edited by S. Voss, 177–94. New York: Oxford University Press, 1993.

Singer, P. *Practical Ethics*. 3rd ed. Cambridge: Cambridge University Press, 2011.

Singer, P., and P. Cavalieri. *The Great Ape Project: Equality beyond Humanity*. London: Fourth Estate, 1993.

Sonego, C. "Italian Star Trek: The Measure of a Man." *Star Trek*. October 15, 2014. http://www.startrek.com/article/italian-star-trek-the-measure-of-a-man.

Sutcliffe, F. E. Introduction to *Discourse on Method and Other Writings*, by R. Descartes, 7–23. Middlesex, UK: Penguin, 1968.

Sweeney, N. C. "The Vanished Legal Rights of Animal Criminals." *Environmental Law and Management* 26 (2014): 24.

Sytsma, J., and E. Machery. "The Two Sources of Moral Standing." *Review of Philosophy and Psychology* 3, no. 3 (2012): 303–24.

Taylor, K., N. Gordon, G. Langley, and W. Higgins. "Estimates for Worldwide Animal Use in 2005." *Alternatives to Laboratory Animals* 36 (2008): 327–42.

US Department of Agriculture. *Annual Report Animal Usage by Fiscal Year*. 2010. Accessed January 19, 2014. https://www.aphis.usda.gov/animal_welfare/efoia/downloads/2010_Animals_Used_In_Research.pdf.

Wolch, J., and J. Emel. *Animal Geographies: Place, Politics, and Identity in the Nature-Culture Borderlands*. London: Verso, 1998.

Harms versus Benefits
A Practical Critique of Utilitarian Calculations

Katy D. Taylor

THE EUROPEAN UNION (EU) directive on the protection of animals used for scientific purposes was significantly revised in 2010.[1] It outlines a framework for the evaluation and authorization of projects involving animal experiments that had to be incorporated into EU member state national legislation by 2013. The revision was very much an exercise in leveling the playing field and is broadly considered to have been modeled on the UK regulatory system. To this end, the revision of the directive represents very little change to the authorization process for animal experiments in the United Kingdom but significant change for other EU countries, such as France, whose authorization process was arguably less rigorous.

The utilitarian approach of weighing the harms done to the animals in animal experiments against the benefits to humans now lies formally at the heart of the directive. A positive harm-benefit assessment (HBA) is now a prerequisite for approval of a project involving harmful use of animals: "Member States shall ensure that no project is carried out unless a favourable project evaluation by the competent authority has been received in accordance with Article 38."[2]

Unfortunately, the directive itself does not explain how the HBA should be performed, stating just that it should "assess whether the harm to the animals in terms of suffering, pain and distress is justified by the expected outcome taking into account ethical considerations, and may ultimately benefit human beings, animals or the environment."[3] The European Commission has produced some more detailed guidance on how project evaluation should be performed,[4] but much of how it will be done in practice has been left to member states to decide.

An HBA has in fact been conducted under the UK regulatory system under the Animals (Scientific Procedures) Act (ASPA) since 1986. However, Cruelty Free International, along with other animal protection organizations, is concerned about the HBA as it is currently being performed. This is not just because the organization does not ascribe philosophically to this approach to deciding whether animal experiments are ethical. For several reasons, discussed here, we are concerned that the process is not being performed in a thorough, unbiased manner. As a consequence, there are some projects that are currently authorized that, under a properly conducted HBA, we argue should not have been—for example, the permitted use of tens of thousands of mice in LD50 (lethal) tests that cause substantial suffering and death in order to test a botulinum toxin product (Dysport™) that is sold in large quantities for cosmetic purposes, or the use of macaques in severe surgical and behavioral procedures for fundamental brain research with no direct human benefit, or the use of rodents in harmful tests to prove the well-known effects of recreational drugs or natural foods on behavior.[5] That is not to say that there is not some limit on the experiments that can be conducted in the United Kingdom, however. Following a review of the cost-benefit assessment, as it was called then, in 1997 the United Kingdom implemented policies to ban the use of animals to test cosmetics (products and ingredients), tobacco and alcohol products, and offensive weapons, as well as the use of great apes or wild-caught primates for any purpose.[6] More recently, the United Kingdom also banned the testing of household products on animals.[7]

In this essay I question the validity of the current approach to HBA based on my experience of the approach in the United Kingdom. I raise a number of practical and theoretical issues with the process, some of which are surmountable and some of which appear to be inherent and unavoidable. My evidence comes from discussions within working groups on the implementation of the EU directive and the ASPA, public statements made by researchers, and project licenses that Cruelty Free International has obtained under the Freedom of Information Act 2000. Using a hypothetical example of a new treatment for stroke being tested on marmosets, I demonstrate the ways in which the harms can be underestimated and the benefits overestimated. The example is based on marmoset research at Cambridge University that was originally uncovered in a Cruelty Free International investigation in 2001,[8] along with data that is, unusually, available regarding the predictivity of animal tests for stroke as a result of extensive research by a group at Edinburgh University called Collaborative Approach to Meta-Analysis and Review of Animal Data from Experimental Studies (CAMRADES).[9]

Surmountable Problems with the HBA

The HBA is utilitarianism in practice. It is intended to be a way of ensuring that only those animal experiments that cause less suffering to the animals than the benefits gained by humans, or by other animals or the environment, are permitted. In practice, however, due in part to the lack of proper ethical debate about animal experiments (see section 1.2, "The Old Debate," in part 1 of the current volume) and lack of guidance, many of those individuals who are part of the HBA process appear to be unclear about why they are doing it.

Lack of Clarity of Purpose

Some confuse the HBA with application of the 3Rs, looking at whether the animal tests being proposed can be replaced, the numbers of animals reduced, or the suffering reduced (refined). It is common to see animal experiments justified in terms of there being no other way to answer the research question at hand rather than in terms of the benefit per se. Whether the experiment can be done another way should be the first consideration, and the absence of this is not a justification for the experiment itself. Indeed, considerations about the 3Rs should be made first, and only then should there be consideration about whether the proposed animal test is ethical in its final form, following adoption of any subsequent 3Rs changes that may have been made to "improve" the experiment. The chief inspector for animal experiments in the United Kingdom admitted in his "note on the cost/benefit assessment" in 1997 that "a considerable proportion of Inspectorate resources is devoted to ensuring that project license applications cannot be further refined"—the implication being that considerations about refinement are done at the expense of considerations about whether the projects should be authorized.[10]

Others rather think that the HBA is a useful tool to get animal researchers to simply consider the ethics of what they are doing. This is more commonly mentioned in discussions, but even according to its own document, the commission thinks it is important that there is "evidence that the applicant has considered and understood all the relevant issues."[11] However, thinking about ethics is not the same as the "practical ethics" of making decisions about whether an animal test should go ahead or not.

One could argue that if performing an HBA doesn't actually result in any rejection of projects (see subsequent discussion), then the HBA is not performing its purpose. Some may argue that our not seeing rejections of projects doesn't necessarily mean that the HBA is not being done properly. What is simply happening is that the applications being received match where the ethical bar should be set. Considerations about how and where the bar should be set aside, there is evidence that the public at large certainly does not agree with where it is currently set.

A recent opinion poll conducted for the UK government found that only 37 percent of people agree that it is acceptable to use animals for "all types of research."[12] When asked whether they supported the use of certain types of animals, support dropped dramatically, with only 14 percent agreeing that it was acceptable to use dogs and only 16 percent supporting the use of macaque monkeys for medical research to benefit people.[13] Despite this public concern, the UK government permits testing on more than thirty-five hundred dogs and nearly two thousand macaques every year.[14]

A recent survey in the United States found that only 47 percent of adults "favor the use of animals in research," compared to 89 percent of scientists.[15] In other words, scientists appear to have a different ethical perspective from the general public. This was raised in the Animals in Scientific Procedures Committee's (APC) 1997 review of ASPA: "There were concerns about the adaptability of the regulatory system to changing attitudes and values on animal use, and whether the cost/benefit assessment reflected generally held values (the view of society), or the particular views and values of more narrowly defined groups (such as the scientific community or industry)."[16] This disparity between scientific and public ethical viewpoints—and its implications regarding how the HBA should be conducted—has yet to be tackled, perhaps in part because members of the public, despite their apparent concern, know very little about the extent of animal experimentation in their country.

Lack of Transparency

The Animals in Science Regulation Unit (ASRU, as it is now known) within the Home Office receives applications to test on animals from individuals (associated with registered establishments), which the ASRU reviews and authorizes on behalf of the secretary of state. However, the process by which ASRU officials review the projects and approve them, based on a favorable HBA, is not transparent. Establishments typically review their own projects within animal welfare and ethical review bodies (AWERBs) before HBAs are sent to the ASRU. The extent to which these committees make an ethical assessment (as opposed to consideration of the 3Rs) also is not typically made public and presumably varies between establishments. There is a note on the cost-benefit assessment by the

chief inspector in the Animals Procedures Committee report for 1997;[17] however, this is only a few pages long and, aside from making some useful points, is largely discursive. Even the APC said in reviewing the inspector's report that as a consequence, "further attention should also be given to the nature of the assessment on which the decision on whether to grant a licence is made, and the comparison of costs and benefits which it involves."[18] Following the revision of the EU directive and the amendment to the ASPA, the ASRU has promised to release a more detailed note on how it currently processes licenses. Tellingly, the *Guidance on the Operation of the Animals (Scientific Procedures) Act 1986* describes only the considerations that *applicants* should make when conducting their own HBAs.[19]

As a consequence, for nearly thirty years, the process (and to some extent the outcome) of the HBA has been secret in the United Kingdom. This is a shocking statement to have to make, especially since a large proportion of the animal research conducted in the United Kingdom is funded by government and therefore the taxpayers. Many of those in animal protection suspect that this is partly because the process is in fact conducted in a rather rudimentary manner. This assertion is based on knowledge of those projects that are approved—that is, the outcomes of project evaluation. Until recently, outcomes were known only by looking at the annual statistics on animal experiments and scientific publications after the research was completed. However, following a successful case by Cruelty Free International against Newcastle University, which tried to block the requirement to release project licenses, it has been possible since 2011 to see some project licenses on a case-by-case basis under the Freedom of Information Act 2000.[20] Release of project licenses by the Home Office, even after they have expired, is still a prisonable offense under section 24 of the ASPA.

Skepticism regarding the robustness of the HBA is also based on the fact that project applications do not tend to get formally rejected. Rather, the Home Office claims that early discussions with applicants mean that "proposals unlikely to meet the Act's stringent requirements are revised or withdrawn before formal refusal becomes necessary."[21] The problem with this—as acknowledged by the APC in 1997—was that no inference can therefore be drawn from the rarity of formal refusals of applications since the system operates in such a way as to encourage applicants to bring forward applications which comply with the terms of the Act or, alternatively, to ensure that applications which are variously unsatisfactory in cost/benefit (or other) terms "fall out" of this process without formally failing a cost/benefit assessment.[22]

This further strengthens the perception we have that there is in fact little or no assessment happening—projects merely match what the scientific community considers acceptable, which is the majority of research.

Poor Breadth of Expertise, and Ethical Perspectives of Evaluators

In the United Kingdom, we understand that project evaluation is initially done within an institution by its AWERB, based on the application from the researcher. The final project application is forwarded to ASRU, where a single inspector reviews the application and makes his or her own ethical judgment, possibly assisted by discussions with colleagues or internal policy. The requirements under the amended ASPA mandate that the institution's AWERB must include at least a veterinarian, an animal care officer, and a scientist. The ASRU inspectors are typically veterinarians or doctors with animal experimentation experience.

The situation in France appears to be even less impartial, with the institution-based ethical assessment effectively being rubber-stamped by an official from the Ministry of Research. The legislation accredits institutionally funded ethical review committees to do project evaluation, which appears to be a mechanism to devolve responsibility from the government.[23] Germany appears to have larger bodies that either are involved in or finalize ethical evaluations. German law says that regional ethical review may be assisted by animal experimentation commissions that contain one-third animal protectionists,[24] although the final assessment is made by, as in the United Kingdom, a single inspector.

So it appears that ethical evaluation (and subsequent authorization) in major EU countries is being done by relatively few individuals. Typically, a small number of individuals do the preliminary assessment internally, and a single individual may make a final assessment externally. This is of concern on a number of fronts. First, article 38(4) of the directive insists that project evaluation is to be conducted in an "impartial manner," but this is impossible if the institution itself is doing its own evaluations! Clearly, an institution has an interest in permitting its researchers to do the work they want to do. The commission agrees in its own guidance that it would be "very difficult" for project evaluation by the institution to meet the requirement for impartiality.[25]

Second, it is unlikely that the small committees involved are going to include individuals with the necessary expertise to properly evaluate the harms and benefits of the research. Animal protectionists are not explicitly required to be involved according to the UK legislation. Lay members, if they are included, may not even understand the purpose of the research fully enough to challenge the likely benefits. The general lack of involvement of a broader spectrum of experts, such as ethicists and economists, is likely to mean the HBA is going to be heavily scientifically focused.

Third, the lack of layperson involvement (at least as a legal minimum in the United Kingdom) is of real concern. This means that the general public's ethical approach (see previous discussion) is not likely to be represented. This imbalance is likely to be exacerbated by the fact that the groups involved in the assessment are usually small in number. It is unlikely that a small group of people will contain a balanced mix of ethical beliefs. The scientific ethical approach, which tends to be in favor of animal experiments, is likely to be overrepresented by the very nature of those who are required to be involved in the process.

As a result, the makeup of the limited groups that are involved in project evaluation appears to be biased toward those who support animal experimentation (possibly in all its forms), such that these persons are actually not utilitarians but are instrumentalists—that is, they believe that it is acceptable to use animals for human ends as long as the animals are not subjected to unnecessary cruelty (which they define). It is therefore concerning if the assessment is meant to be utilitarian but those doing it are fundamentally not.

Incomplete Assessment of Harms and Benefits

It is important that the assessment of both harms and benefits is as complete (i.e., all elements are considered) and, ideally, as quantitative as possible (i.e., is measurable). An HBA that is based on descriptive (qualitative) language is likely, in my view, to be inadequate. The whole point of an HBA is that the harms are "weighed" against the benefits. If there is no element of quantity in the assessment, then how can this be done? Indeed, in other cost-benefit assessments, such as how the National Institute for Health and Care Excellence (NICE) evaluates whether to provide new drug treatments through the National Health Service, numbers factor in very much, even to the extent that monetary value is ascribed to human life (quality-adjusted life years measurement, QALYS).[26]

The assessment of "harms" is arguably easier to do because not only has there been a lot of research into the assessment of animal pain and suffering over the last thirty years but also the researchers know what they intend to do to the animals and to how many. Indeed, often the painful effects themselves are a key part of the experiment—for example, a degree of arthritis may need to be inflicted as a "baseline" before treatment in order to determine whether the treatment results in any improvement. Researchers can write down all the procedures they plan to do to an animal and make a judgment as to how this might affect them, perhaps drawing on how humans might feel in those circumstances and using expert knowledge on how the species in question might feel. This is called critical anthropomorphism.[27] Alternatively, and more commonly, the degree of suffering is assumed based on how other animals fared in previous, similar experiments.

Under the new directive, severity is to be assessed retrospectively at the end of the experiment for every animal. Annex VIII of the directive suggests types of experiments that are likely to cause "mild," "moderate," and "severe" suffering. It is probable that we will see applicants include these qualitative categories to describe the expected severity of their projects in order for evaluators to decide on the harms. Indeed, the United Kingdom already uses these three categories in this way, each procedure having a "limit" that is the worst severity likely to be experienced by any single animal in the study, an approach advocated in the directive.

Nonetheless, the harms to which the animals are subjected are still underappreciated and still unknown to some extent. For example, researchers are only just realizing that pain and distress can be seen in the facial expressions of mice and that these animals vocalize at levels beyond our hearing.[28] The fact that common laboratory procedures can induce stress is also not well recognized.[29] This is perhaps a consequence of the fact that rodents, who are the most commonly used animals, are prey species whose reaction to being harmed may not be to look ill but to hide this fact so that a predator will not see them as an easy prey. I am concerned therefore that assessment of the harms based purely on observing animals is likely to lead to a significant underestimation of their suffering.

In addition, although the scientific animal-welfare community may admit that the normal laboratory environment is woefully inadequate for the animals, in terms of space and complexity, among other things, the fact that animals are kept in "standard" cages that adhere to the dimensions set out in the directive is likely to lead many to forget the impact of just being in the laboratory. According to the commission guidance on severity assessment, however, animals' whole life experience should be considered,[30] but it is not obvious that this will be genuinely done.

The assessment of "benefit" is more complex. Table 1 provides a matrix of the considerations for harms and benefits that need to be made. It builds on the commission's guidance that the probability of the experiment being successful is a material consideration, but it makes a distinction between the probability of the experiment being successful and the probability of the overall aim being achieved.[31] It is my experience that there is a strong tendency for justifications of animal research to focus on the importance of the overall aim (e.g., curing cancer) and to some extent the likely success of the individual experiment (e.g., "we are experienced researchers," "we have done this experiment many times"). However, there is poor consideration of the specific need for the experiment (over and above other ways of treating the disease or other ways of studying cancer, for example) and even less consideration of the likelihood of the experiment (assuming it is successful) translating into a treatment for the disease in question (the overall aim).

Sometimes the need for the experiment is considered under discussion of replacement, but the question is wider than that. The question should be, is this experiment needed to answer a key question upon which the overall aim depends? The proposed research may not actually be key, or a similar, equally key question could be answered without using animals. It is my opinion that, particularly in basic medical research, this is not properly considered. Information obtained from other types of experiments, including human studies, is often shown to have been just as, if not more, useful when one looks at the history of a particular "discovery." See, for example, the debate over the provenance of deep brain stimulation treatment for Parkinson's disease symptoms.[32]

Crucially, it is my experience that current project applications rarely include a proper assessment of the *chances* that the experiment will contribute to the overall aim. In his 1997 note on the cost-benefit assessment, the then chief inspector of ASRU said,

> The essential determinants of "benefit" remain the likelihood of success, and how the data (or other product) generated by the programme of work will be used, rather than the importance of the field to which the research relates: for example, the long-term goal might be to find a cure for cancer, but the benefits relate only to those which might reasonably be expected to arise from the programme of work for which licence authorities are sought. Expressed in these terms, the gulf between "fundamental" and "applied" research is narrower than many people perceive.[33]

A decent evaluation of the chances of the benefit being realized does not seem to be yet demanded from project applications. This is of concern and is discussed more in the following pages.

Inherent Problems with the HBA

Bias in Assessment of Harms and Benefits

Currently, the assessment of harms and benefits is done initially by the researchers themselves. The extent to which this assessment is revised or supplemented by a more external reviewer or committee varies among countries. However, the point is that the person making the judgment at least initially is the one set to benefit directly from the research, either professionally, intellectually, or financially. The individual about to be harmed (i.e., the animal) cannot make the assessment. It is doubtful, therefore, whether the initial assessment can ever be truly unbiased. However, even if the final assessment is made by someone not connected to the research, that person will still not be from the same group (species) as those being harmed. Even if animal protectionists were to be heavily involved on the side of the animals, they would still be from the same group set to benefit. This inherent bias can be seen both in the assessment of harms and benefits and in the weights given to these in the final evaluation (see later discussion in this essay).

This inherent bias can be seen in the discomfort researchers seem to have in considering the worst-case scenario for the animal and using that as the measure of harm (although they must under the directive). They prefer to see these worst cases as rare events or things that should not happen, even if they do. They appear reluctant to consider what they are doing to the animal—on the face of it—but prefer to look at how the animal might feel. This seems to result in a significant underestimating of the severity (for reasons explained previously). This was never more exemplified than in the Cambridge University case in which marmosets who were subjected to a stroke, as well as extensive behavioral testing following water or food deprivation and other interventions, including other surgeries and injections, were considered to be likely to suffer only "moderately." On the face of it, what they were doing to the animals would be considered "severe" if it were done to humans, and indeed it was the assertion of Cruelty Free International (then BUAV), having conducted an undercover investigation at the laboratory, that the marmosets did suffer severely; some died as a result of their surgeries. The Home Office permitted the researchers to assume that the marmosets would be well cared for and monitored (they weren't always), such that any suffering would be kept below "severe."

In fact, it is my experience that researchers may also include the fact that the animals may improve as a result of the test treatment as mitigation of the harm, ignoring the fact that the animals were suffering prior

UNIVERSITY OF WINCHESTER
LIBRARY

to the treatment being applied. The lasting harm of the procedure (i.e., permanent paralysis or brain damage) is often ignored because the animals are usually killed at the end of the experiment anyway. Indeed, as a further example of the inherent bias in the system, the death of the animal is not considered to be a "lasting harm."[34]

The language used by researchers when discussing their research publicly also suggests that they are underestimating the harms. For example, Tipu Aziz famously said of his work inducing Parkinson's in macaque monkeys that "pain is not a feature of any of the experiments we do. . . . He won't really be in the same distress as a human patient."[35] Cruelty Free International raised this in a judicial review case with the Home Office over its underestimation of "distress" in project evaluation. One of the project licenses we had seen claimed that monkeys (who were significantly deprived of water and physically restrained by head posts surgically implanted in their heads for up to eight hours in a primate chair) "will simply not co-operate in chair-sitting and certainly not in actual task performance if they are distressed or in pain."

The assessment of benefit is influenced by the researchers' desire to promote not only the importance of their work but also the chances that a particular experiment will be successful. This desire is only natural, but it is exacerbated by the fact that researchers have to apply for funding for their research in the vast majority of cases and therefore tend to apply the same language in their project application forms as in their funding application forms. It is our experience that these forms can exaggerate the importance and/or severity of the human disease and the validity of the animal model being used, implying that the research will be successful and helpful, even in the absence of any data to support that.

Uncertainty in the Benefits Being Realized

The HBA for animal experiments is complicated by the fact that the benefit is not certain. That there is some risk that the benefit will not occur, even though the harms are certain, is not unusual in utilitarian assessments.[36] However, in the area of animal experiments, there are two independent ways in which the benefit may not be realized, neither of which is, I would argue, being properly considered.

First, there is a chance that the experiment may "fail"—that is, a statistically significant difference may not be shown. By definition, an animal experiment is uncertain; if the results were known, there would be no need to do the experiment! This is strangely ignored in the documents I have seen. It is possible to make a judgment as to how likely it is that an experiment will be successful; this could be done based on experience or systematic review. Systematic reviews looking at the success of animal experiments are sadly quite rare, but there have been systematic reviews of research on animals for stroke. One study found that 62 percent of published tests of new drugs for focal ischemia using animals showed an effect.[37] But a similar study on the same condition estimated that 16 percent of studies go unpublished, presumably because they were unsuccessful, a phenomenon known as publication bias.[38] This therefore results in an estimate that tests of new treatments for stroke in animals are likely to show a positive effect 53 percent of the time. How this should be factored in is discussed in the next section.

Second, there is a risk that the overall aim of the knowledge gained from that single experiment will not be realized. By "realized" I mean, as do others, that there is some advance in medical research that improves the quality of life of humans. However, depending on how far away the animal research is from the medical advance (such as a new treatment), the chances of that being benefit realized—as a consequence of that experiment—can be very low or even not known. I would argue, of course, that in very many cases there is no benefit to animal research. In basic medical research, the potential benefit is often not even known at the time of the experiment. The immediate aim is to improve medical knowledge, with the overall aim being that the experiment will provide a key step in the process toward a medical treatment. The chances of this happening can be reviewed retrospectively, and indeed, a paper reviewing 101 high-impact discoveries in animal tests found that only 5 percent translated into a marketed medical treatment within twenty years.[39]

Even for applied research where the expected medical advancement is known, other animal experiments have to be factored into the harms if the assessment is to be balanced in terms of "potential" benefit. This is because animal experiments rarely sit in isolation. There are usually several animal studies demonstrating efficacy of a new treatment (partly due to a desire to replicate and partly due to unwitting duplication by researchers in other countries). And once a drug company is convinced of the potential of the drug, a number of animal-based safety studies are then conducted before the drug can be tested in humans. Therefore, even if we want to assess the *potential* benefit of a particular animal experiment, we cannot do it in isolation; we have to factor in other animal experiments that will be involved *in the same overall aim*. Otherwise, the same *potential* benefit is being counted over and over again each time a similar experiment is being authorized.

For example, using the stroke example, a review of the animal studies supporting the efficacy of various drugs for stroke found that for drug NXY-059 there had been twenty-nine animal studies published, using a total of 408 animals.[40] Adding on the 16 percent of studies that would have been unpublished (according to the same study) leaves us with thirty-four animal-based efficacy studies involving 478 animals to test just one drug. The animal-based safety studies that would then normally be done would be likely to use in excess of 2,000 animals, including rodents and nonhuman primates.[41] So in this example, at a minimum, we are looking at around 2,500 animals involved in the *same overall aim* of testing the drug to see if it will help humans. This does not include the animals who were involved in the development of the particular method of testing the treatment or other incidental studies.

However, it is practically impossible within a single project authorization to include all other animal studies that are contributing to the same potential overall aim. This is because these other animals are being used in other projects by other researchers, possibly in other countries and at other times. Even in the same country, those doing the efficacy studies are not always the same as those doing the safety studies. Even within the same establishment, there might be different project authorizations, so one could argue that the evaluators have already disabled themselves from doing a proper HBA!

What is even more poorly recognized by those who perform HBAs is the chance of an overall aim being realized. Even following all of these animal-based efficacy and safety studies, the chance of any drug making it through human clinical trials to market is now only 5 percent.[42] Again, because there has been specific research looking at the success of stroke drugs, we can work out the probability that a single drug tested for stroke will be successful. One study found that only 10 percent of successful stroke drugs have progressed to phase 2 human clinical trials.[43] Another study has shown that in general only 11 percent of drugs that make it to phase 2 trials are marketed.[44] So the chances of a successful drug in animal studies for stroke being marketed is 10 percent × 11 percent = 1.1 percent.

Those conducting an HBA are left with two options: Either the benefit is assessed at *the level of the experiment*—for example, thirty marmosets suffer severely in an experiment for a 53 percent chance of increased confidence in the stroke drug being tested—or the benefit is assessed at *the level of the overall aim*, in which case over 2,500 animals are used to test a potential drug treatment for stroke that has a 1 percent chance of being successful. Either way, the equation does not seem to balance; real harms are done to animals to pursue knowledge, or real harms are done to (many more) animals for a very low probability of a medical advance.

Bias in Weighing of Harms and Benefits

As in the assessment of harms and benefits, the individual or group making the final evaluation by weighing these harms and benefits is the one set to benefit either directly or indirectly. The individuals or groups set to be harmed cannot make the judgment because they are nonhuman animals. It is doubtful then if the project evaluation can be "impartial" as the directive requires it to be.

This unavoidable bias can be demonstrated if we look at the types of decisions that should be made if an HBA is done dispassionately. Animal-welfare scientist Patrick Bateson recognized the importance of factoring probability into the benefits when making the decision and illustrated this in the form of his "3D Bateson cube," which is replicated in the commission's guidance.[45] Harms have to be weighed against the size of the potential benefit multiplied by the chances of that benefit being achieved. Bateson's cube uses green, amber, and red cubes to show that—in theory—experiments with very low benefit (irrespective of chances of success), very low chances of success (irrespective of high benefit), or very high severity (irrespective of size of benefit or chances of benefit being realized) should not be authorized. The question therefore is, will projects actually be rejected on these grounds? It would be interesting to map those types of experiments that fall into these categories and look at whether they are (still) being permitted. This may enable us to determine in reality what weights are being given to harms (animals) and what to benefits (humans).

Perhaps most interesting of all, as the stroke example illustrates, is the question of whether evaluators will be brave enough to say no on probability grounds. If they will not, does this show that they are not treating interests equally? If they are prepared to accept low probability of success for high harm, then are they applying Singer's utilitarian view (equal consideration of moral interests) or something more akin to instrumentalism?[46] For basic research the benefits are not even known, so if you say that knowledge—or an unknown chance that knowledge will translate to a medical benefit—is greater than a known serious harm, then are you really applying a utilitarian approach? On this basis should we accept the HBA as a utilitarian approach or expose it as the (instrumentalist) wolf in sheep's clothing?

Conclusions

An HBA is now a prerequisite for animal experiments to be approved across twenty-eight EU member states. However, there are a number of problems with the HBA as it is currently performed in countries that already do it. Some of these problems could be overcome by greater transparency, the production of clearer criteria, and insistence on rigorous and more impartial, wider evaluation involving general society.

However, I argue that we are unlikely to reach a point at which the process is entirely unbiased, both in measuring and in weighing the harms and benefits. This is because this process is dominated by the opinions of those set to benefit and not by the perspective of those set to be harmed, no matter how their views may, or may not, be represented. There is also a disconnect between the point in time at which harms are assessed and the point in time at which the benefit can be realized. In order for the (probability of) absolute benefits to be matched to absolute harms, the projects have to be very large (to capture the long-term aim) or very small (to capture the immediate aim). Herein lies the rub. Those wishing to use animals in experiments are very reluctant to argue that an experiment is justified on the basis of the immediate benefit arising from it, which is in most cases simply knowledge (that might lead to more knowledge or something more tangible). And yet, they cannot, for practical reasons, hope to include all the animals (harms) used in other projects that will contribute *to the same chance* of an overall aim. In reality the potential benefit is being counted many times over, every time a similar animal experiment is evaluated.

What is lacking in the HBA of animal experiments is comparison with how ethical evaluation is done in other sectors, such as government planning, economics, and human clinical trials. Indeed, the APC in 1997 noticed this, and although the APC promised "to compare the way the cost/benefit assessment is currently carried out with other cost/benefit models," it never did.[47] At the moment the fact that animal experiments have to pass a positive harm-benefit assessment is being trumpeted as a significant step for animals when in reality we do not even know how it will be done or how this compares to other sectors that use this assessment. As a result it is difficult to say whether the conduct of an HBA will make any real difference to the numbers and level of suffering of the animals used in scientific research across Europe.

Notes

The author was funded by the Cruelty Free International Trust during the preparation of this manuscript.

1. European Commission, Directive 2010/63/EC of the European Parliament and of the Council of 22 September 2010 on the Protection of Animals Used for Scientific Purposes.

2. Ibid., article 36(2).

3. Ibid., article 38(2).

4. European Commission, "National Competent Authorities for the Implementation of Directive 2010/63/EU on the Protection of Animals Used for Scientific Purposes: Working Document on Project Evaluation and Retrospective Assessment," last modified September 18–19, 2013, accessed March 31, 2017, http://ec.europa.eu/environment/chemicals/lab_animals/pdf/Endorsed_PE-RA.pdf.

5. For examples, see www.crueltyfreeinternational.org.

Table 1. Potential HBA matrix for considering harms and benefits of a single experiment, with examples of considerations for testing a new therapeutic drug

Harms	Benefits			
	Importance of the Objectives		Probability of Achievement	
Cumulative severity of the experiment	**Importance of the overall aim**	**Need for the specific experiment**	**Probability of success of experiment**	**Probability of successful experiment contributing to the overall aim***
Severity of the procedure	Severity of the disease	Other existing disease models	Riskiness of experiment	Chance of treatment being marketed
Numbers of animals	Incidence of the disease	Significance of gap in knowledge	Experience of the researcher	Likely therapeutic size of treatment vs. side effects
Extent/risk to which individual animal will suffer (worst case)	Other existing treatments	Extent to which other experiments could contribute	Type of research question being asked	Proportion of patients who will have access to the treatment

* It is unlikely that a single experiment in isolation will contribute to the overall aim.

6. Animal Procedures Committee, *Report of the Animal Procedures Committee for 1997*, November 26, 1998 (London: Stationery Office, 1998), 4.

7. Lynne Featherstone, Minister of State for Crime Prevention, "Testing of Household Products in Animals," written statement for the House of Commons, March 12, 2015, Hansard source: HC Deb, March 12, 2015, cWS, HCWS385, accessed March 31, 2017, http://www.parliament.uk/business/publications/written-questions-answers-statements/written-statement/Commons/2015-03-12/HCWS385/.

8. *BBC News*, "Cambridge Monkey Experiments Inquiry," May 24, 2002, accessed March 31, 2017, http://news.bbc.co.uk/1/hi/sci/tech/2006643.stm. See also pp. 78–79 in this volume.

9. CAMRADES is found at http://www.dcn.ed.ac.uk/camarades/.

10. Animal Procedures Committee, *Report*, 50.

11. European Commission, " . . . Project Evaluation and Retrospective Assessment."

12. J. Leaman, J. Latter, and M. Clemence, *Attitudes to Animal Research in 2014—A Report by Ipsos MORI for the Department for Business, Innovation, and Skills*, Ipsos Mori, September 2, 2014, accessed March 31, 2017, http://www.ipsos-mori.com/researchpublications/publications/1695/Attitudes-to-animal-research-in-2014.aspx.

13. Ibid.

14. Home Office, *The Statistics of Scientific Procedures on Living Animals Great Britain 2013* (London: Stationery Office, 2014).

15. C. Funk and L. Rainie, "Chapter 3: Attitudes and Beliefs on Science and Technology Topics," in *Public and Scientists' Views on Science and Society*, Pew Research Center, January 9, 2015, accessed August 1, 2015, http://www.pewinternet.org/2015/01/29/chapter-3-attitudes-and-beliefs-on-science-and-technology-topics/.

16. Animal Procedures Committee, *Report*, 48.

17. Ibid., 50.

18. Ibid., 3.

19. Home Office, *Guidance on the Operation of the Animals (Scientific Procedures) Act 1986*, March 2014, accessed March 31, 2017, https://www.gov.uk/government/uploads/system/uploads/attachment_data/file/291350/Guidance_on_the_Operation_of_ASPA.pdf.

20. L. Sherriff, "Animal Rights Campaigners Win FOI Battle against Newcastle University Monkey Experiments," *Huffington Post*, December 19, 2013, accessed March 31, 2017, http://www.huffingtonpost.co.uk/2011/11/16/buav-animal-rights-win-newcastle-university-foi-monkey-experiments_n_1096659.html.

21. M. Hillier, "Written Parliamentary Answer to David Amess, January 12, 2009," Hansard source, HC Deb, January 12, 2009, c266W, accessed March 31, 2017, https://www.publications.parliament.uk/pa/cm200809/cmhansrd/cm090112/text/90112w0056.htm.

22. Animal Procedures Committee, *Report*.

23. Rural and Marine Fisheries Code article R 214–117 to article R 214–126, February 7, 2013, 24, accessed March 31, 2017, https://www.legifrance.gouv.fr/affichCode.do?cidTexte=LEGITEXT000006071367.

24. Third Act amending the Animal Welfare Law (3: TierSchGÄndG), BGBl I 2013/2182, 3911, accessed March 31, 2017, http://dipbt.bundestag.de/extrakt/ba/WP17/451/45177.html.

25. European Commission, ". . . Evaluation and Retrospective Assessment."

26. National Institute for Health and Care Excellence (NICE), "How NICE Measures Value for Money in Relation to Public Health Interventions," September 1, 2013, accessed March 31, 2017, www.nice.org.uk/Media/Default/guidance/LGB10-Briefing-20150126.pdf.

27. F. Karlsson, "Critical Anthropomorphism and Animal Ethics," *Journal of Agricultural and Environmental Ethics* 25, no. 5 (2012): 707–20.

28. D. J. Langford, A. L. Bailey, M. L. Chanda, S. E. Clarke, T. E. Drummond, S. Echols, S. Glick, et al., "Coding of Facial Expressions of Pain in the Laboratory Mouse," *Nature Methods* 7 (2010): 447–49; J. Chabout, A. Sarkar, D. B. Dunson, and E. D. Jarvis, "Male Mice Song Syntax Depends on Social Contexts and Influences Female Preferences," *Frontiers in Behavioral Neuroscience* 9 (2015): 76.

29. J. P. Balcombe, N. D. Barnard, and C. Sandusky, "Laboratory Routines Cause Animal Stress," *Contemporary Topics in Laboratory Animal Science* 43, no. 6 (2004): 42–51.

30. European Commission, "National Competent Authorities for the Implementation of Directive 2010/63/EU on the Protection of Animals Used for Scientific Purposes: Working Document on a Severity Assessment Framework," last modified July 11–12, 2012, accessed March 31, 2017, http://ec.europa.eu/environment/chemicals/lab_animals/pdf/Endorsed_Severity_Assessment.pdf.

31. European Commission, " . . . Project Evaluation."

32. J. Bailey, "Letters re: Monkey-Based Research on Human Disease: The Implications of Genetic Differences," *Alternatives to Laboratory Animals* 42 (2014): 287–317.

33. Animal Procedures Committee, *Report*, 44.

34. European Commission, " . . . Severity Assessment Framework."

35. Adam Wishart, "What Felix the Monkey Taught Me about Animal Research," *London Evening Standard*, November 25, 2006, accessed September 10, 2015, http://www.standard.co.uk/news/what-felix-the-monkey-taught-me-about-animal-research-7220631.html.

36. Peter Singer, *Practical Ethics*, 2nd ed. (Cambridge: Cambridge University Press, 1993).

37. V. E. O'Collins, M. R. Macleod, G. A. Donnan, L. L. Horky, B. H. van der Worp, and D. W. Howells, "1,026 Experimental Treatments in Acute Stroke," *Annals of Neurology* 59 (2006): 467–77.

38. E. S. Sena, H. B. van der Worp, P. M. W. Bath, D. W. Howells, and M. R. Macleod, "Publication Bias in Reports of Animal Stroke Studies Leads to Major Overstatement of Efficacy," *PLoS Biol* 8, no. 3 (2010): e1000344.

39. D. G. Contopoulos-Ioannidis, E. Ntzani, and J. P. Ioannidis, "Translation of Highly Promising Basic Research into Clinical Applications," *American Journal of Medicine* 114 (2003): 477–84.

40. Sena et al., "Publication Bias."

41. Based on the requirements of ICH M3(R2), the International Conference on Harmonisation's main overarching guideline on the nonclinical studies that must be done before a new drug is placed on the market (International Conference on Harmonisation of Technical Requirements for Registration of Pharmaceuticals for Human Use, *ICH Harmonised Tripartite Guideline: Guidance on Nonclinical Safety Studies for the Conduct of Human Clinical Trials and Marketing Authorization for Pharmaceuticals M3(R2)*, June 11, 2009, accessed March 31, 2017, http://www.ich.org/fileadmin/Public_Web_Site/ICH_Products/Guidelines/Multidisciplinary/M3_R2/Step4/M3_R2__Guideline.pdf). Minimum testing includes a single- or seven-day repeated dose test in rodents (20 animals), a one-month repeated dose test in rodents (60 animals), a six-month repeated dose test in rodents (120 animals), a nine-month repeated dose test in nonrodents (20 animals), at least one genotoxicity test in rodents (20 animals), a carcinogenicity test in rodents (400 animals), a prepostnatal developmental study in rats (900 animals) and rabbits (500 animals), and a nonabuse study in nonhuman primates (20 animals) (my analysis).

42. KMR Group, press release, "Annual R&D General Metrics Study Highlights New Success Rate and Cycle Time Data," Chicago, IL, August 8, 2012, accessed March 31, 2017, https://kmrgroup.com/PressReleases/2012_08_08%20KMR%20PBF%20Success%20Rate%20&%20Cycle%20Time%20Press%20Release.pdf.

43. O'Collins et al., "1,026 Experimental Treatments."

44. J. Arrowsmith, "A Decade of Change," *Nature Reviews Drug Discovery* 11 (2012): 17–18.

45. P. Bateson, "When to Experiment on Animals," *New Scientist* 109 (1986): 30–32; European Commission, " . . . Project Evaluation and Retrospective Assessment."

46. Singer, *Practical Ethics.*

47. Animal Procedures Committee, *Review of Cost-Benefit Assessment in the Use of Animals in Research* (London: Stationery Office, 2003).

Bibliography

Animal Procedures Committee. *Report of the Animal Procedures Committee for 1997*. November 26, 1998. London: Stationery Office, 1998.

———. *Review of Cost-Benefit Assessment in the Use of Animals in Research*. London: Stationery Office, 2003.

Arrowsmith, J. "A Decade of Change." *Nature Reviews Drug Discovery* 11 (2012): 17–18.

Bailey, J. "Letters re: Monkey-Based Research on Human Disease: The Implications of Genetic Differences." *Alternatives to Laboratory Animals* 42 (2014): 287–317.

Balcombe, J. P., N. D. Barnard, and C. Sandusky. "Laboratory Routines Cause Animal Stress." *Contemporary Topics in Laboratory Animal Science* 43, no. 6 (2004): 42–51.

Bateson, P. "When to Experiment on Animals." *New Scientist* 109 (1986): 30–32.

BBC News. "Cambridge Monkey Experiments Inquiry." May 24, 2002. Accessed March 31, 2017. http://news.bbc.co.uk/1/hi/sci/tech/2006643.stm.

Chabout, J., A. Sarkar, D. B. Dunson, and E. D. Jarvis. "Male Mice Song Syntax Depends on Social Contexts and Influences Female Preferences." *Frontiers in Behavioral Neuroscience* 9 (2015): 76.

Contopoulos-Ioannidis, D. G., E. Ntzani, and J. P. Ioannidis. "Translation of Highly Promising Basic Research into Clinical Applications." *American Journal of Medicine* 114 (2003): 477–84.

European Commission. Directive 2010/63/EC of the European Parliament and of the Council of 22 September 2010 on the Protection of Animals Used for Scientific Purposes. *Official Journal of the European Community* L 276 (October 20, 2010): 33–79.

———. "National Competent Authorities for the Implementation of Directive 2010/63/EU on the Protection of Animals Used for Scientific Purposes: Working Document on Project Evaluation and Retrospective Assessment." Last modified September 18–19, 2013. Accessed March 31, 2017. http://ec.europa.eu/environment/chemicals/lab_animals/pdf/Endorsed_PE-RA.pdf.

———. "National Competent Authorities for the Implementation of Directive 2010/63/EU on the Protection of Animals Used for Scientific Purposes: Working Document on a Severity Assessment Framework." Last modified, July 11–12, 2012. Accessed March 31, 2017. http://ec.europa.eu/environment/chemicals/lab_animals/pdf/Endorsed_Severity_Assessment.pdf.

Featherstone, Lynne, Minister of State for Crime Prevention. "Testing of Household Products in Animals." Written statement for the House of Commons. March 12, 2015. *Hansard* source: HC Deb, March 12, 2015, cWS, HCWS385. Accessed March 31, 2017. http://www.parliament.uk/business/publications/written-questions-answers-statements/written-statement/Commons/2015-03-12/HCWS385/.

Funk, C., and L. Rainie. "Chapter 3: Attitudes and Beliefs on Science and Technology Topics." In *Public and Scientists' Views on Science and Society*. Pew Research Center, January 9, 2015. Accessed August 1, 2015. http://www.pewinternet.org/2015/01/29/chapter-3-attitudes-and-beliefs-on-science-and-technology-topics/.

Hillier, M. "Written Parliamentary Answer to David Amess, January 12, 2009." *Hansard* source; HC Deb, January 12, 2009, c266W. Accessed March 31, 2017. https://www.publications.parliament.uk/pa/cm200809/cmhansrd/cm090112/text/90112w0056.htm.

Home Office. *Guidance on the Operation of the Animals (Scientific Procedures) Act 1986*. March 2014. Accessed March 31, 2017. https://www.gov.uk/government/uploads/system/uploads/attachment_data/file/291350/Guidance_on_the_Operation_of_ASPA.pdf.

———. *The Statistics of Scientific Procedures on Living Animals Great Britain 2013*. London: Stationery Office, 2014.

Karlsson, F. "Critical Anthropomorphism and Animal Ethics." *Journal of Agricultural and Environmental Ethics* 25, no. 5 (2012): 707–20.

KMR Group. "Annual R&D General Metrics Study Highlights New Success Rate and Cycle Time Data." Press release. Chicago, IL, August 8, 2012. Accessed March 31, 2017. https://kmrgroup.com/PressReleases/2012_08_08%20KMR%20PBF%20Success%20Rate%20&%20Cycle%20Time%20Press%20Release.pdf.

Langford, D. J., A. L. Bailey, M. L. Chanda, S. E. Clarke, T. E. Drummond, S. Echols, S. Glick, et al. "Coding of Facial Expressions of Pain in the Laboratory Mouse." *Nature Methods* 7 (2010): 447–49.

Leaman, J., J. Latter, and M. Clemence. *Attitudes to Animal Research in 2014—A Report by Ipsos MORI for the Department for Business, Innovation, and Skills*. Ipsos Mori, September 2, 2014. Accessed March 31, 2017. http://www.ipsos-mori.com/researchpublications/publications/1695/Attitudes-to-animal-research-in-2014.aspx.

National Institute for Health and Care Excellence (NICE). "How NICE Measures Value for Money in Relation to Public Health Interventions." September 1, 2013. Accessed September 10, 2015. http://www.nice.org.uk/guidance.

O'Collins, V. E., M. R. Macleod, G. A. Donnan, L. L. Horky, B. H. van der Worp, and D. W. Howells. "1,026 Experimental Treatments in Acute Stroke." *Annals of Neurology* 59 (2006): 467–77.

Rural and Marine Fisheries Code. Article R 214–117–26, February 7, 2013, 24. Accessed March 31, 2017. https://www.legifrance.gouv.fr/affichCode.do?cidTexte=LEGITEXT000006071367.

Sena, E. S., B. H. van der Worp, P. M. W. Bath, D. W. Howells, and M. R. Macleod. "Publication Bias in Reports of Animal Stroke Studies Leads to Major Overstatement of Efficacy." *PLoS Biol* 8, no. 3 (2010): e1000344.

Sherriff, L. "Animal Rights Campaigners Win FOI Battle against Newcastle University Monkey Experiments." *Huffington Post*, December 19, 2013. Accessed March 31, 2017. http://www.huffingtonpost.co.uk/2011/11/16/buav-animal-rights-win-newcastle-university-foi-monkey-experiments_n_1096659.html.

Singer, Peter. *Practical Ethics*. 2nd ed. Cambridge: Cambridge University Press, 1993.

Tierschutzgesetzes. *Third Act amending the Animal Welfare Law* (3: TierSchGÄndG), BGBl I 2013/2182, 3911. Accessed March 31, 2017. http://dipbt.bundestag.de/extrakt/ba/WP17/451/45177.html.

Utilitarian Benefit and Uncertainty under Emergent Systems

Robert Patrick Stone Lazo

MOST ARGUMENTS JUSTIFYING nonhuman animal experimentation use some utilitarian model to analyze the benefits versus the costs. Rather than presenting any external critique of these arguments, I offer a critique within utilitarianism. I would like to talk about the problem of predictability. This is probably so obvious that it will hardly seem worth mentioning, but it should be made plain that most contemporary policy concerning nonhuman animal experimentation has at its base the belief that actual benefit will come out of those experiments that are approved and performed, whether that benefit is an application or the knowledge that whatever is being tested will not work for humans.

This assumption of benefit really ought to seem a strange thing. Keep in mind that the whole point of performing any given experiment is to see whether or not a hypothesis is true, which, in this context, typically means whether or not some treatment will be effective or not in humans. Now we come to the thesis of this essay: that there is no way to know ahead of time whether any animal experiment will lead to benefits for humans as defined above, and so there is a deep flaw in any system of evaluation for the approval or not of a nonhuman animal experiment that is willing to claim human benefit will come. Why uncertainty is a necessary component in these sorts of experiments will be covered in detail a little later. For now, a brief discussion of the four possible conclusions of any given experiment will be helpful, as it

will better point toward the sort of uncertainty with which this essay is concerned.

First, an experiment might turn out so that the hypothesis is confirmed and is true, a true positive. Second, a hypothesis might be confirmed but turn out to be false; this is a false positive. Third, a hypothesis might be confirmed false and be false, a true negative. Fourth and last, a hypothesis might be confirmed false but turn out to be true; this is a false negative. Half of the possibilities, then, are accurate, and half are inaccurate. But this is somewhat misleading because there are actually two ways that false positives and false negatives can be misleading in medical research using nonhuman animals. False positives might turn out, on the one hand, to come out positive because of the numerous ways in which confinement alters animals' physiological states, because of mistaken measurements or math, and so on. On the other hand, the hypothesis could come out positive but then turn out to be false in human trials. One catastrophic example of such a mistake was the testing of TGN 1412, a hormonal treatment meant to prevent heart disease and strokes.[1] Humans given the treatment suffered a massive autoimmune response, sending all of them to the hospital, leaving some with permanent organ damage.[2] Notice that these two types of false positives can overlap, though they do not need to.

The ways in which negative results can be false have a similar structure: results can come out negative because of experimental problems or because they do not hold for nonhuman animals but do hold for humans. The favorite example of this possibility—necessarily a theoretical one—is penicillin. Tested on rats, it worked beautifully and was moved to human trials. Had it, however, been tested on guinea pigs, which it may well have been, seeing as they were the more popular choice for animal experimentation at the time, it would have killed them.[3] It may never have reached the human trial stage. Again, these can overlap with one another, though they do not need to. Notice also that mistakes from experimental errors can turn out, from our epistemic standpoint, to look like false positives when they are really false negatives, or vice versa.

With these new possibilities in mind, we may see that there are actually four ways error can come into medical research using nonhuman animals, meaning two-thirds of the possibilities are errors. This is not to say that the actual probability of any of these outcomes is determined so that two-thirds of the time there is an error. Experiments are not like coin tosses. It is to say, however, that are certain special types of unpredictability in those cases where nonhuman experimental results are a stepping-stone toward human trials.

A Cause of Unpredictability

I take probably the primary cause of unpredictability in biological experiments to be that biological systems are complex. Here "complex" is a technical term. Anything that is complex is so because it involves emergent systems or properties. Before continuing to the main thesis, it will be helpful to define and provide examples of these terms and a few others that will make future claims clearer.

Let us begin with the type-token distinction, which rests at the heart of the discussion of complexity and emergence. A type is, to oversimplify and generalize over multiple ontologies, a category of or abstraction from the particulars of the universe. A type might also be called a "kind," as when we discuss natural kinds, like water, or artificial kinds, like chairs. A token, on the other hand, is a particular with unique space-time coordinates. These are the sorts of things we refer to with demonstratives, proper nouns, and definite descriptions: "this," "Abraham Lincoln," "the man over

there with a pipe and a monocle, holding a martini glass." This is still fairly abstract, still crouched in technical language, so consider the following concrete example.

$$3 \qquad 3 \qquad \mathbf{3}$$

We may speak of these three marks on at least two different levels. The most obvious way for us, since we have been so thoroughly trained this way, is that these are all 3. Just like 4 is the same as 4 is the same as 4, these "3"s are the same. Indeed, they are all three identical. None are bigger or smaller than the others, and any other "3" (including this one, as well as the one in the previous sentence) that occurs in the universe will be as identical to them as they are to one another. Not only that but there are even more radically different ways to write 3 than just changing the size of the font. "III," "11," "three," and "trois" are all still 3, the same as the examples above. (We will return to this point a little later in the discussion of emergence proper.) Here, we are discussing the marks as examples of a type, specifically the type 3. There is also, however, another way we may discuss them, a way that is less obvious since we are so thoroughly trained—in this case, at least—to recognize types instead of their token manifestations. We can say that the one on the farthest right is bigger than the other two; it is literally larger in size than the others. It may also be said that the first two, though the same in size, are not the same, because they occupy different space-time coordinates, are made up of unique sets of atoms, and so on. "III," "11," "three," and "trois" are similarly distinct, and even more so, not only made up of different sets of atoms but also made up by totally different arrangements, or patterns, of atoms. Now we are discussing the marks as tokens. Trusting that this discussion has been enough to make clear the type-token distinction, I will move on.[4]

With this distinction laid out, we now turn to it in action. In science and in the philosophy of science, there is much talk of "reductions," of one science being reduced to another. Almost always, whenever someone is discussing reduction, that person means type reduction, which is to say that the types of things discussed by one science, along with their causal powers, can be explained using only the types of things discussed by another. Put a linguistic way, if one science is type reduced to another, it means that every claim in the former can be made using only the latter by translating claims between the sciences. There has been only one successful type reduction in the history of science, and that is the type reduction of chemistry into physics using quantum mechanics in the first half of the twentieth century. All chemical types can be explained using only physical types. A type reduction essentially means that what we thought were two different sciences are actually just the same one. Chemistry is actually physics. All further efforts at type reductions, from biology to chemistry, psychology to neuroscience, and so on, have thus far failed. Token reductionism states that all tokens of one science are tokens of another. That everything is token-reducible to physics is uncontroversial in science. Every object studied by science is a physical token, which is to say something like that everything that science studies just is physical (i.e., is, minimally, physically instantiated),[5] so everything in science is token-reducible to physics. It should be noted that type reduction entails token reduction, but token reduction does not entail type reduction. If there are only physical types, then everything must just be physical. That everything is physically instantiated is no guarantee that every type is physical, even if it only exists thanks to a physical substrate.

There is one last type-token distinction to make clear, between type and token physicalism. According to type physicalism, every property is a physical property. Token physicalism states that every event is a physical event.[6] Whereas type and token reductionism are tools, type and token physicalism are positions. All types do reduce to physical types; all tokens are physical tokens. Again, type physicalism entails token physicalism, but token physicalism does not entail type physicalism. To be perfectly clear, this essay assumes token physicalism but rejects type physicalism.

Emergence

We now have the necessary tools to discuss emergence and complexity. A system or a property of a system in a science is emergent if and only if it does not appear in the system's parts. What this really ends up meaning is that an emergent system or property, though ontologically dependent on the physical substrate—or, to use the previous terminology, since everything is token-reducible to physics—cannot be explained using only the properties and causal powers of its parts.[7] Emergent systems or properties have new properties and causal powers. They also are not so dependent on their physical substrates as to be constituted in just one way. Instead, there are multiple realizations of some emergent system or property; think of the many different versions of the type 3. This last is the telltale sign of emergence. Why this is will be discussed through the following example, largely borrowed from two articles by Jerry Fodor, "Special Sciences (Or: The Disunity of Science as a Working Hypothesis)" and "Special Sciences: Still Autonomous after All These Years."[8]

All money is physical. Every single instance in the history of the human race has been made up of matter, whether gold, silver, paper, porcelain, or cocoa beans.[9] I would venture further and claim that all money that ever has existed, both on Earth and elsewhere in the universe, that ever will exist, and that ever could exist is also physical. Now, according to type physicalist-reductionists, this means that all of the properties of money, and all of the rules that it follows, can be described in physical terms. I do not dispute this claim, but I do dispute the implication that those type physicalists about economics believe follows from it—that therefore economics can be explained using only physics—because I believe they are either misunderstanding or misrepresenting what such a physical law would be about and look like.[10]

Let us take Gresham's law to see what a physical description of it would look like.[11] Given that it is a generalization over all forms of money, the physical reduction of the law must cover every single possible token of money in our universe to be a legitimate reduction. As such, the physical law must describe equally well gold, silver, paper, porcelain, cocoa beans, and so on. This should immediately look suspicious. First, these different types out of which money is made, and the different tokens of money, have so little in common with one another physically that it is thoroughly unclear what physical property, or even set of properties, they might all possess that could indicate they are money. It seems far more likely that anything they all have in common would be so mundane—that they all have electrons; that they all obey the laws of thermodynamics—as to fail to differentiate them from practically anything else.[12]

An alternative to such a law would be that each type has a unique physical description covering all of its causal powers as money. These different descriptions would then be put together by a series of disjunctions (i.e., connected by the inclusive or, so that one side, the other, or both can be true) so that each individual case of money could be covered, turning money into an epiphenomenon. What we would be left with would be, of course, a disjunctive mess, maybe not infinite, but certainly an open set and certainly far too large to practically deal with in day-to-day economic work. It should also be pointed out that the law would then be fantastically weak (i.e., would be making a weak claim, since not much is needed to confirm the whole thing).[13] Confirmation of any single disjunct in the chain would be confirmation of the entire law but would not confirm the truth of any other individual disjunct. A law without disjunctions will always be stronger than a law with them and will be of more practical worth.[14] Last, it should also be asked whether or not such a disjunctive law would be explanatory. It would be descriptive; every causal power of money in all of its different realizations would be laid out to examine in purely physical terms. In some cases this is actually sufficient for explanation, as when the properties of water are described using quantum mechanics. This must be because when the description is done, there is nothing else to say.[15] Here, however, the description is still not everything. This is because so many, probably the majority of, interesting generalizations that can be made about money are simply not about its composition. They are instead about the macrolevel characteristics (e.g., its value and so on) that are shared across its various instantiations, which are just those characteristics the disjunctive law dissolves as epiphenomena. Discussing only the physical description of money will lose these interesting generalizations one could have made with the nonphysical type money.[16]

This is a much-deeper critique than the practical ones previously laid out and stems largely from a further point—namely, that any physical version of Gresham's law will be gerrymandered.[17] The reason all of the tokens of money would be collected together under a physical law would just be that they are all money, that money can be multiply realized. Even supposing, under the best of possible circumstances, that we find some set of properties, causal powers, and so on that, all together, are the type money, this still will not have eliminated the type, so long as it is the set, and not the individual parts, that now possesses the properties and causal powers of money. Nothing will have been explained away, only physically described. In what I take to be the more realistic case, where we might create a disjunctive law, the gerrymandering is only more obvious. This is the underlying reason why the two options open to the type physicalist—that every instantiation of money has some property or set of properties connecting it with all of the others and that property or set of properties identifies them all as money; or that there is an individual law for each instantiation, all of which when connected by a series of disjunctions are the physical law describing money—are, respectively, so unlikely to succeed and so theoretically unappealing.

So this is the sort of thing that I mean when I call a system or property emergent, but there is one further point to be made about emergence—that it leads to a certain level of unpredictability. Abstractly, this is because the shortest description of an emergent system is the system itself.[18] Unlike linear systems, which are easily predictable by an equation once the equation is discovered, emergent systems are nonlinear, meaning their component parts interact in such a way that causation is not one-directional. A change in one place may cascade out and eventually return to the starting point, either restarting the process or causing a totally new one. In such an environment, prediction is possible only by simulation, but these simulations require perfectly measured initial conditions in order to give us accurate predictions. Complex systems are so sensitive to initial conditions that any change in them is capable of causing tremendous changes later on.[19] But it is impossible to perfectly measure initial conditions, since any measurement will have some degree of error, so there is, inevitably, some point at which it becomes impossible to predict how a nonlinear system will behave. To borrow the term from physics, simulations of nonlinear systems suffer from an onset of chaos. This is precisely the same issue of unpredictability as encountered in physics with the n-body problem and in mathematics when trying to algebraically find real solutions to equations of four degrees or higher.

Again, let this abstract discussion be cleared up with a concrete example. We tend to look to physics for how our scientific laws ought to look, so that we expect other sciences to have the predictive power of things like the laws of thermodynamics, or Kepler's laws of planetary motion. Most sciences, though, have nothing like these.[20] Everyone knows economics does a very poor job at making predictions.[21] This poverty comes from the level of complexity that exists in economics' object of study. There is a point to be made here and a corollary to it.

Economics is primarily concerned with results and not so much with how one gets there. This seems to be universal for those concerned with praxis and questions that require immediate action. Simply consider that scientists engaged in pharmaceutical research tend not to know mechanisms of action even though they do know results and are able to give predictions about how humans will react to some chemical. It's common for drugs on the market to have unknown mechanisms of action. Only recently have we discovered how aspirin works, and we have little to no idea about how psychopharmaceuticals operate. I do not mean to insinuate that economists and medical researchers are not concerned with reality and are not trying to accurately map it. I merely mean that in day-to-day decision making, which is usually the concern of the economist consulted by a governing body or by a business, the correspondence of the results to reality is more important than the correspondence of the models to reality. The corollary to this point: it doesn't seem likely that we could even judge the correspondence to reality of a given theory except by comparing its models' predictions to what actually occurs.

Biological Systems as Emergent Systems

Now we finally return to directly arguing for the thesis of this essay: that there is necessary unpredictability in nonhuman animal experimentation that calls arguments from benefit into question. To reiterate, this unpredictability is a by-product of biological systems' ontological status as complex systems, because complex systems have a high degree of unpredictability.

There are two arguments to be made in support of this claim: first, that biological systems really are complex, and second, that this complexity is pervasive enough to establish that even though there have been many success stories, the amount of uncertainty concerning benefit in any given experiment weighs against, rather than for, the practice. Because many of the arguments for enough compatibility between human and nonhuman biology to ensure successful translation of results between species come in the form of genetic comparisons, the discussion will focus there.

It is both popularly and esoterically stated that humans share about 99 percent of our genes with chimpanzees (hence, they are so popular a subject for testing). My first step in arguing for emergence in biology is to claim that this statement is actually false, first and foremost because it misinterprets the concept of a gene.[22] This is not to say that genetics is a flawed research program or that certain strings of genetic code and organization do not suggest the existence of certain traits in an organism, or any other outrageous denial of genetic theory. It is to say, however, that precisely delineated "genes" in the genetic code of some organism that can be neatly compared to genes of the same type in another simply do not exist as they are imagined by this statement, and that any description of genetics as such is an abstraction and idealization that do not neatly map onto the world.

There are at least two big reasons to suppose we cannot neatly divide genetic code into parts with determinate functions. First, the existence of individuated genes would suggest that genetics could be read, like we read an algorithm describing a linear system, where genetic code gives the whole story by way of a one-to-one mapping between genotype and phenotype. Certainly, in a place in the genetic code with two alleles at one locus (e.g., those traits studied by Mendel in his pea plants), there might exist such a simple mapping, but in the overwhelming majority of cases, this will not work out. Consider whether genetic code can tell us the function of a liver or the location of particular red blood cells in my body. There is simply more about organisms than can be said by programs in our DNA; there are variations among organisms not determined by their genetics.[23]

Second, and this is less theoretical and more experiential—read, experimentally confirmed—genetics interact in a way that linear programs don't. Different parts of a genetic code interact with one another similarly to on-off logic gates, where a change in one part will cascade out to others, which will in turn interact with others, which will send even more signals forward and back.[24] A change in one part, whether the addition of some new bit of genetic code or even just the activation of an old bit of it because of environmental factors, will not only add itself to the mix but can actually change what the whole genome is doing. What previously was producing one protein is now producing another. Alternatively, a change can die out almost immediately, never accomplishing anything at all. This is exemplified by changes in the third base of a codon.

It would seem that in attacking the picture of genetics where genes are traits—which is really the type physicalist understanding of morphology and physiology—we have also been arguing for an understanding of organisms as emergent. In the first, theoretical argument, the idea was briefly discussed that genetics simply do not tell the whole story of an organism and all of its parts. Alternatively, there is theoretical stuff left over by the type physicalist's attempt to reduce the organism to its genetic code, just as there seems to be stuff left over by a type physicalist's understanding of economics. The second, experimental argument is a claim about the sensitivity of an organism at the macro level to the initial conditions at the genetic level. The inability to make predictions from a biological system's component parts is just the same as the unpredictability found in economic systems and in those examples from physics and math that are so characteristic of an emergent system.

Finally, examples of the most telltale sign of emergent systems and properties, multiple realizability, are easily seen in biology. Perhaps the most astonishing such case is the eye. There have been at least forty independently evolved instances of the eye.[25] All of these have different genetic substrates, different physical manifestations, and different mechanisms of action.[26] But all of these different eyes are just that: eyes. All of them provide photoreceptivity and the appropriate neurological pathways to be able to react to the received input. This means that all of these different eyes have in common certain causal powers that are particular to them, that classify them all as

eyes. All of the same arguments made from the multiple realizability of money apply in biology, too.

Why Emergence Matters for the Ethics of Animal Experimentation

I believe the preceding discussion is enough to establish the reality of emergence as a phenomenon in biology. This in turn has substantial ethical ramifications for the practice of nonhuman animal testing for the benefit of humans. Particularly, decision making about which experiments are carried out and which are not has generally been seriously misguided. This is primarily for two reasons. First, emergent systems are tremendously sensitive to initial conditions, as has already been covered. From this it may be deduced that we have little theoretical evidence to support that even near identity between genomes will entail similarity of reactions to medical treatments between nonhuman animals and humans, and indeed, the studies actually done on translation rate seem to thoroughly support the theory that it will not.[27] Any claim that benefit will come from any given experiment has little to back it up. Second, the unpredictability of emergent systems means there is a serious misunderstanding of our epistemic abilities when we assume benefit will come. The behavior of an emergent system can be predicted only by simulation. There is no algorithm, no magic percentage of shared genetic material that can be relied upon as predictive. Even if the translation statistics were better than they are, there would still be no way to know, except by actually running the experiment or by using an alternative model (i.e., not actually performing nonhuman animal experiments), whether or not some treatment would be effective for nonhuman animals and for humans. At the very best, a high probability based on the statistical analyses of past experiments could be offered, but even then, the potential benefit would still be theoretical, whereas the suffering caused by the experiment would be all too real.

Where uncertainty necessarily exists, we ought to be cautious. We must keep in mind that the burden of proof is very much on the side of those who wish to perform a nonhuman animal experiment, and with both the statistical evidence against the effectiveness of translational work and the uncertainty inherent in any such experiment, we ought to require strong proof indeed. So be careful. Remember what we do and can't know.

Notes

Thank you to Joel Richeimer, for his patience and perseverance in helping and guiding me through my research on emergence. Thank you to Andrew Linzey and Clair Linzey for their invitations and ceaseless support.

1. See discussion of this event in section 1.3, "The New Scientific Critiques," of the report in the first part of the current volume.

2. Examples of this kind do not, of course, always go so tremendously wrong. In that respect, at least, this is an unfair example likely to produce a biased response. Still, the point behind it, that something can seem to work in nonhuman animal trials and fail to work in human trials, is unaffected.

3. Frank E. Cormia, George M. Lewis, and Mary E. Hopper, "Toxicity of Penicillin for the Guinea Pig," *Journal of Investigative Dermatology* 9 (1947): 261.

4. I know there are some—namely, hardcore nominalists—who do not believe types exist at all, who believe that there are only tokens. I will be implicitly attacking this position later with a discussion of economics, so please forgive my passing over it for now.

5. Of course, the question of what counts as physical is endlessly tricky, thanks to the complications for the materialist position brought on by electromagnetic theory, information theory, and so on. It seems to me that the best solution is to either widen the term "material" or abandon materialism in favor of physicalism, where what counts as physical is simply what is studied by physics. Of course, this is a cheap and unsatisfactory answer for anyone looking for something really deep, but it will do well enough for this paper.

6. Jerry Fodor, "Special Sciences (Or: The Disunity of Science as a Working Hypothesis)," *Synthese* 28, no. 2 (1974): 100.

7. Mark A. Bedau, "Downward Causation and Autonomy in Weak Emergence," *Emergence: Contemporary Readings in Philosophy and Science*, ed. Mark A. Bedau and Paul Humphreys (Cambridge, MA: MIT Press, 2008), 161.

8. Fodor, "Special Sciences (Or: The Disunity of Science)"; Jerry Fodor, "Special Sciences: Still Autonomous after All These Years," Supplement: Philosophical Perspectives, Mind Causation and World, *Nous* 31 (1997): 149–63.

9. Some might argue that this is complicated by digital banking, but seeing as the money exists as certain electric patterns, which are physical according to our working definition, I'd say the point still holds.

10. Do these people even exist? The position is totally absurd. For the sake of the paper, though, let's at least pretend they do.

11. There is no need, I think, to know anything about Gresham's law, other than that it is about money.

12. Notice that any effort to use complexes of physical types to describe money in all of its forms is really to give up on type physicalism, since the complex of physical types would be a new, and hence emergent, entity in the world, existing only in the interaction of its parts and not in the parts themselves.

13. Fodor, "Special Sciences: Still Autonomous," 158.

14. To best appreciate this point, consider the difference between the predictions "It will be sunny tomorrow" and "It will be sunny tomorrow, or it will be rainy, or the president of the United States will have a thought."

15. I am not sure that I precisely believe this point. After all, how water interacts with the world around it, including biological systems, social systems, economic systems, and so on, is determined by its macrolevel properties plus the properties of those systems. I do not know enough physics to say whether phase state can be adequately explained in physics to establish understanding of its macrolevel interactions. I have generally been under the impression that there is some debate in this area. Regardless, the example serves its purpose well enough.

16. Fodor, "Special Sciences: Still Autonomous," 158.

17. Ibid., 156.

18. Bedau, "Downward Causation," 162.

19. Ibid.

20. In fact, physics tends not to, either. Consider the *n*-body problem mentioned above.

21. It has historically been argued that this shows that economics, along with the rest of the social sciences, is not really science at all. I hope that the preceding examples from physics and mathematics help to show how wrong this assumption is. Other examples of unpredictability include meteorology—as anyone who has been let down by a weatherperson knows—and evolutionary biology, which assuredly cannot say ahead of time whether or not a particular organism will be selected.

22. Paul E. Griffiths and Karola Stotz, "Gene," in *The Philosophy of Biology*, ed. David L. Hull and Michael Ruse (Cambridge: Cambridge University Press, 2007), 102.

23. Peter Godfrey-Smith, *Philosophy of Biology* (Princeton, NJ: Princeton University Press, 2014), 87–88.

24. Ibid., 91.

25. Richard Dawkins, *The Ancestor's Tale* (Boston: Houghton Mifflin, 2004), 587–88.

26. I should point out that all of these different eyes use rhodopsin, but this seems more a point about availability of resources than about anything necessarily physically in common. (Thanks to Luke Kresslein for this insight.) A similar point may be made about money—that everything that is used for money must be rare, but what is rare is contingent; there is not some inherent value of the stuff used, save in those

instances when the rarity of the thing would also make it generally unusable. Here I am thinking of fluorine, which bonds too quickly to isolate, or those gray elements at the bottom of the periodic table with half-lives too short to measure their atomic mass, or so on.

27. See section 1.3, "The New Scientific Critiques," especially "The Unreliability of Animal Experiments," in the first part of the current volume.

Bibliography

Bedau, Mark A. "Downward Causation and Autonomy in Weak Emergence." *Emergence: Contemporary Readings in Philosophy and Science*, edited by Mark A. Bedau and Paul Humphreys. Cambridge, MA: MIT Press, 2008.

Cormia, Frank E., George M. Lewis, and Mary E. Hopper. "Toxicity of Penicillin for the Guinea Pig." *Journal of Investigative Dermatology* 9 (1947): 261–62.

Dawkins, Richard. *The Ancestor's Tale*. Boston: Houghton Mifflin, 2004.

Fodor, Jerry. "Special Sciences (Or: The Disunity of Science as a Working Hypothesis)." *Synthese* 28, no. 2 (1974): 97–115.

———. "Special Sciences: Still Autonomous after All These Years." Supplement: Philosophical Perspectives, Mind Causation and World. *Nous* 31 (1997): 149–63.

Godfrey-Smith, Peter. *Philosophy of Biology*. Princeton: Princeton University Press, 2014.

Griffiths, Paul E., and Karola Stotz. "Gene." In *The Philosophy of Biology*, edited by David L. Hull and Michael Ruse, 85–102. Cambridge: Cambridge University Press, 2007.

Do Moral Principles Permit Experimenting on Nonconsenting Beings?

Nedim C. Buyukmihci

I WAS TRAINED AS a veterinarian. In addition to practice and teaching, I spent many years in the laboratory as principal investigator in projects that involved using nonhuman animals in ways to which I now object.[1] My years of exploiting animals culminated in my developing consistent ethical principles that I applied in my personal and professional life. As a result of the latter, I was treated as a pariah among my colleagues, even by those at my university, where there was supposed to be open debate and a search for "truth." Even after I had received tenure, the administration continued to make life difficult, sometimes in onerous ways, rampantly violating my right to free speech and academic freedom. The situation finally resulted in an attempt to terminate my employment when I tried to institute alternatives to the fatal use of dogs in surgical-instruction laboratories, despite my having science and pedagogy on my side. As a result, I filed a lawsuit in US federal court.[2] Fortunately, for the issue of protected speech in general and for me in particular, I prevailed. From that point on, there was a relatively rapid move to eliminate the fatal use of animals in instructional exercises. I have to give credit here to several brave students who insisted—despite being threatened with expulsion—on obtaining an education without resorting to purposefully killing animals.

Although I originally had considered what we do to animals in the name of science to be necessary, this was because I believed we could do it "humanely." It had not immediately occurred to me why what was done to the animals would never be considered humane if done to human beings. Such a duplicitous—and morally inconsistent—view eventually plagued me to the point of reexamining the issue honestly and by avoiding preconceptions. When people consider the issue of using animals in research, there is essentially always the tacit assumption that human concerns tower above those of others. This was a formidable obstacle when debating my colleagues. When I completely rejected this notion, it became clear to me that *human beings do not have a moral right to use other animals if human beings are unwilling to apply the same treatment to fellow human beings.* Human animals, particularly when they claim to be acting as moral agents, do not have a right to use other animals in ways they would not permit themselves or, especially, human moral patients to be used.[3]

A major argument used to denounce using animals for delving into human issues is lack of scientific validity as a result of species differences, the effects of artificial conditions in captivity, and a myriad of other factors that confound the results. Whereas there is unquestionable truth to this argument, I am not going to deal with this complex subject in this discussion; I have prepared critiques previously.[4] My concern about using the validity argument, at least if it is used exclusively, is that it is not insurmountable if one is advocating an end to animal experimentation. What happens when validity is mitigated, for example, by using animals genetically engineered to express human disease? Furthermore, what about when the species used experimentally is the same as the "target" species, such as when cats are used to develop vaccines for other cats? For those whose goal is to end all animal research and who use the validity argument exclusively or even as one of many, these situations diminish the strength of their arguments. The situation is analogous to holding the opinion that eating animals is morally wrong but urging people to discontinue this because of health issues. The industry simply modifies the "product" to be more healthful—as witnessed, for example, by feeding omega-3 fatty acids to animals being raised for human consumption.[5]

The major defense put forth for our destructive use of animals is that human beings—or other animals—derive benefits from this use. This notion, that the "end justifies the means," is something we reject when it comes to our interactions with each other.[6] We do not condone harming or killing other human beings—even just a few—regardless of how beneficial it might be to the majority. When we do this to other animals, we need to ask ourselves if we are behaving in a manner that is consistent with the essence of our own code of conduct or consistent with the best we could be as a species.

Furthermore, when we try to justify this conduct by claiming that we are helping other animals, we need to admit that such claims are specious at best and dishonest at worst. Almost always, the "other animals" are those from whom human beings will be deriving a benefit; if we are providing treatment to a cow who is lame, we are hardly looking out for her best interests given that we plan to kill and eat her at some point.

Even if the animal is not going to be consumed—for example, when the animal is someone's companion dog—what we are really concerned about in almost all instances is the person to whom the dog is attached. Otherwise, how could we justify killing a *different* dog in a surgical-training laboratory for veterinary medical students, or why would there be concern about veterinary medical students doing something for the first time on a client's dog? There are no morally relevant differences between one dog and another. Any argument supporting the destruc-

tion of one dog to "help" or "save" another is necessarily incoherent and morally bankrupt.

There is little question that the primary issue with respect to using animals in research, particularly for the benefit of human beings, is one of morality. If it was not, then we would be compelled on a purely scientific or practical basis to use human beings for all research aimed at understanding human diseases or tests of drugs for toxicity, even if it meant harming or killing them. An appeal to utilitarian principles would demand this. It is irrefutable that this would provide human beings, as a whole, with far greater benefits and safety—and far more quickly—because a human being is the perfect and only reliable "model" of another human being. When people say that we could not have done certain things without the use of animals or that we could not continue doing these things, that is not strictly true; anything we have done using other animals could also have been done using human beings. But to subject human beings to most of the things to which nonhuman beings have been—*and continue to be*—subjected would be immoral. I do not advocate such treatment of human beings regardless of whether we might derive benefits. It is, however, *precisely* for the same reasons that such treatment must be considered immoral if applied to other animals.

When it comes to human beings, we do not accept the notion of a master race. We do not believe that there is an inferior race of people that could be practiced on or used for the benefit of others. Nor do we believe that having the strength or other ability to overpower someone gives us the right to exploit that person. We do not allow the prospect of benefits to the human species as a whole—*no matter how monumental they might be*—to guide our conduct toward each other. Further, we refrain from harming each other not just out of fear of retaliation. These restraints are part of our moral code. This is, of course, the ideal. I realize that not all people treat each other with respect or hold to the highest moral principles. It would be inappropriate and self-defeating, however, to consider a moral principle invalid simply because not all adhere to it.

In the case of animals other than human beings, the vast majority of human beings disregard this moral code. In the name of science and other activities as well, we do to other animals things we would consider abhorrent if done to each other—or to our companion animals, even if they are of the same species we are exploiting. We do not even do these things to people who are guilty of vile transgressions against society—people who have committed the most heinous of crimes and have forfeited their right to freedom, pursuit of their interests, and sometimes even their lives. We are nevertheless willing to do these things to other beings who are "guilty" only of being alive on this earth. No one, however, has ever put forth a coherent, *non-self-serving* argument demonstrating that other animals are not deserving of the same degree of moral concern we have for members of our own species or for those animals we consider our companions.

Our sense of morality in dealing with each other stems from our highest capacity for benevolent action. This is not simply because we call ourselves human beings. If I labeled a chair a "human being," that would not make the chair an object of moral concern. Cutting off one of its legs would not matter to the chair. But it would matter to a human being, even if an anesthetic or analgesic was used and regardless of whether this was done for her or his benefit, for the benefit of others, or gratuitously.

The reason it is wrong to harm another human being, therefore, is not simply because he or she is called a human being. Nor is it only because pain or suffering might result. It is wrong to harm human beings because it *is* possible to harm them. That is, there is no question in our minds that we *can* cause harm to each other. A person has certain qualities that are important to consider and protect. A person is an individual who has a life that fares better or worse depending on what happens to that life; no such claim can be made for inanimate objects. A person has value that is independent of his or her utility to another; the value of an inanimate object is negotiable. A person has interests whose pursuit is an important component of her or his life; such a notion does not appear to make sense in the case of inanimate objects.[7] These traits are fundamental to the so-called inalienable rights we confer on each other. Even people who have no concept of what is right or wrong and who have no obligations to others—moral patients—are granted these minimal rights.

Unlike chairs, nonhuman animals are just like human beings in these important ways, certainly infinitely more so than they are like inanimate objects. In fact, we use these individuals in research because we recognize their similarities to us. Unfortunately, we stop short of anything other than physical similarities in governing our behavior toward them. We cannot, however, rationally deny that at least other mammals share with us more than just anatomical or physiological features. We are learning more and more that these individuals share emotions, intelligence, self-will, and other traits that we value in ourselves. Moreover, it is unquestionable that these animals can experience more than just physical pain; we recognize, for example, that they also demonstrate anxiety, fear, and depression, which we exploit in studies on these phenomena while, sadly, failing to allow this to affect our willingness to continue this subjugation.[8]

We cannot provide an adequate defense against changing our treatment of animals in the light of their overwhelming similarities to us. Animals *can* be harmed. They have lives that fare better or worse depending on what happens to those lives. Their lives can be enriched or impoverished, especially at our hands. What happens to them *does matter* to them. Like human beings, other animals have interests, although they may be difficult to define and may be different from those of human beings. Other animals can experience pain and pleasure, and most can probably suffer in the general way in which human beings do. When we examine the issue without prejudice—and with humility rather than arrogance—there do not appear to be any *morally relevant* differences between humans and other animals that justify denying other animals similar consideration, respect, or treatment, based upon their interests or whether what we propose to do *matters* to the individual. There are no morally compelling differences between human beings and other animals that justify treating other animals so markedly differently from the manner in which we treat human beings or even our companion animals.

Physical or intellectual equality is not mandatory in order to propose equal consideration. Human beings want inalienable rights not because all people are created equal. Quite the opposite, such rights are a means of protecting disadvantaged or other individuals from subjugation by some people. The differences between various people—for example, differences in intelligence or physical strength or differences in gender or race—are *biological* and are irrelevant from a moral perspective. In the case of other animals, the major differences from human beings also are biological and are usually a difference in degree—not in kind. But more to the point, every characteristic stated to be important and uniquely human is shared to some degree with many other animals and does not even exist in some human beings. Language—in a broad sense, not just the artificially narrow human construct—thinking, intelligence, and other characteristics that people try to use to separate human beings from others exist in many other animals.[9] For example, experiments have shown that animals can seriate and that they use at least some of the important information-management processes exploited by human beings.[10] Some other animals have memory similar to that of human beings.[11] Other arguments put forth by some—for example, that other animals do not have political systems or do not compose symphonies—are nonsensical, vacuous, or morally irrelevant.

People who defend the harming and killing of animals in research argue that the individuals are "protected" by review committees and laws and are treated "humanely."[12] This is patent nonsense, especially when the animals are deprived of a normal life or are purposefully harmed or killed. One has to wonder whether people who believe they are being "humane" or that the animals are "protected" have critically evaluated these issues or whether they are in deep denial. Would they consider it "protection" if someone was legally allowed to subject them to surgery unnecessary for their health or to kill them as long as it was in the name of science? When a committee reviewing animal subjects determines that a particular project is "reasonable," the obvious question begged is, reasonable to whom? Certainly, no animal, human or other, would knowingly submit to experiments—even if they were nonpainful—if they knew that death was the end point. My many years of experience on such committees or similar bodies have shown me that even if a person who is an advocate for animals is on such a committee, it is a token gesture because the control of the vote is made up of people who in some way have a vested interest in having the projects done.

To be humane is to have sympathy for another, to be merciful and compassionate. If you provide pain relief after you have done surgery on a dog or a rat as part of an experimental study, in what way can this be considered humane? If it were not for you, there would have been no pain in the first place. It is particularly disingenuous—and repugnant—to take credit for helping victims you have created. Considering yourself to be acting humanely in this instance is a little like breaking someone's leg and then offering her analgesics and a crutch to use. Even if you support the use of animals in ways that are harmful to them or result in their destruction—even if painlessly—considering the situation to be "humane" is deplorable and dishonest. If you do not believe this, take any paragraph that describes a use of animals that is acceptable to you and that you believe to be "humane." Then substitute the words "human child" or similar for each reference to an animal. Read it back to yourself and see if you still think this constitutes humane treatment. For example, consider the following taken from the "Experimental Procedures" section of a 2015 paper reporting a UK study using rhesus macaques, approved by the UK Home Office and Oxford's Committee on Animal Care and Ethical Review:[13]

> The monkeys were . . . sedated . . . and anesthetized throughout surgery. . . . A bone flap was raised over the . . . cortex, the dura mater was cut and reflected, and the craniotomy was extended . . . to provide access to make the lesion. All cortex anterior to the limit of the lesion . . . was removed. . . . The operated animals rested for 2 wk after surgery before . . . testing. . . . At the conclusion of the experiments, the . . . animals were deeply anesthetized . . . perfused through the heart with . . . formol-saline. . . . Their brains were . . . removed from the skull.[14]

Now consider this description with the substituted words:

> The [children] were . . . sedated . . . and anesthetized throughout surgery. . . . A bone flap was raised over the . . . cortex, the dura mater was cut and reflected, and the craniotomy was extended . . . to provide access to make the lesion. All cortex

anterior to the limit of the lesion . . . was removed. . . . The operated [children] rested for 2 wk after surgery before . . . testing. . . . At the conclusion of the experiments, the . . . [children] were deeply anesthetized . . . perfused through the heart with . . . formol-saline. . . . Their brains were . . . removed from the skull.

Does this still sound "humane"? Can you honestly say this is an ethical way to treat someone? Bear in mind that "humane" and "ethical" logically have nothing to do with the purported purpose of the study.

Those who support research on nonconsenting beings usually point out that people are suffering, often using highly emotive scenarios of children with birth defects or cancer. There is, of course, no incontrovertible proof that using animals as human surrogates will ameliorate human suffering. When a claim is made to the contrary, a good scientist would want to know whether a controlled study comparing advances with and without the use of animals had been done to support this.[15] Nevertheless, appealing to the suffering of some to justify causing even more suffering in others is surely not only contrary to our own moral principles; it also begs the question of why one group of individuals is morally superior to another. These same people often ask questions such as, "Who would you save in a situation where your mother and your dog were in mortal danger?" Such questions, although stimulating, do not bear on the question of whether human or nonhuman life is more valuable. Rather, they deal with the question of which *individual* is more valuable to *another individual*. Suppose that the situation were a life-or-death scenario between two human beings in which a person had to choose between saving her or his daughter or someone else's daughter. I believe that most people would choose their own child over another. This does not mean that they are callous or that they do not value other human life. They simply have a closer, more familiar, and more compelling relationship with their own child. Furthermore, such situations are exceptional, and we do not base our standards of behavior on them.

If other animals are so similar to us, if they clearly have moral value based on our own definition of morality, if what we do to them matters to them, what is absent that renders them unworthy of serious moral concern that should provide them with true protection from harm by us? I submit that there is nothing absent; we are simply blinded by our self-centeredness, fear, greed, arrogance, and self-deception. When we critically and honestly evaluate the situation, it becomes clear that we do to other animals what we do not out of some moral imperative and not because it is right or "humane." Instead, we do these things because it is believed that we—or someone we care about—will benefit in some way *and because we have the power to dominate those animals*. We tacitly act on the morally repugnant principle that might makes right: we *can* do it, so that makes it right.

Most of us even delude ourselves into thinking that we are acting morally under these circumstances. If we consider ourselves to be acting morally, however, we should not be basing our decisions on whether we might derive benefits from exploiting other animals. Nor is it relevant whether there are adequate alternatives to situations in which we currently use animals. The questions we should be asking ourselves are these:

- Is our domineering behavior appropriate for such a highly developed, intelligent, and potentially compassionate species as ours?
- Is our behavior consistent with the best we could be as a species, intellectually and spiritually?
- Is our subjugation of animals consistent with the reasons we care about each other?

If we consider ourselves to be so much better than others, we behave in a most despicable—and self-degrading—manner by subjugating and destroying those we consider to be below us. We set standards of behavior for ourselves, based on compassion, fairness, and kindness—the best of human qualities—and then we systematically deny others the benefit of these standards because those "others" appear to be different from us or because they are not our cherished companions. To consider other animals the moral equivalent of human beings in no way demeans human beings.

I accept that there are certain forms of research that might be permissible to do on nonconsenting beings but only when this research has the potential for direct benefits to them as individuals, does not result in appreciable harm, and importantly, allows them to continue living their lives with dignity and freedom after the research has ended. Unless these or similar criteria can be assured, my answer to the question of whether human moral principles permit experimenting on nonconsenting beings, whether human or other, is an unequivocal and resounding no.

Notes

1. Purely for the sake of convenience, I will primarily refer to animals other than human beings as "animals," recognizing that all are animals of one kind or another; there is no intention to imply that any animal, even a human being, is morally superior to or intrinsically more valuable than another.

2. *Nedim C. Buyukmihci v. Regents of the University of California et al.*, CIVS-89-0067-LKK-PAN, US District Court, Eastern District of California (1989).

3. By "moral agents," I mean individuals who can develop, articulate, and apply principles of right and wrong. By "moral patients," I mean individuals, regardless of species, who cannot logically be expected to understand and live by the principles developed by moral agents, nor can they necessarily give their consent to be research subjects. There are, of course, ways in which such individuals show their lack of consent, including hiding, biting, or other behavior. A. P. Silverman, "Rodents' Defence against Cigarette Smoke," *Animal Behaviour* 26, no. 4 (1978): 1279–81.

4. Nedim C. Buyukmihci, "The Draize Eye Irritancy Test," November 20, 2016, accessed March 24, 2017, http://escholarship.org/uc/item/5ds7v9tj; Nedim C. Buyukmihci, "'Safety' Testing of Products for Human Use: Irrefutable Necessity or Morally Indefensible False Sense of Security?" November 19, 2016, accessed March 24, 2017, http://escholarship.org/uc/item/0kw5q9s5; Nedim C. Buyukmihci, "Amblyopia and Non-Human Animal Research," October 26, 2016. accessed March 24, 2017, http://escholarship.org/uc/item/3fx028nz; Nedim C. Buyukmihci, "Experimenting on Individuals without Their Consent," November 12, 2016, accessed March 24, 2017, http://escholarship.org/uc/item/1kp253b7.

5. Lauren Milligan Newmark, "Getting More Omega-3 Fatty Acids from Milk," *Splash! Milk Science Update*, April 2014, accessed March 24, 2017, http://milkgenomics.org/article/getting-omega-3-fatty-acids-milk/.

6. I realize that there are legitimate situations in which the end does justify the means. For example, in order to expedite the healing process in the case of a fractured femur or severe laceration, you may have to subject the patient to restraint, anesthesia, and medications. A human child or dog so injured may be terrified at such treatment, and the postoperative recovery phase may be very unpleasant. The intent in situations such as this, however, is to help the individual directly. No one is being used as a means to another's ends.

7. The pursuit of interests, of course, must be balanced against the impact on others.

8. Yan Liu, Liu Yang, Jin Yu, and Yu-Qiu Zhang, "Persistent, Comorbid Pain and Anxiety Can Be Uncoupled in a Mouse Model," *Physiology and Behavior* 151 (2015): 55–63; Klaus A. Miczek, Aki Takahashi, Kyle L. Gobrogge, Lara S. Hwa, and Rosa M. M. de Almeida, "Escalated Aggression in Animal Models: Shedding New Light on Mesocorticolimbic Circuits," *Current Opinion in Behavioral Sciences* 3 (2015): 90–95; Stephanie L. Willard and Carol A. Shively, "Modeling Depression in Adult Female Cynomolgus Monkeys (*Macaca fascicularis*)," *American Journal of Primatology* 74, no. 6 (2012): 528–42.

9. David Barner, Justin Wood, Marc Hauser, and Susan Carey, "Evidence for a Non-Linguistic Distinction between Singular and Plural Sets in Rhesus Monkeys," *Cognition* 107, no. 2 (2008): 603–22; Marc Bekoff, "'Do Dogs Ape?' or 'Do Apes Dog?' and Does It Matter? Broadening and Deepening Cognitive Ethology," *Animal Law* 3 (1997): 13–23; Elizabeth M. Brannon and Herbert S. Terrace, "Ordering of the Numerosities 1 to 9 by Monkeys," *Science* 282, no. 5389 (1998): 746–49; A. S. Chamove, "Cage Design Reduces Emotionality in Mice," *Laboratory Animals* 23, no. 3 (1989): 215–19; Lars Chittka and Jeremy Niven, "Are Bigger Brains Better?" *Current Biology: CB* 19, no. 21 (2009): R995–1008; Graziano Fiorito and Pietro Scotto, "Observational Learning in *Octopus vulgaris*," *Science* 256, no. 5056 (1992): 545–47; Ashley J. Frost, Alexandria Winrow-Giffen, Paul J. Ashley, and Lynne U. Sneddon, "Plasticity in Animal Personality Traits: Does Prior Experience Alter the Degree of Boldness?" *Proceedings of the Royal Society B: Biological Sciences* 274, no. 1608 (2007): 333–39; Marc D. Hauser, David Glynn, and Justin Wood, "Rhesus Monkeys Correctly Read the Goal-Relevant Gestures of a Human Agent," *Proceedings of the Royal Society B: Biological Sciences* 274, no. 1620 (2007): 1913–18; Tetsuro Matsuzawa, "Form Perception and Visual Acuity in a Chimpanzee," *Folia Primatologica: International Journal of Primatology* 55, no. 1 (1990): 24–32; John C. Mitani, Toshikazu Hasegawa, Julie Gros-Louis, Peter Marler, and Richard Byrne, "Dialects in Wild Chimpanzees?" *American Journal of Primatology* 27, no. 4 (1992): 233–43; Francesco Natale, Patrizia Poti, and Giovanna Spinozzi, "Development of Tool Use in a Macaque and a Gorilla," *Primates: Journal of Primatology* 29, no. 3 (1988): 413–16; Sue Savage-Rumbaugh and Roger Lewin, *Kanzi: The Ape at the Brink of the Human Mind* (New York: Wiley, 1994); Justin N. Wood, Marc D. Hauser, David D. Glynn, and David Barner, "Free-Ranging Rhesus Monkeys Spontaneously Individuate and Enumerate Small Numbers of Nonsolid Portions," *Cognition* 106, no. 1 (2008): 207–21.

10. Brendan Oliver McGonigle, "Cognitive Psychology: Non-verbal Thinking by Animals?" *Nature* 325, no. 6100 (1987): 110–12.

11. Gema Martin-Ordas, Dorthe Berntsen, and Josep Call, "Memory for Distant Past Events in Chimpanzees and Orangutans," *Current Biology: CB* 23, no. 15 (2013): 1438–41.

12. The relief of pain is an integral part of "humane" treatment. However, we often cannot be certain when an individual is in pain. John F. Bradfield, Todd R. Schachtman, Ron M. McLaughlin, and Earl K. Steffen, "Behavioral and Physiologic

Effects of Inapparent Wound Infection in Rats," *Laboratory Animal Science* 42, no. 6 (1992): 572–78.

13. Although the following is taken verbatim from the report, I have arranged the wording to make my point, without in any way altering the truth of what was done.

14. Erica A. Boschin, Carinne Piekema, and Mark J. Buckley, "Essential Functions of Primate Frontopolar Cortex in Cognition," *Proceedings of the National Academy of Sciences of the United States of America* 112, no. 9 (2015): E1020–27.

15. This would be virtually impossible at this point in our history, but without this, claims that medical discoveries depend (or depended) on or could not occur without the use of animals are pure speculation.

Bibliography

This bibliography of sources cited in this essay is not intended to be exhaustive on any particular subject. Rather, I have provided just a few examples in this essay to emphasize certain points.

Barner, David, Justin Wood, Marc Hauser, and Susan Carey. "Evidence for a Non-Linguistic Distinction between Singular and Plural Sets in Rhesus Monkeys." *Cognition* 107, no. 2 (2008): 603–22.

Bekoff, Marc. "'Do Dogs Ape?' or 'Do Apes Dog?' and Does It Matter? Broadening and Deepening Cognitive Ethology." *Animal Law* 3 (1997): 13–23.

Boschin, Erica A., Carinne Piekema, and Mark J. Buckley. "Essential Functions of Primate Frontopolar Cortex in Cognition." *Proceedings of the National Academy of Sciences of the United States of America* 112, no. 9 (2015): E1020–27.

Bradfield, John F., Todd R. Schachtman, Ron M. McLaughlin, and Earl K. Steffen. "Behavioral and Physiologic Effects of Inapparent Wound Infection in Rats." *Laboratory Animal Science* 42, no. 6 (1992): 572–78.

Brannon, Elizabeth M., and Herbert S. Terrace. "Ordering of the Numerosities 1 to 9 by Monkeys." *Science* 282, no. 5389 (1998): 746–49.

Buyukmihci, Nedim C. "Amblyopia and Non-Human Animal Research." October 26, 2016. Accessed March 24, 2017. http://escholarship.org/uc/item/3fx028nz.

———. "The Draize Eye Irritancy Test." November 20, 2016. Accessed March 24, 2017. http://escholarship.org/uc/item/5ds7v9tj.

———. "Experimenting on Individuals without Their Consent." November 12, 2016. Accessed March 24, 2017. http://escholarship.org/uc/item/1kp253b7.

———. "'Safety' Testing of Products for Human Use: Irrefutable Necessity or Morally Indefensible False Sense of Security?" November 19, 2016. Accessed March 24, 2017. http://escholarship.org/uc/item/0kw5q9s5.

Buyukmihci, Nedim C., v. Regents of the University of California et al. CIVS-89-0067-LKK-PAN (1989), US District Court, Eastern District of California.

Chamove, A. S. "Cage Design Reduces Emotionality in Mice." *Laboratory Animals* 23, no. 3 (1989): 215–19.

Chittka, Lars, and Jeremy Niven. "Are Bigger Brains Better?" *Current Biology: CB* 19, no. 21 (2009): R995–1008.

Fiorito, Graziano, and Pietro Scotto. "Observational Learning in *Octopus vulgaris*." *Science* 256, no. 5056 (1992): 545–47.

Frost, Ashley J., Alexandria Winrow-Giffen, Paul J. Ashley, and Lynne U. Sneddon. "Plasticity in Animal Personality Traits: Does Prior Experience Alter the Degree of Boldness?" *Proceedings of the Royal Society B: Biological Sciences* 274, no. 1608 (2007): 333–39.

Hauser, Marc D., David Glynn, and Justin Wood. "Rhesus Monkeys Correctly Read the Goal-Relevant Gestures of a Human Agent." *Proceedings of the Royal Society B: Biological Sciences* 274, no. 1620 (2007): 1913–18.

Liu, Yan, Liu Yang, Jin Yu, and Yu-Qiu Zhang. "Persistent, Comorbid Pain and Anxiety Can Be Uncoupled in a Mouse Model." *Physiology and Behavior* 151 (2015): 55–63.

Martin-Ordas, Gema, Dorthe Berntsen, and Josep Call. "Memory for Distant Past Events in Chimpanzees and Orangutans." *Current Biology: CB* 23, no. 15 (2013): 1438–41.

Matsuzawa, Tetsuro. "Form Perception and Visual Acuity in a Chimpanzee." *Folia Primatologica: International Journal of Primatology* 55, no. 1 (1990): 24–32.

McGonigle, Brendan Oliver. "Cognitive Psychology: Non-verbal Thinking by Animals?" *Nature* 325, no. 6100 (1987): 110–12.

Miczek, Klaus A., Aki Takahashi, Kyle L. Gobrogge, Lara S. Hwa, and Rosa M. M. de Almeida. "Escalated Aggression in Animal Models: Shedding New Light on Mesocorticolimbic Circuits." *Current Opinion in Behavioral Sciences* 3 (2015): 90–95.

Mitani, John C., Toshikazu Hasegawa, Julie Gros-Louis, Peter Marler, and Richard Byrne. "Dialects in Wild Chimpanzees?" *American Journal of Primatology* 27, no. 4 (1992): 233–43.

Natale, Francesco, Patrizia Poti, and Giovanna Spinozzi. "Development of Tool Use in a Macaque and a Gorilla." *Primates: Journal of Primatology* 29, no. 3 (1988): 413–16.

Newmark, Lauren Milligan. "Getting More Omega-3 Fatty Acids from Milk." *Splash! Milk Science Update*, April 2014. Accessed March 24, 2017. http://milkgenomics.org/article/getting-omega-3-fatty-acids-milk/.

Savage-Rumbaugh, Sue, and Roger Lewin. *Kanzi: The Ape at the Brink of the Human Mind*. New York: Wiley, 1994.

Silverman, A. P. "Rodents' Defence against Cigarette Smoke." *Animal Behaviour* 26, no. 4 (1978): 1279–81.

Willard, Stephanie L., and Carol A. Shively. "Modeling Depression in Adult Female Cynomolgus Monkeys (*Macaca fascicularis*)." *American Journal of Primatology* 74, no. 6 (2012): 528–42.

Wood, Justin N., Marc D. Hauser, David D. Glynn, and David Barner. "Free-Ranging Rhesus Monkeys Spontaneously Individuate and Enumerate Small Numbers of Non-solid Portions." *Cognition* 106, no. 1 (2008): 207–21.

Can Animal Experiments Be Ethically Acceptable When They Are Not Scientifically Defensible?

Jarrod Bailey

OF PARAMOUNT importance to the debate surrounding animal experiments is the central tenet of those who advocate them: the issue of human relevance and benefit. If human benefit is minimal—and I believe evidence suggests animal experiments are, in fact, counterproductive—then such experiments should not be conducted in the first place. This means that an ethical consideration of them, as important as this is, must be secondary: if the benefit side of the harm-benefit equation is absent or even negative, then the consequent harm and ethical costs to animals become academic. Arguably, the human harms born of such widespread use of a research approach from which little or no benefit is derived, especially in the face of superior and humane alternative methods of inquiry, become salient.

Much has been published in this regard, especially in recent years, with numerous articles outlining the failure of use of animals in many areas of research. Examples include stroke, heart failure and disease, neurological diseases, cancers, multiple sclerosis, Alzheimer's and Parkinson's diseases, head injury, amyotrophic lateral sclerosis, and osteoporosis, among many other areas of investigation,[1] as well as critical opinions surrounding animal use in Alzheimer's, Parkinson's, and HIV/AIDS research, for example, as well as in the testing of new human drugs.[2]

In contrast to the systematic, comprehensive, evidence-based approach to the critical evaluation of the translation of animal studies to human benefit, however, claims that animal research is necessary for or even a helpful part of human disease research and drug development are generally based on evidence-free assumptions of human relevance, supported by anecdotes of the involvement of animals in certain experiments associated with various areas of research and medical breakthroughs. Further, these anecdotes are often historical and irrelevant in any case in light of the current and developing array of cutting-edge alternative methods. This justification is unacceptable because involvement of animals per se is no measure at all of their necessity or even contribution, and anecdotal examples have no weight unless they are backed up by broad and comprehensive data.

To illustrate, prior to the US Institute of Medicine declaring that "most current biomedical use of chimpanzees is unnecessary" following a comprehensive inquiry in 2011,[3] supporters of chimpanzee research claimed the exact opposite: that chimpanzee research not only had contributed to many past advances in medicine but also was crucial to any future advances, particularly in areas such as HIV/AIDS, hepatitis C, and malaria, among other diseases.[4] The defense of using chimpanzees in HIV/AIDS research, for instance, rested on the fact that chimpanzees are the only nonhumans who can be infected with HIV, the fact that there are some commonalities in the infectious process and pathology, and the fact that some aspects of the virus and disease might have been first discovered in chimps. But this is a superficial and misleading defense because we must also consider that chimpanzees don't get AIDS when infected with HIV, as a result of major differences in chimpanzee biology, immune responses, and genetics; that "discoveries" in HIV-infected chimps were, on examination, "rediscoveries" of information gleaned from the study of human beings and/or human cells and tissues; and that almost one hundred vaccines that worked in chimps went on to fail in human trials.[5] A more informed appraisal, therefore, taking into account all available information, including interspecies differences as well as similarities, is essential when considering the value and human relevance of any animal "model."

Over the past ten years, I have conducted, published, and coauthored several critical studies on the human relevance, or lack of relevance, of animal experiments, including studies on teratology or developmental toxicity;[6] nonhuman primate research in general;[7] the use of chimpanzees in general[8] as well as in HIV/AIDS,[9] cancer,[10] and hepatitis C[11] research; the use of animals in the research and development of human drugs;[12] and the interspecies genetic differences that underpin the poor human relevance of animal experiments in these and other areas.[13] The latter two topics constitute the main focus of this review.

Animal Testing of New Human Drugs

In common with many other areas of animal use in science, the assertion that animal testing of new drugs is predictive of human response—of efficacy and safety—has always been made and continues to be made with little or no scientific basis;[14] indeed, this has even been acknowledged by some within the pharmaceutical and chemical industries and their regulatory bodies.[15] In spite of this and coupled with the fact that these tests are central to a development and testing paradigm that has contributed to increasing and current record levels of drug attrition standing at 95 percent,[16] regulators continue to require animal tests involving at least two species (one rodent and one nonrodent).[17] This is, of course, troubling from just a human perspective, given that so many drugs are failing in late development and that adverse drug reactions (ADRs) from drugs that make it to market constitute the fourth direct leading cause of death in developed countries.[18] From the perspective of animal welfare and ethics, however, it is also of major concern: over and above the nature of life in a laboratory and drug testing in animals and their degree of suffering,[19] almost three hundred thousand animals were used for the purposes of "pharmaceutical safety and evaluation" in the United Kingdom alone in 2013.[20]

It may be considered remarkable, therefore, that efforts to evaluate the human relevance of animal drug tests and their contribution to drug development and safety have been exceedingly scarce over the past sixty years or so and far from comprehensive. The relatively few analyses reflect unfavorably on animal tests, nonetheless. Briefly, for example: a 2012 study that expressly set out to minimize bias showed that 63 percent of serious ADRs had no counterparts in animals, and less than 20 percent of serious ADRs had an actual positive corollary in animal studies.[21] An extensive study of publicly available nonrodent data on twelve hundred compounds revealed false-negative and false-positive rates of up to 51 percent and 33 percent, respectively, and showed that combining nonrodent (mostly dog) data with rodent data increased human concordance by only 2 to 3 percent, from 46 to 49 percent.[22] Experiments on dogs did not provide valuable additional data to the experiments on rats in 92 percent of cases, and in the remaining 8 percent, the dog data did not result in a change of course for the development of the drug.[23] Other similar examples exist for testing generally[24] and more specifically—for example, in teratology[25] and drug-induced liver injury.[26] One oft-cited study claimed a good concordance between animal and human toxicology,[27] though neither the actual predictive nature of the animal data for humans nor the evidential weight provided by those data was addressed.[28]

The inadequate analysis has been due largely to the difficulty in accessing data: Most studies are unpublished, and pharmaceutical companies continue to refuse to share proprietary data, even suitably anonymized to protect confidentiality; to conduct their own studies; or to facilitate data analysis in any way. My coauthors and I wished to address this and perform our own study, and though our requests for access to data were rebuffed, we obtained collated, publicly available data from a commercial enterprise. Relevant details of these data and of the large scope of our study and advantages of our statistical approach are detailed in our previous publications.[29] In summary, our evaluation was based on data for 2,366 pharmaceutical compounds and 3,275 comparisons of effects in each animal-human pair, and we used "likelihood ratios" (LRs—namely, the positive LR [PLR] and inverse negative LR [iNLR])[30] in our analyses, which we argue are more statistically appropriate, comprehensive, and inclusive than metrics commonly used previously.[31] They enable the assessment of the salient question at issue with animal models, which is *whether or not they contribute significant weight to the evidence for or against the likely toxicity of a given compound in humans.*

An LR that is statistically significantly higher than 1.0 can be regarded as contributing evidential weight to the probability that the compound under test will be toxic or not toxic in humans. The median values and the ranges for dogs, mice, rats, and rabbits are shown in table 2.[32] These may be summarized as follows: first, the PLRs were generally high for all species, suggesting that drugs that are toxic in animals are also likely to be toxic in humans; and second, the iNLRs were very low, indicating that if a new drug shows no toxic effects in animals, this result provides essentially no insight into whether that drug will also show no toxic effects in humans. Although the PLR values suggest the animal tests do add evidential weight to toxicity testing when toxicity is detected, the ranges are considerable, and the values vary enormously, meaning there is no obvious pattern with regard to the type of toxicity, which undermines the reliability of this specific aspect of animal testing.

The iNLR results are much more significant, however, and bear repeating. The very low median value for all four species—just greater than unity— supports the view that at least these four species provide essentially no evidential weight to this aspect of toxicity testing. Specifically, the fact that a compound shows no toxic effects in animals provides essentially no insight into whether the compound will also show no toxic effects in humans. Indeed, this can be quantified. For example, with respect to dogs, suppose a drug is thought, based on prior data and the drug's relationship to similar compounds and so on, to have a 70 percent probability of freedom from ADRs in humans. Based on our data, if the compound shows no sign of toxicity in dogs, the probability that the compound will also show no toxic effects in humans will have been increased by the dog testing from 70 percent to 72 percent. The dog testing thus contributes essentially no additional confidence in the outcome but at considerable extra cost, both monetary and in terms of animal welfare.

This lack of evidential weight has serious implications for the role of dogs and other animals in toxicity testing, especially for the pharmaceutical industry, because the critical observation for deciding whether a candidate drug can proceed to clinical trials—to testing in humans—is the absence of toxicity in tests on animals. However, our findings show that the predictive value of the animal tests in this regard is barely greater than by chance. Further, we conducted and published a third study incorporating data from nonhuman primates, which also examined the ability of toxicity data to be extrapolated between any two species, not just nonhumans and humans.[33] Broadly, the results are similar to those found in the two articles already published, and in fact nonhuman primates were the most poorly predictive of all nonhuman

Table 2. Positive likelihood ratios (PLR) and inverse negative likelihood ratios (iNLR) (median values) and ranges for four species commonly used in preclinical drug testing, with respect to evidential weight provided by the animal test for human toxicity or lack of toxicity

	PLR (median)	iNLR (median)	PLR range	NLR range
Rat	253	1.82	24–2360	1.02–100.00
Mouse	203	1.39	23–2361	1.03–50.00
Rabbit	101	1.12	13–1348	1.01–2.33
Dog	28	1.10	5–549	1.01–1.92

UNIVERSITY OF WINCHESTER
LIBRARY

species for humans when there were no toxic effects in testing.[34] All of this is, of course, entirely consistent with reports (such as those cited in this article) highlighting the failure of animal tests in general to provide guidance on likely toxicity or lack of toxicity ahead of clinical trials. The least the pharmaceutical industry and regulators should do, therefore, in light of these findings, is commit to their own, transparent analysis of proprietary data. In the absence of such an analysis and evidence to the contrary, the available evidence strongly argues against the use of animals and underpins a status quo that is dire for both human and animal health and welfare.

Failure to Translate to Humans— Genetic Differences

Not only is it becoming ever more appreciated that one species cannot reliably be used to investigate and predict the biology of another but it is also being increasingly understood *why* this is so. Simply put, the genes of one species—and probably more important, the manner in which those genes operate and are controlled—are very different indeed from those of another species. Such differences render false the superficial claims from advocates of animal experiments that many species are very similar to one another and that therefore data from one species must translate well to another (see, for example, claims surrounding chimpanzee experiments in the United States before they were deemed unnecessary by an Institute of Medicine review).[35]

These differences are present in every aspect of gene expression, from what genetic material is present or absent in one species and how it compares with another through all of the many aspects of gene expression (how genes are used as templates to produce the proteins that make up the fabric of the body and carry out the chemical reactions that sustain life). Though poorly researched and underappreciated for decades, these differences are being investigated to a greater degree as improved technologies have made and continue to make this easier, quicker, and cheaper and as explanations for the confounding nature of animal research with respect to humans demand attention. In this regard and to further elucidate the debate, I authored two comprehensive, detailed reviews of the genetic differences among humans, chimpanzees, and other nonhuman primates; these reviews both explain the failures of using nonhuman primates as models for human research and caution against any future reliance on their use.[36] What follows is a précis of these reports, which should be consulted for specific references that may not be given herein (due to the number of citations).

Broad Genetic Similarity and Comparisons

First, species differ by more than superficial comparisons suggest. It is claimed that humans and chimps are up to 99 percent genetically similar, though if comparisons are made more rigorously, the similarity is more like 93 to 94 percent or even less.[37] Similarly, it is claimed that macaques are 93 percent similar to humans, though the true figure is more like 89 percent.[38] These levels of similarity may still seem quite encouraging, but many of the differences are in genes that are involved in areas of biology that are intensively researched, and so these differences particularly negatively affect the translation of data to humans.[39] Second, the real dissimilarities among species that underpin species differences are not in the genes themselves but in the mechanisms and processes involved in gene expression, and crucially, many of these minor differences result in major biological differences that are associated with very important biological processes and diseases.[40]

Types and Importance of Genetic Differences

These genetic differences range from major rearrangements of the genetic material, including chromosomal fusions, inversions, and translocations, to the transposition and duplication of genetic material facilitated by various different mobile DNA elements; differences in gene complement (i.e., genes are present in one species but absent in the other); differences in the coding sequences of genes that result in differences in the gene product(s) and therefore functional differences; differences in the regulatory regions of genes, leading to differences in expression; and differences in other factors that control and affect gene expression, such as epigenetic factors, transcription factors, micro-RNAs, and RNA editing.[41]

To illustrate, genetic rearrangements are important because of the "position effect"—whereby an identical gene in a different position in the genome and/or in an altered genomic neighborhood may be expressed differently. This may be due to altered accessibility of promoters, enhancers, and such (the control regions of gene expression) to transcriptional machinery—the apparatus within a cell that conducts the first main phase of gene expression—as well as other factors that promote and/or inhibit gene expression.[42] Between humans and other primates, there may be around a thousand species-specific inversions, fusions, and other rearrangements of chromosome sections that have been associated with hemophilias and muscular dystrophies, mental retardation, diabetes and renal disease, susceptibility to multiple sclerosis, and other diseases.[43] Gene expression can also be affected in this way by transposition of DNA, as well as via the disruption of genes and of genetic control elements at the site of insertion of a transposed section of DNA, for instance. This is mediated by mobile DNA elements, which differ in prevalence and type across species: One type is present in around a million copies in the average primate genome, but this number can differ across primate species by approximately a hundred thousand. The importance of mobile DNA elements is illustrated by their association with various diseases, including muscular dystrophy, several cancers (retinoblastoma, leukemia, and breast and colon cancers), hemophilia, neurofibromatosis, type 2 diabetes, Alzheimer's disease, and various syndromes.

It has therefore been acknowledged that interspecies and intraspecies differences in mobile elements, their locations, their proximity to specific genes, and so on differentially affect gene complement and expression and also disease susceptibility and pathology among species, including susceptibility to HIV infection and other infectious agents and response to toxic substances, including drugs and chemicals. One of the ways in which this manifests is alteration of "gene copy number," in which certain transposition events involve duplication of DNA, resulting in changes in the number of gene copies present in the genome. This "copy number variation" (CNV) is acknowledged to be a major cause of genetic variation even among humans—that is, within the same species, let alone among different species—and is known to affect, among other things, disease susceptibility, immune responses, and the formation of tumors. Notably, it

has greatly influenced the evolution of a family of genes pivotal to the function of the immune system: major histocompatibility complex (MHC; in humans, human leukocyte antigen, or HLA). This is, of course, absolutely critical since the immune system is central to much biomedical research. Yet, it is known that CNV differentially affects immune functions of even different types of macaques from different parts of the world, leading to claims that "although the macaque has been extensively used to model the human immune response, there may be substantial and previously unappreciated differences in HLA function between these species."[44] Such differences have been associated with different responses to and outcomes of simian immunodeficiency virus (SIV)/HIV infection, insulin-dependent diabetes, rheumatoid arthritis, ankylosing spondylitis, common variable immunodeficiency, and IgA deficiency—and consequently, with different disease susceptibility and pathology.

It is also known that various species, through evolution, have gained and lost genes, leading to differences in their complement of genes. For example, several hundred genes have been lost and gained in humans and chimpanzees,[45] and a comparative study of cynomolgus macaques and humans showed that almost half of gene transcripts (one of the intermediates in gene expression) in the macaque could not be matched to humans, suggesting these gene transcripts were unique to the macaque.[46] Notably, many of these were associated with immune function. It is also astounding to note that in spite of macaques being used extensively in drug testing, very little investigation has been conducted into the nature of their liver enzymes that metabolize drugs. Most of this metabolism is down to cytochrome P450 (CYP) enzymes, and it has been shown among multiple species, such as various monkeys, dogs, and rodents, that there is, specifically with regard to CYP genes, "considerable variation in gene content"; that even shared genes are only between 94 and 99 percent similar (bearing in mind that small differences are known to cause differences in specificity and activity of P450 enzymes); and that both rhesus and cynomolgus macaques have only around two-thirds of the genes involved in drug processing and metabolism that humans have.

Gene expression differences, caused by mechanisms such as those briefly described previously, cause significant differences in expression across species in many different organs and tissues. For example, several thousand genes are differently expressed in the brain, liver, kidney, heart, and other organs of various species of monkeys and apes and in humans. Many of these genes are associated with immune function, cancer, and cardiovascular disease. Hundreds of genes are differently expressed just in different types of macaques from different parts of the world, leading some researchers to conclude that "gene expression levels of certain cytochromes p450 can complicate the interpretation of primate drug metabolism experiments with respect to their translational relevance for humans."[47] Studies of gene expression in immune cells of humans and rhesus and cynomolgus macaques have shown different responses to viral infections, in which hundreds of genes are differently expressed and/or are unique to one species.[48]

Conclusions

These are just a small, illustrative sample of the myriad differences that exist between humans and other animals, many of which are detailed in my two published reviews.[49] The salient point is that small, ostensibly minor differences in genes and/or their control regions often exert promiscuous influences with far-reaching and significant effects. These effects belie claims of overall interspecies genetic similarity underpinning biological similarity that is sufficient in degree to support the use of animals as reliable and translatable models for human biomedical research. Many genetic differences affect the expression of dozens or even hundreds of genes, and further, the combined effects of these numerous differences are greater than the sum of their parts. Therefore, not only do the results of animal experimentation in many, if not all, areas of research demonstrate nonhuman animals' lack of relevance to human biology and disease but increasing knowledge of functional genetic differences also *proves* their lack of relevance and shows *why* there is a lack of relevance.

In short, given what we now know about the failures and lack of translation of animal research, about the reasons behind these failures, about nonhuman sentience, and about the suffering intrinsic to animal experimentation, as well as its financial and ethical cost, I believe it is hard to see how animal research can ever be sanctioned. Further, this is not something that can be improved. Although suffering can be ameliorated to some degree, arguably it is impossible to make this amelioration significant—and crucially, it is impossible to make animals significantly better (or "less bad") models for humans: their genetic modification can never make them "human enough" for experiments on them to be truly relevant to and predictive of human biology. There are too many differences; there is too much intricate and exquisite regulation of tens of thousands of genes to make this a possibility, even if this were desirable and there were no good alternatives. We must use the current and burgeoning knowledge we possess to conclude that not only is animal research not working but that also it can never "work." The need to move on from it—to embrace, adopt, and use superior, human-specific clinical, in vitro, and in silico research instead—has never been more pressing.

Notes

The author is grateful to Cruelty Free International and to the New England Anti-Vivisection Society for their support of much of the work discussed herein.

1. See, for example, P. Perel, I. Roberts, E. Sena, P. Wheble, C. Briscoe, P. Sandercock, M. Macleod, L. E. Mignini, P. Jayaram, and K. S. Khan, "Comparison of Treatment Effects between Animal Experiments and Clinical Trials: Systematic Review," *BMJ* 334, no. 7586 (2007): 197; P. Pound, S. Ebrahim, P. Sandercock, M. B. Bracken, and I. Roberts, "Where Is the Evidence That Animal Research Benefits Humans?" *BMJ* 328, no. 7438 (2004): 514–17; P. Pound and M. B. Bracken, "Is Animal Research Sufficiently Evidence Based to Be a Cornerstone of Biomedical Research?" *BMJ* 348 (2014): g3387; D. G. Hackam, "Translating Animal Research into Clinical Benefit," *BMJ* 334, no. 7586 (2007): 163–64.

2. See, for example, J. Bailey, "An Assessment of the Role of Chimpanzees in AIDS Vaccine Research," *Alternatives to Laboratory Animals* 36, no. 4 (2008): 381–428; J. Bailey, M. Thew, and M. Balls, "An Analysis of the Use of Dogs in Predicting Human Toxicology and Drug Safety," *Alternatives to Laboratory Animals* 41 (2013): 335–50; J. Bailey, M. Thew, and M. Balls, "An Analysis of the Use of Animal Models in Predicting Human Toxicology and Drug Safety," *Alternatives to Laboratory Animals* 42 (2014): 189–99; J. Bailey, "Monkey-Based Research on Human Disease: The Implications of Genetic Differences," *Alternatives to Laboratory Animals* 42 (2014): 287–317.

3. Institute of Medicine, *Chimpanzees in Biomedical and Behavioral Research: Assessing the Necessity* (National Academies Press, 2011), http://www.nap.edu/openbook.php?record_id=13257.

4. For example, see J. L. VandeBerg and S. M. Zola, "A Unique Biomedical Resource at Risk," *Nature* 437, no. 7055 (2005): 30–32.

5. Bailey, "Assessment of the Role"; J. Bailey, "Lessons from Chimpanzee-Based Research on Human Disease: The Implications of Genetic Differences," *Alternatives to Laboratory Animals* 39, no. 6 (2011): 527–40.

6. J. Bailey, A. Knight, and J. Balcombe, "The Future of Teratology Research Is In Vitro," *Biogenic Amines—Stress and Neuroprotection* 19, no. 2 (2005): 97–145; J. Bailey, "Developmental Toxicity Testing: Protecting Future Generations?" *Alternatives to Laboratory Animals* 36, no. 6 (2008): 718–21.

7. J. Bailey, "Non-Human Primates in Medical Research and Drug Development: A Critical Review," *Biogenic Amines* 19, no. 4 (2005): 235–56; J. Bailey, T. Capaldo, K. Conlee, M. Thew, and J. Pippin, "Experimental Use of Nonhuman Primates Is Not a Simple Problem," *Nature Medicine* 14, no. 10 (2008): 1011–12; J. Bailey and K. Taylor, "The Scher Report on Non-Human Primate Research—Biased and Deeply Flawed," *Alternatives to Laboratory Animals* 37, no. 4 (2009): 427–35.

8. J. Bailey, J. Balcombe, and T. Capaldo, "Chimpanzee Research: An Examination of Its Contribution to Biomedical Knowledge and Efficacy in Combating Human Diseases," 2007, accessed March 29, 2016. www.neavs.org/resources/publication/chimpanzee-research.

9. Bailey, "Assessment of the Role."

10. J. Bailey, "An Examination of Chimpanzee Use in Human Cancer Research," *Alternatives to Laboratory Animals* 37, no. 4 (2009): 399–416.

11. J. Bailey, "An Assessment of the Use of Chimpanzees in Hepatitis C Research Past, Present, and Future: 1. Validity of the Chimpanzee Model," *Alternatives to Laboratory Animals* 38, no. 5 (2010): 387–418; J. Bailey, "An Assessment of the Use of Chimpanzees in Hepatitis C Research Past, Present, and Future: 2. Alternative Replacement Methods," *Alternatives to Laboratory Animals* 38, no. 6 (2010): 471–94.

12. Bailey, Thew, and Balls, "Analysis of the Use of Dogs"; Bailey, Thew, and Balls, "Analysis of the Use of Animal Models."

13. Bailey, "Lessons"; Bailey, "Monkey-Based Research."

14. G. P. Aithal, "Mind the Gap," *Alternatives to Laboratory Animals* 38, Suppl. 1 (2010): 1–4.

15. N. Hasiwa, J. Bailey, P. Clausing, M. Daneshian, M. Eileraas, S. Farkas, I. Gyertyan, et al., "Critical Evaluation of the Use of Dogs in Biomedical Research and Testing in Europe," *ALTEX* 28, no. 4 (2011): 326–40.

16. For example, see G. Duyk, "Attrition and Translation," *Science* 302, no. 5645 (2003): 603–5; I. Kola and J. Landis, "Can the Pharmaceutical Industry Reduce Attrition Rates?" *Nature Reviews Drug Discovery* 3, no. 8 (2004): 711–15; M. Wehling, "Drug Development in the Light of Translational Science: Shine or Shade?" *Drug Discovery Today* 16, no. 23–24 (2011): 1076–83; J. A. DiMasi, "Pharmaceutical R&D Performance by Firm Size: Approval Success Rates and Economic Returns," *American Journal of Therapeutics* 21, no. 1 (2014): 26–34.

17. European Parliament, Directive 2004/27/EEC of the European Parliament and the Council of 31 March 2004, on the Community Code Relative to Medicinal Products for Human Use," http://ec.europa.eu/health//sites/health/files/files/eudralex/vol-1/dir_2004_27/dir_2004_27_en.pdf; US Congress, Federal Food, Drug and Cosmetics Act (1938), accessed September 11, 2013, http://www.fda.gov/regulatoryinformation/legislation/federalfooddrugandcosmeticactfdcact/fdcactchaptervdrugsanddevices/default.htm.

18. J. Lazarou, B. H. Pomeranz, and P. N. Corey, "Incidence of Adverse Drug Reactions in Hospitalized Patients: A Meta-Analysis of Prospective Studies," *JAMA* 279, no. 15 (1998): 1200–1205; M. Pirmohamed, S. James, S. Meakin, C. Green, A. K. Scott, T. J. Walley, K. Farrar, B. K. Park, and A. M. Breckenridge, "Adverse Drug Reactions as Cause of Admission to Hospital: Prospective Analysis of 18820 Patients," *BMJ* 329, no. 7456 (2004): 15–19.

19. For example, see J. P. Balcombe, N. D. Barnard, and C. Sandusky, "Laboratory Routines Cause Animal Stress," *Contemporary Topics in Laboratory Animal Science* 43, no. 6 (2004): 42–51; British Union for the Abolition of Vivisection, "Next of Kin—A Report on the Use of Primates in Experiments" (2006), available from Cruelty Free International, London.

20. UK Home Office, *Statistics of Scientific Procedures on Living Animals: Great Britain 2013*, 2014, March 27, 2017, https://www.gov.uk/government/publications/statistics-of-scientific-procedures-on-living-animals-great-britain-2013.

21. P. J. van Meer, M. Kooijman, C. C. Gispen-de Wied, E. H. Moors, and H. Schellekens, "The Ability of Animal Studies to Detect Serious Post Marketing Adverse Events Is Limited," *Regulatory Toxicology and Pharmacology* 64, no. 3 (2012): 345–49.

22. S. Spanhaak, D. Cook, J. Barnes, and J. Reynolds, "Species Concordance for Liver Injury" (Cambridge: Biowisdom, 2008), accessed July 8, 2015, http://www.biowisdom.com/files/sip_board_species_concordance.pdf.

23. C. L. Broadhead, *Critical Evaluation of the Use of Dogs in the Regulatory Toxicity Testing of Pharmaceuticals* (Nottingham, UK: Fund for the Replacement of Animals in Medical Experiments [FRAME], 1999).

24. T. Igarashi, S. Nakane, and T. Kitagawa, "Predictability of Clinical Adverse Reactions of Drugs by General Pharmacology Studies," *Journal of Toxicological Sciences* 20, no. 2 (1995): 77–92; J. T. Litchfield Jr., "Symposium on Clinical Drug Evaluation and Human Pharmacology; XVI: Evaluation of the Safety of New Drugs by Means of Tests in Animals," *Clinical Pharmacology and Therapeutics* 3 (1962): 665–72.

25. Bailey, "Developmental Toxicity Testing."

26. Aithal, "Mind the Gap"; Spanhaak et al., "Species Concordance."

27. H. Olson, G. Betton, D. Robinson, K. Thomas, A. Monro, G. Kolaja, P. Lilly, et al., "Concordance of the Toxicity of Pharmaceuticals in Humans and in Animals," *Regulatory Toxicology and Pharmacology* 32, no. 1 (2000): 56–67.

28. R. A. Matthews, "Medical Progress Depends on Animal Models—Doesn't It?" *Journal of the Royal Society of Medicine* 101, no. 2 (2008): 95–98.

29. Bailey, Thew, and Balls, "Analysis of the Use of Dogs"; Bailey, Thew, and Balls, "Analysis of the Use of Animal Models."

30. D. G. Altman and J. M. Bland, "Diagnostic Tests 2: Predictive Values," *BMJ* 309, no. 6947 (1994): 102.

31. For explanation, see Bailey, Thew, and Balls, "Analysis of the Use of Dogs"; Bailey, Thew, and Balls, "Analysis of the Use of Animal Models."

32. Ibid.

33. J. Bailey, M. Thew, and M. Balls, "Predicting Human Drug Toxicity and Safety via Animal Tests: Can Any One Species Predict Drug Toxicity in Any Other, and Do Monkeys Help?" *Alternatives to Laboratory Animals* 43, no. 6 (2015): 393–403.

34. Bailey, Thew, and Balls, "Analysis of the Use of Dogs"; Bailey, Thew, and Balls, "Analysis of the Use of Animal Models."

35. Institute of Medicine, *Chimpanzees*; VandeBerg and Zola, "Unique Biomedical Resource."

36. Bailey, "Lessons"; Bailey, "Monkey-Based Research."

37. See Bailey, "Lessons."

38. R. A. Gibbs, J. Rogers, M. G. Katze, R. Bumgarner, G. M. Weinstock, E. R. Mardis, K. A. Remington, et al., "Evolutionary and Biomedical Insights from the Rhesus Macaque Genome," *Science* 316, no. 5822 (2007): 222–34.

39. Bailey, "Monkey-Based Research."

40. Ibid.

41. Bailey, "Lessons"; Bailey, "Monkey-Based Research."

42. D. J. Kleinjan and V. van Heyningen, "Position Effect in Human Genetic Disease," *Human Molecular Genetics* 7, no. 10 (1998): 1611–18.

43. Maria Francesca Cardone, Zhaoshi Jiang, Pietro D'Addabbo, Nicoletta Archidiacono, Mariano Rocchi, Evan E. Eichler, and Mario Ventura, "Hominoid Chromosomal Rearrangements on 17q Map to Complex Regions of Segmental Duplication," *Genome Biology* 9, no. 2 (2008): R28; National Library of Medicine, "Conditions Related to Genes on the X Chromosome," 2016, accessed March 29, 2016. https://ghr.nlm.nih.gov/chromosome/X/show/Conditions.

44. Gibbs et al., "Evolutionary and Biomedical Insights."

45. Matthew W. Hahn, Jeffery P. Demuth, and Sang-Gook Han, "Accelerated Rate of Gene Gain and Loss in Primates," *Genetics* 177, no. 3 (2007): 1941–49; J. P. Demuth, T. De Bie, J. E. Stajich, N. Cristianini, and M. W. Hahn, "The Evolution of Mammalian Gene Families," *PLoS One* 1 (2006): e85.

46. Wei-Hua Chen, Xue-Xia Wang, Wei Lin, Xiao-Wei He, Zhen-Qiang Wu, Ying Lin, Song-Nian Hu, and Xiao-Ning Wang, "Analysis of 10,000 ESTs from Lymphocytes of the Cynomolgus Monkey to Improve Our Understanding of Its Immune System," *BMC Genomics* 7 (2006): 82.

47. Martin Ebeling, Erich Küng, Angela See, Clemens Broger, Guido Steiner, Marco Berrera, Tobias Heckel, et al., "Genome-Based Analysis of the Nonhuman Primate Macaca Fascicularis as a Model for Drug Safety Assessment," *Genome Research* 21, no. 10 (2011): 1746–56.

48. See Bailey, "Monkey-Based Research."

49. Ibid.; Bailey, "Lessons."

Bibliography

Aithal, G. P. "Mind the Gap." *Alternatives to Laboratory Animals* 38, Suppl. 1 (2010): 1–4.

Altman, D. G., and J. M. Bland. "Diagnostic Tests 2: Predictive Values." *BMJ* 309, no. 6947 (1994): 102.

Bailey, J. "An Assessment of the Role of Chimpanzees in AIDS Vaccine Research." *Alternatives to Laboratory Animals* 36, no. 4 (2008): 381–428.

———. "An Assessment of the Use of Chimpanzees in Hepatitis C Research Past, Present, and Future: 1. Validity of the Chimpanzee Model." *Alternatives to Laboratory Animals* 38, no. 5 (2010): 387–418.

———. "An Assessment of the Use of Chimpanzees in Hepatitis C Research Past, Present, and Future: 2. Alternative Replacement Methods." *Alternatives to Laboratory Animals* 38, no. 6 (2010): 471–94.

———. "Developmental Toxicity Testing: Protecting Future Generations?" *Alternatives to Laboratory Animals* 36, no. 6 (2008): 718–21.

———. "An Examination of Chimpanzee Use in Human Cancer Research." *Alternatives to Laboratory Animals* 37, no. 4 (2009): 399–416.

———. "Lessons from Chimpanzee-Based Research on Human Disease: The Implications of Genetic Differences." *Alternatives to Laboratory Animals* 39, no. 6 (2011): 527–40.

———. "Monkey-Based Research on Human Disease: The Implications of Genetic Differences." *Alternatives to Laboratory Animals* 42 (2014): 287–317.

———. "Non-Human Primates in Medical Research and Drug Development: A Critical Review." *Biogenic Amines* 19, no. 4 (2005): 235–56.

Bailey, J., J. Balcombe, and T. Capaldo. "Chimpanzee Research: An Examination of Its Contribution to Biomedical Knowledge and Efficacy in Combating Human Diseases." 2007. Accessed March 29, 2016. www.neavs.org/resources/publication/chimpanzee-research.

Bailey, J., T. Capaldo, K. Conlee, M. Thew, and J. Pippin. "Experimental Use of Nonhuman Primates Is Not a Simple Problem." *Nature Medicine* 14, no. 10 (2008): 1011–12.

Bailey, J., A. Knight, and J. Balcombe. "The Future of Teratology Research Is In Vitro." *Biogenic Amines—Stress and Neuroprotection* 19, no. 2 (2005): 97–145.

Bailey, J., and K. Taylor. "The Scher Report on Non-Human Primate Research—Biased and Deeply Flawed." *Alternatives to Laboratory Animals* 37, no. 4 (2009): 427–35.

Bailey, J., M. Thew, and M. Balls. "An Analysis of the Use of Animal Models in Predicting Human Toxicology and Drug Safety." *Alternatives to Laboratory Animals* 42 (2014): 189–99.

———. "An Analysis of the Use of Dogs in Predicting Human Toxicology and Drug Safety." *Alternatives to Laboratory Animals* 41 (2013): 335–50.

———. "Predicting Human Drug Toxicity and Safety via Animal Tests: Can Any One Species Predict Drug Toxicity in Any Other, and Do Monkeys Help?" *Alternatives to Laboratory Animals* 43, no. 6 (2015): 393–403.

Balcombe, J. P., N. D. Barnard, and C. Sandusky. "Laboratory Routines Cause Animal Stress." *Contemporary Topics in Laboratory Animal Science* 43, no. 6 (2004): 42–51.

British Union for the Abolition of Vivisection. "Next of Kin—A Report on the Use of Primates in Experiments." 2006. Available from Cruelty Free International, London.

Broadhead, C. L. *Critical Evaluation of the Use of Dogs in the Regulatory Toxicity Testing of Pharmaceuticals*. Nottingham, UK: Fund for the Replacement of Animals in Medical Experiments (FRAME), 1999.

Cardone, Maria Francesca, Zhaoshi Jiang, Pietro D'Addabbo, Nicoletta Archidiacono, Mariano Rocchi, Evan E. Eichler, and Mario Ventura. "Hominoid Chromosomal Rearrangements on 17q Map to Complex Regions of Segmental Duplication." *Genome Biology* 9, no. 2 (2008): R28.

Chen, Wei-Hua, Xue-Xia Wang, Wei Lin, Xiao-Wei He, Zhen-Qiang Wu, Ying Lin, Song-Nian Hu, and Xiao-Ning Wang. "Analysis of 10,000 ESTs from Lymphocytes of the Cynomolgus Monkey to Improve Our Understanding of Its Immune System." *BMC Genomics* 7 (2006): 82.

Demuth, J. P., T. De Bie, J. E. Stajich, N. Cristianini, and M. W. Hahn. "The Evolution of Mammalian Gene Families." *PLoS One* 1 (2006): e85.

DiMasi, J. A. "Pharmaceutical R&D Performance by Firm Size: Approval Success Rates and Economic Returns." *American Journal of Therapeutics* 21, no. 1 (2014): 26–34.

Duyk, G. "Attrition and Translation." *Science* 302, no. 5645 (2003): 603–5.

Ebeling, Martin, Erich Küng, Angela See, Clemens Broger, Guido Steiner, Marco Berrera, Tobias Heckel, et al. "Genome-Based Analysis of the Nonhuman Primate Macaca Fascicularis as a Model for Drug Safety Assessment." *Genome Research* 21, no. 10 (2011): 1746–56.

European Parliament. *Directive 2004/27/EEC of the European Parliament and the Council of 31 March 2004, on the Community Code Relative to Medicinal Products for Human Use*. http://ec.europa.eu/health//sites/health/files/files/eudralex/vol-1/dir_2004_27/dir_2004_27_en.pdf.

Gibbs, R. A., J. Rogers, M. G. Katze, R. Bumgarner, G. M. Weinstock, E. R. Mardis, K. A. Remington, et al. "Evolutionary and Biomedical Insights from the Rhesus Macaque Genome." *Science* 316, no. 5822 (2007): 222–34.

Hackam, D. G. "Translating Animal Research into Clinical Benefit." *BMJ* 334, no. 7586 (2007): 163–64.

Hahn, Matthew W., Jeffery P. Demuth, and Sang-Gook Han. "Accelerated Rate of Gene Gain and Loss in Primates." *Genetics* 177, no. 3 (2007): 1941–49.

Hasiwa, N., J. Bailey, P. Clausing, M. Daneshian, M. Eileraas, S. Farkas, I. Gyertyan, et al. "Critical Evaluation of the Use of Dogs in Biomedical Research and Testing in Europe." *ALTEX* 28, no. 4 (2011): 326–40.

Igarashi, T., S. Nakane, and T. Kitagawa. "Predictability of Clinical Adverse Reactions of Drugs by General Pharmacology Studies." *Journal of Toxicological Sciences* 20, no. 2 (1995): 77–92.

Institute of Medicine. *Chimpanzees in Biomedical and Behavioral Research: Assessing the Necessity*. Washington, DC: National Academies Press, 2011. Accessed March 27, 2017. http://www.nap.edu/openbook.php?record_id=13257.

Kleinjan, D. J., and V. van Heyningen. "Position Effect in Human Genetic Disease." *Human Molecular Genetics* 7, no. 10 (1998): 1611–18.

Kola, I., and J. Landis. "Can the Pharmaceutical Industry Reduce Attrition Rates?" *Nature Reviews Drug Discovery* 3, no. 8 (2004): 711–15.

Lazarou, J., B. H. Pomeranz, and P. N. Corey. "Incidence of Adverse Drug Reactions in Hospitalized Patients: A Meta-Analysis of Prospective Studies." *JAMA* 279, no. 15 (1998): 1200–1205.

Litchfield, J. T., Jr. "Symposium on Clinical Drug Evaluation and Human Pharmacology. XVI. Evaluation of the Safety of New Drugs by Means of Tests in Animals." *Clinical Pharmacology and Therapeutics* 3 (1962): 665–72.

Matthews, R. A. "Medical Progress Depends on Animal Models—Doesn't It?" *Journal of the Royal Society of Medicine* 101, no. 2 (2008): 95–98.

National Library of Medicine. "Conditions Related to Genes on the X Chromosome." 2016. Accessed March 29, 2016. https://ghr.nlm.nih.gov/chromosome/X/show/Conditions.

Olson, H., G. Betton, D. Robinson, K. Thomas, A. Monro, G. Kolaja, P. Lilly, et al. "Concordance of the Toxicity of Pharmaceuticals in Humans and in Animals." *Regulatory Toxicology and Pharmacology* 32, no. 1 (2000): 56–67.

Perel, P., I. Roberts, E. Sena, P. Wheble, C. Briscoe, P. Sandercock, M. Macleod, L. E. Mignini, P. Jayaram, and K. S. Khan. "Comparison of Treatment Effects between Animal Experiments and Clinical Trials: Systematic Review." *BMJ* 334, no. 7586 (2007): 197.

Pirmohamed, M., S. James, S. Meakin, C. Green, A. K. Scott, T. J. Walley, K. Farrar, B. K. Park, and A. M. Breckenridge. "Adverse Drug Reactions as Cause of Admission to Hospital: Prospective Analysis of 18820 Patients." *BMJ* 329, no. 7456 (2004): 15–19.

Pound, P., and M. B. Bracken. "Is Animal Research Sufficiently Evidence Based to Be a Cornerstone of Biomedical Research?" *BMJ* 348 (2014): g3387.

Pound, P., S. Ebrahim, P. Sandercock, M. B. Bracken, and I. Roberts. "Where Is the Evidence That Animal Research Benefits Humans?" *BMJ* 328, no. 7438 (2004): 514–17.

Spanhaak, S., D. Cook, J. Barnes, and J. Reynolds. "Species Concordance for Liver Injury." Cambridge: Biowisdom, 2008. Accessed July 8, 2015. http://www.biowisdom.com/files/sip_board_species_concordance.pdf.

UK Home Office. *Statistics of Scientific Procedures on Living Animals: Great Britain 2013*. 2014. Accessed March 27, 2017. https://www.gov.uk/government/publications/statistics-of-scientific-procedures-on-living-animals-great-britain-2013.

US Congress. *Federal Food, Drug and Cosmetics Act (1938)*. Accessed September 11, 2013. http://www.fda.gov/regulatoryinformation/legislation/federalfooddrugandcosmeticactfdcact/fdcactchaptervdrugsanddevices/default.htm.

van Meer, P. J., M. Kooijman, C. C. Gispen–de Wied, E. H. Moors, and H. Schellekens. "The Ability of Animal Studies to Detect Serious Post Marketing Adverse Events Is Limited." *Regulatory Toxicology and Pharmacology* 64, no. 3 (2012): 345–49.

VandeBerg, J. L., and S. M. Zola. "A Unique Biomedical Resource at Risk." *Nature* 437, no. 7055 (2005): 30–32.

Wehling, M. "Drug Development in the Light of Translational Science: Shine or Shade?" *Drug Discovery Today* 16, no. 23–24 (2011): 1076–83.

2.9

A Rawlsian Case against Animal Experimentation

Carlos Frederico Ramos de Jesus

EVERY THEORY OF JUSTICE applies to equals. Who are the equals? John Rawls answers:

> Moral persons are distinguished by two features: first they are capable of having (and are assumed to have) a conception of their good (as expressed by a rational plan of life); and second they are capable of having (and are assumed to have) a sense of justice, a normally effective desire to apply and to act upon the principles of justice, at least to a certain minimum degree.[1]

Moral persons are rational and reasonable: they want to pursue their plans for life and their conception of a good life, but they accept doing so while following common rules that allow others to pursue their plans as well. Rawls calls "two moral powers" the capabilities for a conception of good and for sense of justice.[2]

Then animals are clearly out. Rawls acknowledges that it is wrong to be cruel to animals and that they should be objects of "duties of compassion and humanity" but not duties of justice. Rawls says that an adequate conception for our relations with animals depends on the place of the human species in the world, in relation to nature. But if justice as fairness "is sound as an account of justice among persons, it cannot be far too wrong when these broader relationships are taken into consideration."[3]

A Contractarian Theory of Animal Rights?

Even though animals are explicitly out, can Rawls's "justice as fairness" be rethought so that it may render a better conception of animal entitlements than utilitarianism? Justice as fairness was reframed in order to extend to international justice (*The Law of Peoples*). If it is adequate for human affairs, as Rawls says, it can't be that far from the point when animals are included.

For Martha Nussbaum and Tom Regan, the answer to the previously posed question is a sound no. Nussbaum states that an original position with animals can't even be thought of.[4] Although an original position is not a historical situation, it should be a "coherent fiction," and a contract between animals and humans is not coherent.[5] Moreover, the initial hypothetical agreement should be of mutual advantage.[6] If one is not to gain from the agreement, why engage in it? Why should humans make an agreement with animals if humans can simply dominate them? No party in the contract should be strong or clever enough to dominate the others. If a party is, the contract is not even a possibility.

Tom Regan argues that according to Rawls, humans would have only indirect duties to animals. These would not be direct duties because animals are not in the social contract. Only those who are in the social contract can be subjects of rights and objects of duties of justice.[7] As Rawls states, "those who can give justice are owed justice."[8] Thus, there would be, in Rawlsian theory, only indirect duties to animals.

Regan points out that it is inconsistent that Rawls excludes animals from duties of justice because other moral patients (e.g., humans with severe disabilities) should be subjects of duties of justice. Society has duties toward them, even after they lose exercise of two moral powers (which are capability for a conception of good and for sense of justice, as stated above).[9] Why would it be different with animals? It would be only if Rawls were speciesist.

It seems to me that both Regan and Nussbaum dismiss too fast the potentiality of Rawls's theory for animal rights. They say that Rawls did not address the question, and they explain why animals do not fit Rawls's theory. But they do not try to rethink the theory, as Rawls did in *The Law of Peoples*. Could there be such a thing as a "Law of Animals"?

I will sketch some reasons for a positive answer. First, a disclaimer: I believe that the matter of animal rights poses two questions: Why? And how? I don't think that Rawls can say something about the first, but once the first is answered, he can say something about the second. Rawls cannot offer foundations for animal rights, especially because he does not offer them even for *human* rights, although this connection can be made. He is concerned not with foundations but with justification of fair institutional arrangements. He takes the foundations for granted: he does not need to argue that human beings are "ends in themselves" and therefore need rights for the important things in their lives.[10] He argues *from* this point on. He intends to ask *how* we can articulate liberty and equality in a fair society, presupposing that some kind of liberty and some kind of equality are important for humans. To be sure, his justification helps to square out which conceptions of liberty and equality are more reasonable. But for his purpose, he does not need to ask *why* equality and liberty are important because he does not need to ask whether respect is due to human beings. Rawls neither needed nor wanted to write a new *Foundations of Metaphysics of Morals*.

This is the reason I do not expect to extract from Rawlsian theory any answers on *why* animals have or do not have rights. Many authors (including Regan and Nussbaum) have already addressed the *why* subject, reaching different conclusions. But I do claim

that Rawlsian theory might have a say about *how* animals have rights, once we acknowledge that they might have some.

An Extended Original Position

In Rawls's well-known original position (OP), parties (or proxies) are under veil of ignorance.[11] Each one knows the same things and ignores the same things. They know the "traditional conceptions of justice" (such as utilitarianism, liberalism, socialism, libertarianism) and what the "primary goods" are.[12] Rawls defines these as "means for all ends":[13] whatever one's plan of life is, one will prefer having more primary goods than fewer primary goods. For humans, Rawls says the main primary goods are basic liberties, access to positions of power, wealth, income, and social bases of self-respect.[14]

Parties (or proxies) also ignore the "concrete position" of represented ones in society. A proxy does not know whether the one she represents is poor or rich, talented or nongifted, healthy or constantly sick, and so on. Because she does not know whether the represented one will fare well or badly, she tends to choose alternatives that leave the person she represents in the best possible position, if everything turns out poorly.[15] That is, if the represented person is poor, belongs to a group (or perhaps two groups) that suffer social prejudice and discrimination, has a bad health condition, and has meager talents (not well paid for in the market), there still should not be any deprivation of primary goods because of these unfortunate conditions. The party (or proxy) in the original position is someone who cuts the pizza without knowing which slice the person she represents will get: it is rational that she will cut equal-sized slices.[16]

It is clear that the Rawlsian OP is a hypothetical situation that stresses the constraints to which we should defer when thinking morally.[17] It is a "heuristic device."[18] Its basic motto could be "it could happen to you." Anyone could be the worst off. OP, then, is about impartiality.

Up to now, I have mentioned that the OP is composed of parties, not real people. Rawls made this important clarification—that the OP is composed of parties, not persons—exactly in order to stress the point that it is a moral device, not an actual situation.[19]

The OP is composed of (abstract) proxies, representatives, and each individual has her proxy.

That's why Nussbaum's first critique misses the point: why is the existence of animals' proxies less imaginable than people's proxies? It is not essential to state *whom* the proxies represent because they do not know the individuals' identities. An original position in which we find proxies for humans and for animals is a fiction as credible (or incredible) as an original position with humans' proxies.

So in the extended OP, parties would know different primary goods that apply to animals and humans.[20] Inasmuch as these goods vary greatly from species to species, it is necessary to "recognize a wide range of types of animal dignity and of corresponding needs for flourishing."[21] There will be, of course, general goods (life, liberty, physical integrity) and species-specific ones (such as social bonds and mental integrity).[22]

In this extended OP, parties would ignore another important fact: they would ignore whether they represent a human or a nonhuman animal. Ignoring this fact leads them to choose principles that render the worst-off in the best possible condition. In this case, it is hard to admit that some nonhuman animals could live miserable lives in farms and be eaten by humans—who do not need at all to eat them.[23] A proxy would never cut the pizza in a way that leaves the possibility that her represented would receive this dreadful share. This share would not be a rational possibility.

But we need to face another criticism. Can the OP occur with so great an inequality of powers as that between human and nonhuman animals? Yes, because representatives do not know whether the beings they represent are animals or humans. And there is another particular compelling reason for accepting OP between individuals with unequal powers, which is the very reason that the OP exists: engaging in the hypothetical OP makes sense only if the individual who is actually better off thinks she could be worse off. Then it does not matter whether the worst-off is the poorest human being in society or the confined ox doomed to slaughter. The ones better off do not have bargaining reasons to make an agreement either with the poorest human or with the confined ox.[24] If the difference of bargaining power is a reason to believe

that an OP with animals' and humans' representatives is not feasible, then Rawls's OP is also not feasible. The OP wants to build political fairness, starting from concrete inequality. Whether real inequality is extended to animals and humans or is only between humans, it does not matter. The egalitarian aim is the same: building fairness that still does not exist from inequality that exists.

Indeed, this objection fails because it reads Rawls as if he were closer to Thomas Hobbes's contractarianism than to Immanuel Kant's:

> The Hobbesian contractarian sees the contract as *constitutive* of moral right and wrong: these are constituted or defined by the tacit agreements reached by rational contractors of roughly equal power. The authority of the contract, therefore, derives from our tacit agreement to its conditions. Contained in the idea of Kantian contractarianism, on the other hand, is an at least minimal conception of moral *truth* or *objectivity* that is independent of the contract and the agreements reached by contractors.[25]

Rawls does not see his "justice as fairness" as a private compact or as a bargaining agreement.[26] He does not defend the idea that whatever the OP creates is right. On the contrary, the OP is a heuristic device to think better (that is, impartially) about political principles. The OP is not about "might makes right." On the contrary, whatever one *might* do, one *should* do what is right.

Moral Lottery and the Difference Principle

In the classical OP account, Rawls's concern with moral lotteries is clear: "moral lotteries" are the morally arbitrary facts that make people better or worse off.[27] They are morally arbitrary in the sense that they are undeserved. From Rawls's theory, we can extract four moral lotteries: natural (intelligence, health, talent), social (wealth, structured family), strict luck (being in the right place at right time), and time (being born in a time of affluence or famine).[28]

Inasmuch as lotteries are morally arbitrary, a well-ordered society should not count on them for distributing primary goods. That's why Rawls says that "natural distribution is neither just nor unjust; nor is it unjust that persons are born into society at some particular position. These are simply natural facts. What is just and unjust is the way that institutions deal with these facts."[29]

Rawls's difference principle tries to correct moral arbitrariness:[30] bad luck in the life lottery is not a legitimate basis for one having fewer primary goods than the fortunate ones. Luck alone does not justify inequality in a well-ordered society. What, if anything, can justify it? Inequality can be justified if and only if it renders the worst-off in a better position than they would be in a situation of absolute equality. Inequality should be a *service* to the worst-off. If it is not, it is illegitimate. For Rawls, that is what might justify different wages for different functions and professions: the more specialized the function, the greater the incentive one needs in order to be motivated to do it. A physician or an engineer might earn more than, say, a coconut seller on the beach. The reason is not the physician's effort to graduate or the engineer's talent in complex and mysterious fields, such as math and physics. Effort and talent are part of the moral lottery. The reason is that a community won't have good physicians or engineers unless it pays them well enough. If they are paid only as much as the coconut seller, what is the incentive to be a physician? Granted, many people would follow this career because of vocation (like many of us defend animal rights without receiving one cent for it). But not enough people would do it. And this would be much worse for the coconut seller when he had a health problem or wanted to build his house.

If moral lotteries do not justify inequality because they are morally arbitrary, why shouldn't we take into account the lottery of being born human or animal? Indeed, this is a very influential lottery: being born a human or an ox makes a great difference for flourishing. Being born one or the other is not fair or unfair, but what institutions make from this natural fact is fair or unfair. Being born an ox is not a moral reason for having a miserable life and being slaughtered.[31]

When is an inequality fair to animals? When this inequality is justified to them—that is, when this inequality leaves them in the best possible position and leaves them better than they would be without this inequality. In human justice, natural lotteries alone do not justify inequalities. The same should apply for interspecies justice.

Animal Experimentation

Is animal experimentation fair to animals? One might think that it is because only humans perform science and save lives with its achievements. Animals do not perform science and might benefit from human research. Why not contribute to it? Cognitive difference between animals and humans would seem to justify animal experimentation.

However, even if animals were, today, absolutely necessary to science progress and to new medications, current animal experimentation would never be justified. It is the practice of animal experimentation that it is "against the individual interests" of the animal.[32] From the outset, it is clear that this inequality, by which animals are objects of experimentation and humans are not, is not justified to each of the animals. The difference principle would not endorse the position that animal experimentation is fair because this inequality does not render the worse-off in the best possible position. Participation of animals in experiments could be justified by the difference principle only if animals would be left in a better position than if there were no experiments at all. This is not what actually happens: animals who are used in experimentation as a mere means to human ends would be in a much-better position *without* being forced into experimentation.

What is left of experimentation, then, is almost nothing. Testing a new drug or a new procedure in a sick dog who is not recovering with regular treatment is possible and fair—but that would be the case with a human as well. And of course, behavioral studies and experiments are also justified, as long as they are harmless or cause only slight distress.

How can we know whether a specific experiment with animals is fair or not? If we really adhere to the Rawlsian difference principle applied to animals, we can have only an institutional answer—that is, a *general* rule to be followed. This comparison is possible: if we would allow a young child to be used to test a new drug or a new procedure, then it could also be tested with animals. That is, we could allow someone who is inviolable and cannot consent to undergo an experiment if it would render the subject in a better condition than she would be without the experiment. Comparing animals with children is enlightening because today we have a consensus that experiments with children are extremely unfair because every child is a subject of rights. As a consequence, a child can undergo an experiment only if she might profit from it. Granted, once the experiment is performed, it may have bad and unforeseeable results. But the reason an inviolable subject might undergo an experimental medication or a medical procedure can only be that this subject will *most likely* be better off after the procedure. Regarding inviolable subjects, experimentation should be carried on *in the interest of the individual being experimented on.*

Finally, I would like to briefly address one question: if we are really convinced that Rawlsian principles apply to interspecies justice, why should we think animal experimentation is connected with the difference principle and not with the liberty principle? Indeed, regarding inviolable subjects, it would make more sense to think of the liberty principle, which states, "Each person has an equal right to a fully adequate scheme of equal basic liberties which is compatible with a similar scheme of liberties for all."[33] And animals' basic needs are not "index goods,"[34] in which some optimal inequality could favor the worst-off.

I concede this point. Nonetheless, the difference principle better suits animal experimentation for the following reason: it might account much better for the biological difference between humans and other animals, which enables humans to seek scientific progress through experimentation. Inasmuch as animals do not do science and humans do it, one might wonder if this fact is a justification for humans to use animals in science. The difference principle allows one to ask whether this biological difference may render animals better off through experimentation. On the other hand, the liberty principle does not even allow this hypothesis to be thought about. The liberty principle is question-begging on this important point. To sum up, one should prefer the difference principle over the liberty principle because of the principle of charity: with the difference principle, animal experimentation could perhaps be justified (although it is not), whereas with the liberty principle, it could never be justified.

It seems clear that parties in the OP would not choose the principle that nonhuman animals can be used by humans for necessary and noble human ends. Such a principle is not justified for the worst-off. It would be too risky to cut a pizza slice so small.

Conclusions

The different capabilities possessed by humans and animals do not allow the former to use the latter as mere means to their ends, unless one holds that natural lotteries have moral significance. As a consequence, animal experimentation can be justified only by one who makes a strong case against the irrelevance of the natural lottery of being born human or animal. An animal-rights theory with Rawlsian inspiration would deem animal experimentation unthinkable. It might be surprising that a contractarian theory has this implication, but it is a mere consequence of including animals in an extended OP and properly understanding Rawlsian concepts.

Then why not a "Law of Animals"? The author who renewed contractarian doctrine and changed the subject of talk in political theory may inspire an institutional approach for interspecies justice. Until we are convinced that Rawls's theory cannot give a good answer, it is worth trying this exercise of impartiality and otherness offered by Rawls's contractarianism.

Notes

1. John Rawls, *A Theory of Justice* (Cambridge, MA: Harvard University Press, 1971), 442.

2. John Rawls, *Political Liberalism* (New York: Columbia University Press, 1995), 49.

3. Rawls, *Theory of Justice*, 448–49.

4. An original position is an imagined moral device, in which each person in society is represented by a proxy, who has limited information about the person's life. A proxy does not know which conceptions of good are possessed by the person he or she represents. Neither does a proxy know a person's social position. Proxies only know general facts: they know that everyone wants *primary goods*, which are life, liberty, opportunities, wealth, income and the social bases of self-respect. In this context of limited information, all the proxies decide which principles of justice society will endorse. This account will be deepened later. For original position's general description, see Rawls, *Theory of Justice,* 10–19.

5. Martha Nussbaum, "Beyond 'Compassion and Humanity': Justice for Nonhuman Animals," in *Animal Rights: Current Debates and New Directions*, ed. M. Nussbaum and Cass Sunstein (New York: Oxford University Press, 2004), 301.

6. Nussbaum, "Beyond 'Compassion and Humanity,'" 301.

7. Tom Regan, *The Case for Animal Rights* (Berkeley: University of California Press, 1983), 165–69.

8. Rawls, *Theory of Justice*, 446.

9. Regan, *Case for Animal Rights*, 170–71.

10. Immanuel Kant, *Grundlegung zur Metaphysik der Sitten* (Frankfurt: Suhrkamp, 1974), 60.

11. Rawls, *Theory of Justice*, 17.

12. Ibid., 106–7, 123.

13. Rawls, *Political Liberalism*, 76.

14. John Rawls, "Social Unity and Primary Goods," in *Collected Papers*, ed. Samuel Freeman (Cambridge, MA: Harvard University Press, 2001), 362–63.

15. Rawls, *Theory of Justice*, 118–19.

16. Mark Rowlands, *Animals like Us* (New York: Verso, 2002), 59.

17. Rawls states it clearly: "It may be helpful to observe that one or more persons can at any time enter this position, or perhaps better, simulate the deliberations of this hypothetical situation, simply by reasoning in accordance with the appropriate restrictions." Rawls, *Theory of Justice*, 119.

18. Rowlands, *Animals like Us*, 66.

19. John Rawls, "Justice as Fairness: Political, not Metaphysical," in *Collected Papers*, ed. Samuel Freeman (Cambridge, MA: Harvard University Press, 2001), 404–5.

20. Robert Elliot states: "The idea of judging how things are from an animal's point of view makes sense. . . . We are capable of empathetic understanding with regard to animals and we can make comparative judgments about different lifestyles for them based on our understanding of the propensities, desires, interests and preferences that they have." "Rawlsian Justice and Non-human Animals," *Journal of Applied Philosophy* 1, no. 1 (1984): 103.

21. Nussbaum, "Beyond 'Compassion and Humanity,'" 300.

22. In OP, proxies do not know whether individuals have life plans or simply have a life that matters for the latter. Contrary to what Lilly-Marlene Russow argues, it is not necessary that an individual have a life plan to be a subject of justice in Rawls's theory ("Animals in the Original Position," *Between the Species* 8 [1992]: 226). Rawlsian rejection of utilitarianism is not based solely on the importance of life plans to each individual. Steve Sapontzis notes: "What a desire to overcome the distributive shortcomings of utilitarianism inevitably leads to, then, is not a procedure that respects just those who have life-plans; rather, it leads to principles which protect all those who might be sacrificed for the general welfare against such sacrifice and which assure all concerned that they will receive an equitable share of available goods." Steve Sapontzis, "On the Utility of Contracts," *Between the Species* 8 (1992): 230.

23. Vegetarian and strict vegetarian diets are healthy, and the evidence is summarized in American Dietetic Association, "Position of the American Dietetic Association: Vegetarian Diets," *Journal of American Dietetic Association* 109 (2009): 1266–82, doi:10.1016/j.jada.2009.05.027.

24. Bargaining reasons play a role in actual private agreements, in which both sides will only endorse the agreement if they profit from it, for example, a seller only sells a product if she can get enough money for it. In OP, these reasons play no role because OP's agreement takes place between proxies who do not know the actual conditions of individuals they represent. For a comparison between private agreement and OP's agreement, see Rawls, *Political Liberalism,* 276–78.

25. Mark Rowlands, *Animal Rights: Moral Theory and Practice*, 2nd ed. (Basingstoke, UK: Palgrave, 2009), 125–26. For a similar argument extending contractualism to justify duties to animals, see Matthew Talbert, "Contractualism and Our Duties to Nonhuman Animals," *Environmental Ethics* 28 (2006): 201–15.

26. Basic justice is, then, morally prior to bargaining compacts. That is why Sapontzis says that "matters of moral or social justice and associated basic rights differ from special rights and privileges in being guarantees one does not have to earn." Sapontzis, "On the Utility of Contracts," 231.

27. "Moral lottery" is an expression by Brian Barry, *A Treatise of Social Justice*, vol. 1 (Berkeley: University of California Press, 1991), 226.

28. Rawls acknowledges only three groups of contingencies, excluding time lottery. Rawls, *Theory of Justice*, 83. But we can extract time lottery from his "just savings" proviso, included in his difference principle: "It is a natural fact that generations are spread out in time and actual economic benefits flow only in one direction. . . . What is just or unjust is how institutions deal with natural limitations and the way they are set up to take advantage of historical possibilities. Obviously if all generations are to gain (except perhaps the earlier ones), the parties must agree to a savings principle that insures that each generation receives its due from its predecessors and does its fair share for those to come." Rawls, *Theory of Justice*, 254.

29. Ibid., 87.

30. Rawls's difference principle: "Social and economic inequalities are to be arranged so that they are both: (*a*) to the greatest benefit of the least advantaged, consistent with the just savings principle; (*b*) attached to offices and positions open to all under conditions of fair equality of opportunity." Rawls, *Theory of Justice*, 266.

31. Donald VanDeVeer rightly enquires: "If knowledge of race or gender or social position is excluded from participants OP in order to insure their neutrality in choosing principles to govern interaction among beings with morally relevant interests, must not species identification be excluded as well?" "Of Beasts, Persons, and the Original Position," *The Monist* 62, no. 3 (1979): 373.

32. Tom Regan states that animal experimentation is animal use in "harmful, non-therapeutic medical research." Tom Regan, "Empty Cages: Animal Rights and Vivisection,"

in *Contemporary Debates in Applied Ethics*, ed. A. Cohen and H. Wellman (Lanham, MD: Rowman, 2005), 77.

33. Rawls, *Political Liberalism*, 291.

34. "Index goods" is the expression by Thomas Pogge meaning "powers and prerogatives of offices and positions of responsibility; income and wealth; and the social bases of self-respect"—that is, goods that can be unequally distributed in order to fulfill the difference principle. Freedom is not among these goods. Thomas Pogge, *Realizing Rawls* (Ithaca: Cornell University Press, 1989), 162.

Bibliography

American Dietetic Association. "Position of the American Dietetic Association: Vegetarian Diets." *Journal of American Dietetic Association* 109 (2009): 1266–82. doi:10.1016/j.jada.2009.05.027.

Barry, Brian. *A Treatise of Social Justice*. Vol. 1. Berkeley: University of California Press, 1991.

Elliot, Robert. "Rawlsian Justice and Non-human Animals." *Journal of Applied Philosophy* 1, no. 1 (1984): 95–106.

Kant, Immanuel. *Grundlegung zur Metaphysik der Sitten*. Frankfurt: Suhrkamp, 1974.

Nussbaum, Martha. "Beyond 'Compassion and Humanity': Justice for Nonhuman Animals." In *Animal Rights: Current Debates and New Directions*, edited by M. Nussbaum and Cass Sunstein, 299–319. New York: Oxford University Press, 2004.

Pogge, Thomas. *Realizing Rawls*. Ithaca: Cornell University Press, 1989.

Rawls, John. "Justice as Fairness: Political, not Metaphysical." In *Collected Papers*, edited by Samuel Freeman, 388–414. Cambridge, MA: Harvard University Press, 2001.

———. *The Law of Peoples*. Cambridge, MA: Harvard University Press, 1999.

———. *Political Liberalism*. New York: Columbia University Press, 1995.

———. "Social Unity and Primary Goods." In *Collected Papers*, edited by Samuel Freeman, 359–87. Cambridge, MA: Harvard University Press, 2001.

———. *A Theory of Justice*. Cambridge, MA: Harvard University Press, 1971.

Regan, Tom. *The Case for Animal Rights*. Berkeley: University of California Press, 1983.

———. "Empty Cages: Animal Rights and Vivisection." In *Contemporary Debates in Applied Ethics*, edited by A. Cohen and H. Wellman, 77–90. Lanham, MD: Rowman, 2005.

Rowlands, Mark. *Animal Rights: Moral Theory and Practice*. 2nd ed. Basingstoke, UK: Palgrave, 2009.

———. *Animals like Us*. New York: Verso, 2002.

Russow, Lilly-Marlene. "Animals in the Original Position." *Between the Species* 8 (1992): 224–29.

Sapontzis, Steve. "On the Utility of Contracts." *Between the Species* 8 (1992): 229–32.

Talbert, Matthew. "Contractualism and Our Duties to Nonhuman Animals." *Environmental Ethics* 28 (2006): 202–15.

VanDeVeer, Donald. "Of Beasts, Persons, and the Original Position." *The Monist* 62 (1979): 368–77.

The Harms of Captivity within Laboratories and Afterward

Elizabeth Tyson

ANIMAL EXPERIMENTATION has been the focus of concern for nonhuman animal advocates for over a century. The main reason for this concern, and thus the focus of most discussion in relation to the use of animals in this way, is the welfare impact that the often invasive and painful experiments carried out have on the individuals in question. With some exceptions, the lifelong captive state of the individuals involved in animal experimentation is either overlooked or deemed a secondary welfare concern when compared to the specific procedures that the animals might be forced to endure.

Considering recent work in this area, this essay seeks to explore narratives surrounding concepts of captivity, freedom, release, and rehabilitation in the context of experimentation on nonhuman primates, from animal welfare, legal, ethical, and public perception viewpoints. I suggest that the failure to properly consider captivity in the context of animal experimentation as harmful in itself may lead to the suffering of animals used in purely behavioral studies or of animals who continue to suffer postprocedure not being given the critical attention that is warranted.

This essay focuses specifically on the captivity of nonhuman primates for a number of reasons. First, because all nonhuman primates are considered to be nondomesticated (or free-living) animals, captivity in and of itself can be deemed problematic. In addition, there are a number of high-profile and widely publicized case studies involving nonhuman primates in

experimentation, thus allowing for the examination of narratives surrounding their captivity. The present discussion will consider four case studies relating to the captivity of nonhuman primates in the context of animal experimentation. The first two are concerned with the "retirement" of nonhuman primates previously used in laboratories. The third considers a purely behavioral experiment (involving no explicitly painful or invasive procedures) carried out on a chimpanzee, and the final case study considers ongoing legal proceedings that seek "bodily liberty" for two chimpanzees held in a biomedical research center.

The reason captivity may be considered problematic for nonhuman primates is closely associated with the fact that all species of nonhuman primates, as noted previously, are considered nondomesticated. This means that they have not been subjected to the process of domestication, which takes place over thousands of years and changes animals genetically. As such, all nonhuman primates, whether born in captivity or in their natural habitat, share largely the same physiological and behavioral needs and interests as other members of their species. These might include but are not limited to the need to live in specific (and often very large and complex) social groups, the need to develop interpersonal relationships, the need to travel over a home range freely (sometimes covering long distances), the need to eat a certain diet, the need to live in a particular climate or habitat, and the need to procreate and raise offspring. It is widely agreed that at least some of these needs or interests are inevitably frustrated when these animals (and other animals belonging to nondomesticated species) are held captive. The extent to which it can be agreed that captivity is harmful will differ depending on a variety of factors; for example, an animal-rights advocate may hold a different stance on this issue than a zookeeper. The differences of opinion with regard to the extent to which captivity is harmful will, however, not be addressed as part of this discussion. Instead, the present argument will proceed on the basis that despite differing opinions regarding the extent to which captivity is deemed problematic for nondomesticated animals, there are developed, evidence-based arguments founded in welfare and ethics that recognize that captivity can reasonably be considered harmful in and of itself.

In 2014 the essay "Sanctuary, Not Remedy," by philosopher Karen Emmerman, was published in the anthology *The Ethics of Captivity*. Emmerman states in this piece that "it is common for people to believe that sanctuaries provide restitution to animals for harms they have suffered at human hands. This belief is reflected in public discourse." She suggests that restitution can be considered a way "to make [the victim] whole again or at least to provide her with compensation commensurate with her losses." The people she refers to as holding this belief exclude sanctuary workers themselves, who are well aware, she says, that sanctuary cannot provide full restitution for the animals, but includes "policymakers and the general public."[1]

She then speculates that "the belief that sanctuaries provide restitution is prevalent enough that policymakers may justify harm to animals with the idea that restitution through sanctuary is possible."[2] In effect, she suggests that animal experimentation may be deemed more palatable and acceptable as long as "retirement" of animals to a sanctuary is believed to provide a "happy ending" for the animals involved. For the remainder of the article, Emmerman makes a strong case for how provision of sanctuary to nondomesticated animals previously used in exploitative practices should not be conflated with provision of full restitution. The main premise of her argument is based on the previously mentioned position that captivity for nondomesticated animals is harmful in

itself and that these animals, having no opportunity to be released into their natural habitat, will remain in captivity for their lifetimes.

An area not explored in Emmerman's article is the origin of the "public discourse" that she believes results in the ostensibly genuinely held belief that the provision of sanctuary can provide full restitution. The remainder of the present essay seeks to consider the public discourse surrounding captivity in the context of vivisection, with a view to understanding its origins and driving forces.

The first case study under consideration is referenced both in Emmerman's work and in Stephen Ross's article "Captive Chimpanzees,"[3] published in the same volume. The case can be summarized as follows.

As a result of the fast growth of the chimpanzee population in laboratories in the United States following the establishment of the 1986 National Chimpanzee Breeding and Research Program, there were around fifteen hundred chimpanzees in laboratories in the United States by 1994. In 1997 the Institute for Laboratory Animal Research (ILAR) released the report *Chimpanzees in Research: Strategies for Their Ethical Care, Management, and Use*,[4] which had been commissioned by the National Institutes of Health (NIH). The report stated that there was a "moral responsibility" for the long-term care of chimpanzees used in research. In 2000 the Chimpanzee Health Improvement, Maintenance, and Protection (CHIMP) Act was implemented in order to "provide the means to fund a national sanctuary system for former research chimpanzees."[5] The act was based on the recommendations made in the government-commissioned report.

It was in this case that Emmerman suggests policymakers may have been influenced by the public discourse of "sanctuary as restitution," leading them to an apparently genuinely held belief that offering retirement to ex-laboratory chimpanzees could undo past wrongs. However, the commissioning body for the report was the same government department responsible for the chimpanzee breeding program and one that, at that time, advocated the continued use of chimpanzees in this way. As such, it seems reasonable to reach the conclusion that policymakers, rather than being influenced by genuine belief that sanctuary would provide full restitution, instead played a significant role in developing and driving the discourse in order to justify ongoing harm to animals.

The narrative from the president at the time, Bill Clinton, on the passing of the act explicitly included themes of "moral obligations," "lifelong care," and "retirement" and opened as follows: "This Act is a valuable affirmation of the Federal Government's responsibility and moral obligation to provide an orderly system to ensure a secure retirement for surplus Federal research chimpanzees and to meet their lifetime needs for shelter and care."[6]

However, at the same time, the Association of Sanctuaries and the American Sanctuary Association raised serious concerns, particularly over the fact that the NIH would retain "ownership" of the retired chimpanzees and thus would be able to "yank them back into research use at any time, along with any offspring born to them."[7] The concerns of the sanctuary organizations suggested that the idea that true sanctuary was being provided was disingenuous and that the system would, in fact, simply provide a holding facility for the animals.

In the foregoing two examples, it can be noted how the same situation has been communicated very differently to the public by two key stakeholders in the debate surrounding sanctuary as restitution—policymakers, on the one hand, and sanctuaries themselves, on the other.

The second case under consideration involves the Colombian scientist Manuel Elkin Patarroyo and the operation of his research lab, the Fundación Instituto de Inmunología de Colombia (FIDIC), which was based until 2012 in Leticia, a town in the Colombian Amazon. Patarroyo's research was focused around the development of a malaria vaccine, and his test subjects were the *Aotus* spp., or owl monkeys, small nocturnal primates native to South America, including the forests of Colombia, Peru, and Brazil. All animals used in the laboratory were captured from their natural home for the purpose of experimentation. In 2012, as a result of work carried out by Fundación Entropika,[8] the FIDIC lab's license was revoked when it was concluded that the lab was using animals taken from both Peruvian and Brazilian territories. The license issued to the laboratory allowed capture of animals only from Colombian territory.

The narrative that was promoted by the FIDIC was that the monkeys were captured from the forest, used for a number of months to carry out the relevant tests, and then released back into the area that they had been taken from. Patarroyo stated in interviews in the press that he had worked with over twenty-five thousand monkeys in his thirty-five years of operation.[9] The process that the lab claimed the animals were subjected to was described in the press as follows:

If the monkey did not contract [malaria] after being injected with the parasite, it would be returned to the wild once scientists had evaluated the possible causes. The procedure was to place the monkey in quarantine and then release it at the site in the jungle where the seller reported it had been captured. If the monkey did get sick, it was treated with drugs and then a similar release protocol was followed.[10]

Patarroyo said in an interview, "I must insist on clarifying that all of the monkeys are kept in excellent general conditions, which is agreed on by the environmental authorities and many people who visit our institute."[11]

The FIDIC's narrative focused strongly on the kind treatment offered to the animals during the months they were in the laboratory, as well as their eventual release back into their natural habitat. This went further than the suggestion of sanctuary as restitution for the animals and instead gave a clear message to the public that full "restitution" for the monkeys, via release back to their natural habitat so that they could live out their lives, was being achieved. My own experiences of visiting the lab and caring for animals who had been used in the FIDIC's experiments, plus eyewitness accounts from field researchers and officials, have contradicted the laboratory's narrative in various aspects.

My personal experience of the operation of the FIDIC laboratory came as a result of being entrusted by the local environmental agency, Corpoamazonia, with the care of four monkeys previously housed at the FIDIC, after they were deemed "unfit for release." Due to my previous experience working in a sanctuary for rescued monkeys, I was known to the environmental agency and acted as a temporary carer for confiscated animals while permanent homes were sought. One of the monkeys from the lab was a male owl monkey whom I named Tango. Tango was emaciated, suffering from serious muscular atrophy and a skin condition called dermatophilosis. The skin condition resulted in sores all over Tango's body that seeped and undoubtedly caused him discomfort and pain. He had lost a lot of his fur. Despite being given round-the-clock care, the physical toll on his body was too much, and he died in his sleep around four weeks after being removed from the laboratory.

During their time housed in the laboratory, the animals were housed singly—something that is behaviorally alien to most primates and that likely caused significant distress. The cramped living conditions, in the form of a metal cage measuring no more than fifty centimeters (about twenty inches) in height and depth, did not allow the most basic of locomotive activity. This had a direct impact on the animals' health. The lack of movement for what was thought to be around six months was what led to the muscular atrophy that Tango experienced and was, according to veterinarians, a direct contributor to his weakened state and subsequent death.

With regard to the release protocol, an official from the environmental agency Corpoamazonia spoke to the Colombian magazine *Cambio* in 2007, stating that she had "discovered during a visit carried out at the [FIDIC center] on October 19 that some animals were in a terrible state of health, others had stayed longer than the allotted time allowed and, most worryingly, there was no plan for the rehabilitation for those that were to be released."[12]

This view was reiterated by the researchers involved in the monitoring work carried out by Fundación Entropika. The organization published statements alleging that local people had reported the presence, close to their crops, of carcasses of night monkeys with tattoos on their legs. The tattoos identified them as monkeys used in the FIDIC laboratory who had apparently been released in very poor states of health. Fundación Entropika reiterated concerns raised by the Corpoamazonia official in 2007: that no rehabilitation process was in place, nor was any postrelease follow-up carried out by the laboratory.

A study carried out in 2014 as a joint initiative between the Sinchi Center and the Universidad Nacional de Colombia found worryingly low body weights in animals who had survived release. Fundación Entropika concludes in an overview of its Aotus Project, published on its website, that in light of the evidence, "although released animals *can* survive, it is almost impossible to determine survival rates owing to the lack of follow-up."[13]

It would appear that the persistent narrative in the press from the laboratory itself focused on release and thus full restitution of the animals used in research. This was coupled with themes of high standards of care during the captive period. In reality, almost every aspect of the discourse promoted by the laboratory has been countered, in part or in full, by at least some evidence to the contrary.

In this case study, it could be considered that the discourse of freedom, liberation, and restitution is again being driven by the industry itself in order to justify, or at least mitigate, harm caused to animals. In reality, the capture and release of animals from and to the forest was likely the most cost-effective approach for the FIDIC because breeding and housing twenty-five thousand owl monkeys in thirty-five years in captivity would have proven costly and complex. Captive-bred monkeys could not be released to their natural habitat and therefore would have needed to be either euthanized or provided with sanctuary. The former might have resulted in public outcry, and the latter would have been hugely expensive. As such, the capture and release of free-living monkeys and the accompanying narratives surrounding freedom arguably serve to benefit the laboratory, despite not necessarily being in the best interests of at least some of the animals, who simply did not survive the process.

The third case under consideration is that of a chimpanzee called Nim Chimpsky. Nim was the seventh baby taken from his mother, Caroline, at the Institute for Primate Studies (IPS) in the United States in 1973. He was sent to live with a human family in a New York townhouse. The family was given the mandate to raise Nim as they would a human child and to teach him American Sign Language. His story was well known at the time and was reported in major news outlets. Rather than focus on the way in which the experiment was received at the time, however, this case study is focused on the 2011 documentary *Project Nim*, which was adapted from the 2008 book *Nim*

Chimpsky: The Chimp Who Would Be Human.[14] The film is presented from the perspective of participants in the project and their family members. Although discussions of the rights and wrongs of the finer details of the experiment are raised throughout, wider moral discussion was notably absent of whether or not the experiment, which subjected Nim to a lifetime of captivity and many years without any contact with others of his own kind was justified. In fact, many of the participants appeared to believe that Nim had benefited from his upbringing in captivity. For example, although chimpanzees have a natural maternal dependency period of up to five years and Nim was removed from his mother at just two weeks old, the head of the experiment stated, in reference to the woman who looked after Nim in her New York home, that "a chimp could not have had a better mother."

When Nim was less than a year old, he was moved to a property owned by the university that was funding the research. The property had large grounds, and Nim was given opportunities to go outside—something he had had limited opportunity to do when housed in New York City. One of his carers said of his move to the new base that "he was free" there. After some time, Nim was moved back to IPS and then, to the horror of his previous carers, sold to the Laboratory for Experimental Medicine and Surgery in Primates (LEMSIP). Nim was not used in any invasive experiments, but his move to LEMSIP triggered a campaign to "free" him. A lawyer who wanted to take on Nim's case to get him out of LEMSIP based his proposed legal proceedings on the fact that Nim had been raised like a human child. The lawyer argued that for Nim the experience in the LEMSIP laboratory was worse than for the other chimpanzees housed there because he had had such a "privileged upbringing." References to Nim being "spoiled" and being a "spoiled child" were used throughout by his carers, implying that his handrearing in a human environment had been a form of pampering or benefit to him.

After a short campaign, Nim was removed from LEMSIP and moved to a "sanctuary," where he spent the remainder of his days. Much of his time was spent alone, and participants in the documentary criticized the standards at his new home initially. By the time Nim passed away from a heart attack at twenty-six

years old, he was living with two other chimpanzees. A carer who had worked with Nim when he was housed at IPS said of his final living arrangements, "It wasn't perfect, but it was pretty damn good." The final word in the documentary was given to a former member of the LEMSIP staff. The last words heard before the final credits are, "They will forgive you"—a statement made in relation to how forgiving animals were in light of their past treatment.

At a film screening in Manchester, England, in August 2011, which I attended,[15] producer Simon Chinn confirmed in a question-and-answer session that he had deliberately in the making of the film avoided addressing the ethical or animal-rights concerns surrounding Nim's treatment. Chinn told audience members that this was, in part, to ensure that he could secure the involvement of the relevant participants, who might not have agreed to be involved if the film was deemed to be overly critical. He said he wanted his audience to draw their own conclusions on the ethical and moral questions that the film raised. Thus, a conscious decision was made to deliberately omit discussion of ethical concerns.

The resulting narrative was one that was largely silent on Nim's captive state. It drew a bright line between the horror of Nim's captivity in a traditional vivisection laboratory and his "privileged" captive upbringing as part of the behavioral study. The film tended toward the idea of sanctuary as retribution, reinforced by the idea that the animals themselves would forgive past unkind treatment. This had the effect of presenting audiences with something of a happy ending.

An alternative view of Nim's story could be that he suffered the trauma of being removed from his mother, was raised in a completely unnatural environment, was given alcohol and marijuana by his carers, and spent years of his life without any contact with other chimpanzees and was, indeed, frightened when introduced to them. In his so-called sanctuary, which was a concrete and metal construction with little apparent enrichment and no foliage or green space, he spent most of a decade living alone before being joined in his final years by two other ex-laboratory chimpanzees. He then died at half his natural age. Nim was not subjected to invasive experiments, but his lifelong captivity arguably resulted in his welfare being severely compromised over many, many years as part of a behavioral study that lasted for just a few years before being closed down when funding was discontinued.

The final case study under consideration is that involving chimpanzees Leo and Hercules. The two chimpanzees are, at the time of this writing, being held at New Iberia Research Center, having been moved in early 2016 from the biomedical research center at State University of New York at Stony Brook. They have been the focus of a major legal challenge led by the Nonhuman Rights Project, a groundbreaking initiative that seeks legal rights for animals via court proceedings. Of the four cases under consideration in this discussion, the case of Leo and Hercules appears to offer the strongest example of how the ethical and welfare implications of lifelong captivity for nonhuman primates used in research are overlooked. It also presents sanctuary as directly related not just to restitution but to liberation, freedom, and rights.

The Nonhuman Rights Project describes its purpose on its website as follows: "It is the first and only organization petitioning courts to recognize that, based on existing scientific evidence, certain nonhuman animals—specifically great apes, dolphins, and elephants—are entitled to such basic legal rights as bodily liberty and integrity." It further defines "bodily liberty" as the right "not to be imprisoned."[16]

The organization explains that the process in cases such as Hercules and Leo's is as follows: "We argue that our first chimpanzee plaintiffs should be freed, then transferred to a sanctuary where they can live out their days with many other chimpanzees in an environment as close to the wild as is possible in North America." Finally, the Nonhuman Rights Project states, "We are asking the courts to recognize, for the first time, that these cognitively sophisticated, autonomous beings are legal persons who have the basic right to not be held in captivity."[17]

Here, sanctuary and freedom are clearly conflated, and the principles of "imprisonment" or "captivity" and "sanctuary" are promoted as mutually exclusive. According to the project's narrative, after the animals are freed, they will be moved to a sanctuary, where their right to "bodily liberty" will implicitly be upheld. But because a sanctuary is simply another (albeit arguably better-intentioned) form of "imprisonment" and is unarguably a form of captivity, the terminology used by the project can be considered somewhat problematic.

It seems highly unlikely that the members of the Nonhuman Rights Project hold a genuine belief that sanctuary is not a form of captivity. Rather, it can be speculated that because the project is dealing with complex principles of law, there is a need for its work to be presented in a way that helps those with little to no understanding of law or the principles of animal rights and ethics (particularly complex principles such as nonhuman personhood) understand clearly its objective. This perhaps inevitably means creating a simplified and clear narrative that allows people to effectively understand what the key objectives of the organization's work are, without the need to have a full understanding of the legal and ethical principles underpinning that work. However, in failing to properly address the fact that the chimpanzees' "freedom" from the laboratory means neither full restitution nor that they will have truly gained "bodily integrity," the project mirrors the narratives of some of the previous case studies. These previous examples, it has been argued, may serve the purpose of justifying ongoing harm to animals by manipulating the discourse surrounding sanctuary and freedom—the antithesis of what the Nonhuman Rights Project seeks to achieve. It is therefore argued that clarity could be offered on this point as part of the Nonhuman Rights Project's own narrative. At present, such clarification can be found nowhere within the group's website or publications.

Conclusions

This essay has considered four case studies relating to the use of nonhuman primates in experimentation. The case studies have provided an insight into how the concepts of captivity, freedom, retirement, and liberty are dealt with by those seeking an end to experimentation, those working within experimentation, and those who appear to have no clear interest in either position but who are instead exploring the issue as a matter of interest (in the case of *Project Nim*).

The case of the National Institutes of Health documented policymakers driving discourse on the provision of sanctuary and retirement, potentially as a result of a genuine belief that full restitution via sanctuary is possible or possibly as a deliberate attempt to justify the continued use of animals in invasive procedures. It may even be that, as suggested by some stakeholders at the time, there was never any real intention to provide sanctuary, but, rather, the intention was to create a holding facility for animals in the event that they were needed for future experiments. The case study surrounding the FIDIC center in Colombia provided an example of people who work as vivisectionists promoting narratives of "life after the laboratory" in terms of complete freedom and "life in the laboratory" as a situation where animals benefit from high welfare standards and the best care. These claims have been contradicted in part or in full by evidence from researchers and from my own firsthand experience. In the case of Nim the chimpanzee, his captors questioned many aspects of his treatment in retrospect but avoided questions surrounding his lifelong captivity, despite there being evidence within their own narrative accounts that he likely suffered as a result of it. Finally, the conflation of sanctuary, freedom, and "bodily liberty" and even the notion of sanctuary as something other than "captivity" has been considered in the work of the Nonhuman Rights Project.

Nondomesticated animals removed from laboratories almost certainly will live a better life in a good sanctuary than in a laboratory, but they will remain in captivity for their lifetimes and may suffer ongoing trauma, health issues, and behavioral problems as a result of this and their past treatment. The impact of these factors on their welfare should not be underestimated. Given that narratives surrounding sanctuary and freedom may be, knowingly or otherwise, manipulated by those seeking to justify ongoing animal experimentation, it can be concluded that there is a need for animal advocates to incorporate into their own narratives open and honest discussion surrounding the welfare and ethical impacts of captivity. Failure to do so may leave largely unchallenged the situation of animals, such as Nim, who are being held captive for purely behavioral research, while also serving to perpetuate the industry's own use of the concept of sanctuary or release as full restitution to justify the ongoing use of animals in experimentation or make it appear more palatable. In contrast, the incorporation of truthful narratives surrounding captivity and associated concepts of freedom may serve both to strengthen the call for an end to animal experimentation and to inform the public and key stakeholders of the lifelong suffering endured by those animals used in research.

Notes

1. Karen Emmerman, "Sanctuary, Not Remedy: The Problem of Captivity and the Need for Moral Repair," in *The Ethics of Captivity*, ed. Lori Gruen (New York: Oxford University Press, 2014), 217, 215.

2. Ibid., 217.

3. Stephen Ross, "Captive Chimpanzees," in *The Ethics of Captivity*, ed. Lori Gruen (New York: Oxford University Press, 2014), 57–76.

4. National Research Council, *Chimpanzees in Research: Strategies for Their Ethical Care, Management, and Use* (Washington, DC: National Academy of Sciences, 1997).

5. Chimpanzee Health, Improvement, Maintenance, and Protection Act (CHIMP Act, 2000), Public Law No. 106–551; Ross, "Captive Chimpanzees," 67.

6. William J. Clinton, "Statement on Signing the Chimpanzee Health Improvement, Maintenance, and Protection Act," December 20, 2000, *The American Presidency Project*, December 20, 2000, accessed May 8, 2015, http://www.presidency.ucsb.edu/ws/?pid=1263.

7. "Chimp Haven or NIH Holding Facility?" *Animal People*, January–February 2002, accessed May 8, 2015, http://www.animalpeoplenews.org/02/1/chimpHaven0102.html.

8. For full disclosure the author of the current chapter helped to found Fundación Entropika in 2006 and worked as part of the organization in Leticia until 2009.

9. Carlos Fernández, "El Día Que Patarroyo Casi Gana el Nobel," *Bocas*, March 29, 2014, accessed May 8, 2015, http://www.eltiempo.com/bocas/manuel-elkin-patarroyo-en-entrevista-con-revista-bocas/13748377.

10. Lisbeth Fog, "Row over Court Closure of Colombian Monkey Research Lab," *SciDev.Net*, August 7, 2014, accessed May 8, 2015, http://www.scidev.net/global/governance/news/colombian-monkey-research-lab.html.

11. Carlos Fernández, "Vacunas que salvarían a 17 millones de personas, en vilo por fallo," December 14, 2014, accessed May 8, 2015, http://www.eltiempo.com/archivo/documento/CMS-13286089. Quote translated by author from Spanish.

12. "Los Micos de Patarroyo: Cambio Revela Pruebas que Ponen en Aprietos al Científico por el Tráfico Ilegal de Especies para Su Centro Experimental de Leticia," *El Tiempo*, November 21, 2007, accessed May 8, 2015, http://www.eltiempo.com/archivo/documento-2013/CMS-3825952. Quote translated by author from Spanish.

13. Entropika, "Conservation Projects," no date, accessed July 31, 2015, http://www.entropika.org/en/projects.html.

14. *Project Nim*, DVD, dir. James Marsh, 100 minutes, New York: Red Box Films, Passion Pictures in association with

BBC Films (2011); Elizabeth Hess, *Nim Chimpsky: The Chimp Who Would Be Human* (New York: Bantam, 2008).

15. Screening, *Project Nim* (plus producer's question-and-answer session), The Cornerhouse, Manchester, August 11, 2011.

16. "Q&A about the Nonhuman Rights Project," *Nonhuman Rights Project*, no date, accessed March 9, 2016, http://www.nonhumanrightsproject.org/qa-about-the-nonhuman-rights-project/.

17. Ibid.

Bibliography

Chimpanzee Health, Improvement, Maintenance and Protection Act (CHIMP Act, 2000). Public Law No. 106–551. https://www.gpo.gov/fdsys/pkg/PLAW-106publ551/content-detail.html.

"Chimp Haven or NIH Holding Facility?" *Animal People*, January–February 2002. Accessed May 8, 2015. http://www.animalpeoplenews.org/02/1/chimpHaven0102.html.

Clinton, William J. "Statement on Signing the Chimpanzee Health Improvement, Maintenance, and Protection Act." December 20, 2000. *The American Presidency Project*, December 20, 2000. Accessed May 8, 2015. http://www.presidency.ucsb.edu/ws/?pid=1263.

Emmerman, Karen. "Sanctuary, Not Remedy: The Problem of Captivity and the Need for Moral Repair." In *The Ethics of Captivity*, edited by Lori Gruen, 213–30. New York: Oxford University Press, 2014.

Entropika. "Conservation Projects." Accessed July 31, 2015. http://www.entropika.org/en/projects.html.

Fernández, Carlos. "El Día Que Patarroyo Casi Gana el Nobel." *Bocas*, March 29, 2014. Accessed May 8, 2015. http://www.eltiempo.com/bocas/manuel-elkin-patarroyo-en-entrevista-con-revista-bocas/13748377.

———. "Vacunas que salvarían a 17 millones de personas, en vilo por fallo." December 14, 2014. Accessed May 8, 2015. http://www.eltiempo.com/archivo/documento/CMS-13286089.

Fog, Lisbeth. "Row over Court Closure of Colombian Monkey Research Lab." *SciDev.Net*, August 7, 2014. Accessed May 8, 2015. http://www.scidev.net/global/governance/news/colombian-monkey-research-lab.html.

Hess, Elizabeth. *Nim Chimpsky: The Chimp Who Would Be Human*. New York: Bantam, 2008.

National Research Council. Institute for Animal Research. *Chimpanzees in Research: Strategies for Their Ethical Care, Management, and Use*. Washington, DC: National Academy of Sciences, 1997.

Project Nim. DVD. Directed by James Marsh. 100 minutes. New York: Red Box Films, Passion Pictures in association with BBC Films, 2011.

"Q&A about the Nonhuman Rights Project." *Nonhuman Rights Project*, no date. Accessed March 9, 2016. http://www.nonhumanrightsproject.org/qa-about-the-nonhuman-rights-project/.

Ross, Stephen. "Captive Chimpanzees." In *The Ethics of Captivity*, edited by Lori Gruen, 57–76. New York: Oxford University Press, 2014.

When Harry Meets Harry

An Ethical Assessment of Harry Harlow's Maternal Deprivation Experiments

Kurt Remele

HARRY FREDERICK HARLOW was born Harry Israel in 1905 in the city of Fairfield, Iowa, in the American Midwest.[1] He received his PhD in psychology from Stanford University in 1930. Due to the widespread anti-Semitism of the time, Harry changed his blatantly Jewish-sounding surname to Harlow, his father's middle name, at the suggestion of one of his professors. After graduation he accepted an academic position at the University of Wisconsin–Madison. As an experimental psychologist, he counted on doing biomedical and behavioral research on rats but ended up with monkeys. From the 1950s onward, Harlow became both famous and infamous for his various excessively harsh and cruel experiments with rhesus monkeys, also called rhesus macaques. He separated quite a number of monkeys from their mothers at birth and reared them with surrogate cloth or wire mothers. Moreover, he examined the effects of partial or total isolation on rhesus macaques.

According to his biographer Deborah Blum, "in his prime, Harlow was almost universally acclaimed. He was a scientific hero, one of those rare researchers who could charm both his colleagues and the general public."[2] In 1958 he was elected president of the American Psychological Association. He received numerous awards for his scientific achievements, among them the National Medal of Science in 1967. Gradually and steadily, though, his research started to be criticized for its cruelty to a large number of rhesus macaques and its questionable benefit to human

beings. Harlow and his monkey experiments were causal and crucial for the rise of the animal-liberation movement. To animal activists, his research clearly was sadism cloaked in scientific jargon and false promises of aid to humans.

The first part of this essay is an overview of Harlow's most important and most contested monkey studies. The second part analyzes Harlow's research from the perspective of a type of animal ethics that is rooted in both philosophical ethical theory and social psychological science. The third and final part compares Harry Harlow to Harry Lime, the racketeer and diluter of penicillin from the famous 1949 movie *The Third Man* and from Graham Greene's subsequently published novella of the same title.[3] By doing this, I intend to demonstrate both the obvious differences and the surprising commonalities between the real person and famous scientist Harry Harlow and the fictional character and vile criminal Harry Lime.

Harlow's Experiments on Rhesus Monkeys

Harlow's maternal-deprivation experiments can be divided into the categories of affection experiments, isolation experiments, and separation experiments,[4] although the demarcation lines between them are a bit blurred. Let's start with the affection category or, as Harlow called them himself, his experiments on "the nature of love."[5]

Terry-Cloth Mothers and Bare-Wire Mothers

Almost every introductory course in psychology will cover Harry Harlow's affection experiments with newborn or—to use the technical term—neonatal rhesus monkeys. Harlow's affection research was triggered by his random discovery that newborn monkeys who had been deprived of their mothers became psychologically attached to cloth pads or cloth diapers that were used to cover the floors of their cages. Harlow resolved to discover whether touch and cuddling—he used the term "contact comfort"—was desired by the baby monkey even more than food. Two different surrogate mothers were designed and constructed: One was a cloth surrogate mother. In his presidential lecture "The Nature of Love" at the annual convention of the American Psychological Association in 1958, Harlow described her as "a block of wood, covered with sponge rubber, and sheathed in tan cotton terry cloth . . . with a light bulb behind her [that] radiated heat."[6] The other surrogate mother was a bare-wire construction, although she also was warmed by an electric light placed inside her.

Among the diverse experiments Harlow conducted with newborn monkeys, the one that pitted a cloth mother without a feeding milk bottle against a wire mother providing milk became the most famous. Within days after the separation from their real mothers, the baby macaques transferred their affections to the cloth surrogates, which they hung on to and cuddled. The cloth mother, however, had no milk, so when the little monkeys got hungry, they darted over to the wire mothers. Yet, after drinking they immediately ran back to the comfort and safety of the cloth mothers. Harlow recorded the mean amount of time the monkeys spent nursing versus cuddling. According to Harlow, the imbalance was "so great as to suggest that the primary function of nursing as an affectional variable is that of insuring frequent and intimate body contact of the infant with the mother."[7] This insight, of course, was a severe blow to the behaviorist assumptions on child-rearing that prevailed at the time. Today, however, we are aware that Harlow grossly underestimated the value and importance of nursing itself.

What is true for rhesus monkeys, Harlow concluded, would also be true for other animals. His article is interspersed with short poems that praise the need of every baby animal for physical contact: hippo, rhino, elephant, and even crocodile and snake. Harlow then went one step further in the practical application of his monkey experiments: from his discoveries with the monkeys, Harlow drew decisive conclusions for newborn human beings. In his distinctive phrasing, "the baby, human or monkey, if it is to survive, must clutch at more than a straw," and "certainly, man cannot live by milk alone."[8]

Although Harlow came across to many of his students and colleagues as a nice and humorous guy, a darker side of him is already present and recognizable in these early studies on maternal deprivation. The experiments were quite stressful and psychologically damaging to the baby monkeys. In fact, it later became apparent that inanimate surrogate mothers were not at all sufficient to prevent monkey infants from becoming psychologically disturbed. Moreover, the monkey mothers, whose children were taken away right after birth, undoubtedly grieved over their loss.

Bare-Wire Cages and "Rape Racks"

The researchers at the University of Wisconsin psychological primate laboratory distinguished two types of isolation conditions: "partial isolation" and "total isolation." Partial isolation (or semisocial isolation) "involves rearing infants alone in bare-wire cages. The infants can see and hear other monkeys, but not touch them. . . . 'Total isolation' involves rearing infants in isolation chambers that exclude all forms of interaction between monkeys."[9]

Fifty-six rhesus infants were subjected to partial isolation for twenty-eight to twenty-nine months during the early 1960s. It is hardly surprising that these experiments produced monkeys who were severely disturbed. Their abnormalities included blank staring; stereotyped, repetitive circling of cages; and self-mutilation of limbs. In a considerable number of instances, the injuries caused by self-mutilation were so severe that the animals had to be killed or "sacrificed,"[10] which is scientific jargon for slaughtering laboratory animals. The total isolation experiments, in which monkeys were housed in stainless steel chambers from a few hours after birth until three, six, or twelve months old, had even more dramatic negative effects on the survivors.

In follow-up studies, Harlow and his colleagues examined the maternal behavior of females who had been deprived of their own mothers throughout infancy. Many of these "motherless mothers," as Harlow termed them, were unable to be in contact with other monkeys, let alone sexual contact with males, and therefore were impregnated while restrained on a device that Harlow had designed and given the graphic name of "rape rack."[11] Most of the motherless mothers ignored and neglected their infants; some even abused them—for example, by crushing the infant's face to the floor or chewing off the infant's feet and fingers.

"Pits of Despair" and "Iron Maidens"

One of the alleged rationales of Harlow's so-called separation experiments, which were extremely cruel and highly bizarre, was the creation of animal models for human depression, a psychological state Harlow suffered from himself during his second wife's experience with cancer and after her death in 1971, depression for which he was treated at the prestigious Mayo Clinic in Minnesota.

Because depression in humans has often been characterized as a state of helplessness and hopelessness and a sense of being trapped in a well of despair, Harlow and Stephen Suomi, one of his doctoral students, designed a device that was termed the "well of despair" or "pit of despair."[12] It was shaped like a narrow inverted pyramid, wider at the mesh-covered top and slanting downward. It was also described as a vertical chamber with stainless-steel sides sloping inward to form a rounded bottom. According to Blum, "most of the chambered monkeys were at least three months old. . . . The whole point was to take animals who had an established bond—and then break it."[13] The unprompted separation from others and the consistent incarceration in a vertical chamber, sometimes up to six weeks at a time,[14] devastated the animals: "you could take a perfectly happy monkey, drop it into the chamber, and bring out a perfectly hopeless animal within half a week."[15]

Harlow and his fellow researchers also devised other methods of inducing depression in monkeys. Infants were reared with cloth surrogate mothers whose bodies could be made so cold that the little monkeys got scared and let go of them. Other versions of these evil mothers attacked the infant monkeys with compressed air, vigorous shaking, or sharp brass spikes that were ejected over all of the ventral surface of the their bodies. The latter were termed "iron maidens" by Harlow.[16] He observed that no matter what the torture, afterward the little monkeys returned to their mothers and clung to them.

William Mason, one of Harlow's students, admits that his teacher kept his experiments "going to the point where it was clear to many people that the work was really violating ordinary sensibilities, that anybody with respect for life or people would find this offensive."[17] It's high time for an ethical assessment of professor Harry Harlow's rhesus monkey experiments.

Philosophical Ethics and Social Psychology

To his fans, Harry Harlow was a twentieth-century hero, a scientific pioneer whose work on monkey cognition and social development, contrary to the prevailing behaviorist thinking of the time, fostered a view of these animals as having rich subjective lives filled with intention and emotion. Even more so, Harlow's fan community is convinced that by his monkey research on "contact comfort," he altered the way we raise our children, for at the time of his surrogate mother experiments, cuddling children was regarded critically by most health professionals. Psychologist John Watson, for example, had argued that parental affection should be withheld in response to any behavior one did not want to reinforce. Attending to a crying baby would reinforce needy, whiny behavior and spoil a child. To his critics, however, Harlow was an opportunist, subjecting animals to the most cruel experiments to boost his own fame, and a sadist, who by his own admission despised cats, dogs, and monkeys and cared only whether a monkey would turn out a property he could publish.[18] Besides, his experiments were of little or no scientific value.

If you are a strict animal-rights advocate and/or are convinced that scientific experiments on sentient animals are as unjustified as scientific experiments on human beings, your ethical verdict on Harlow and his colleagues at the University of Wisconsin psychological primate laboratory is quick and clear: causing extreme suffering to sentient fellow creatures such as rhesus monkeys to satisfy intellectual curiosity and scientific research is intrinsically wrong and morally illicit. Such a rigorous deontological rejection of animal experiments is argumentatively made more accessible when it can be shown that viable alternatives to animal models do indeed exist. With regard to mother-child attachment, this is the case: the importance of maternal contact had already been conclusively shown two decades before Harlow by research on the effects of human infants' and young children's separation from their mothers in hospitals and institutional care, research done by psychoanalysts John Bowlby and René Spitz. (Due to cultural and era-specific circumstances, these psychoanalysts did not explore and know of good "father-child interactions as a secure [filial] base for exploration and a safe haven in times of distress.")[19]

From a teleological ethical position, in which all the consequences of an action are weighed, further arguments against Harlow's experiments can be made: what if Harlow's experiments were not only unnecessary, unsubstantiated, and of no benefit to human beings but also in some respects even scientifically misleading? Both a profound mistrust of Harlow's research findings and a rejection of the extreme violence against sentient creatures taking place in his experiments are crucial to utilitarian ethicist Peter Singer's strong disapproval of Harlow's research. In his book *Animal Liberation*, Singer points out that Gene Sackett, a former student of Harlow, continued deprivation studies after leaving Wisconsin, at the University of Washington. Sackett studied rhesus macaques, pigtail macaques, and crab-eating macaques. Sackett, though, found considerable differences in the personal and social behavior of the different monkey species and started to question the generality of behavior in isolation across primate species. Singer justly concludes, "If there are differences even among closely related species of monkeys, generalizations from monkeys to humans must be far more questionable."[20] How true. William Mason, a former student and coworker of Harlow, discovered in later studies with South American titi monkeys that infant titi monkeys have a much closer relationship to their fathers than to their mothers. The infants are more upset by separation from their fathers than by separation from their mothers. This is, in fact, quite different from rhesus macaques, where the infants cling fiercely to their mothers.[21]

In his 2007 book *The Lucifer Effect: How Good People Turn Evil*, US social psychologist Philip Zimbardo mentions that if people behave violently, one often "searches for sadistic personality traits."[22] This personal or dispositional perspective, as Zimbardo calls it, is not entirely wrong, yet Zimbardo insists that it ought to be complemented by a situational and systemic understanding of our actions. Indeed, violent and inhumane treatment of animals sometimes is approached too exclusively as a matter of individual choice and character flaws, with the social dimension thereby neglected. In the case of Harlow's experiments, one may point out the situational context and historic fact that for a long time cruelty to animals was, as the Oxford Centre report puts it, "defined, wholly or largely, in terms of stabbing, kicking, or hitting another creature, for example. That it was possible to harm animals by emotional or psychological means was almost entirely absent from the notion of cruelty as previously defined."[23] This tradition might have contributed to making Harlow less sensitive to the suffering he caused. With regard to a systemic approach, one has to point out that scientific academic research by and large to this day is characterized by using animals without a qualm. Whoever questions animal experiments is confronting, as the Canadian scholar and cultural critic Henry Giroux calls it, "the military-industrial-academic complex."[24] (Zimbardo, on the other hand, uses the equally provocative term "military-corporate-religious complex.")[25] Confrontation with and opposition to the ruling academic elite, though, are not conductive to a career in academia.

According to Zimbardo, the situational and systemic influences we experience are underrated. Yet, Zimbardo also insists "that attempting to understand the situational and systemic contributions to any individual's behavior does not excuse the person or absolve him or her from responsibility in engaging in immoral, illegal, or evil deeds."[26] This statement applies both to actors and agents and to bystanders. "No one said stop," Marc Bekoff remarked with regard to the latter. "Harry Harlow was very famous and you don't tell famous people to stop."[27]

When Harry Harlow Meets Harry Lime

For a final ethical assessment of Harry Harlow, I use the device of a comparison of characters, which ethicists are likely to assign to the field of virtue ethics: I compare Harry Harlow, award-winning scientist from the University of Wisconsin–Madison, with Harry Lime, despicable racketeer from the classic movie *The Third Man* and from Graham Greene's subsequently published novella of the same title. To satisfy his intellectual curiosity and to succeed in academia, Harry Harlow became responsible for the suffering and deaths of numerous infant rhesus monkeys in midwestern laboratories. To make money, Harry Lime stole penicillin and sold it in a diluted form, thereby causing the deaths of numerous children from meningitis in postwar Vienna. Of course, Harry Harlow was a real person and an acclaimed scientist. His research was both legal and popular. Harry Lime, on the other hand, is a fictional character and a vile criminal hunted by the American occupation force in postwar Vienna. What they have in common, though, is an alarming, possibly pathological detachment from the suffering and deaths of their victims. When Harry Lime joins his old friend Rollo Martins for a ride on the Ferris wheel in the Vienna Prater, Martins asks him whether he has ever seen any of his victims. Harry replies, "Don't be melodramatic, Rollo. Look down there. . . . Would you really feel any pity if one of those dots stopped moving—forever? If I said you can have twenty thousand pounds for every dot that stops, would you really, old man, tell me to keep my money—without hesitation? Or would you calculate how many dots you could afford to spare? Free of income tax, old man. Free of income tax."[28]

In an article published in 1997 about Harry Harlow and his work, his former graduate student John P. Gluck, an emeritus professor of psychology at the University of New Mexico, for ethical reasons rejects "any organizational scheme that limits scientists' actual contact with the impact of their work on the animals."[29] Direct observation, on the other hand, according to Gluck, may incite the scientists' empathic potential.

The Oxford Centre report featured in the first part of this book refers to the psychological distance from events in the laboratory that brings the scientist to turn a blind eye to the animals' "struggling, cries, bleeding, repetitive behavior, moans, agitation, anxiety, pain, fear, depression, and vomiting."[30]

Gluck, who collaborated with him on rhesus monkey experiments, is not this kind of scientist, not anymore. He is one of the signatories of the Oxford Centre's report, which rejects all animal research as unethical. At a time when academia, ethics, and religion by and large still give their blessing to the use of animals in research, even research quite similar to Harry Harlow's, both human and nonhuman animals need people like John Gluck.

Notes

1. For biographical details of Harry Harrow's life, see Deborah Blum, *Love at Goon Park: Harry Harlow and the Science of Affection* (New York: Berkley Books, 2002).

2. Deborah Blum, *Monkey Wars* (New York: Oxford University Press, 1994), 81.

3. Graham Greene, *The Third Man and the Fallen Idol* (Harmondsworth, UK: Penguin, 1979), first published by Heinemann, 1950.

4. Martin L. Stephens, *Maternal Deprivation: Experiments in Psychology, A Critique of Animal Models*, report for the American Anti-Vivisection Society, the National Anti-Vivisection Society, and the New England Anti-Vivisection Society, 1986, accessed August 31, 2015, http://neavs.org/docs/NEAVS_-_Maternal_Deprivation_-_A_Critique_of_Animal_Models.pdf. The second category of experiments is called "deprivation experiments" by Stephens instead of "isolation experiments," the term I prefer.

5. Harry F. Harlow, "The Nature of Love," *Classics in the History of Psychology*, March 2000, accessed August 31, 2015, http://psychclassics.yorku.ca/Harlow/love.htm, first published in *American Psychologist* 13 (1958): 673–85.

6. Ibid., 3.

7. Ibid., 5.

8. Ibid., 2, 5.

9. Stephens, *Maternal Deprivation*, 18–19.

10. Alison Christy, "Sacrifice: When Scientists Have to Kill," *LabLit.com*, July 6, 2008, accessed August 31, 2015, http://www.lablit.com/article/394.

11. Stephens, *Maternal Deprivation*, 23.

12. Ibid., 44.

13. Blum, *Love at Goon Park*, 219.

14. See Peter Singer, *Animal Liberation*, 2nd ed. with new preface (London: Pimlico, 1995), 34; Blum, *Love at Goon Park*, 219.

15. Blum, *Love at Goon Park*, 219.

16. Lauren Slater, "Monkey Love," *Boston Globe*, March 21, 2004, accessed August 31, 2015, http://www.boston.com/news/globe/ideas/articles/2004/03/21/monkey_love/?page=full.

17. Blum, *Monkey Wars*, 96.

18. Ibid., 92.

19. Glen Palm, "Attachment Theory and Fathers, " *Journal of Family Theory and Review* 6 (2014): 294, accessed August 31, 2015, http://onlinelibrary.wiley.com/doi/10.1111/jftr.12045/pdf.

20. Singer, *Animal Liberation*, 35. See also Stephens, *Maternal Deprivation*, 3.

21. See Bloom, *Monkey Wars*, 101.

22. Philip Zimbardo, *The Lucifer Effect: How Good People Turn Evil* (London: Rider, 2009), 7.

23. See section 1.2, "The Old Debate," in part 1 of the current volume.

24. Henry A. Giroux, *The University in Chains: Confronting the Military-Industrial-Academic Complex* (Boulder: Paradigm, 2007).

25. Zimbardo, *Lucifer Effect*, 10.

26. Ibid., xi.

27. Quoted in Blum, *Love at Goon Park*, 303.

28. Greene, *Third Man*, 104.

29. John P. Gluck, "Harry F. Harlow and Animal Research: Reflection on the Ethical Paradox," *Ethics and Behavior* 7 (1997): 149–61.

30. See "The Distorting Power of Language" in section 1.6, "The Problem of Institutionalization," in part 1 of the current volume.

Bibliography

Blum, Deborah. *Love at Goon Park: Harry Harlow and the Science of Affection*. New York: Berkley Books, 2002.

———. *Monkey Wars*. New York: Oxford University Press, 1994.

Christy, Alison. "Sacrifice: When Scientists Have to Kill." *LabLit. com*. July 6, 2008. Accessed August 31, 2015. http://www.lablit.com/article/394.

Giroux, Henry A. *The University in Chains: Confronting the Military-Industrial-Academic Complex*. Boulder: Paradigm, 2007.

Gluck, John P. "Harry F. Harlow and Animal Research: Reflection on the Ethical Paradox." *Ethics and Behavior* 7 (1997): 149–61.

Greene, Graham. *The Third Man and the Fallen Idol*. Harmondsworth, UK: Penguin, 1979. First published by Heinemann, 1950.

Harlow, Harry F. "The Nature of Love." *Classics in the History of Psychology*, March 2000. Accessed August 31, 2015. http://psychclassics.yorku.ca/Harlow/love.htm. First published in *American Psychologist* 13 (1958): 673–85.

Palm, Glen. "Attachment Theory and Fathers." *Journal of Family Theory and Review* 6 (2014): 282–97. Accessed August 31, 2015. http://onlinelibrary.wiley.com/doi/10.1111/jftr.12045/pdf.

Singer, Peter. *Animal Liberation*. 2nd ed. with new preface. London: Pimlico, 1995.

Stephens, Martin L. *Maternal Deprivation: Experiments in Psychology. A Critique of Animal Models*. Report for the American Anti-Vivisection Society, the National Anti-Vivisection Society, and the New England Anti-Vivisection Society, 1986. Accessed August 31, 2015. http://neavs.org/docs/NEAVS_-_Maternal_Deprivation_-_A_Critique_of_Animal_Models.pdf.

Zimbardo, Philip. *The Lucifer Effect: How Good People Turn Evil*. London: Rider, 2007.

About the Editors, Contributors, and Members of the Working Group

AYSHA AKHTAR (member of the working group) is a board-certified neurologist and public health specialist. She works for the Office of Counterterrorism and Emerging Threats, US Food and Drug Administration. She specializes in biosurveillance, medical ethics, and understanding the crossroads between animal welfare and public health. She writes here in a personal capacity. She has served on several institutional review boards for the protection of human subjects in research. She has published numerous letters and opinion-editorial pieces and has been interviewed by major newspapers, scientific journals, and radio and TV news programs. She also appeared in the television show *30 Days* produced by Morgan Spurlock discussing medical research. She has been published in peer-reviewed journals, including the *Lancet, Pediatrics, Reviews in the Neurosciences*, and the *American Journal of Preventive Medicine*. Her book *Animals and Public Health: Why Treating Animals Better Is Critical to Human Welfare* (2011) examines how the treatment of animals impacts human health.

JARROD BAILEY (contributor) is a senior research scientist at Cruelty Free International. For the past thirteen years, he has applied his knowledge and expertise toward evaluating the scientific validity and human relevance of animal models in biomedical research and testing. He was a chief author of a substantial scientific petition submitted to the US Food and Drug Administration by a coalition of organizations requesting that the FDA require scientists to use valid nonanimal methods in research and testing in place of animal methods, and he has submitted scientific evidence to a variety of British and European inquiries into the validity of animal research, some of which has been published in peer-reviewed scientific journals.

MARK H. BERNSTEIN (member of the working group) holds the Joyce and Edward E. Brewer Chair in Applied Ethics at Purdue University. He specializes in animal ethics, more specifically in the issues of animals' moral status and the extent, scope, and content of human obligations to nonhuman animals. In addition to working on articles in these areas, he is writing a book arguing that both the considerability of nonhuman animals and the value of the lives of nonhuman animals are as significant as those of their human counterparts. His books include *Fatalism* (1992), *On Moral Considerability* (1998), *Without a Tear* (2004), and *The Moral Equality of Humans and Animals* (2015).

NEDIM C. BUYUKMIHCI (contributor) is an emeritus professor of veterinary medicine at the University of California School of Veterinary Medicine at Davis. He is board-certified in ophthalmology by the American College of Veterinary Ophthalmologists. His research interests include ethics, retinal disease, and ophthalmic pathology.

DARREN CALLEY (member of the working group) is a lecturer in law at the University of Essex and the director of the university's animal welfare and wildlife law undergraduate program. He was awarded an LLB in 2002 and a PhD in 2009 from the University of Essex for his research into the manner in which restrictive international trade measures can be employed in the fight against the effects of high-seas fishing practices that impact marine-dependent species, and in 2011 he published his first book on this subject, *Market Denial and International Fisheries Regulation: The Targeted and Effective Use of Trade Measures against the Flag of Convenience Fishing Industry*. He has published numerous articles on the subject of animal protection law, including most recently "Developing a Common Law of Animal Welfare" (2011), "The Aggregation of Suffering in the Regulatory Context: Scientific Experimentation, Animals, and Necessity" (2013), and "The International Regulation of the Food Market: Precedents and Challenges" (2013).

JODEY CASTRICANO (member of the working group) is an associate professor of English and cultural studies at the University of British Columbia, Okanagan, Canada. A scholar in the history of ideas of the nineteenth century as well as a lifelong animal rights advocate, she has turned her research toward the ethical obligations that humans have toward their nonhuman counterparts. Her collection of essays, to which she is also a contributor, is titled *Animal Subjects: An Ethical Reader in a Posthuman World* (2008) and is concerned with the lag in the field of cultural studies, where critiques of racism, sexism, and classism have radically changed the face of the humanities and social sciences but which also has historically withheld the question of ethical treatment from nonhuman animals. In this regard, she organized the first panel ("The Question of the Animal: Why Now?") of its kind at the Canadian Association of Cultural Studies to critique the division between human and nonhuman animals in this field.

GRACE CLEMENT (member of the working group) is a professor of philosophy at Salisbury University in Maryland, where she teaches a wide variety of courses related to animals, feminism, the history of ethics,

human nature, modern philosophy, and logic. She is especially interested in questions of animal ethics as they relate to fundamental questions about the nature and boundaries of morality, and she has written on the roles of justice and care in human moral relations to nonhuman animals and on questions about human-animal friendship and animal moral agency. Her publications include a book on feminist ethics, *Care, Autonomy, and Justice: Feminism and the Ethic of Care* (1996), and a number of articles on animals and ethics appearing in journals such as *Between the Species* and the *Journal of Animal Ethics* and in anthologies such as *The Feminist Care Tradition in Animal Ethics* (2007).

LYDIA DE TIENDA (member of the working group) is a Japan Society for the Promotion of Science postdoctoral research fellow in the Department of Philosophy at Hokkaido University. She graduated with degrees in both philosophy and law and received her PhD in philosophy from the University of Valencia. Her doctoral dissertation focuses on the work of Martha Nussbaum and her capabilities approach. She has published various articles in peer-reviewed journals and book chapters in academic books, including "How to Evaluate Justice?" and "La noción plural de sujeto de justicia," and has presented papers at international conferences at the University of Tübingen, Hokkaido University, and Trento University/Complutense University. She is working on a research project on the correlations among capabilities, emotions, and values. She is deeply interested in examining the epistemological role of compassion in relation to justice for especially vulnerable groups, in particular nonhuman animals.

SAMUAL A. GARNER (contributor) is a bioethicist and scholar. His interests include research ethics and animal ethics. He holds a master's degree in bioethics from the University of Pennsylvania and possesses numerous years of professional experience in the field.

LAWRENCE A. HANSEN (member of the working group) is a professor of neuroscience and pathology at the University of California, San Diego (UCSD). He received his bachelor of arts degree in English literature in 1974 from North Central College in

Naperville, Illinois, and was awarded a medical degree in 1977 from Loyola University Stritch School of Medicine in Maywood, Illinois. Following an internship in psychiatry at Loyola in Maywood, he spent four years in combined anatomic and clinical pathology training, also at Loyola. He followed this with three years of neuropathology residency at Emory University in Atlanta, Georgia, and then went to UCSD for a two-year fellowship in geriatric neuropathology and dementia. After an additional year of surgical pathology fellowship at William Beaumont Hospital in Royal Oak, Michigan, he joined the faculty at the UCSD School of Medicine in the departments of neurosciences and pathology in 1988. His research remains focused on the pathology and pathogenesis of dementing illnesses, in particular Lewy body diseases and Alzheimer's disease, in which his work is very well known. He led the neuropathology core of the Alzheimer's Disease Research Center based in the UCSD Department of Neurosciences for twenty-five years. He is also an attending on the clinical neuropathology service at UCSD, working with neurosurgeons and neuro-oncologists on brain tumor diagnosis and treatment.

ROBYN HEDERMAN (contributor) is an associate fellow of the Oxford Centre for Animal Ethics and the principal law clerk for a New York State Supreme Court justice. She has worked on various publications on behalf of the Animal Law Committee of the New York City Bar Association, assisted with the publication "Reporting Suspected Animal Cruelty and Neglect in New York State," and contributed to the search-and-seizure section on animal fighting of *Prosecuting Animal Fighting and Live Depictions: Legal Issues under New York and Federal Law.* Her research interests include the commonalities between animal advocacy and other nineteenth-century reform movements in the United States.

LISA JOHNSON (member of the working group) is an associate professor at the University of Puget Sound, where she teaches environmental law and animal law. She received her PhD from Portland State University in public affairs and policy, with a dissertation in political theory. She received her juris doctorate from the Northwestern School of Law of Lewis and Clark College, along with a certificate in environmental and natural resources law. She received her MFA from the Rainier Writing Workshop at Pacific Lutheran University. She received her MPA from Indiana University's School of Public and Environmental Affairs, with a focus on international environmental policy. Her BA in history is from Indiana University. She is the author of *Power, Knowledge, Animals* (2012). Her primary research interests include the legal status of animals, religion and animals as the former has informed political and secular modern thought, moral theory relating to animals, and animal ethics.

ROBERT PATRICK STONE LAZO (contributor) is an associate fellow of the Oxford Centre for Animal Ethics. His research interests include the philosophy of science, Hellenistic and Roman philosophy, and animal ethics. His articles include "Lucretius' Venus and Epicurean Compassion toward Nondomesticated Animals" in the *Journal of Animal Ethics.*

ANDREW LINZEY (coeditor, contributor, and member of the working group) is director of the Oxford Centre for Animal Ethics, an honorary research fellow at St. Stephen's House, Oxford, and a member of the Faculty of Theology at the University of Oxford. He is a visiting professor of animal theology at the University of Winchester and a professor of animal ethics at the Graduate Theological Foundation in Indiana. He is the author or editor of more than twenty books, including *Animal Theology* (1994), *Why Animal Suffering Matters* (2009), and *The Global Guide to Animal Protection* (2013). In 2001, he was awarded a DD (doctor of divinity) degree by the archbishop of Canterbury in recognition of his "unique and massive pioneering work at a scholarly level in the area of the theology of creation with particular reference to the rights and welfare of God's sentient creatures." This is the highest award that the archbishop can bestow on a theologian and the first time it has been awarded for theological work on animals.

CLAIR LINZEY (coeditor, contributor, and member of the working group) is deputy director of the Oxford Centre for Animal Ethics. She holds an MA in

UNIVERSITY OF WINCHESTER
LIBRARY

theological studies from the University of St Andrews and an MTS from Harvard Divinity School. She is currently pursuing a doctorate at the University of St Andrews on the ecological theology of Leonardo Boff with special consideration of the place of animals. She is associate editor of the *Journal of Animal Ethics* and associate editor of the Palgrave Macmillan Animal Ethics Series. She is also director of the annual Oxford Animal Ethics Summer School.

LES MITCHELL (member of the working group) is the director of the Hunterstoun Centre of the University of Fort Hare, South Africa. He gained a doctorate at Rhodes University in Grahamstown for his dissertation titled "Discourses and the Oppression of Non-human Animals: A Critical Realist Account." He has worked in pathology, community health, and education in the United Kingdom, Tanzania, Zambia, Zimbabwe, Malawi, and South Africa, where he taught sciences in a township school in Grahamstown. His master's dissertation from the University of Malawi is titled "The Relevance of the Malawian MSCE Science Syllabus to the Lives of Young Malawians." He gives talks at schools and has made a number of presentations at Rhodes University, where he is a member of the Ethics Committee, and at the Ethics Society of South Africa. He organized the Hunterstoun Symposium on Nonhuman Animals, the first of its kind in southern Africa. His research interests are critical realism, nonhuman animals, discourses, power in society, genocide, moral disengagement, and alternatives to violence.

KATHERINE MORRIS (member of the working group) is a supernumerary fellow in philosophy at Mansfield College at the University of Oxford. Her special interests include phenomenology (particularly of the human body), Descartes, Merleau-Ponty, Sartre, and Wittgenstein. Her DPhil thesis discusses Freud and Sartre, and she recently completed an MPhil in medical anthropology, with a thesis on cosmetic surgery, gender, and embodiment. She is the author of *Descartes' Dualism* (with Gordon Baker, 1996), *Sartre* (2008), and *Sartre on the Body* (2009).

KAY PEGGS (contributor and member of the working group) is honorary professor of sociology at Kingston University, a visiting fellow at the University of Portsmouth, and a fellow of the Oxford Centre for Animal Ethics. She has contributed to books about human-animal studies, and her articles have appeared in *Sociology, Sociological Review*, the *Journal of Animal Ethics*, and *Society and Animals*. Her recent book *Animals in Sociology* was published in 2012. She is working currently on a single-authored book about experiments, animal bodies, and human values and on a coauthored book about consuming animals, environment, ethics, and lifestyle choices. Peggs is coeditor of *Observation Methods* (2013) and *Critical Social Research Ethics* (in press), both with Barry Smart and Joseph Burridge.

SIMON PULLEYN (contributor) is an independent scholar. He has published two books: *Prayer in Greek Religion* (1997) and *Homer: Iliad I with Introduction, Translation, and Commentary* (2000) and has written a number of articles and reviews about classics, law, and canon law. He is currently writing a book about Homer's *Odyssey*. He is a fellow of the Royal Historical Society and of the Oxford Centre for Animal Ethics.

CARLOS FREDERICO RAMOS DE JESUS (contributor) is a lawyer and PhD candidate at São Paulo University (USP, Brazil) Law School. He coordinates the USP Law School's study group on ethics and animal rights, Grupo de Estudos de Ética e Direito Animal. His main research field is animal rights. His book *John Rawls* was published in 2011. He has also written papers on normative theory and human rights.

KURT REMELE (contributor) is an associate professor of ethics and Catholic social thought at the University of Graz, Austria. He was a visiting professor at the University of Minnesota in Minneapolis and at Gonzaga University in Spokane and is a fellow of the Oxford Centre for Animal Ethics. He has voiced his concern for animals in academic journals, newspaper articles, and lectures and on radio and television. His most recent book is *Die Würde des Tieres ist unantastbar: Eine neue christliche Tierethik* (Animal dignity is inviolable: A new Christian animal ethics) (Kevelaer, 2016).

FRANCES MARGARET CECILIA ROBINSON (member of the working group) graduated from the University of Glasgow Veterinary College in 1971 with a degree in veterinary medicine and surgery. From 1971 to 1980, she worked in private veterinary practice in Glasgow, Epsom, and the Isle of Arran, and from 1981 to 1986, she worked for the PDSA in Nottingham. In 2000 she graduated with a BA in philosophy and environmental management from the University of Keele. In 2001 she was awarded an MA in values and the environment from the University of Lancaster, with a dissertation titled "The Relevance of Chaos to Environmental Ethics." She returned to the University of Lancaster to research the relevance of complex adaptive systems to environmental ethics—with particular focus on the epistemological basis for the use of animals in scientific experimentation. The study was multidisciplinary in nature, and she graduated with an MPhil in 2011. Her thesis was titled "Animal Experimentation, Complexity, and Animal Ethics."

JOHN ROSSI (contributor) is an assistant professor at the Drexel University School of Public Health and the codirector of the school's program in public health ethics and history. His research areas include public health ethics, research ethics, animal and environmental ethics, and the philosophy of risk. He is trained in veterinary medicine, bioethics, and public health.

MARK ROWLANDS (member of the working group) is a professor of philosophy at the University of Miami, Florida. He received a DPhil from Oxford University, and over the past two decades, he has worked at several universities in the United Kingdom, the United States, and Ireland and has held visiting fellowships at universities in Iceland, Finland, and Australia. His research has primarily focused on issues in the philosophy of mind and moral philosophy. In the former area, his published work includes *Supervenience and Materialism* (1995), *The Body in Mind* (1999), *The Nature of Consciousness* (2001), *Eternalism* (2003), *Body Language* (2006), and *The New Science of the Mind: From Extended Mind to Embodied Phenomenology* (2010). In the area of moral philosophy, he has written extensively on the moral status of nonhuman animals and the natural environment. Here his publications include *Animal Rights* (1998; 2nd ed., 2009), *The Environmental Crisis* (2000), *Animals like Us* (2002), and *Can*

Animals Be Moral? (2012). His memoir *The Philosopher and the Wolf* was published by Granta in 2008 and became an international best seller.

JOHN SIMONS (member of the working group) is deputy vice chancellor (academic) at Macquarie University. He was educated at the University of Wales, Aberystwyth. Before taking up his role at Macquarie University, he worked at the universities of Wales, Exeter, Winchester, Edge Hill, and Lincoln in the United Kingdom, and he has held several visiting professorships and research fellowships in the United States, where he is also an alumnus of the State Department's International Visitor Program. He has published widely on topics ranging from Middle English chivalric romance to Andy Warhol and from codicology to the history of cricket. Since the late 1990s, he has mainly concentrated on the issue of animals, and his chief publications in the field are *Animal Rights and the Politics of Literary Representation* (2002), *Rossetti's Wombat* (2008), *The Tiger That Swallowed the Boy* (2012), and *Kangaroo* (2012).

JORDAN SOSNOWSKI (member of the working group) holds a juris doctor degree from Monash University and is currently working in the field of legal research. Previously, she was awarded a bachelor of arts from the University of Queensland, having majored in philosophy and English literature. She also studied animal law as a visiting student at Bond University. She has written numerous articles on animal topics, including free-range labeling and consumer law rights, whaling in the Antarctic, empathy in the human and animal rights movements, and how meaningful change for animals can be created via international law mechanisms. She has also cowritten various papers on animal welfare and human rights law with Stephen Keim. She has recently undertaken work with the Environmental Defenders' Office, drafting and editing material for its online legal handbook. In 2012 she was awarded first prize in the NSW Young Lawyers Animal Law Essay Competition and the second prize in the Australian Legal Philosophy Student Association Essay Competition. Her present academic research focuses on how the animal law movement can be furthered through an international law framework.

DAVID SPRATT (member of the working group) is the former manager of the Department of Cellular Pathology for the North Middlesex University Hospital NHS Trust and was formerly the lead scientist and manager for the Department of Cellular Pathology at Epsom General Hospital. He has also held the position of Designated Individual under the Human Tissue Act for the Epsom and St. Helier University Hospitals NHS Trust. He is a chartered scientist, chartered biologist, fellow of the Linnean Society of London, fellow of the Institute of Biomedical Science, zoologist, fellow of the Royal Society of Medicine, and member of the Pathology Council of the Society. His current research interest is in the field of zoonotic diseases, how animal captivity leads to the proliferation of such diseases, and how these impact animal and human health and the environment.

KATY D. TAYLOR (contributor) is the director of science at Cruelty Free International, chief science adviser to the European Coalition to End Animal Experiments (ECEAE), and secretariat of the International Council for Animal Protection in Pharmaceutical Programs. She holds a doctorate in veterinary behavioral epidemiology from De Montfort University and represents the ECEAE as the official animal protection observer at the European Chemicals Agency, the European Medicines Agency, European Commission's Competent Authority for REACH and CLP (CARACAL), and European Centre for the Validation of Alternative Methods. Her publications include "Reporting 3Rs Parameters in Animal-Based Scientific Research Papers: Are We Making Any Progress?" and "Estimates for Worldwide Laboratory Animal Use in 2005" (with N. Gordon, W. Higgins, and G. Langley) in *Alternatives to Laboratory Animals*.

NATALIE THOMAS (member of the working group) holds a PhD in philosophy from the University of Waterloo in Ontario, Canada. Her dissertation is titled "Agency and Autonomy: A New Direction for Animal Ethics." In this thesis she develops a new theory of animal ethics that focuses on the importance of autonomy and the ability to form a self-concept in animals, using current research in animal cognition and self-awareness, including an analysis of the concept of autonomy in moral theories. Her first degree is in philosophy from the University of Guelph, and her master's degree (also at Guelph) is in the area of environmental ethics and the concept of intrinsic value—an area in which she continues to research, with an emphasis on the relationships between humans, nonhuman animals, and nature. She has taught at the University of Waterloo, the University of Guelph, and Wilfrid Laurier University in the area of applied ethics. She currently teaches at the University of Guelph-Humber in media studies and continues to teach environmental philosophy online through the University of Guelph and Humber College.

ELIZABETH TYSON (contributor) is a doctoral candidate at the School of Law in the University of Essex. Her research addresses the efficacy of regulatory licensing regimes as a means of guaranteeing effective animal protection in the United Kingdom. Tyson has worked for over a decade on the conservation and care of nonhuman primates. Her publications include "Regulating Cruelty: The Licensing of the Use of Wild Animals in Circuses" in the *Journal of Animal Welfare Law*.

CLIFFORD WARWICK (member of the working group) is an independent consultant biologist and medical scientist whose current main role is senior scientific adviser to the UK Emergent Disease Foundation. Among his numerous qualifications, he holds a postgraduate diploma in medical science, a charter award in biology, and a charter award in science, and he is a registered European Professional Biologist. Since the early 1980s, he has specialized in reptile biology, welfare, and protection, graduating from the Institute of Biology, London, in 1990. Since 2004 he has also specialized in zoonoses (diseases transmittable from nonhuman animals to humans), graduating from University Medical School, Leeds. His research interests include reptile behavior, euthanasia, anatomy, physiology, wildlife biology, ecology, and species and environmental conservation. He has over one hundred publications across his research fields. His major book project *Health and Welfare of Captive Reptiles* (coedited with Fred Frye and James B. Murphy, 1995) is the world's leading scientific volume dedicated to reptile welfare.

Index

genetically modified (GM) animals, 15, 17, 29–30, 56, 169
genetic animal/human differences, 28–32, 89, 132n20, 164–65, 178–80
genetic research, 17, 30, 56
German Guidelines on Human Experimentation (1931), 39
Giroux, Henry, 203
Gluck, John P., 204
Godlee, Fiona, 28
Godlovitch, Ros, 3
Godlovitch, Stanley, 3
Granger, James, 2, 9n11
Great Ape Project, 142
Greene, Graham, 204
Gresham's law, 162–63
Grier, Katherine C., 112
Gross, Daniel M., 24

Halliday, M. A. K., 59
Hansen, Lawrence A., 209
Hare, R. M., 51
Harlan UK, 77–78
Harlow, Harry Frederick, 8, 200–204
harm-benefit assessment (HBA), 148–57
    incompleteness of, 152
    inherent problems with, 153–56
    potential HBA matrix, 157
    surmountable problems with, 149–53
Harris, John, 3
Dr. Hawden Trust, 31
Hederman, Robyn, 209
    chapter by, 6, 112–16
Helsinki, Declaration of, 39
Himmler, Heinrich, 86
Hippocratic writers, 103–4
Historia Animalium (Aristotle), 104
Hobbes, Thomas, 35, 187
Hoggan, George, 24–25
Holder, Tom, 140
Hooke, Robert, 24
hormone replacement therapy (HRT), 30–31
Horrobin, David, 30
hospital fire thought experiment, 51–52, 54n40
human-based experimentation, 31–32, 87
    chimpanzees as near-humans, 132n20, 164, 178
    consent and, 39
    cost-benefit assessments and, 49
    medical progress and, 129, 131
    moral objections to, 50–51, 53n13, 169
    in science fiction, 143
Humane Research Trust, 31
Hume, David, 35
hysteria, 115–16, 118n40

Imperial College London, 81–82
index goods, 189, 191n34
institutional animal care and use committees (IACUCs), 71–72, 121–22, 133n23

institutionalization, 55–61, 90
instrumentalism, 35–37, 89
investigations, undercover, 75–83

John Paul II (pope), 45
Johnson, Lisa, 209
Johnson, Samuel, 4

Kant, Immanuel, 36, 187
King, Edward, 2
Korsgaard, Christine, 36

Laboratory for Experimental Medicine and Surgery in Primates (LEMSIP), 196
laboratory inspections, 63–66, 90, 194–95
LaFollette, H., 28
Lazo, Robert Patrick Stone, 209
    chapter by, 7, 160–66
legal status of animals, 139–40, 144
Lewis, C. S., 1, 4, 10n10, 37
licensing, 66–68, 73n3
Liddon, H. P., 3, 9n16, 9n17
"lifeboat" situation, 129–30
Linzey, Andrew, 4, 209–10
    chapter by, 1–9
Linzey, Clair
    chapter by, 1–9
Livesey, Jane, 8
Livingstone, Richard, 1
Lord Dowding Fund, 31
Lovell, Mary F., 113–14
Lucretius, 103
Lyons, Dan, 141

Mackarness, John, 3
Makinson, John, 25
Marlene-Russow, Lilly, 190n22
Mason, William, 203
maternal-deprivation experiments, 8, 200–204
Matthissen, C., 59
medical progress, 121–31
    animal experimentation and, 32, 47, 122–25, 128–31, 138, 140
    "least harm" principle and, 129–30
    medical research and, 18
    as moral imperative, 6, 126–31
    specification of, 127
military experiments, 15–16
Mitchell, S. Weir, 113, 117n10
moral agency, 41–42, 53, 168, 173n3
moral anthropocentrism, 34–35, 37, 47–53, 85, 89, 124, 168–73
moral consideration, 6, 38, 42, 90, 124–26, 130–31
moral disengagement, 59
moral distance, 8
moral innocence, 41–42, 45, 51
moral lottery, 7, 187–88
moral solicitude, 38–42
moral standing of animals, 120, 124, 126, 127, 130–31, 133n29, 138, 143–44

Morantz-Sanchez, Regina, 115

National Commission for the Protection of Human Subjects of Biomedical and Behavioral Research, 39
National Council of Women (NCW), 114, 117n24
National Institute for Health and Care Excellence (NICE), 152
National Research Act (1974), 39
Nazis, 86–87
necessity, concept of, 6–7, 47–51, 120–29, 131, 153
New Iberia Research Center, 197
Newman, John Henry, 2
Nicholson, E. B., 2–3
Nim Chimpsky, 195–98
nonhuman primates, 30, 75–76, 78, 155, 192–98
    as genetically distinct from humans, 178–79
    as genetically similar to humans, 30, 132n20, 164, 178
    ineffectiveness of experiments on, 31
    international trade in, 75–76
    laboratory conditions of, 7, 121, 192–98, 201–2
    legal rights of, 142
    maternal-deprivation experiments and, 200–204
    prohibitions on use of, 127, 149
    suffering of, 40, 47, 76, 154, 201–3
    See also chimpanzees
Nonhuman Rights Project, 197
Nuremberg Code, 39
Nussbaum, Martha, 185, 187

O'Leary, Hazel, 5
original position (OP), 185–87, 189n4, 190n22
Owen, Carla, 8
Oxford Group, 3–4
Oxford University, 1–5, 204

Patarroyo, Manuel Elkin, 194
Peggs, Kay
    chapter by, 7, 137–44
Perelandra (Lewis, 1943), 1
"personhood" of animals, 142–43, 197
pharmaceutical industry, 28, 57, 177–78
Phelps, Elizabeth Stuart, 116
physicalism, 162, 166n5
Pius IX (pope), 36
Pogge, Thomas, 191n34
primates, international trade in, 75–76. *See also* chimpanzees; nonhuman primates
The Problem of Pain (Lewis, 1940), 1
product testing, 17–18
Pulleyn, Simon
    chapter by, 6, 103–9

radiation experiments, 4–5

The University of Illinois Press
is a founding member of the
Association of American University Presses.

Cover designed by Dustin J. Hubbart
Cover illustration: Mouse (tcheres/Shutterstock.com)

University of Illinois Press
1325 South Oak Street
Champaign, IL 61820-6903
www.press.uillinois.edu